LOUIS RIEL *v.*
CANADA

The Making of a Rebel

by J. M. BUMSTED

GREAT PLAINS
PUBLICATIONS

Great Plains Publications
3 - 161 Stafford Street
Winnipeg, MB R3M 2W9
www.greatplains.mb.ca

Great Plains Publications gratefully acknowledges the financial support provided for its publishing program by the Government of Canada through the Book Publishing Industry Development Program (BPIDP).

Design & Typography by Gallant Design Ltd.

Printed in Canada by Friesens

CANADIAN CATALOGUING IN PUBLICATION DATA

Bumsted, J.M., 1938-

Louis Riel v. Canada

ISBN 1-894283-25-2

1.   Riel, Louis, 1844-1885.   I.   Title.
FC3217.1.R53B85   20001   971.05′1′092   C2001-910926-1
F1060.9.R53B85   2001

To my students,
present and past.

Table of Contents

Thomas Scott

J.C. Schultz

Colonel Garnet
Wolesley

Sir John A.
Macdonald

Introduction

The title of this book has been cast quite deliberately in the form of a legal citation for a court case. Despite the high drama of Louis Riel's life, few individuals in Canadian history have had their actions so defined by, and bound up with, the law and legalities. On one level, Riel was not so much a personality as a litigant — sometimes the prosecutor but more frequently the defendant — in an ongoing legal struggle with the government of Canada.

The declaration of a provisional government in Red River late in 1869 raised the legal question of whether Riel was a rebel against the Queen and Canada or the head of a legitimate government. For the execution of Thomas Scott not to be regarded as murder depended on the legality of the government that tried and executed him. From first news of the death of Scott, the Canadian government insisted that Scott had been indeed murdered, a point of view which greatly influenced the admission of Manitoba into Confederation and certainly controlled the subsequent life of Riel.

Although Riel was never tried for the death of Scott, his associate Ambroise Lépine was put in the dock, and in a very real sense stood in for his colleague. The legal arguments in the Lépine trial were the same ones that would have been at issue in a Riel trial, and the outcome was in many ways far more conclusive than the ambiguities of the evidence warranted. Riel was finally tried by Canada in 1885, this time for treason, and once again the legal issues were complex and ambiguous.

Since his first emergence on the historical stage in 1869, Louis Riel has had the power to fascinate historians, and especially biographers. No figure in Canadian history has been the subject of more biographical study than Riel, and his collected papers remain the only attempt at a complete edition of all papers for a Canadian. In the process of all this study, no figure has become more misunderstood than Louis Riel. Some of the biographers go so far as to invent dialogue for the key moments in

his life, and — like most biographers — they are fond of inferring important pieces of information, context, and interpretation from scattered bits
of innuendo, rumour, and second-hand accounts. One of Canada's leading biographers has recently described his role as follows:

> Although a life-writer must collect evidence in the most
> complete and rigorous manner possible, his most important
> duty is to interpret the life, to offer a "reading" of the subject to
> his audience. In so doing, the biographer places himself in
> danger because he takes the chance of getting things wrong, of
> misunderstanding the clues from the past and of providing a
> false and misleading characterization of his subject. So be it, the
> risk must be hazarded. Without interpretation, there can be no
> genuine life-writing.*

As James King suggests, the biographer's task is to make his or her
character come to life, usually by getting inside the subject's head. The
biographer must of necessity explain why his subject acts or behaves as
he does, which requires some fixed conception of his personality.
Whether or not that conception of personality is actually explained in
detail, it is always inherent in the explanations the biographer gives of
motivation and the descriptions he or she offers of inner feelings.
Although it is quite possible to write an unsympathetic biography, and
some of Riel's at least border on the unsympathetic, most biographers
end up identifying fully with their subjects; such identification, after all,
is the typical way to write biography, for it makes it possible for the
biographer to get inside of the subject's mind.

Because of all the dangers involved with subject identification as
well as because of the importance of the legal complications, which are
not always necessarily much illuminated by what was going on in Riel's
head, I do not wish to write a biography of Louis Riel. I wish instead to
write a historical study of Riel and his times, one which focuses on his
lengthy confrontation — mainly a legal one — with Canada. For me the
difference between a biography and a history is that a biography interprets the life, while a history interprets the context and times in which the
life is played out. Whether this approach succeeds in illuminating a
subject as vast and complex as Louis Riel is for the reader to decide.

This work is based on a variety of primary and secondary sources.
A full bibliography can be accessed at <www.greatplains.mb.ca>.

---

* James King, review of G.E. Bentley's *The Stranger from Paradise: A Biography of William
Blake,* in *The Globe and Mail Books*, 7 July 2001, p. D9.

-1-

Becoming A Leader

Louis Riel was born in St. Boniface, on 22 October 1844, into one of the community's leading Métis families. His maternal grandmother, Marie-Anne Gaboury Lagimodière, had been successfully wooed by the fur trader Jean-Baptiste Lagimodière in Maskinongé, Lower Canada. She married him in April 1806 and accompanied him to Fort Gibraltar at the forks of the Red and Assiniboine rivers. She was the first woman and mother in the West from Quebec, providing Riel with an impeccable ancestry as a member of the founding (non-aboriginal) family of the area. She added to this general reputation a particular service: as the only Catholic woman in the settlement in 1818, she served as godmother to more than 100 aboriginals and Métis who were baptized soon after the arrival of the first missionaries. Extremely pious in a conventional Catholic way, Marie-Anne passed this piety on to her family. Additionally, Riel's maternal grandfather, Jean-Baptiste Lagimodière, had become a trusted servant of the Earl of Selkirk in 1812, and in a famous adventure had travelled by foot all the way to Montreal to bring Selkirk the news of the destruction of the settlement in 1815.

Riel's parents were Julie Lagimodière Riel and Louis Riel Sr., who had married in 1843 in the Cathedral of St. Boniface. Louis Riel Sr. was a powerful Métis leader. Born in what is now Saskatchewan, he was educated in Lower Canada and was briefly a member of the Oblate Order, which he left for want of vocation. In Red River, he was a spokesman for the Métis free traders in their conflict with the Hudson's Bay Company in 1849. He also advocated Métis representation on the Council of Assiniboia and the use of French in the courts of the settlement. Julie Lagimodière Riel was very strong-minded and very religious. She had hoped to become a nun. She prayed, and had a vision of an old man who ordered her to follow the wishes of her parents, who wanted her married. According to her daughter's later account, Julie was just leaving church, when "she was suddenly enveloped in flames. Dazzled,

9

frightened, she raised her eyes and there in the clouds, she saw an old man, flashing with light and encircled with fire, who in powerful voice boomed out: 'Disobedient child...when you return to your home you will tell your parents that you will obey them.'" She bore the elder Louis 11 children, nine of whom survived infancy.

In a later letter, Riel Junior described his image of his mother in childhood. "Family prayers, the rosary, were always in my eyes and ears. And they are as much a part of my nature as the air I breathe. The calm reflective features of my mother, her eyes constantly turned towards heaven, her respect, her attention, her devotion to her religious obligations left upon me the deepest impression of her good example."

The Métis Background

The Red River Métis were descendants of the relationships between aboriginal or mixed-blood women and francophone *voyageurs* employed by the North West Company. Such descendants were to be found everywhere in the western fur trade country, from Detroit through the Ohio Valley to the Mississippi south of the Great Lakes, and from the Sault to the Athabasca. Red River was probably the largest single concentration of Métis in the West. Like other mixed-bloods in the western country, those in Red River had few fixed national allegiances. As early as 1815, they had raised a distinctive Métis flag in opposition to the Selkirk Settlement, apparently as a symbol of their sense of autonomy from existing governments. After the arrival of Roman Catholic missionaries in 1818, the Métis became devout Catholics.

The territory of the Hudson's Bay Company north of the 49th parallel, especially after the merger of the HBC and the NWC in 1821, was British territory — and its people were British subjects. But it was not part of any government except the local Council of Assiniboia set up around the Red River settlement by the Hudson's Bay Company in 1835. The people of Red River celebrated the Queen's Birthday every year, wrote one observer, "as royally as possible." The Indian population of the huge western territory possessed acknowledged aboriginal rights, especially with regard to the land, but nobody was clear whether the Métis shared in those rights or not. Some inconclusive discussion over aboriginal rights for the mixed-bloods had occurred in Red River in 1861.

The Métis, of course, were not the only mixed-blood people in either the settlement or in the West generally. There were also anglophone mixed-bloods, the descendants of Cree women and Hudson's Bay Company employees, who were mainly Anglicans. The two mixed-blood groups were not only separated by linguistic and confessional characteristics, but by residency as well. The Métis lived south of The Forks on the Red River. The mixed-bloods lived north of The Forks on the Red River. The two groups shared the banks of the Assiniboine River, but in quite different communities.

The traditional view of the Red River settlement's two mixed-blood groups insisted that the anglophones were more thoroughly assimilated into farming, while the francophones were more likely to follow the buffalo hunt. That distinction was increasingly breaking down over time, however, as was the sharp line between the two communities. When Johnny Grant — a mixed-blood born at Fort Edmonton who had spent most of his early years in the United States — came to Red River to visit relations in 1867, he found his kinfolk and his friends on both sides of the divide. The aunt he stayed with was Mrs. James McKay, one uncle was Pascal Breland of White Horse Plains, another aunt was Mrs. Ross at the Stone Fort. Grant became part of a bachelor group that included Bob O'Lone and Alfred H. Scott — both bartenders in Fort Rouge — and made "warm friends" with Pierre Léveillier and the three Genthon brothers. He insisted that the coming of the Canadians polarized the mixed-bloods in new ways.

While most contemporary observers liked to see the Métis element of the mixed-blood community as less "civilized" than their anglophone cousins, not everyone agreed. According to one correspondent of the Montreal *Herald* in the autumn of 1869,

> Almost every man above twenty years of age is a freeholder, and would be entitled to vote under the Canadian franchise. Most of them have received a common education, and nearly all of them have made frequent journeys as freighters with their own cattle to St. Paul's and St. Cloud in the state of Minnesota…. For some years past they have abandoned the buffalo hunt and every family cultivates more or less the soil. They contrast their position with that of the pure Indian and appreciate their own high standing in the scale of civilization. Their frequent visits to the United States have given them at least no dislike to democratic institutions…. Their character however is not understood readily by Canadians, and a misconception of it by the authorities may lead to much misery in the future of the Country.

The British government in the late 1840s had, in the course of dealing with a petition from Alexander Kennedy Isbister, managed to evade making any decision on the land rights of the mixed-bloods, who passed naturally from one side of the American border to the other depending on circumstances. Most buffalo hunting was done to the south of the line, for example.

What was clear, however, was that the Red River Métis, particularly, felt very little connection with or loyalty to the eastern provinces of British North America that would confederate in 1867. Insofar as they had any connection with the East, it was with Quebec via the clergy and nuns of the Catholic Church, many of whom had come to Red River from Lower Canada. A few Métis, including Louis Riel himself, had been educated in Quebec. But most Métis had no historic reason to feel any more attachment to Canada than to the government of the United States in Washington, beyond a very real sense of loyalty to and affection for the symbol of the British Crown.

The Early Life of Riel

L ouis was the eldest surviving son in a family of nine siblings. He was brought up by parents who hoped for him to become a priest. He was sent to school in St. Boniface at the age of seven, and became fluent in French, English, and Cree. The last language he had apparently picked up in the settlement. He and his younger sister Sara had spent their childhood roaming in the woods and fields of St. Boniface. In 1857, at the age of 13, he had been picked out by Bishop A. A. Taché — along with three other youngsters, Daniel McDougall, Louis Schmidt, and Joseph Nolin — to go to Quebec for further schooling preliminary to admission to holy orders. In the end Nolin did not go, and none of the other three became priests, which suggests that the educational experiment was not altogether successful.

At the *petit séminaire* of the College of Montreal, Louis had initially done very well. He was usually first in his class. The death in 1864 of his much-admired father, so far away in Red River, appears to have hit him very hard and unsettled him. Within a year he left the College to attempt to make his way in the world.

During this period he also seems to have suffered through an unhappy love affair. Whether or not he met Marie-Julie Guernon before or after his departure from the College is not clear. She was the daughter of neighbours of Louis's aunt and uncle, the Lees, who lived in the village of St. Louis de Mile-End. Louis had stayed with the Lees in 1864 and had moved in with them upon quitting the College in 1865. In any event, the two young people fell in love, exchanging passionate poems. One poem by Riel entitled "My First Love" describes his affection for a girl named Marie. The young couple signed a marriage contract on 12 July 1866 without consulting the girl's parents, who raised objections when the banns were published at the local church. The match was called off. We do not understand why the Guernons objected to Riel. Since they were not rich and Louis seemed a potentially good catch, several biographers speculate that the problem was that he was a Métis. But it was also true that he had not yet found a proper career when the relationship was terminated.

As he would often do later in his life, Riel evidently lived in the United States for most of the two years between his departure from Canada and his reappearance in Red River in early 1869. Like most Métis, he seemed quite comfortable on the southern side of the 49th parallel. He may have spent much of that time working on the Red River cart transport brigades, although some reports have him working in a dry goods store in St. Paul.

Louis's first public appearance was in the Quebec newspaper *Nouveau Monde* of 1 February 1869, in the form of a letter to the editor from a "Métis" who signed himself "L.R." The letter answered one from recent Red River arrival Charles Mair that had appeared in several Ontario newspapers. Mair's patronizing comments about mixed-blood women in the settlement had already won him a public horse-whipping from Annie Bannatyne, the mixed-blood wife of A.G.B. Bannatyne, the postmaster of the settlement. Mair had also suggested that the only reason famine assistance had been necessary in Red River in 1868 was because of "halfbreed" indolence. "L.R." insisted that famine aid had been given to people of "all colours." He went on, "There are some half-breeds who do not ask for charity, as there are some English, some Germans, and some Scots, who receive it every week."

"L. R." continued: "It was not, of course, enough for these gentlemen to come to mock the distress of our country by making unfortunate people driven by hunger, work dirt cheap. They had also to spread falsehoods among the outside world, to lead people to believe that the relief sent to R. R. was not needed." He concluded: "In other circumstances than those in which we are, I should not have taken note of the falsehoods of this letter. We are accustomed to see strangers arrive every year who come to look us up and down, and who then print in the newspapers or in big books their reflections more or less queer on us and our country; but after the bad times which have befallen on us, driven as we are to have recourse to public charity, I have thought that it was my duty to protest against falsehoods which could give the impression elsewhere that there was no need of relief in Red River." "L.R.," of course was Louis Riel, and this was his first known appearance in print. His response, probably reflecting that of many of the settlement's Métis, reveals a sensitivity both to racial stereotyping and to condescending outsiders.

The letter to *Nouveau Monde* made it apparent not only that Louis Riel was prepared to act as spokesman for his people, but that he was capable of doing so in quite elegant French prose. At the same time, there was a considerable difference between writing a letter of protest and leading, a short time later, a rebellion. In the early autumn of 1869, few residents of Red River, francophone or anglophone, could have predicted that Louis Riel would become the leader of the Métis resistance to Canada which would result in the creation of the province of Manitoba. Riel himself has left us few clues to his thinking or his inner life in these early days in Red River. Any attempt to ascribe motives to Riel for this period is fraught with danger, and biographers who do so are sailing close to the historical abyss. All our available testimony describes Riel's actions, but little more.

One of the first evidences of Métis objections to the Canadians came on 5 July 1869, when a meeting resolved to organize mounted patrols to protect Métis land from speculators, who were rumoured to be buying up large chunks of unoccupied land in the region. This meeting elected Jean Baptiste Tourond as president and J.B. Lépine as secretary. It probably led later in the month to a second meeting held at the court house at Fort Garry on 29 July, called by a number of mixed-bloods, most of whom would later support John Christian Schultz and oppose Riel. William Dease, one of those who had called the meeting, said it was being held to consider the recent transfer of the country by the HBC to Canada and to question "the right of the Company to dispose of any territorial claims without the consent of the natives of the country." William Hallett rose to ask whether the land belonged to the Company or to the mixed-bloods and aboriginal inhabitants of the region. There were a number of questions intertwined in this discussion. One was the issue of whether aboriginal rights had ever been dealt with by treaty or purchase. The governor of the HBC, William McTavish, at this meeting insisted that Lord Selkirk had purchased land from the Saulteaux. But the purchase at best had only included land stretching for two miles on either side of the Red and Assiniboine rivers, and the Saulteaux insisted that the land had been leased and never purchased.

According to Alexander Begg, the meeting had moved on to insist that the £300,000 purchase price received by the HBC actually belonged to the aboriginals and the mixed-bloods. William Dease also proposed, with much less support than his insistence on aboriginal rights, that the mixed-bloods should set up an independent government of their own to negotiate with Canada. Begg thought this strategy had been suggested by land speculators who decided it would be easier to obtain land from aboriginals than from the Canadian government. Riel would later return to the insistence that the purchase price for the territory actually belonged to the community. It is worth noting that Red River knew perfectly well what was happening to it in the summer of 1869. News of the purchase and transfer had been in the Canadian newspapers, some of which circulated freely in the settlement. But there is no sign of Louis Riel at this juncture.

Three factors seem crucial in explaining Riel's subsequent rise to power. One was that Red River was a deferential society in which family mattered. Louis Riel's family background was designed for leadership. The second factor was the absence of any clearly recognized leader among the younger, more militant Métis at the start of the formal resistance to Canada. Many of the influential older Métis, figures like Roger Goulet and Pascal Breland, had been co-opted by the Hudson's Bay Company to the Council of Assiniboia, and were not eager for new directions. While the men leading these early meetings were involved in the later events of 1869 and 1870, neither Tourond nor Lépine were ever particularly prominent in the inner ranks of Métis leadership, and William Dease and William Hallett supported the Canadian Party. Riel was still very young in 1869, although it must be remembered that most of the leading players in the rebellion were of his generation, at most slightly older. John Christian Schultz had been born in 1840, James Ross in 1835, Charles Nolin in 1837, and Ambroise Lépine in 1840. The final factor in the equation, of course, was Riel's burning ambition to do something worthy. A leadership role was there to be seized in the late summer of 1869, and Louis Riel would seize it. In the very narrative of events one can hear Riel emerging as the leader of the settlement's opposition to the Canadian takeover of Red River.

The Canadian Takeover

The Province of Canada (the predecessor of the Dominion of Canada) had long regarded the Hudson's Bay Company Territory as its natural hinterland. George Brown's Toronto *Globe* called for the eventual unification of the "destinies of this immense country" with "our own" as early as 1850. The Canadians had called for a parliamentary enquiry into the Hudson's Bay Company, and a Canadian minister was one of the first to testify at the enquiry of 1857. John Ross — a political associate of Sir John A. Macdonald — told the hearing that Canada did not want the HBC administration in the western region to cease immediately. At present the West could not be administered or governed by Canada, he testified, and should not be until better communications were opened up. One of the major reasons for Canadian reticence was the sense that the "half-breeds" would be difficult to govern. The halfbreed population, said Ross, was "less governed by those rules of order and that sense of propriety which prevail in a white population." This sort of racist thinking, combined with ignorance, would infect Canadian dealings with Red River throughout the period of attempted annexation. The great Macdonald-Brown coalition of 1866 affirmed its

Louis Riel v. Canada

belief that "The future interests of Canada and all British North America" were "vitally concerned in the immediate establishment of a strong Government" in the North-West. At the same time, it must be emphasized that the French and English sections of the province of Canada before Confederation were not equally interested in westward expansion. Most of the enthusiasm for the North-West came from Canada West.

Canada created a constitutional mechanism for expansion in section 146 of the British North America Act. Newfoundland, Prince Edward Island, and British Columbia were designated "Colonies or Provinces" to be admitted by joint action of their legislatures and the Canadian Parliament, while Rupert's Land and the North-Western Territory — which were the territorial units into which the West in the final drafting of the BNA Act was divided — were not described as colonies. Unlike the Quebec resolution of 1864 on the admission of new provinces, which simply called for "the admission into the Union on equitable terms of Newfoundland, The North-West Territory, British Columbia and Vancouver" (the places in British North America not represented at Quebec), the BNA Act distinguished between provinces or colonies and the units of the North-West, the admission of which to the union was to be by action of the Canadian Parliament alone, and not according to rules spelled out in the constitution. In section 147, the Senate representation of the North-West — unlike that of the three "Colonies or Provinces" — was not described.

Canada and Canadians had an opportunity to demonstrate their attitudes toward the North-West late in 1867, when the Canadian Parliament debated eight resolutions introduced into it by William McDougall, minister of public works. The third resolution read: "That the welfare of a sparse and widely scattered population of British subjects, of European origin, already inhabiting these remote and unorganized territories, would be materially enhanced, by the formation therein of political institutions bearing analogy, as far as circumstances will admit, to those which exist in the several Provinces of the Dominion." The fifth resolution requested Britain to allow Canada to "assume the duties and obligations of Government, and Legislation," and the seventh acknowledged that the claims of "the aborigines" would have to be considered and settled according to "equitable principles." The resolutions acknowledged a population of British subjects of European origin and a population of aboriginals, but did not specifically mention the "half-breeds." They also avoided the question of the rights of the Hudson's Bay Company in the region.

In the subsequent debate, Liberal David Mills objected to the wording of these resolutions because they did not spell out "on what principles we intended to govern" these territories. Mills wanted the sorts of rules the Americans employed, which specified the terms under which territories were organized and subsequently admitted as states. He wanted, he said, "to add to the fifth resolution words which would secure to the people of the new territory the same rights of local self-government, free from federal control, that are enjoyed by the provinces already within the Dominion." Prime Minister Macdonald, when he eventually spoke on the matter, argued that the constitution of the territory could be determined later, according to the "wisdom of the Parliament of Canada," although he acknowledged that representative institutions should be immediately introduced and that the people of the territories "should all have representation in the Parliament of Canada." But Macdonald also observed that the natives of the region were "incapable of the management of their own affairs," which was why the final constitution should be adapted "to the growing requirements of the new country." This was a euphemistic way of saying that the constitution should not be decided until enough British subjects of European origin had moved there.

At the same time, while most Quebec Members of Parliament supported the ministry on partisan grounds, there was little Quebec enthusiasm for expansion into the West. The region was generally regarded as a desolate land that could not support settlement. When Bishop A.A. Taché in 1869 published his *Equisse sur le Nord-Ouest de l'Amérique* — intended to introduce Quebeckers to their new possession — newspapers in Quebec responded by observing how disagreeable the bishop made the region sound. One newspaper editorialized that it was prepared to view the North-West as a worthy acquisition for Canada, but held that Quebec needed to continue to keep its population at home, colonizing the wastelands to the north. Other editorial opinion fostered by the Cartier faction in the province held that the new territory would benefit Quebec through the increased economic activity it would generate, not least as serving as a link with the Pacific. This argument was necessary because many newspapers and most French-Canadian public opinion saw Ontario as the supplier of the settlers for the North-West. Moreover, francophones in Quebec did not in the late 1860s view the French-speaking Métis as an integral part of French Canada. Most of the Quebec press would respond to the early reports of the 1869-70 insurgency in the same way as the Ontario press. Opposition papers would criticize the government for its bungling, but most newspaper opinion saw the Métis as untamed rebels.

As it turned out, the Canadian government was frustrated in its hopes to obtain the North-West without dealing with the Hudson's Bay Company. The law officers of the Crown decided that a special formula involving the HBC would be required for the transfer, and this process was spelled out in the Rupert's Land Act, passed by the Imperial

Louis Riel v. Canada

Parliament in July 1868. This Act also established the power of the Canadian Parliament "to make, ordain and establish within the Land and Territory so admitted as aforesaid all such Laws, Institutions, and Ordinances, and to constitute such Courts and Officers, as may be necessary for the Peace, Order, and good government of Her Majesty's Subjects and others therein…" once the transfer was completed. Shortly after the British Parliament had completed the transfer, the Canadian government moved unilaterally in the West. William McDougall as minister of public works authorized the construction of a road from Lake of the Woods to Upper Fort Garry to be supervised by John Allan Snow.

The construction of the road was ostensibly designed to provide relief in the form of employment for the inhabitants of Red River, who were suffering from a very serious famine and for whom various agencies (including Canadian churches) were collecting money. Snow consulted with Governor William McTavish of the HBC as he was instructed to do, but while McTavish was agreeable to proceeding with the project, the London Committee of the HBC protested that the work was "being undertaken by the Canadian government as a matter of right, as though the territory through which it is to pass were Canadian." This project was in part what "L.R." had protested in his letter to *Nouveau Monde* of February 1869. It was undertaken with the permission of the governor of Assiniboia, and it would obviously have benefits to Canada, beyond relieving the settlers, by providing an improved overland communication link. The Canadian government in 1868 was fully aware that all transportation and communication of Canada with Red River went via the United States.

The terms of the transfer, negotiated in March 1869, insisted that land titles granted to the residents of the country by the HBC would have to be honoured by the Canadian government. The land title business was not spelled out in detail, however. As Parliament had discovered in an enquiry into the Hudson's Bay Company's rule in the West in 1857, land titles in the settlement were quite complicated. Not all titles had been properly recorded, and there was a serious question over what land could be properly included in titles. The land ceded by the aboriginals extended only two miles in either direction from the banks of the Red and Assiniboine Rivers. The land beyond this cession was claimed by the aboriginals, but was also claimed by those settlers on the river lots as "hay privilege." Once the transfer had been agreed to, it should have been the responsibility of the Hudson's Bay Company — or perhaps the imperial government — to inform the local population of the region of what had transpired. For some inexplicable reason, this step was not taken. The Canadian government would subsequently blame much of its subsequent difficulties in the North-West on Great Britain.

Sir John A. Macdonald would later complain to George Stephen that: "It was the business of the Hudson's Bay Company to instruct their officers in Rupert's Land of the arrangements as they made progress in London." To Sir George-Étienne Cartier, Macdonald had added, "No explanation, it appears, has been made of the arrangement by which the country is handed over to the Queen, and that it is Her Majesty who transfers the country to Canada with the same rights to settlers as existed before. All these poor people know is that Canada has bought the country from the Hudson's Bay Company, and that they are handed over like a flock of sheep to us." In truth, however, the information which the residents really wanted was not about the transfer or about their alleged rights as British subjects — they could read about these in the newspapers — but about the policy the Canadian government would be following with regard to its new acquisition, particularly the extent to which the existing population would be consulted and involved by the Canadian government in their eventual fate. It was the responsibility of Canada, not the Hudson's Bay Company, to communicate these matters of future policy with the inhabitants of Red River.

That policy perfectly reflected the personality of Canada's prime minister, Sir John A. Macdonald. Like most political brokers — Macdonald once described his occupation as "cabinet maker" — Macdonald preferred not to elaborate future policy on paper. By not spelling things out, he allowed himself room to remain flexible and capable of responding to different political breezes. The process in Ottawa began on 31 May 1869, when Parliament addressed the Crown "praying for the annexation of the North-West." On 4 June, Macdonald introduced a bill. Although the constitutionality of this legislation was subsequently questioned in 1871, it was not doubted at the time. The act dealt with the "temporary government of Rupert's Land and the North-Western Territory when united with Canada." It provided for a lieutenant-governor who was single-handedly responsible "generally to make, ordain, and establish all such laws, Institutions and Ordinances as may be necessary for the Peace, Order and good Government of Her Majesty's subjects and others therein." A council could be established "to aid the Lieutenant-Governor in the administration of affairs." It was to be composed of between seven and 15 persons and its powers would be defined by the Governor in Council, that is, by the Canadian cabinet. The present laws of the region remained in force and present officials remained in office until specifically altered by the cabinet. Prime Minister Macdonald insisted that the act was intended to cover only the period until the "end of the next session," and that within a year the "provisional" government would be replaced by "a more permanent government," and indeed this was emphasized in both the preamble and the final section.

Louis Riel v. Canada

Canada obviously needed to put some kind of temporary government in place in the territory it was acquiring. The Americans might well have moved into a total vacuum. Canada apparently did not consider continuing the Council of Assiniboia in power, perhaps because it governed only Red River rather than the entire North-West. Instead, as the prime minister himself put it, "the lieutenant-governor will be for the time paternal despot, as in other small Crown Colonies, his Council being one of advice, he and they however being governed by instructions from Head Quarters." To another correspondent, the Hon. Sidney Smith, he explained in early July that "our intention is simply to send up some person as Lieutenant Governor to take command of the ship," noting "We are in utter darkness as to the state of affairs there; what the wants and wishes of the people are — or, in fact, how the affairs are carried on at all." At first glance a temporary despotism does not sound an unreasonable expediency, given the "utter darkness" in which the government was operating.

But of course there was no need for this darkness, even though it might have been a bit tricky to consult formally with the residents in advance of the transfer. Nevertheless, someone in Ottawa could have been set to work to do some research on the historic development of the settlement in the substantial printed literature about it, including the published report of the Parliamentary Enquiry of 1857; an individual or a party might have been sent to the settlement to talk informally with the residents (as Joseph Howe subsequently did, feeling guilty about it all the time); or the government might have consulted properly with the existing leaders of Red River, two of whom were in the nation's capital in June and July of 1869. For example, Governor William McTavish, who visited Ottawa sometime in June of that year specifically to deal with the transfer, reported to Bishop Taché upon his return to Red River that "I have not been able to make any of my recommendations to be accepted by the Government."

The Canadians would subsequently deny that McTavish had offered any useful advice in his June visit, not the only time that testimony of Bishop Taché would be disputed by the government. While it is true that either side might be lying, it is also possible that McTavish was asked the wrong questions — or that the government simply failed to listen to him carefully. Taché's story is independently substantiated by a letter written to the Canadian Governor-general by Anglican Bishop Robert Machray in March of 1870. In it Machray insists that he had been in Ottawa in 1868 and had been unable to impress upon members of the government that there was reason for concern over the transfer. Certainly McTavish's presence in 1869 meant that he might have been asked in person to be one of the councillors, which was not done. Similarly, Bishop

Taché on one of his two visits to Ottawa in July and September, might have been asked to serve on the council. Instead, Sir George-Étienne Cartier swept aside Taché's misgivings about the government policy with the words, "We know all about it, and we have made provision respecting matters."

Indeed, what seems clear is that the Canadian government did not really want to become illuminated about Red River. The darkness in which it operated was exactly suitable to its needs. The "small Crown Colonies" which were being compared with Red River were all places with indigenous populations of some sort, and in his letter to the Hon. Sidney Smith, Prime Minister Macdonald had added unambiguously, "We shall expect the Lt. Governor to make a report early enough to have legislation of some kind next Session, and to grant them a Constitution suitable to the present scattered state of the few Whites that there are there." The fact of the matter was that from the Canadian perspective, the resident "half castes" (as Prime Minister Macdonald preferred to call them) did not really count as potential citizens, and the delay was to permit further European settlement. Macdonald wrote J.Y. Bown in October 1869 that "In another year, the present residents will be altogether swamped by the influx of strangers who will go in with the idea of becoming industrious & peaceable settlers." Like most imperialist governments, Canada wanted Red River to be a settlement populated mainly by an ignorant and semi-savage people unworthy to be given self-government or otherwise taken seriously into account. In such a settlement, the indigenous inhabitants could be quietly ignored until replaced by European settlers. Louis Riel was quite accurate in his perception that the Canadians had no interest in taking the Métis into account in the government of Red River.

The potentially disastrous nature of Canadian policy for the North-West was reinforced by the government's choice for lieutenant-governor. William McDougall was selected partly because of his involvement with the acquisition of the region for Canada, but also because he was a political liability being shunted to one side. McDougall was a pre-Confederation Liberal who had remained in the Macdonald coalition. But the coalition was dead by 1869, and members of Macdonald's Conservative party mistrusted McDougall as a renegade. Moreover, McDougall had been associated with an unsavoury business earlier in the decade on Manitoulin Island, in which the aboriginal people had been badly treated. George Brown's Toronto *Globe* was opposed to McDougall because he was a turncoat Liberal, and the Montreal *Herald* had long disliked McDougall as a sleazy politician. These two newspapers were the Canadian papers most frequently read in Red River. When the government failed to spell out its policy for Rupert's Land, these newspapers had a field day.

Both Canadian papers deliberately overstated the nefarious implications of McDougall's entourage of officials. Only three were actually appointed in advance: D. R. Cameron, A. N. Richards, and J.A.N. Provencher. The remainder of McDougall's council was to be chosen once he had taken office, with Governor McTavish and Recorder John Black — as well as other local officials — high on the list to be asked to serve. The newspapers made these three Canadian appointments sound like a much larger collection of carpetbaggers by including in their ranks individuals (like the other Alexander Begg) who were brought along to assist the new government as hired officials but not councillors. The *Herald* mentioned a team of "six Canadian adventurers, who are going there to try to make their fortunes in the scramble which is likely to take place for any good thing which might turn up, in the way of town lots, mines, or especially valuable agricultural property."

Canadian intentions were further rendered suspicious within Red River by the appointment of J. S. Dennis to survey the territory in advance of settlement. Surveying had to be done before new settlers could obtain land, of course, and since upon the arrival of new settlers depended the end of the temporary government of McDougall, there were some good reasons for haste. Moreover, Parliament's Rupert's Land Act of 1868 called for the existing residents to have their grants from the Hudson's Bay Company confirmed. Canada did observe the decencies and consult with the HBC in London and in the colony on the surveying. But there was a basic incompatibility between confirming existing grants and the new survey. Canada had decided to emulate the Americans in their square layout of townships and lots, which hardly accorded with the existing landholding practice in Red River. Dennis never did manage to explain to the settlement how the new survey and the confirmations of existing titles could be made to mesh. Given the way in which the Canadians were proceeding, there seemed no good reason to believe his assurances that everybody's interests would be protected. The Canadians were always very good at adopting a posture of wounded innocence, but nothing in their procedures encouraged trust.

Emergence of Riel as Rebel Leader

We have various testimonies about Riel's activities in the early autumn of 1869. Father Noel Ritchot noted that a "young man," undoubtedly Riel, helped organize a small number of Métis to meet together to "consider the state of the country and see if there were some means at least of making a clear protest against the injustice and injuries done the country by Canada." But Ritchot provides no dates, and it is difficult to find very many chronological signposts in his surviving testimony. According to John Dennis, the chief Canadian surveyor, he met with Louis Riel on 1 October 1869. This was the first occasion that Riel stepped forward publicly. At this point Riel wanted to know the intentions of the Canadian government regarding the extinction of Indian title and land occupied by settlers. Dennis reported: "He said that having some education, his brethren the half-breeds who were in state of great excitement being in ignorance of what was going to be done with the country, had requested him to see me, and obtain explanations." Whether this meant that Riel was more than merely a spokesman is not clear. In any event, Dennis responded that the people need have no fears. The government would survey the lands occupied and give parties in possession Crown deeds without charge. It would extinguish Indian title upon equitable terms.

Dennis obviously thought that these assurances had satisfied Riel's concerns. He later wrote to the Toronto *Globe* that Riel "expressed himself as delighted to hear of the just and even liberal intentions of the Government toward the occupants of land, and left me, promising that he would take very opportunity of making those intentions known among the class mentioned." Dennis turned to surveying land not in crop at Oak Point, apparently never giving a thought to the possibility that his assurances to Riel did not necessarily preclude opposition to new surveying. He would continually emphasize that the surveys which were later confronted by armed locals were not on "settled farms," but were on the "hay privileges" claimed by custom as part of those farms. Even the prime minister could recognize that Dennis had exceeded his brief. On 20 November he wrote William McDougall that Dennis had been "exceedingly injudicious." Macdonald added that Dennis "was in the country simply on sufferance, in anticipation of its future transfer to Canada: on finding any serious dissatisfaction amongst the natives or residents, he should have at once struck and waited your arrival."

A few days after the meeting between Dennis and Riel, on 6 October, a letter was written from St. Boniface to the Quebec newspaper *Le Courier de Saint-Hyacinthe* (which was edited by a former College de Montreal classmate of Louis Riel). The letter was pseudonymously signed by "Two Métis," but it is difficult not to detect Riel's hand in it. The letter offered to tell the newspaper's readers what the people of Red River themselves thought about the Canadian takeover. It reported on the resolutions passed by the first assembly of the people held in the settlement, each parish represented by two delegates. The representatives declared themselves loyal subjects of the Queen and beholden to the HBC for protection. They further declared that the surveyors had disregarded "the law of nations" in coming to Red River to survey "in the name of an alien authority without paying any attention to the authority today existing in the country." This assertion was not entirely true, since the local HBC people had been consulted about the surveying, but it was certainly the case — as the prime minister himself would privately acknowledge — that the surveys were being conducted before the Canadian government was actually in possession of the territory. The people of Red River were willing to submit to the proposed change, the letter continued, but they wanted to insist on their indisputable rights and the "privileges accorded so liberally by the Crown of England to every English colony respected on their behalf." The "Two Métis" letter, not published until 28 October in Quebec, was carefully calculated to appeal for eastern sympathies. It emphasized loyalty to the Crown, and the rights of the people of Red River. And it provides one of the few clues available to Riel's thinking in this formative period.

On 9 October, Canada's Secretary of State Joseph Howe arrived in the settlement for an "unofficial" visit. Howe was the Nova Scotia politician who had led the opposition to Confederation in that province, and had only recently capitulated to the Canadians in return for "better terms." His cabinet post, which included responsibility for Canada's soon-to-be territories, was part of the symbol of Nova Scotia's acceptance of Confederation. What Howe thought he was doing in Red River has never been entirely clear. Had he come in the official capacity to which he was entitled, and had he thus consulted with the people of the settlement, his visit might have proved quite useful. But he was apparently in the settlement on a reconnaissance without the official approval of the Canadian cabinet, supremely ignorant of the possibility that there should be any resistance to the Canadian takeover.

As soon as Howe learned of the local opposition to Canada, he retreated into describing himself as a purely private visitor. He refused to make public speeches, obviously embarrassed by the absence of a specific Canadian policy for governing Red River to which he could make reference. He realized that any public utterances that he made would help make government policy, and he knew this would get him in trouble with his cabinet colleagues, especially Sir John A. Macdonald. Instead, as Howe subsequently reported to Macdonald, he offered vague assurances "that the same constitution as the other Provinces possessed would ultimately be conferred upon the country; that in the provisional arrangements to be made, the feeling and interests of the resident population would be considered — that leading men enjoying their confidence, would be at once taken into the Government, and that the young men, without distinction of blood, would be drawn into the public service as they were fitted by education to fill places of trust and emolument." On the basis of Canada's showing thus far, anyone who believed such assurances had to be exceptionally trusting.

Howe spent two days reading the records and the laws of the Council of Assiniboia, a process which provided him with a series of what he later described as revelations. The settlement *did* have a history, a constitution, and a familiarity with political process, points which came as a shock to a man who had been listening to Canadian yahoo expansionists run down and sneer at the government of the settlement. According to his own account, Howe consulted with the "leading men, who largely represent the resident population." He defended Canada at the house of William Kennedy, who must have given him an earful about Canada's inequitable treatment of Red River, although most of his conversations probably took place in the bar of Emmerling's hotel, where he was staying. In a later parliamentary exchange with William McDougall, Howe made clear that he was fairly familiar with the liquor stock carried by Dutch George.

If Howe thought he had "cleared the air" with mixed-bloods like Kennedy, he was sadly mistaken. More to the point, however, Howe did not talk to any of the francophone leaders at all in his ten-day visit, although the first act of overt resistance occurred during this period and was very publicly led by Louis Riel. His failure to include Riel, John Bruce, or Father Ritchot among those who represented the resident population is inexplicable on any other terms except that he did not conceive of the Métis as a legitimate part of that population. But Howe's lack of communication with the Métis meant that he cleared no air with that portion of the community.

Howe's visit offers us a perfect example of how ignorance can be greatly escalated and even transformed by events. Even without talking to the Métis leaders, Howe left Red River convinced that there was no hope for a "peaceable transfer." He subsequently met William McDougall, heading toward the settlement, on the trail between Georgetown and Fort Abercrombie. The two men met briefly in the midst of a blinding snowstorm, and Howe did not brief the incoming governor on his visit beyond warning him that the Métis had been greatly aggravated by the behaviour of Canadians in the settlement. Weather conditions were not conducive to a lengthy meeting, and what else could Howe have said? He could not report on Métis opinion in detail because he had not spoken to the Métis. He did have any idea of the lengths to which the Métis would go. He could not know that McDougall would be prevented from entering into the settlement to discover the nature of public opinion for himself. McDougall convinced himself that Howe had blindsided him, and the two men were involved in months of nasty recriminations in the Canadian Parliament over their meeting. In the larger sense, Howe's visit represents an opportunity that was missed because the minister had not arrived properly briefed and prepared, and consequently could not take full advantage of the situation into which he was dropped.

A few days after the drafting of the "Two Métis" letter, and while Joseph Howe was still in Red River, John Dennis's survey party was halted on 11 October 1869 by 18 Métis headed by Louis Riel. The Métis did not use any violence, but simply stood on the chain and refused to allow the survey to continue. A day later, Governor William McTavish wrote to the HBC that the Métis had said "that they consider, if the Canadians wished to come here, the terms on which they were to enter should have been arranged with the local government here, as it is acknowledged by the people in the country."

Dennis's memorandum of 12 October recorded that he had spoken to Dr. William Cowan, who was effectively in charge of the HBC government during the illness of William McTavish, and was informed that Cowan and Roger Goulet had sent for Louis Riel, who merely repeated that the Canadian government had no right to make surveys in the territory without the permission of its residents. A day later, McTavish wrote the HBC that he had spoken to one of the leaders of the hostility to the survey, presumably Riel, and confirmed an earlier suspicion that "the priests have somehow countenanced the movement." By mid-October, therefore, Riel had emerged as the man with whom the HBC government was doing its discussions, but this did not necessarily mean that he was already the undisputed leader of his people. For Riel to parlay his articulateness in English with the HBC's memories of the role of his father in the Sayer Trial of 1849 would have been eminently good strategy, however, and this is probably what he did.

On 16 October the Métis met at St. Norbert to decide on further action. Later, Father Ritchot testified that "The old custom of the country was that when a difficulty arose in which it was necessary to take up arms, the inhabitants used to organize of their own accord, after the manner in which they organized for the hunting in the prairies. This custom was chiefly confined to such of the French and English half-breeds who were in the habit of hunting. Those meetings never had reference to municipal affairs at all, and were only held when it was necessary to take up arms to repel enemies from within." This assemblage, which went on for several days, elected John Bruce as president and Louis Riel as secretary.

Bruce has often been described as ill-educated and weak, a mere figurehead for Riel, who some suspected had put the older man's name forward. But contemporaries were not so certain that Bruce was merely a paper leader. Bruce had some facility in the many languages of Red River, and "Justitia" would later insist that he was seen as above "the ordinary run of French half-breeds in intelligence." The American consul described him as "a man of sound judgment within a limited sphere."

Riel may well have chosen to remain in the background because he knew that many of his compatriots preferred someone less volatile at the helm, at least in these early stages of development. This "National Committee" met often over the next week, talking about the codification of the "natural, wise and just laws of the prairie" and organizing a military force to repel intruders. The Committee learned that William McDougall would soon arrive in Pembina and that he apparently had arms in his baggage. The arms were stored by McDougall in Fort Abercrombie, but the Métis would probably not have known about this disposition.

The authorities in Red River decided that they had done all they could to dampen the Métis hostility to the Canadian takeover, and the Governor and Council of Assiniboia met on 19 October to draft a proper welcome of address to Governor William McDougall, the Canadian appointee as head of the territory, who was waiting at Pembina for the official transfer on 1 December 1869. That same evening, a meeting of anglophone mixed-bloods at the Rapids School House debated another address welcoming McDougall. Only Captain William Kennedy opposed this address, arguing that he was suspicious of McDougall's character and antecedents. Kennedy was a mixed-blood who had been successful in the outside world, leading several expeditions to search for Sir John Franklin. He had subsequently attempted to establish a postal service between Red River and Canada. At this point, the people of Red River, Kennedy argued, should join Confederation on equal terms with Canada. Since Kennedy had for many years been one of the principal advocates in the settlement of Canadian annexation, his position illustrates just how deeply hostility to Canada's policy of colonial status for Red River had bitten into all factions in the settlement.

On 20 October, Constable James Mulligan informed John Dennis that a meeting had just taken place at John Bruce's house, which had resolved to send an armed party to meet the governor and prevent him from entering the settlement. One outcome of this gathering was a brief letter to McDougall, dated 21 October. It read: "The National Committee of the Métis of Red River orders William McDougall not to enter the Territory of the North-West without special permission of the above-mentioned committee." It was signed by Louis Riel, Secretary "by order of the President, John Bruce." The Métis subsequently set up a barricade at St. Norbert. "Nor-West" in a letter to the Montreal *Herald* dated 30 October described the roadblock. Before the barricade were two armed sentries. When a traveller was halted, a spokesman came forward to enquire in French the nature of the business in "our country." If satisfied, he opened the gate. "Nor-West" talked with this spokesman, who insisted the Métis would offer violence only if the governor attempted to cross the line. "We want to govern ourselves. We will accept no concessions." Whether

Louis Riel v. Canada

Louis Riel was this spokesman was not clear, but it does sound like his voice.

Around this time Louis Riel and John Bruce met at the home of magistrate Thomas Sinclair in St. Andrew's parish. The two men attempted unsuccessfully to convince those present to join the Métis in opposing the entry of McDougall. The gathering probably told Riel and Bruce roughly what John Dennis reported a few days later to the governor-in-waiting as the attitude of the English-speaking mixed-bloods and the Scottish in the settlement. The anglophones were outraged at Métis behaviour, wrote Dennis, but were not happy that they had not been consulted by Canada. "Should an appeal to arms be necessary, we could hardly justify ourselves in engaging in a conflict which would be, in our opinion, certain to resolve itself into one of nationalities and religions, and of which we could hardly see the termination." In short, the anglophone mixed-bloods were understandably not prepared to fight a civil war on behalf of the Dominion.

It was Louis Riel alone who spoke to the congregation at the Catholic Cathedral as it was leaving the building after Sunday morning Mass on 24 October. He told his listeners that it would be easier to allow Governor McDougall to enter the settlement. But in this case people would be going on without their political rights, and the only means to arouse them "was to force them to some such action as that contemplated. He suggested that should anyone fall, a handkerchief be dipped in his blood and it become their national flag. Opposition to impending changes "must begin somewhere," and it had been decided to begin by opposing the entrance of the future governor. In this address, Riel appeared in a new public role, that of demagogue.

John Bruce and Riel together attended the lengthy meeting of the Governor and Council of Assiniboia held on Monday 25 October. The council unanimously condemned the roadblock, but hoped the parties were ignorant of the "highly criminal character" of their actions. It was Riel who addressed the council. He came with a list of 12 points, and his discussion was long and "somewhat irregular." As was typical of Riel's public speeches, he tended to ramble. Riel insisted that the Métis were "perfectly satisfied with the present Government and wanted no other." His people objected, he said, to a government being sent without a previous negotiation of the terms under which the Métis would acknowledge that government. Riel continued — in the vein of his earlier conversation with John Dennis — that his people were "uneducated and only half civilized and felt that if a large immigration were to take place they would probably be crowded out of a country which they claimed as their own; that they knew they were in a sense poor and insignificant, but that it was just because they were aware of this, that they had felt so much at being treated as if they were even more insignificant than they in reality were." Once in power, claimed Riel, McDougall and the Canadians would be difficult to dislodge. The Métis did not expect opposition from the English-speaking population, said Riel, and they were ready to deal with the Canadian Party in the settlement. Riel agreed to convey to his people the Council's feelings and report back by the following Thursday.

Riel and Bruce then left the meeting, which proceeded to debate the matter at great length. As Joseph Hargrave reported in a letter to the Montreal *Herald*, the meeting decided that the settlement was "quite indifferent about Canadian rule, and the prevailing feeling was that, as the business had not yet practically come before them, they would decline to encounter danger at the hands of their fellow settlers in defence of a body of officials, in the appointment of which they had no voice, and in support of a government hitherto known to them only by report." The Canadian failure to contact the incumbent government officially about the takeover was coming home to roost. Should Governor McDougall choose to remain at Pembina, that was something over which the Council had no control. The meeting also decided to send William Dease and Roger Goulet, both members of the Council, with as large a party of Métis as they could collect, to attempt to convince those manning the barricades to cancel their actions. This mission was, of course, a total failure.

From Pembina, William McDougall wrote to Sir John A. Macdonald on 31 October. He was "charmed with the prospect which everywhere opens to the eye of the tiller of the soil," but reported that there was talk around Pembina of insurrection, based on false rumours that "all the *law* was to come from Canada" and that "no one in Red River would be in the law (meaning the Council). McDougall was able to deny these stories, which he was certain had originate with the Canadian newspapers, especially the *Globe*. He had, of course, no real idea at this point of what the insurgents really wanted, but like most Canadians, preferred to believe the most outrageous possible accounts, which were easier to counter than the truth.

Sometime around the end of October, Louis Riel had a meeting with William McTavish, the terminally-ill governor of the HBC. McTavish began by recalling Riel's father, and praised him. Riel acknowledged the praise and insisted that "I will try to imitate him and, as he did, render service to my country." McTavish argued that it would be better to give the Canadian government a chance to prove itself. Riel disagreed. The anglophone settlers would allow the Canadians to establish themselves, he said, but this was not the Métis preference. "It is, it seems to me, only prudence to prevent the wolf's entry into the sheep-pen; it looks to us as if it would be easier to keep the wolf outside in the first place than to have to throw it out later. To us, the Canadian Government *is a wolf*, and to sum up, we are determined to prevent its entry into our country, where it has no right. We remain loyal subjects of her Majesty, but we refuse point-blank to recognize the authority of Canada."

This statement did not fully reflect the position which the Métis had developed, but it came close enough. The resistance to Canada would be within the context of loyalty to the Queen, but the Métis also were prepared to negotiate terms and conditions with the Canadians on the basis of resident "rights" which ought to have been discussed much earlier. If Riel and the Métis were to accomplish this end without a bloodbath, the greatest necessity was to unite the entire mixed-blood population of the settlement in support of such negotiations. The problem was not simply that the Métis could not go it alone, but that the alternative to unification was civil war. To the complex process of unification, therefore, Riel now turned.

-2-

Uniting the Mixed-Bloods

On 1 November 1869 the Métis council met in the evening. It called for armed horsemen, led by Ambroise Lépine, to escort members of the Canadian government in waiting — residing just north of the 49th parallel — across to the American side of the line. This was the first real use of the Métis horsemen in such a role. According to Governor McDougall, he was subsequently forced across the border by men bearing arms, who claimed they acted in the name of "the Government they had made." McDougall sent J.A.N. Provencher — who was distantly related to the former Catholic bishop of Red River and who spoke French — northward to negotiate with the rebels. Provencher got as far as St. Norbert, where he assured a gathering of Métis at the blockade that "many members of the New Council would be taken from amongst the population of this country, so as to represent as faithfully as possible all the various interests of the people, and that the policy of the Canadian Government could be ascertained by their general dealings with other Provinces, and by the speeches of ministers on this very question."

A more fatuous assertion was hard to imagine. How or why should the residents of Red River examine the relationship of Canada with other provinces, and where were they to find the speeches of the ministers? More immediately to hand was the record of the dealings of Canada with Red River, which suggested a considerably different interpretation. "The people of Canada," Provencher continued, "would be only too glad to be relieved of a portion of their responsibility, by granting to those people free political institutions and self-government as soon as practicable." The Métis were not fools, and they saw through phrases like "as soon as practicable." What was Canada waiting for? Provencher was told that these assurances were too late. The Métis and the anglophone mixed-bloods were already talking about a common front, following which they would negotiate with the Canadian government. Provencher informed the Canadian government that he had been told at St. Norbert that "if the

Canadian Government was willing to do it, they [the Métis] were ready to open negotiations with them, or with any person vested with full powers, in view of settling the terms of their coming into the Dominion of Canada." He was then politely escorted back across the border. This seemed straightforward enough. The insurgents had told a representative of the Canadian government what they wanted, and the Canadian government received this information on 26 November. Unfortunately, it did not act.

As Provencher was being returned to the United States from his effort at diplomacy, Captain Donald Cameron tried another strategy, based on the standard British imperial assumption that a solitary Briton, armed with nothing but panache, could always face down an angry mob of indigenous people. Cameron, driving a team of magnificent black horses, decided to run through the barricade, which was only three feet high. Muttering about "being accustomed to such matters," he urged his horses to a gallop and literally drove over one of the rebels before his horses were seized and halted. He demanded to be allowed to drive to Winnipeg for supplies, but he was forced to join Provencher under armed escort back to Pembina.

The United States and Red River

S ome considerable irony was connected with the fact that Governor McDougall and his party were blocked from entrance into Red River and were forced to cool their heels in the United States. As the West had developed after 1840, the connection between Red River and the United States — particularly St. Paul, Minnesota — had become an increasingly close one. By 1869, the major trade, transportation, and communications routes into Fort Garry all came via the United States rather than through British territory. The Red River carts transported the bulk of the settlement's trade goods north and south, and St. Paul was its chief market and supply centre. The most expeditious transportation route to Red River was by American railway to the railhead at Georgetown, transferring in the summer to a steamboat. McDougall himself had travelled to his new assignment via the American route. Postal communications to the settlement from the East and from Europe ran through Pembina, employing the American post office.

American expansionists like James Wickes Taylor (1819-93) and Minnesota Senator Alexander Ramsey confidently expected that, in the fullness of time, Red River and the Canadian North-West would fall within the American political orbit as well. When the news of the transfer of the British Northwest to Canada reached Minnesota in 1869, the *St.*

Paul Daily Press commented of Rupert's Land: "If politically it belongs to Canada, geographically and commercially it belongs not to Canada but to Minnesota. Shut off and walled out from Canada by the wild and rugged uplift of primary rocks which divides the Hudson and Superior basins...nothing but an imaginary line...separates it from Minnesota." The expansionists were quite pleased to point out that the people of the settlement were being treated like cattle. Senator Ramsey had personally added an amendment to the annual American consular appropriations bill which had established a consulate in Winnipeg, and Oscar Malmros had appeared in the village in August of 1869, opening his consulate in Emmerling's Hotel. "Dutch George" Emmerling was himself an American, and the place had the only decent rooms and bar (plus pool tables) in town. It became the watering place for the small American presence in Red River, which consisted of Malmros, a handful of merchants, and the occasional visitor from south of the border like Enos Stutsman, the legless lawyer from Dakota, who was the treasury agent at the customs house in Pembina and occasionally practised law in the settlement's courts.

Without doubt, the Americans were fishing in the troubled waters of Red River discontent. Canadians tended to be paranoid about the United States at the best of times, still remembering the vast territorial claims north of the 49th parallel the Americans had advanced after the Civil War. Moreover, the Canadian government could hardly help but realize how tenuous were the physical connections between Red River and Ottawa. The entire situation conspired to encourage Canada to take American activities in Rupert's Land far more seriously than they should have been.

By all rational arguments, the Métis should have been far more attracted to the Yankees than ever was the case. While we can never get inside the head of Louis Riel, it is quite likely that he took as much advantage as he could of Canadian fears in order to increase Métis leverage with Ottawa over the terms of annexation.

In the late summer and autumn of 1869, the American press in St. Paul assiduously followed the Red River story. Most of its information had come second-hand from its listening post at Pembina, home of the American post office and, after the beginning of November, the future Canadian government of Red River in exile. Many of the exaggerated reports of developments in the settlement probably originated with the McDougall party. The fastest way for McDougall to communicate with Ottawa was via the American telegraph. The American newspapers jumped on any news of discontent in the settlement. They were fond of exaggerating Yankee influence with the Métis and especially of associating Métis resistance with the substantial Indian restlessness in the West, a consequence of the speed of the expansion of American settlement and lack of concern for the niceties of aboriginal-white relationships. The Canadian government in Ottawa usually learned of events in Red River from reports in the St. Paul newspapers, which usually had the latest "intelligence" several weeks ahead of the Canadian newspapers. The reports from St. Paul tended to make the Métis resistance sound like something that had been orchestrated in the Minnesota capital. The Americans certainly approved of what was happening at Fort Garry.

The Seizure of Upper Fort Garry

On 2 November, the same day that McDougall was escorted back to American territory, another armed party of Métis, 120 strong, took decisive action in the settlement itself. Brandishing their rifles, they marched into Fort Garry through an open gate and took possession of the HBC post. With typical politeness, Louis Riel met William Cowan — the officer in charge — inside the fort, and said he was sorry to have come, assuring the HBC official that Company property would be respected and nobody would be hurt. Officials of the Company had been warned several times over the past few days of the risk of such a takeover, but no measures of protection were taken, prompting many in the settlement to think that the occupation was a result of collusion between the Métis and HBC officialdom, particularly Governor McTavish. Both William McTavish — in his sickbed dying of consumption — and William Cowan always vehemently denied connivance, although Cowan admitted in 1874 that he and McTavish had contemplated defending the fort, but decided that "those who were best affected to the Company" were those in insurrection. McTavish subsequently wrote to Joseph Howe that neither he nor Cowan had suspected a takeover, but even if they had, "we were powerless to prevent it." The settlement boasted 26 former soldiers remaining from the Chelsea Pensioners and Royal Canadian Rifles, argued McTavish, who were mostly "old worn out men, and those among them who are otherwise have already publicly and repeatedly refused to acknowledge the Company's right to command them to take up arms during civil disturbances."

While the armed party of Métis were riding on their way to the fort, wild rumours circulated around the village of Winnipeg about their intentions. Some said that an attack was to be made on Dr. Schultz's store, other that Schultz and editor Walter Bown of the Nor'-Wester were the targets. Another rumour circulating was that an oath of allegiance was to be administered to all "foreigners. " Instead, the villagers discovered that those occupying the fort were kept under firm discipline. They took over policing of the streets, and a number of drunks ended up in the local gaol. "The Government, so far," wrote one observer, "is generally acknowledged to be an improvement upon that of the Company."

In any event, Riel — without bloodshed — had now established a central base for his movement. He also apparently had a flag, which at this point was described as being "composed of a white ground, upon which are displayed three crosses — the centre one large and scarlet coloured, the side ones smaller and gold coloured. A golden fringe binds the white ground." One correspondent to the Montreal *Herald* reported that 402 men had answered the muster roll, all bearing arms, and another 100 had taken the oath while Provencher was in St. Norbert. Whether Riel actually moved into the fort at this point is an open question. The newspaper correspondence of Joseph James Hargrave, who continued to reside in the Fort, certainly suggests that Riel was in residence. According to one of his letters written on 20 November, both Riel and John Bruce were living in apartments in the fort. What is certain is that the insurgents were by this point stopping and searching all mail travelling in both directions. Letters to the McDougall party were being taken to Pembina by roundabout routes across the plains.

As for William McDougall, he fulminated in correspondence to all and sundry, including Governor McTavish, about the lack of action by the officials of Red River, but as he himself acknowledged, in noting that McTavish did not call for assistance from the community: "I must, therefore, conclude that your better knowledge of the disposition of the people and of the means at your disposal to enforce your authority, convince you that such a call would prove ineffectual." McTavish would respond by pointing out that the local authorities had no official information about the takeover. McDougall pressed for a proclamation from McTavish which declared the opposition to Canada to be illegal. In the short run, the only proclamation that was issued — written on 6 November — was "By order of the President, Louis Riel, Secretary."

Red River had always been a rumour-mill. As a result of its small interrelated population with a strong oral tradition, its limited area, and the unavailability of daily communications media, rumours spread rapidly. Three centres of rumour-mongering were the bar of Emmerling's hotel, the post-office in the store of Alexander Begg and A.G.B. Bannatyne — where everyone went to pick up their mail — and now the guard-room of Upper Fort Garry. In addition to rumours, Red River in late 1869 was subject to the dissemination of information by what a century later would be called "unattributed sources." There seems little other way to describe some of the material that was sent to the eastern press by Red River correspondents in this period. Take, for example, this statement sent to the Montreal *Herald* by "Fort Garry", dated 6 November. "Fort Garry" was sympathetic to the insurgents, and in general well-informed. He wrote:

I hear there is to be a proclamation, and that the reasons assigned for rising will be that their consent was not asked by the Canadian people — that they were 'sold like so many sheep'; that the Canadian Government should, before entering into negotiations with the Hudson's Bay Company, have consulted the natives of the country, and that if this had been done, they would have listened to what the Commissioners of the government had to say; but having been transferred in the way they were, nothing was left to them as brave men but to resent the insult. My informant [could he have been Riel himself?] was not sure that it will not be stated that if the Canadian Government still sends a Commissioner they will hear him, but will listen to no one sent in the capacity of Governor. As to their future intentions they are, I believe, to communicate their position to the Imperial Government. They are anxious that it should be clearly understood that their actions have been solely directed against the Canadian and not at all against the Imperial Government. They will not submit to be the 'colony of a colony.'

This sounds very much like a deliberate "leak" to the press on someone's part. Surely the Canadians would get the signal.

On behalf of the President and representatives of the French-speaking population of Rupert's Land in Council, the inhabitants of Rupert's Land were invited to send 12 representatives to "form one body with the above Council…to consider the present political state of this Country and to adopt such measures as may be deemed best for the future welfare of the same." The meeting was called for 16 November. According to "Red River" (Joseph James Hargrave writing to the Montreal *Herald*), considerable trouble occurred over the printing of this proclamation. When Riel as secretary of the Métis committee brought the proclamation to Dr. Walter Bown of the *Nor'-Wester* — who had the only operational press in town — Bown refused to print it. But "the Secretary," wrote "Red River," ordered his armed men to take over Bown's press and type, and found two experienced workmen, supervised by James Ross (the leading mixed-blood in the settlement), to do the work. This little incident is not often mentioned in Riel biographies.

It is interesting to observe Riel's unsympathetic attitude toward the independence of the press, the beginning of a pattern that would be continued over the ensuing months. The Métis and the *Nor'-Wester* had clashed since its ownership had been assumed by John Christian Schultz, but Riel clearly saw the press as an instrument that should be in the hands of the people in power, to be used solely for their purposes. The Bown incident is perhaps even more interesting in several other respects.

For one thing, it provides evidence of the beginning of co-operation between Louis Riel and James Ross, who had returned to Red River from the East in August. For another, it indicates that Riel now felt secure enough to order personally the use of force to achieve what he felt needed to be done.

The Council of Twenty-Four

On 16 November the representatives of the anglophone and francophone mixed-blood communities — 12 from each side — assembled at the Red River courthouse to discuss what was to be done about the crisis with Canada. The delegates assembled at noon, and 150 armed men escorted them into the council chamber. The escorts fired off a "feu de joie" in welcome, while there was a 24-gun salute from the cannon at the fort. These salutes became the first item of business at the meeting. The English-speaking delegates saw them as an unwarrantable display of military force, while the Métis denied coercive intentions, seeing the salutes merely as "light-hearted" celebration. The 12 anglophones attending the meeting were a cross-section of the community they represented. The delegation consisted of three mixed-bloods, one full-blooded aboriginal, six long-time Scottish settlers, and two newcomers — a Canadian and an American — known to be sympathetic to American annexation.

The settlement's anglophone mixed-bloods were under-represented, but the anglophone members were hardly otherwise stacked in favour of anything or anybody. As for the francophone delegation, none of its 12 members had any connection with those who had before the resistance been regarded as leaders of the Métis community. In short, these represented a new generation of Métis, most not of previously prominent families. We do not have a sufficiently detailed knowledge of the undercurrents of Métis society and politics to know whether these new Métis figures had naturally surfaced because of the crisis or whether they had been handpicked by Louis Riel. No reporters or visitors were allowed at this council, although rumours of what was said inevitably leaked out.

Several observations can be made about these meetings. In the first place, Louis Riel did most of the talking for the Métis, and the fact that he was allowed to dominate the debate says something both about his influence and the degree of Métis homogeneity, at least among the ranks of the delegates. The anglophones were less united from the beginning. Although the mixed-bloods were under-represented, it was a mixed-blood — James Ross — who served as the principal counter-spokesman to Louis Riel. Ross was the son of Alexander Ross, only recently returned to Red River from a journalistic career in Ontario; he intended to open a newspaper to compete with the Nor'-Wester. Other voices were heard in the English delegation as well. Nevertheless, the entire discussion revolved around the assumption — often stated explicitly by Riel — that there were two communities in Red River, francophone and anglophone, that needed to act in concert.

Riel may not have been very well prepared for these meetings, but it is hard to know what he ought to have done, particularly at the outset when he did not know what the anglophones thought or how they had been instructed. The meeting may have been premature, but Riel was operating against the looming deadline of 1 December. If some sense of internal unity among the major communities of Red River could not be achieved before the date of the official transfer, the Métis resistance would be in serious trouble. Some notes for these meetings do survive, in the hand of Riel. They are neatly written in French, suggesting that these were later copies rather than hurried originals. But the only detailed first-hand perspective we have on these important discussions about the future of Red River comes from Riel himself, who may well have suppressed all sorts of things, including other voices from his own side.

After the initial jostling over the salutes, there were several more rounds of sparring. The anglophones requested fresh elections, in which the French concurred — once the two sections had agreed on a line of conduct. For their part, the French wanted all instructions from con-stituents put on the table, so that the "true intentions" of the two sections could be known. The anglophones complained about the taking up of arms, the occupation of Fort Garry, the illegal opposition of the entrance of the Queen's representative. The French answered that their custom was to repel with arms all enemies, adding that the HBC had sold the rights of government, "yet neither England nor the Company has warned us of this." Although the mixed-bloods were critical of what the Métis had done, they stopped short of walking out of the gathering.

At this point, Governor McTavish's secretary Joseph James Hargrave knocked at the door with a communication from the governor. The anglophones wanted it read immediately; Riel — sensing that it was probably a proclamation declaring resistance illegal — proposed that it be read at the close of the present session. An interchange then occurred between Riel and James Ross over the occupation of the fort. Ross said the means employed by the Métis were "unconstitutional" because McDougall and McTavish were the Queen's representatives. Riel answered that the Métis "have never refused to obey the Queen of England" and thought highly of McTavish. Well, then, said Ross, you can't object to reading his proclamation. Riel conceded.

The governor's proclamation was read. The text was not quite what William McDougall had demanded from his isolation in Pembina. McTavish noted that a large number of unlawful acts had been committed, including an avowal of resistance to the transfer of the government of Red River to Canada. Instead of adopting lawful and constitutional means — neither McTavish nor anyone else ever outlined a practical policy of lawful and constitutional objections to what governments far away had decided — some people had resorted to behaviour that threatened "the evils of anarchy and the horrors of war." McTavish urged everyone to disperse peaceably lest they provoke a "crisis out of which may come incalculable good or immeasurable evil." The governor had not totally condemned resistance, but had talked instead about a crisis which could produce either positive or negative results. At the conclusion of the reading of this document there was an understandable silence.

In many ways, what followed this silence was a major turning point, perhaps the major turning point, in the history of Red River. Had the anglophone delegates gone home at this juncture, co-operation between the different communities would probably never have been achieved. James Ross rose and stated that he was awaiting with confidence the Métis evacuation of Fort Garry. Riel answered, "Not yet." Ross replied, "You can no longer protest ignorance." Riel riposted, "A Proclamation, however emphatic, still does not remove what is just in our pretensions." Ross pressed his point: "Your acts are now acts of rebellion." Riel put his oratory into high gear: "If we rebel against the Company which sold us and against Canada which wishes to buy us, we do not rebel against the English government, which has not yet given its approval to the actual transfer of the country. What! We recognize the government of Assinboia so far as it exists." This last raised laughter, which says much about the settlement's opinion of the existing government.

Ross tried again. "You make a pretence of recognizing it." Riel turned to his Métis compatriots, asking, "Do we indeed only pretend to recognize it? Come, speak." The Métis answered in unison, "Non, Non." Riel continued. "Moreover, we are faithful to our native land. We shall protect it against the dangers which menace it. We wish that the people of Red River be a free people." Riel then appealed for unity. "Let us help one another. We are all brothers and kindred, says Mr. Ross, and it is true. Let us not separate." Then he picked out McTavish's words about good and evil from the proclamation. "See what Mr. McTavish [says]. He says that from this assembly and from the decisions of this assembly can come inestimable good. See how he speaks. Is it surprising? His children are of mixed-blood like ourselves." At this point, according to Riel's notes, there was an adjournment. What would the mixed-bloods do? On the second day of the council, the anglophone delegates appeared promptly at the appointed hour of 10 a.m. at the courthouse. Riel had won his gamble.

Louis Riel v. Canada

The Métis delegates did not themselves appear until noontime for the council meeting, but the discussions this day were on a more friendly basis. It was still difficult to come to an understanding. The chief disagreement was between those who wanted a pre-emptive strike against Canada (the Métis), and those who preferred to negotiate after the fact. The emerging anglophone position, Riel recorded, was to admit McDougall, ask him the essential questions, and then send him back if he did not grant what was wanted. In contrast, the French "say that if McDougall is once settled in, nothing will get rid of him." He would have official papers and be acting in the name of the Queen. "It would be really an act of rebellion to try to turn him out when he had established himself." Although agreement between the two communities was not reached, they were still talking. Moreover, there was no evidence that the mixed-bloods would take up arms in aid of the Canadians.

Walter Bown would bring out a newspaper "extra" on 17 November, called *The Nor'-Wester and Pioneer*. The extra printed an address to Governor McTavish and his proclamation. As several letter-writers to the eastern newspapers noted, the newspaper missed out the governor's fifth point, apparently because it had obtained a copy surreptitiously. In any event, it was to be the last issue of the newspaper to be circulated in the settlement. Riel closed down the *Nor'-Wester* (and the *Pioneer*) in early December, turning the offices into a guard-room. In the wake of the first days of meeting between the Métis and the mixed-bloods, Walter Bown — the editor of the *Nor'-Wester* — apparently obtained a statement of the "rights" claimed by the Métis, perhaps by the same means as he got a copy of the Governor McTavish's proclamation. Bown forwarded the list to his brother in Ontario, who in turn forwarded it to Sir John A. Macdonald. We have absolutely no idea of the precise provenance of this listing, but it was probably another "unattributed" statement from Riel or another of the Métis leadership which somehow got into Bown's hands. The demands are both credible and sensible, and gives us some notion of what the National Committee would have said to a Canadian commissioner if one were sent to Red River. The list read:

1. That the Indian title to the whole territory should be at once paid for.

2. That on account of their relationship with the Indians a certain portion of this money shall be paid over to them.

3. That all their claims to lands should be at once conceded.

4. That 300 acres shall be granted to each of their children.

5. That they and their descendants shall be exempted from taxation.

6. That a certain portion of lands shall be set aside for the support of the R.C. Church and Clergy.

7. That the Council shall be elective and at once chosen.

8. That Dr. Schultz and others shall be sent out of the Territory forthwith.

It was a pity that these terms had not been given to Joseph Howe when he had visited the settlement a few weeks earlier, for this might have given them some standing in Ottawa. As it was, even if the list was authentic, the Canadians could do nothing with it.

From our modern standpoint, the demands represent the earliest detailed statement we have of what the Métis wanted as a condition of agreeing to allow Governor McDougall into the country, probably generated before the Americans began advising them on what they should insist upon. The list is interesting both for what it includes and what it omits. Confirmation of existing land claims and further land grants based upon aboriginal rights were obviously important. Canada would have to recognize that the Métis were entitled to a share of the aboriginal land rights, something the British had refused to do earlier. Were the Indian title settled, the Métis claims for lands in the "hay privilege" could also be confirmed. Some legal recognition of and provision for financial support of the Roman Catholic Church was also important. Also essential was an immediate election of members of the Council. One suspects the banishment of leaders of the Canadian Party was intended to be negotiable. No mention is made of provincial status at this point. Almost without exception, these conditions were implied, if not made explicit, in previous actions and statements of the Métis.

What seems absolutely crucial however, is that these conditions go considerably beyond what the Canadians were prepared to offer as guarantees to the residents of Red River. Canada was talking about guaranteeing existing titles, not confirming Métis land rights as a part of aboriginal land rights. Canada had said nothing about the place of the Catholic Church in a Canadian colony, and it was only planning an appointive council in the short run. The Canadians had no reason to think that their assurances would be sufficient to make a smooth takeover possible, even if the Métis were prepared to listen to them.

The meeting of the council was interrupted so that the Court of Quarterly Sessions could use the courthouse, virtually the only public meeting place in the settlement outside Upper Fort Garry. J. J. Hargrave used the occasion to explain the workings of court in Red River for his eastern readers, emphasizing that "substantial justice has been generally administered." One of the cases heard at this session was a charge of aggravated assault against four Canadians working on the road crew.

They were accused of seizing and threatening to drown John Snow in the course of a dispute over wages. Two of the men were found guilty and ordered to pay a fine within 30 days. Alexander Begg in his journal suggested that a better defence might have ended in acquittal. One of the men, a tall, well-built, Irish-Canadian named Thomas Scott, was overheard to say as he left the courtroom that "It was a pity they had not ducked Snow when they were at it as they had not got their money's worth." This was Thomas Scott's first appearance in the records of Red River. Unfortunately for him, it would not be the last.

Making the Provisional Government

In a meeting of the two sides on 22 November, James Ross insisted upon the gains that would come from the admission of Red River into Confederation, maintaining that the union "of this vast country to Canada is necessary to the dearest interests of British North America." Riel concurred, but argued that the country needed to be put on a footing so that existing residents could continue to live prosperously, while outsiders "may find institutions all ready to make them happy by bestowing on them those liberties which all America likes to see its children enjoy without distinction." He continued to refuse to allow the French to lay down their arms. A number of other events occurred on the same day as the reconvening of the council.

The meeting of the mixed-blood communities seemed to be serving as a lightning rod for other interests. In the morning of the 22nd, Enos Stutsman arrived in the village from Pembina. He regaled the drinkers at the bar at Emmerling's Hotel with satiric descriptions of the Canadian officials caught at the border. It was probably Stutsman who brought a copy of the St. Paul *Daily Press* containing a statement from Canadian businessman W. E. Sanford, who had accompanied Joseph Howe to Red River. Sanford told the newspaper that word of the uprising was greatly exaggerated, and subsequently admitted that he had planted the story to discourage American troublemakers from rushing to the settlement.

It was certainly Stutsman who circulated a letter from the Chippewa Indians to Governor McDougall, dated 26 September, which he claimed had not been presented by the aboriginals because they did not want its claims confused with those of the Métis. The Chippewa wanted to know "the intention of the Government you represent respecting our people and lands." The letter wondered what interests the Canadians had purchased from the Hudson's Bay Company, since the aboriginals had never sold their lands and had only allowed the company to occupy a limited district for a limited amount of time. The white men from Canada, moreover, had started to divide the land into small lots without consultation and any treaty negotiation. This statement of aboriginal land rights and complaint about the Canadians only emphasized the ham-handedness of the Canadian procedures on the takeover.

Also on the 22nd, Dr. Schultz circulated a petition calling for the council to admit the Canadian officials. Postmaster A.G.B. Bannatyne refused to sign it because "those engaged in getting it up have been to a very great extent the cause of all our present troubles." Bannatyne sent a letter to the council denying that he was in collusion with the rebels and insisting that he had not tampered with the mail. He admitted, however, that he was in sympathy with the efforts of the Métis to claim "the unassailable rights of a free people worthy of having a thorough & complete voice in the management of their own affairs."

On the following day — 23 November — Louis Riel demanded at Upper Fort Garry all the records connected with the public business of the settlement, and had them carried to his "office" in the fort. Our best account of the seizure comes from J. J. Hargrave in a "Red River Settlement" letter to the Montreal *Herald*. Hargrave wrote as a first-hand observer, as indeed he was. According to his story, Mr. John H. McTavish, the accountant of the HBC at Upper Fort Garry, had been summoned early in the morning to Louis Riel's office in the fort. He was told to hand over to Riel the land register and accounts of the council of Assiniboia. When he refused he was escorted under armed guard to the public office, which was next door to the room Hargrave occupied as the governor's secretary. McTavish asked Hargrave "to make haste and witness a transaction of an irregular nature about to take place on the spot." Riel again demanded the records of the public business of the settlement, and when McTavish refused, Riel himself searched the shelves for the books he wanted, and had them carried to his own office. Most of the books taken dealt with the accounts between the HBC and residents of the settlement. The land register was the official record of titles to all surveyed land in the settlement. Riel's men also subsequently seized the customs records, and he threatened to begin collecting all debts for import duties owed by the merchants of the settlement. This series of actions much frightened many in the settlement. The anglophone delegates about to attend a reconvened council debated their response to these acts of aggression, but decided to meet and continue their discussion.

At the meeting, both sides agreed on the need for stronger government and on the weaknesses of the government of Assiniboia in recent years. The anglophones concluded from this that Canadian government was a necessity. Riel answered that it was time the people of the colony considered the formation of a provisional government to protect themselves and to treat with Canada to "force it to grant us a form of responsible government." Although he did not say so, his earlier actions that morning in sequestering the records of the government of the settlement were probably closely connected with the intention to create a provisional government to supplant the existing one. He asked the English-speaking delegates to check with their constituents, inviting the latter to send delegates empowered to join the Métis in organizing a provisional government. James Ross warned of a Canadian military expedition if the settlement did not adopt a moderate position. Riel answered that winter protected Red River. We have six months, Riel predicted, to get a settlement. This prophecy proved quite accurate. The meeting adjourned with Riel recording, "Adjournment, no understanding, little hope of one."

Following adjournment, the Métis met well into the night. Louis Riel spoke for seven hours in an effort to convince his "National Committee" to agree to form a provisional government. A number of Americans were consulted. "No one was ready," Riel recorded. "What fears and hesitations there were to overcome. It is incredible what misgivings I had to overcome in them." The principal Métis fear was that their actions would be perceived as rebellion against the Queen. Riel insisted that they could remain faithful to the Queen while taking over a government too weak to act. If the Queen knew what the Métis wanted, said Riel, she would listen to them. Riel said he was willing to wait until after 1 December (when the Canadian takeover supposedly would become effective) to proclaim the formation of the provisional government, although how waiting would make the action any less rebellious was never made clear.

The Fort Garry council met again on 24 November. When asked what the Métis would do, Riel responded by querying whether the anglophones would join with them to resolve the present difficulties. The anglos were equivocal. Riel said, "You will know indeed what we want, on our side. We want what all the French parishes want. And they want to form a provisional government for our protection and to treat with Canada. We invite you to join with us sincerely. That government will be composed equally of French and English. It will be only Provisional." Just how much of a bombshell the suggestion of a provisional government was is open to dispute. In any event, the anglophones requested time to consult their constituents, since their instructions did not authorize such actions. The council then adjourned until 1 December.

A conference of English-speaking inhabitants was held in Winnipeg at the office of Messrs. Bannatyne and Begg on 26 November. Present were Bernard Rogan Ross, Dr. Curtis Bird, Alexander Logan, A.G.B. Bannatyne, Alexander Begg, Oscar Malmros (the American consul in Winnipeg) and W.B. O'Donoghue. Although these were influential residents, the gathering was in no way representative of public opinion in the settlement. All parties present agreed that the best plan would be to allow the old HBC rule to continue in the form of a legislative council, with the people electing an executive council, in order to treat with the Canadian government. This plan had the great merit of continuing the legitimate government of Red River, which would have made charges of rebellion much more difficult. It had even more merit than this meeting realized. The Canadian government had cabled to Britain this very day to request a delay of the transfer until "peaceable possession" of the territory could be guaranteed. However clever a plan, however, this proposal of 26 November had taken too long to be formulated. Louis Riel had already decided on another option, and he was not about to be deflected from it.

Louis Riel spoke at the new fire engine house in Winnipeg on that same evening at a public meeting of anglophones, mainly Americans and Canadians. He had entered the hall with his bodyguard and was spontaneously applauded. Pensioner Michael Power asked Riel for the source of his authority. Riel answered hesitantly in English. He said he drew his authority from the people, and that the Métis did not wish to impose their provisional government on anyone who did not wish to owe allegiance. He had no money, and would have been better off working to support his family. He and his supporters could not really afford to give so much time to public affairs. He concluded by insisting that the provisional government was not inspired by the Catholic Church. According to Alexander Begg, even Schultz supporters applauded Riel in the course of his remarks.

Power himself rambled on about loyalty to the British flag, and a shoemaker named McPherson opposed the provisional government, telling the humorous story of his early victimization by Thomas Spence's "Republic of Manitobah" in 1868 to great laughter. The story involved a chase through the snow after McPherson, clad only in his underwear.

J. J. Hargrave reported that after this gathering he visited with three friends. He made fun of the idea that most of the participants at the meeting had been armed, but modified his opinion, he wrote, "when my three friends pulled, each man from a belt concealed under his coat, a revolver pistol."

The following day another meeting held in Winnipeg discussed the earlier selection of delegates to the gathering of the two mixed-blood groups. It was decided that any householder, property owner, or resident of seven months tenure could vote in future elections. John Christian Schultz argued for one week's residency, but was defeated by a vote of 19 to 13, which suggests how many were present. At about the same time, Louis Riel wrote Schultz that his house was suspected of being the centre of dissidence. Riel added in a veiled threat how sorry he would be to have to take energetic action against the Canadian. At issue was some Canadian government pork stored in Schultz's house, which Riel wanted to take over and certainly did not want removed to the Stone Fort at Lower Fort Garry.

Riel subsequently accepted and then later rejected on 30 November the scheme for the continuation of HBC rule. The HBC government was "dead already," he insisted latterly, "& therefore not in force nor able to protect the people." Riel's assumption was that the Canadian takeover would go ahead, and therefore the HBC rule would be superseded. That same day, the British colonial secretary responded to Canadian Governor-General Sir John Young about the Canadian decision to delay the transfer. Earl Granville insisted that it had never been suggested that the settlement of Red River was being handed over in a state of tranquillity. Instead, he argued, William McDougall had caused the disturbance by his behaviour. Granville added acerbically, "The Canadian Government, having by this measure given occasion to an outbreak of violence in a Territory which they have engaged to take over, now appear to claim the right of postponing indefinitely the completion of their engagements to the company, and of imposing on her Majesty's Government the responsibility of putting down the resistance which has thus arisen." The British could not now accept the surrender of the territory from the Hudson's Bay Company, which was therefore still legally in control of Red River.

Thus the decision not to work with the existing HBC government turned out to be a mistake on Riel's part — albeit an understandable one — for the takeover of the Council of Assiniboia by the residents would simultaneously have relieved the insurgents of the charge of rebellion against the Queen and united both sections of the settlement. At an assemblage of anglophone leaders on 30 November, gathered for the meeting of the council the next day, the concept of reforming the Council of Assiniboia was endorsed. Nobody in the settlement disputed the need for better terms. Riel's decision to press on with a provisional government became even more of an error when, due to the refusal of Canada to take over the West on 1 December, the HBC government formally remained by default the one still in force after that date. But from Riel's perspective, to reform the Council of Assiniboia after McDougall had declared the Canadian takeover, would be no less radical a step than the declaration of a provisional government, and a good deal less satisfactory.

The whole question of the legitimacy of the HBC government was a tricky one. The existing government remained in force when the Canadians did not assume authority on 1 December. At the same time, nobody in Red River — or in Pembina — knew that the transfer had not gone through. At the end of November, Prime Minister Sir John A.

Macdonald had warned William McDougall of the dangers of precipitate action in a letter the Canadian governor-in-waiting would not receive until well into December. "An assumption of the government by you," Macdonald had written, "of course puts an end to that of the Hudson's Bay Company's authorities." Macdonald continued, "There would then be, if you were not admitted into the country, no legal government existing, and anarchy must follow. In such a case, no matter how the anarchy is produced, it is quite open by the law of nations for the inhabitants to form a government *ex necessitate* for the protection of life and property, and such a government has certain sovereign rights by the *ius gentium*, which might be very convenient for the United States, but exceedingly convenient to you." McDougall, of course, did not receive this letter, any more than he received an earlier warning dated 19 November from Joseph Howe reminding him that he had no authority until officially given it. The warning from Howe merely confirmed McDougall's earlier commitment not to usurp authority without approval from Ottawa.

In what had become a familiar occurrence in this prolonged comedy of errors, William McDougall and Ottawa miscommunicated. McDougall assumed that his pledges and Ottawa's warnings all dealt with assuming power prematurely, before the date of the transfer, which he assumed would be 1 December 1870. It did not occur to the man appointed to be lieutenant-governor that the government of Canada might postpone the date, particularly an action taken so close to the date that there was no time to get word to Pembina. On the day of the transfer, William McDougall walked defiantly north of the boundary and read a proclamation that ought to have made him legally the lieutenant-governor of the North-West Territories. He did subsequently issue and circulate in the settlement this same proclamation, which, in the name of the Queen, proclaimed McDougall the lieutenant-governor of the North-West Territories and advised "our loving subjects of the said Territories...to take notice and govern themselves accordingly." The document was quite illegal, but its assumption of power also quite understandable.

The story of the circulation and subsequent printing of this document is a fascinating one. Louis Riel had stopped the publication of the local newspapers and seized the presses, partly to prevent Canadian material from circulating in the settlement. Nevertheless, Colonel John Dennis had smuggled a copy of the proclamation into Red River and had managed to get several copies of it printed out by hand — in large letters — in French and English. The problem then became to find type and a printing press. George Winship, a young Canadian who had worked for the *Nor'-Wester*, contrived, under pretense of cleaning up the newspaper office, to smuggle enough type out from under the noses of the guards to print the proclamation. He and Patrick Laurie, another *Nor'-Wester* employee, found an old hand-printing press, used cardboard boxes to hold the type, and laboriously ran off 300 copies of the document. Copies of the original which survive illustrate the difficulties of printing and the shortage of type. The printer had to use inverted commas instead of apostrophes, for example. McDougall also granted to Colonel John Dennis a commission as "my Lieutenant and a Conservator of the Peace in and for the Northwest Territories," calling upon Dennis to raise an armed force to "attack, arrest, disarm or disperse" any men committing acts of lawless violence. Dennis would try to do so over the next few days, but found nobody but Charles Arkoll Boulton anxious to join him. He apparently ran off copies of this commission on the same hand printing press, which he had carried to the Stone Fort in a blinding snowstorm.

Although the Canadian prime minister would never publicly admit the fact, McDougall may indeed have opened the Pandora's box. He had assumed the mantle of government, however erroneously, but was not able to exercise authority. He had thus voided the rule of the HBC and produced anarchy. By Macdonald's own calculation, McDougall's actions had made the establishment of a provisional government legitimate. When the Canadian and British governments subsequently insisted that there had been no formal interruption of governance in Red River, since the HBC government continued in force, both governments conveniently forgot that William McDougall's proclamation had effectively ended the HBC system, at least for the duration of time that the settlement did not know that Canada had refused to assume authority. That period was most of December, a long time to believe there was no government. Technically the HBC was still in power, but this was a technical fiction only. It was in this time period that the provisional government had been proclaimed.

The French and the English mixed-bloods resumed their meeting on 1 December. Riel insisted that the proclamation changed nothing. All McDougall had to do was prove that he intended to treat the inhabitants well. "If he guarantees our rights," Riel maintained, "I am one of those who will go to meet him in order to escort him as far as the seat of his government." James Ross asked the critical question, "What will we ask of him?" A period of "disorderly discussion followed," and at 4 p.m. the French requested an adjournment of two hours to formulate something in writing. Riel apparently consulted with several Americans hanging around one of the local hotels, and produced a document incorporating four clauses of a Dakota bill of rights sent a month earlier to the St. Paul *Daily Press*.

The resulting document, the first Red River "List of Rights," was printed under date of 4 December on one of the printing presses held by

Riel. It began by claiming the right of the people to elect their own legislature, which had the power to pass all local laws by a two-thirds majority over an executive veto. It was thus considerably more detailed, and much more American, than the earlier statement of rights forwarded by Dr. Bown to the prime minister. Gone was the demand for continued support for the Roman Catholic Church, gone was the insistence on Métis sharing in aboriginal rights. In this version, the Dominion Parliament could make no local act binding on the territory without the consent of its legislature. All local officials (sheriffs, magistrates, constables) were to be elected by the people. The document called for a free homestead and pre-emption land law — very American — and for bilingualism in French and English in both the legislature and the courts — very Canadian. It called for a full and fair representation for Red River in the Canadian Parliament and the continuation of "all privileges, customs and usages existing at the time of the transfer." Whether the earlier Métis conditions had been modified by American influence or by the need to appeal to the wider mixed-blood community is not clear. Probably both played their part. In any event, the new demands for opening negotiations with the Canadians were much more political than the old. The delegates to the council discussed these clauses *seriatim*, and there was general agreement on all sides that they were "fair."

This particular version of Red River "rights" was very strong on political and constitutional matters, especially those required after the transfer to Canada. Except for homestead and pre-emption, however, it was not very explicit about land or aboriginal rights. While the anglophone delegates were anxious to send delegates to negotiate with McDougall on the basis of these conditions, Riel brought such enthusiasm to a quick halt by insisting that the Métis were not interested in any promises, written or oral, from Mr. McDougall. Let him secure these rights to the people of Red River by an act of the Canadian Parliament, Riel proclaimed. Then he would be admitted into the settlement. The English-speaking delegates refused to meet with McDougall under these obviously impossible conditions. Riel responded, "Go, return peacefully to your farms. Rest in the arms of your wives. Give that example to your children. But watch us act. We are going to work and obtain the guarantee of our rights and of yours. You will come to share them in the end."

As "Justitia" wrote somewhat ruefully later in the *Globe*, the "point of an Act of Parliament" had "split the meeting without the two sides uniting, as had been expected." The disagreement was not really over a minor point, however, but was simply a continuation of the previous impasse in a new guise. The anglophones were willing to petition for their rights as supplicants before the Canadians, while Riel wanted to negotiate them from a position of strength. As it turned out, neither approach worked very well. But Riel would certainly be proved right that the Canadian politicians were not to be trusted. Moreover, although none in the settlement were to know it, the Canadians themselves were running well behind local events in their thinking about policy for Red River.

On 4 December 1869, Joseph Howe, as Canadian secretary of state for the provinces, instructed the Very Reverend Grand Vicar Jean-Baptiste Thibault, who was one of those chosen to travel to Red River to attempt to assist "in putting down the unlawful assemblage of people on the Red River, and obtaining access for the Canadian Authorities into the North-West." Thibault had spent many years in Red River and was well known to the Métis. The other representative of the government was Charles de Salaberry, who would accompany Thibault to Red River. De Salaberry was the son of a hero of the War of 1812. He spoke French, but otherwise had little connection with the settlement. The instructions were replete with arguments which Thibault was obviously intended to pass on to the mixed-bloods, who were to be informed that in Canada "men of all origins, creeds and complexions, stand upon one broad footing of perfect equality in the eye of the Government and the law."

Certainly that was the way things were supposed to be, but only if one ignored the previous Canadian treatment of the aboriginal people. Howe was willing to blame part of the problems of transition upon the imperial government, but he insisted that the residents had been artfully misled. The instructions of 28 September to McDougall, he maintained, demonstrated how groundless were the suspicions of unfair treatment that had been widely circulated in some Canadian newspapers. The secretary of state did not specify which suspicions were groundless, however, and his very letter to Thibeault made quite clear that Canada was still committed to "a probationary period, till the growth of population, and some political training" prepared Red River for "self-government." The American example was noted. Thibault was authorized only to assure the residents of the settlement "that the Governor-General and his Council will gladly welcome the period when the Queen can confer, with their entire approbation, the largest measure of self-government on her subjects in that region, compatible with the preservation of British interests on this Continent, and the integrity of the Empire." Not surprisingly, a provisional government committed to the "List of Rights" of 1 December would find such attitudes and "trust us" assurances both useless and patronizing when Thibault appeared at the settlement.

On December 7, Howe wrote to William McDougall with another version of the current line of the Canadian government. It was basically unaltered. Printed copies of the earlier instructions to the governor were included for distribution in the settlement; they were supposed to demonstrate the groundlessness of the suspicions. Copies of a proclamation from the Governor-general were also included for distribution. As we shall see, it is doubtful that either of these documents were ever put in the hands of the residents. McDougall was now to assure the people of the North-West that their civil and religious liberties and privileges, as well as their "properties, rights, and equities of every kind, as enjoyed under the Government of the Hudson's Bay Company," would be continued. He was also allowed, however, to state that the land policy of granting titles would be an unspecified "most liberal," that the Governor's council could establish municipal self-government at once "and in such manner as they think most beneficial to the Country," and that existing customs duties (apart from alcoholic beverages) would continue for two years.

What the concession on municipal government meant is not entirely clear. The Council of Assiniboia was sometimes regarded as a municipal government, often referring to its jurisdiction as the "Municipal District of Assiniboia," but there was no other municipal government in the settlement. In their debates, the Fathers of Confederation had often referred to provincial governments as "municipal governments." Sir John A. Macdonald would subsequently insist that the Temporary Government Act had envisaged the continued existence of the Council of Assiniboia. It would appear, therefore, that the Canadians were now prepared to introduce a two-tiered system of government for Red River, an arrangement which is not transparently obvious anywhere in the documentation and was never clearly explained to anybody.

A two-tiered government would make some sense, of course, for the Canadians were intending to take over and govern the North-West Territories, a huge chunk of land of which Red River was only a small part. Most of the inhabitants of the larger territory were nomadic aboriginals, and Red River clearly was different. If Canada had in mind to give Rupert's Land territorial government without an elected assembly, and Red River municipal government with an elected council, it should have said so much more clearly, particularly since the existing Council of Assiniboia which Macdonald claimed was continued in the Temporary Government Act was not an elected body. More likely, McDougall would merely continue the existing Council of Assiniboia. It may be that the Canadians were as confused over "municipal government" in 1869 as they had been in their earlier formulations of the British North America Act. In any case, Howe in his letter to McDougall, emphasized that the governing arrangements remained temporary, as before. There would be a "liberal constitution" later, but not at the beginning. In short, the Canadians still wanted keep the settlement in colonial tutelage, and to have their good-will accepted on trust.

Louis Riel v. Canada

Apparently in response to the McDougall proclamation, many of the young Canadians around Winnipeg gathered at the house of Dr. John Christian Schultz, waiting for the arrival of a large party of reinforcements recruited by John Dennis from among the anglo mixed-bloods down the river. When it became clear that there were no reinforcements, the house should have been evacuated. But by the time the inhabitants decided to abandon the house, it was surrounded by hundreds of armed Métis. On the morning of 7 December, Riel arrived in front of the Schultz house. He read aloud Dennis's proclamation of the previous day calling for loyal men to rise in arms, and then "threw it on the ground and stamped on it, amid the cheers of his followers." Some Canadians would make much of this gesture of contempt for the proclamation, since Riel did not at this point know it was illegitimate. But few in Canada would admit the corollary of such a characterization of Riel's action, which was to acknowledge there was a state of anarchy in the settlement. The besieged Canadians chose three delegates, including Thomas Scott, to negotiate an arrangement to permit the ladies in the building to retire. They returned to report that Riel refused to make a deal. Those in the house subsequently surrendered unconditionally on promise of protection, and were taken off as prisoners to Upper Fort Garry. The prisoners were, with one exception, Canadians. Their ranks included John Christian Schultz and his wife, John O'Donnell and his wife, Charles Mair and his wife, Thomas Scott, and more than 40 others.

A day later, a proclamation signed by John Bruce and Louis Riel was issued in English and French as the "Declaration of the People of Rupert's Land and the North West." It was printed by William Coldwell at *The Red River Pioneer* office. Coldwell told John Dennis that he had been forced to print it "by threats of armed men." The Declaration was a highly erudite document, obviously familiar with abstruse political theory and the "law of nations." The French version of the Declaration included reference to several obscure royalist political theorists. Some small differences existed between the manuscript French version, which may have been drafted by Father George Dugas, and the printed English version. It began by insisting that a people lacking a government which "commands the obedience and respect of its subjects" was free "to adopt one form of Government in preference to another to give or to refuse aliegance [sic] to that which is proposed." This *ex necessitate* argument was the one anticipated by the prime minister in his letter of 27 November to William McDougall. Curiously enough, however, the declaration continued by eschewing a justification based on the McDougall proclamation of 1 December. Instead, it argued that the HBC had abandoned the people when it had surrendered to Canada all its rights "by transactions with which the people were considered unworthy to be made acquaint-ed." By implication, therefore, Red River was in a state of anarchy from March 1869, although the people had not decided on a form of govern-ment to replace the HBC until 24 November 1869, when a provisional government had been established.

The Declaration then declared a refusal to recognize the authority of Canada, which sought to impose upon the population a despotic form of government. The provisional government was now the only lawful authority in Rupert's land and the North-West, it insisted. The document concluded by stating a readiness to negotiate with the Canadian govern-ment if such were favourable to the "good government and prosperity of this people." The backdating of the assumption of power before 1 December does not negate the assumption of power after 1 December, when McDougall had plainly put the settlement into a state of anarchy by assuming an authority he could not exercise. Those issuing the Declaration did not yet know that McDougall's assumption of authority had been premature, and for some reason they did not wish to rely on the argument that McDougall had claimed power but still could not enter the territory, which had obviously created a vacuum. The neglect of this argument is quite curious, since much of Riel's strategy was based on the creation of anarchy by the blockade of the new government. The most likely explanation is that Dugas, rather than Riel, was responsible for the political theory. In any case, the situation was legally further complicat-ed by the fact that Canada had already cancelled the transfer, unbe-knownst to the people of Red River, and had explicitly continued the Hudson's Bay government and the Council of Assiniboia as the official government of the settlement. At the same time, no one in the settlement doubted that the existing government was bankrupt. All this may seem legal nitpicking, but much of Louis Riel's subsequent history would revolve around the question of whether the provisional government he headed was the legitimate government of the settlement.

On 10 December a celebration was held at the Forks. Riel addressed the Métis at Upper Fort Garry. He hoped that all his men were loyal to the Queen, and that they would be loyal to the new flag of the provi-sional government until their rights "as free born subjects of Queen Victoria" were recognized. At 4 p.m. the flag of the new government was raised for the first time over Upper Fort Garry. The flag contained a fleur-de-lis and a shamrock, the latter allegedly in honour of Mr. O'Donoghue rather than in reference to the Fenians. Governor McTavish arrived just in time to see the flag hauled up the mast. He exclaimed, "Oh, the fools! the fools!" Following the flag-raising, the boys' brass band from St. Boniface, directed by Father Dugas — played a number of tunes, and salutes were fired "until they thought they had wanted powder enough."

The band, still serenading the citizens, continued up Main Road to "Dutch George's" hotel, where cakes were distributed among the crowd. American consul Oscar Malmros reported to Washington, "The revolutionists fulfil the principal function of a government, protection of persons and property, in a highly satisfactory degree." As for Louis Riel, nobody in Red River doubted that the provisional government was his creation and that he was in complete charge. The process of becoming a rebel leader was now complete.

Up to this point, Riel's performance, improvised as he went along, had been quite masterful. His only important error was in refusing to accept Hudson's Bay Company authority as the *de facto* position, and this mistake was quite understandable. More significantly, Riel had shepherded the settlement into rebellion without the loss of a single life.

-3-

Trying to Negotiate with Canada

With the proclamation of the provisional government on 10 December 1869, Louis Riel had crossed the first of a long series of obstacles that would have to be overcome before the Red River situation could be resolved satisfactorily. The American consul Oscar Malmros reported to Washington in the wake of the Métis flag-raising: "The revolutionists fulfil the principal function of a government, protection of persons and property, in a highly satisfactory manner."

Riel had improvised well under very fluid and volatile circumstances. He had kept his goal and his strategy simple. His goal was to force Canada to recognize that the Métis, Scots, and anglophone mixed-bloods, as the long-standing residents of Red River, had rights that could not simply be pushed aside in the takeover. Although he took advice from the Americans and would subsequently allow vague talk of American annexation, there is absolutely no evidence that Riel had any other intention except integration into Canada. His strategy toward this goal was to keep the mixed-blood communities together in the struggle, or at least to prevent the anglophones, including many of the Scottish settlers, from collapsing into the Canadian Party's open arms. The initial provisional government, composed only of Métis, did no more than this. Understandably, he had little hesitancy about treating the recalcitrant resident Canadians roughly. Whether Riel positively sought a bloodless rebellion is not known, but so far he and his followers had achieved one.

Beginning the Provisional Government

Riel and his provisional government faced a number of problems in December of 1869. The first was to continue to provide the settlement with effective government. A collapse into chaos or anarchy would destroy the creditability of the insurgency. To govern the settlement, a source of revenue was necessary, especially to pay for the re-establishment of Upper Fort Garry, which consisted of both Métis "soldiers" and Canadian captives. On 22 December Riel tried to borrow money from the HBC. But Governor McTavish refused to lend any, so Riel and W.B. O'Donoghue took whatever cash they could find in the Company safe and paid off most of the Métis at Upper Fort Garry. Rumour had it that accountant John McTavish allowed himself to be searched for the key to the safe.

Internally, Riel had also to try to enlarge the base of support for his provisional government — and to find a better system of government than martial law. The obvious solution was to bring the anglophones into it. In a private meeting with a Kildonan Scot settler just before Christmas, Riel suggested a council of 24, with 12 representatives from each group, with a president elected from the council, which would act as a court in civil cases. The overture was not immediately successful. The government spent much of December attempting to find a formula for releasing its prisoners, but most of them refused to swear loyalty to the new regime or to promise not to oppose it. Some dissent emerged in the ranks of the prisoners when they learned that they enlisted under false pretenses, since Canada had not assumed control of the settlement on 1 December as expected.

The external problems of the government were manifold. In the first place, there were constant rumours about an Indian war. To some extent these stories were dealt with by a meeting in Silver Heights at the end of the month with a visiting band of Sioux who had arrived in the settlement. Riel distributed 25 pounds of tobacco to them and each visitor was allowed to touch the live wire attached to a large galvanic battery. This produced great hilarity amongst the Sioux, and the Indian menace seemed "galvanized" away. There were also rumours of an American takeover, although Riel and the Métis council did little to give them any credence. Finally, there was the problem of Canada. Securing the rights of the people of Red River within Confederation by negotiation would have to be accomplished swiftly, or the Canadians — whose honour and pride had been badly shaken — would doubtless attempt to settle the matter by force.

Attempting to Negotiate with Canada

The chief problem with negotiation was the need to find someone authorized to negotiate. The Métis had been sending signals to Canada for months about wanting to bargain, but no-one seemed to respond. Governor McDougall and most of his party had left Pembina in mid-December. Contrary to popular opinion then and later, McDougall had not been recalled in disgrace. He left for home when he learned that the date of the transfer had been postponed. Regardless, he and his entourage were now out of the picture, although Riel had made clear that he would negotiate with McDougall only before his admission to the territory, which the Canadian would have not accepted as a condition. A number of Canadian emissaries subsequently arrived, but none of them appeared to have any real authority to deal with the rebels. Colonel Charles de Salaberry and Father Jean-Baptiste Thibault were both francophones. But neither man was Métis nor had much influence in Métis circles. Moreover, their instructions were merely to "confer" with the Métis and "if possible, disabuse their minds of the erroneous impressions that have been made upon them."

The proclamation from Governor-General Sir John Young, which de Salaberry and Thibault carried in their luggage, spoke of misunderstanding and the redress of all well-founded grievances. It assured the residents of Red River that civil and religious rights and privileges would be respected, property would be secured, and the country would be governed under British laws and the spirit of British justice, as in the past. All would forgiven, wrote Young, providing the insurgents immediately stopped their resistance and went home. There would be considerable subsequent debate over the fate of this proclamation, which was apparently seized by the rebels and never communicated to the inhabitants of the community. But the proclamation demonstrated that the Canadians still didn't get the point. These reassurances should have been made in advance of the dispatch of McDougall and his colonial government. Moreover, they did not deal with the question of power, giving the majority Métis no mechanism by which they might be able to control their own fate.

Donald A. Smith, a tough-minded HBC executive with a career spent largely in Labrador, arrived at Upper Fort Garry on 27 December, accompanied by his brother-in-law. He had left his official papers behind in Pembina, he said, but he had a commission from the Canadian government which he would produce in good time. Riel must have suspected that Smith was without authority to deal. In his first letter to the prime minister on 28 December, Smith reported, on the basis of his brief visit in Pembina, that "the drift of the whole thing is evidently annexation." Smith had talked with Enos Stutsman, who was certain that Red River would fall to the United States.

Initially more promising was the arrival of Charles Tupper in Fort Garry on 28 December. Tupper was a principal Father of Confederation who was not yet in the cabinet but would soon be. He was known to be a man of power in Ottawa. He had also accompanied Smith to the border from the East, but had stopped there to visit his daughter, married to one of Governor McDougall's entourage. Tupper insisted that he had come to Red River as a private citizen solely to take his daughter back to Nova Scotia, and there is no evidence that his visit really had anything to do with the Canadian government, although Sir John A. Macdonald would later write favourably of its value. Tupper had come to Fort Garry to collect his daughter's luggage, which had been seized by the Métis when her husband had tried to drive his wagon through the barricade north of the border. Tupper did meet with Father Ritchot and even with Riel himself. In his memoirs he subsequently insisted that once Riel arrived, "I avoided anything but general conversation."

We do not know how Riel explained to himself the arrival of two major Canadian politicians — Howe and Tupper — in isolated Red River over a three-month period, both claiming a singular unwillingness to talk officially with the insurgents. Several explanations are possible. Both the Canadians were Nova Scotians, elected representatives of a province still committed to taking Nova Scotia out of Confederation. They were still regarded as political outsiders in Ottawa, even though Howe was a cabinet minister. Howe would have considerable trouble in Parliament explaining his visit to Red River. He was forced to answer charges that he had "encouraged" the insurgents. Moreover, the Canadians initially had no intention of negotiating with the resident population. Louis Riel probably did not understand anything about these Canadian nuances. What he did appreciate was that the Canadians continued to refuse to legitimize the rebellion by negotiating with the rebels, especially on the understanding that they were the *de facto* government. Riel and Donald A. Smith had already held a verbal tussle over the question of whether the provisional government was legal or illegal. Tupper was told that Smith had said "he was prepared to acknowledge the only government he had found in the country," an interpretation of Smith's position which the HBC man would deny strenuously.

From Pembina, on his return to Ottawa, Tupper had written Sir John A Macdonald that he thought an amicable settlement was possible if a "*statesman* of standing and ability, armed with large discretionary power" was sent to Red River. Tupper was probably quite right. A negotiated settlement was easily possible, providing the Canadian government was willing to negotiate. No evidence existed that it was so disposed, however. From the Canadian perspective, William McDougall should have been admitted into the territory, taken it over, and then paternally entertained petitions from the residents. Although Riel did not know it, Prime Minister Macdonald had already set in motion the process necessary for raising a military expedition to conquer Red River by force. As 1869 ended, the ultimate problem which faced Riel — whether he was aware of it or not, and he probably was — was to find some way to bring the Canadians to the bargaining table.

On the first day of the new year in 1870, Riel rode out to Oak Point, on the southeastern shore of Lake Manitoba. There he told a meeting of Métis who had not been very supportive of the provisional government that he was a loyal British subject who desired only the welfare of the settlement. Some accounts reported that he repudiated annexation to the United States, other that he "pledged himself for Canada on proper terms." Perhaps he did both.

A day later Prime Minister Macdonald wrote to Donald A. Smith from Ottawa. He had read the claims from the insurgent halfbreeds, he wrote. Whether these claims referred to the list submitted to Macdonald by Walter Bown or the List of Rights printed in the settlement on 4 December is not at all clear, but probably the latter. Thanks to their Red River correspondents, the List of Rights was printed in the Montreal *Herald* and the Toronto *Globe* on 31 December 1869, and so Macdonald should have had access to the latter version. The prime minister found some of the claims "altogether inadmissable." He laid out for Smith "what we are willing to concede," which fell far short of what was being demanded, but did suggest for the first time some movement on the part of the government. It was always Canada's intention to continue the present Council of Assiniboia, the prime minister wrote, and two-thirds of its number could be selected from the residents. Elections would have to wait for recommendations on how to proceed with them. Representative institutions would eventually be granted to Rupert's Land "as soon as the Territory is in a position to bear the burdens and assume the responsibilities of such institutions." Macdonald did concede that elected municipal institutions and school boards could be introduced at once, as in Ontario and Quebec, if the council so wished.

Smith was authorized to invite a delegation of at least two from Red River to visit Ottawa "for the purpose of representing the claims and interests of Rupert's Land." For the first time, the Canadian government was indicating a willingness to talk with the residents of the settlement. Had this occurred a year or even six months earlier, all difficulties might have been avoided. The expenses of the government of Rupert's Land would be, for the moment, defrayed by the Dominion, and the present tariff would be continued for two years. Indian claims, "including the claims of the half-breeds who lived with and as Indians," would be equitably settled. Macdonald was thus willing to recognize some mixed-blood claims to aboriginal rights, but only if the mixed-bloods were for all intents and purposes Indians. Most of the inhabitants of Red River would not have qualified as possessors of aboriginal claims under this definition. For the residents of Red River, all titles to land held in peaceable possession would be confirmed, he wrote. What the prime minister meant by his end statement to Smith that he would honour "any pecuniary arrangements that you may make with individuals, in the manner we spoke about" can only be a matter of speculation. But it sounded very much like an authorization for bribery, and Smith's subsequent reports certainly sounded as if he had engaged in some.

Louis Riel v. Canada

A few days later the provisional government's council met to talk about the possibility of a united council, with equal representation of the linguistic sections. Alexander Begg thought that bringing the anglophones on side would be very difficult, but added that "to be able to treat properly with the Commissioners from Canada the people should be united — and...if these commissioners are not treated with now, the golden chance is lost and God knows where the country will drift to." Riel began talking about unifying the settlement in order to produce a list of demands that could be taken back to Ottawa by the visiting commissioners. He increasingly suspected that the visitors were simply not authorized to deal, that they were — as he put it — "not able to grant what the people want." Riel succeeded in bringing A.G.B. Bannatyne into the government as postmaster and "Head of the Courts," and he appeared close to adding James Ross, the mixed-blood leader, as well.

The first issue of the *New Nation*, the newspaper which Riel allowed to replace the *Nor'-Wester*, appeared on 7 January. The *Pioneer's* printing press had been bought by Enos Stutsman and Colonel Henry Robinson in late December, and the American Robinson was in the editor's chair. The first issue editorialized strongly on behalf of annexation to the United States, which upset Riel considerably. The American consul in Winnipeg in a report to Washington insisted that there was little support in Red River for Canada because the "historical life" of the Métis was unconnected with Canada, and because the Métis feared an influx of Protestant anglophone settlers would drive them to the plains. In any event, meetings in some of the anglophone parishes had begun to produce support for co-operation with the provisional government.

A number of the prisoners at Upper Fort Garry escaped from confinement in mid-January. The method of their escape tells us a good deal about the mindsets of the prisoners. We have an account of the flight from the journal of Henry Woodington, who accompanied Thomas Scott out of a window on a cold January night. According to Woodington, the sound that night of the wrenching of a window frame out of the wall in the prisoners' room was covered by the noise of the prisoners "piling on" Joseph Coombs. "Piling on" was, along with chess, cards, and checkers, one of the principal recreations of the men in confinement. It was indeed their particular favourite. "It begins," explained Woodington, "with one catching hold of another and throwing him down or against the wall, yelling 'pile on.' There is a general rush to the scene, and pity the poor fellow that gets under." The popularity of such schoolboyish antics in captivity reminds us that most of the prisoners were young men with their hormones raging. Apart from going down the hall to relieve themselves, this was apparently the only exercise enjoyed by the prisoners. "Piling on" obviously happened frequently, since the Métis guards did not bother on the night of the escape to check the room where it was occurring.

Most of those who got free were quickly rounded up and returned to the fort, but Charles Mair and Thomas Scott managed to elude recapture. From Riel's perspective their presence in the community was disturbing, since these Canadians were men around whom resistance to the provisional government might collect. He made strenuous efforts to recapture all the escapees, but without success. After holding discussions with them, an angry Riel ordered Colonel de Salaberry and Father Thibault out of the settlement. These representatives of Canada had never been allowed free access to the community, probably because Riel did not want them reassuring people of Canadian benevolence. He well knew that many in the settlement, including some in his own party, would have been quite willing to welcome the Canadians on the strength of vague promises of fair treatment.

Dealing with Donald A. Smith

What could be expected from Donald A. Smith was another matter. Smith had been sent by the Canadian government less as an emissary than to generate an opposition to Riel by spreading money around judiciously. He had been given no powers to make any commitments. He might even be characterized as an *agent provocateur*. Riel had kept Smith under confinement from his arrival in the settlement, but although Smith was not allowed free access to the community, he was allowed to entertain visitors and talk with them. On 14 January Riel called on Smith and asked to see his commission, observing that the instructions to Thibault and de Salaberry merely allowed them to "calm the halfbreeds." Smith's own account of the discussion which followed made clear the war of wills waged by the two men. Smith's documents were finally brought from Pembina and opened in the house of Dr. William Cowan in Upper Fort Garry in front of a large crowd. Several participants testified to a considerable tussle over the papers on the trail, with several Métis hired by Smith guarding the papers which Riel and his followers tried desperately to intercept. With the papers in his hands, Smith insisted on being freed and allowed to communicate with the people. By his own admission, his goal was "of making the people both French and English fully acquainted with the liberal views of the Canadian Government so that a peaceful transfer of the Territory might be afforded." The gathering at Dr. Cowan's had a heated discussion over what to do with Smith. Not all were supportive of Riel. The outcome was to send messengers all over the settlement calling the people to a public gathering at Fort Garry to hear Smith read his papers.

While Riel and the settlement waited to hear what Donald A. Smith had to say for himself, a curious if revealing incident occurred at Upper Fort Garry. It was reported in the *Globe* on 28 January and tells us a good deal about the way Riel and the Métis would be regarded in Canada and treated in the Canadian press. Two Canadian reporters, Robert Cunningham of the *Globe* (and Montreal *Gazette*) and John Ross Robertson of the *Telegraph* had finally arrived in Red River to provide a first-hand account of events, supplementing the letters these newspapers had been printing from correspondents in the settlement. They had headed straight for the fort to interview Louis Riel, and had waited overnight in the guard room to meet with him. Obviously Riel should have put all other business to one side to deal with these representatives of the press.

Cunningham, in the subsequent story he filed, insisted that he realized the "French half-breeds" had been grossly maligned. They had a "pretty comprehensive idea of the political system at work in the States and Territories of the United States," insisted the Toronto reporter, and "some true appreciation of what rights naturally belong to them in any connection whatever." He quoted at length from conversations he had enjoyed with Métis guards in the guard room of the fort. According to one of his informants, "We want to be treated as free men. Your Canada Government offered to pay £300,000 to the Hudson Bay Company for the Rivière Rouge Territory. Now what we want to know, and we will not lay down our arms till we know what they mean to buy. Was it the land? If so, who gave the Hudson Bay Company the right to sell the land? When the Canada Government bought the land did they buy what was on it? Did they buy us? Are we the slaves of the Hudson Bay Company?" These were good rhetorical questions, suggesting a familiarity with the concept of aboriginal rights extended to the Métis.

The reporter's informant continued, "We are not the cruel murderous men we have been described. We do not want to kill any one in this quarrel. We have hurt no one yet, nor do we mean to do so." Either he or Cunningham (or both) had a pretty good idea of what Canadians normally thought about Métis. As it turned out, of course, Riel's actions would more than fulfil the negative characterization. For the moment, however, the guard emphasized, "Let the Canadian Government come and treat with us as free men, and we will lay down our arms, and go to our homes." The journalist concluded that the "half-breeds are not savages by any means," but if "properly treated, they might be a peaceable, industrious harmless people."

For Riel, this was his first exposure to the outside media and an easterner's first assessment of him, and the result was far less sympathetic than the earlier descriptions and characterizations presented by J. J. Hargrave or Alexander Begg or the St. Paul newspapers. *The Globe* on 1 December 1869 had reprinted an item from the St. Paul *Dispatch*, which had begun by countering an earlier comment about Riel that he was "of no particularly mental ability" and that his emergence as a leader had astounded his friends and acquaintances. The writer described himself as an acquaintance of Riel, and insisted that he was "a man of strong mental ability, thoroughly educated for his age, and possessing high aspirations though not exceeding the limits of his talents." The piece described Riel as from a poor family who had clerked in Minnesota grocery stores. "Justitia" (Alexander Begg) had subsequently written to the *Globe* (in a letter published on 6 January 1870) describing the team of Riel, John Bruce, W.B. O'Donoghue, and Father Ritchot which was leading the insurgency. It observed that Riel was a fine orator whose eloquence had united the Métis. His father had been a Métis political leader, but "from what I hear the present Riel is more persevering, energetic and clever than his father was."

The Toronto reporter's subsequent treatment of his meeting with W. B. O'Donoghue and Riel was quite different — a hatchet job from beginning to end. It was true that Riel had ended up summarily expelling the journalists from the settlement and forcing Cunningham to Pembina to file his report. But no CNN reporter describing a meeting with Saddam Hussein could possibly have been any nastier. It was pure character assassination. In his description of the Métis leaders, Cunningham made no attempt at a fair appraisal of the two men. What the reader got instead was a pen portrait dipped in venom and hostility from the opening words. Without offering any explanation for his animus, Cunningham described O'Donoghue as a "Uriah Heep: — "of a semi-priestly appearance, fair-haired, closely shaven, with a cringing, cunning way with him." Riel was "a man about thirty years of age, about five feet seven inches in height — rather stoutly built." His head was "covered with dark, curly hair; his face had a Jewish appearance, with a very small and very fast receding forehead." Cunningham insisted that he tried to visualize a Napoleon, but only saw a Linen Draper's Assistant, dressed in a light tweed coat and black trousers. He even managed to repeat the story circulating in the settlement that Riel had bought these clothes with money from the sale of his mother's only cow. The reference to a Jewish appearance and to Napoleon were both intended to invoke negative responses from Cunningham's readers.

Cunningham insisted that in their brief subsequent discussion he had trouble understanding Riel, who "spoke in the most broken of English." This comment would have surprised most of those who knew Riel, since his English was quite good. The Canadian concluded that those who credited Riel with military genius and ambition had misread him, failing to appreciate that "he was a vain-glorious creature so elated by the position he had attained to, that any particle of common sense he ever had owned had been eliminated from his being." Cunningham further maintained that Riel "was the mere tool of a certain party," presumably the Americans, "who used him their purposes as they listened and laughed at him." In the lengthy report filed by Cunningham, what the reader learned above all was the patronizing way with which the Canadians wished to visualize and deal with both the Métis and with Riel, who quite appropriately gave him short shrift.

A meeting called at short notice in mid-January drew a considerable crowd. The audience was more than 1,000, meaning that the meeting had to be held in the open air of the courtyard of Upper Fort Garry rather than indoors. The temperature on the day stood at minus 20 degrees Fahrenheit. It was a classic January day on the prairies. The sky was blue, the sun was shining, the weather was clear, and the wind chill was considerable. Many of the crowd huddled inside the Company houses that surrounded the courtyard, so that not everyone was actually outside for the entire proceedings. Others who were outside dashed indoors from time to time, ostensibly to get warm but also to consume some liquid fuel that would insulate their bodies against the outside temperatures. All present were well bundled, the anglophones in their fur caps and coats, the francophones in their capotes belted at the waist with brightly coloured woolen scarves. Outside the walls waited a number of sleighs, their horses and ponies standing patiently while their breath showed white in the cold crisp air. The best shorthand reporter in the settlement, William Coldwell, was on hand as reporter for the *New Nation* to keep a record of the proceedings.

For a second time, Riel would be called upon to manoeuvre his way around an unruly public gathering, this one considerably larger than the meetings of November and early December. Over the hours before the opening of this crucial gathering, Riel's supporters had worked desperately behind the scenes to make sure that the settlement presented a unified front to Donald A. Smith. When the meeting first opened, Riel was immediately on his feet, nominating Thomas Bunn to be the chairman. The nomination was seconded by Pierre Léveiller. Smith himself recognized the great significance of this seemingly simple action. Bunn was an anglophone mixed-blood from the lower settlements, and Léveiller was one of those most critical of Riel's policies. Father Lestanc and Grand Vicar Thibault had apparently persuaded the defectors to close ranks. Smith regarded this reconciliation as a "sad blow" for Canada, but he was forced to carry on. Riel's task was to prevent Smith from carrying the crowd by use of expressions of loyalty to the Queen or the desirability of ultimate annexation to Canada. Ideally he also needed to prevent the crowd from joining in demands for the release of the prisoners being held at Upper Fort Garry.

Bunn opened the assembly, calling it "the most important meeting ever held in the Settlement." The first item of business was the election of an interpreter. Most of the audience recognized the significance of the interpreter, who to some extent controlled the way in which arguments presented in one language were couched in another. Nominated by

Charles de Salaberry, Louis Riel was chosen. This was another serious blow to Smith in several respects. In the first place, Smith had insisted that Riel had withheld vital information from the francophone settlers. That same Riel would be responsible for putting the French words in Smith's mouth. Smith had hoped that de Salaberry would agree to be interpreter, but he had begged off and suggested Riel instead. Not only did Smith's colleagues from Canada refuse to join him on the platform, but they had colluded with the opposition. The platform party was now completed with the nomination of Judge John Black as secretary to the meeting. Another anglophone who had been sitting on the fence appeared to have been successfully added to the rebel ranks. Smith made one final effort to wrest control of the day by insisting that arms be laid down and the flag of the provisional government, flying on the flagpole of the fort, be replaced by the British ensign. The chairman thought that this could be done later, but it never was.

Introduced to the meeting by the chairman, Donald A. Smith began his presentation by reading his letter of appointment, dated 10 December and signed by Joseph Howe. It named him special commission to enquire and report on the causes of discontent and dissatisfaction in the region. He was to explain to the inhabitants "the principles upon which the Government of Canada intend to govern the country," and to remove any misapprehensions on this point. He was also to act in concert with Mr. McDougall and Governor McTavish to effect the peaceable transfer of the territory to Canada. Enclosed with the letter were a number of documents: a copy of the instructions to McDougall of 18 September; a further letter to McDougall of 7 December; and a copy of the governor-general's proclamation on 7 December, promising an amnesty for misguided settlers who laid down their arms immediately. Because of the incomplete information available to Ottawa, Smith was not hampered with specific instructions but told to use his own best judgment. The reading of the letter in English being completed, it was then translated into French by Louis Riel, who now knew that Smith had been given no special powers to negotiate a settlement with the rebels.

Smith then turned to a letter sent personally to him by the governor-general. Riel queried whether this letter was public or private, and was informed it had been sent to Smith in his official capacity. The crowd stirred at this information. The chairman ordered the letter read. In it the governor-general noted that he had sent letters to Governor McTavish and the heads of the Anglican and Catholic churches in the settlement, enclosing copies of the telegraphic message from Her Majesty's government. Sir John Young emphasized that all who wished to complain could do so to him as the Queen's representative. The imperial government intended to act in good faith toward the inhabitants of Red River, said Young. There would be respect and protection for the different religions (loud cheers from the assembly), titles to all property would be perfectly guaranteed (more cheers), and all existing franchises or those "which the people may prove themselves qualified to exercise" would be continued or conferred. The ancient formula "Right shall be done in all cases" was safe to use. Riel complained that the letter was not signed "Governor," but Smith answered it was signed "in my capacity as Her Majesty's Representative," which was the same thing. Riel translated the letter into French for the crowd.

Matters then got more interesting. Smith asked Grand Vicar Thibault to produce the copies of letters entrusted to him, notably those from Canada to Governor McTavish. Riel protested, but the crowd cried, "We will hear it," and cheered. Judge Black objected to documents being withheld from the meeting. A voice from the assembly shouted, "Who had the documents?" Another voice answered, "Mr. O'Donoghue has them." After considerable verbal scuffling, A.G.B. Bannatyne moved that O'Donoghue be asked "in the name of the people of Red River" to produce the documents. Sensing the spirit of crowd, Riel himself seconded this demand. O'Donoghue and Pierre Léveiller went off to search up the documents in question, although the governor-general's proclamation of 7 December could not be found. Smith had to make do with a telegram from Earl Granville to Sir John Young which began, "Make what use you think best of what follows," and then offered some formulas for a royal response, such as "The Queen has heard with surprise and regret" and viewed "with sorrow and displeasure" the "unreasonable and lawless proceedings which have taken place." These were not enough to move the crowd, which had been standing for five hours in the open air. A move from Mr. John Burke to call for the release of the prisoners was voted down at the end of the meeting.

The following day was not as cold. The assembly should have started at 10 a.m. but did not begin until noon. The audience considered, according to the *New Nation*, "that during the present doubtful state of affairs it would be premature to let loose the prisoners." Numbers were larger than the previous day. Smith read his letters intended to reassure the people of Red River that Canada's intentions were honourable, but such declarations were about a year too late and were not believed by everyone. According to Thomas Bunn in testimony before an 1874 parliamentary enquiry, the governor-general's proclamation calling for the people to lay down their arms and disperse was still not read. Smith spoke at great length, insisting that the interests of Canada and those of Red River were identical. He read a letter to William McDougall which gave him instructions on what to do upon taking office by listing all the matters he was supposed to investigate. Smith said he would carry all complaints back to Ottawa. The meeting then adjourned for 30 minutes.

When the meeting resumed, Louis Riel, seconded by A.G.B. Bannatyne, moved that: "20 representatives shall be elected by the

English population of Red River to meet 20 other representatives of the French population, on Tuesday the 25th inst., at noon, in the Court House, with the object of considering the subject of Mr. Smith's commission, and to decide what would be best for the welfare of the country." This resolution was easily carried. Cheers were offered for Father Lestanc, Bishop Machray, Father Ritchot, Louis Riel, W.B. O'Donoghue, and the commissioners. Then someone in the audience spoke out: "That resolution seems to cast a doubt on Mr. Smith's commission." Riel answered, "We accept the commission as genuine and are merely to consider what is to be done under it." On motion of Judge Black, seconded by O'Donoghue, a committee was chosen to apportion the English representation to the proposed convention, and to decide on the means of election. The committee was broad-bottomed, consisting of Thomas Bunn, Judge John Black, Bishop Machray, John Sutherland, and John Fraser. Father Ritchot spoke favourably of the ecumenical nature of the meeting just concluded, and Bishop Machray answered in the same vein. He thought all present could agree "on all reasonable propositions" and he hoped the gathering the following week "would lead to a happy settlement of public affairs. (cheers.)" He then added that he "hoped we would be as united in the future as we had been in the past." This remark, according to the newspaper report of the meeting, brought loud and repeated cheers.

Louis Riel had the last word. In his concluding speech, Riel admitted that he had begun the meeting with "fears." He insisted that those fears were for the possible animosity of the two peoples of Red River, conveniently forgetting his concerns that Smith would walk away with the meeting. Now he could see that both sides shared "just rights." To repeated cheers he emphasized, "We claim no half rights mind you, but all the rights we are entitled to. These rights will be set forth by our representatives, and what is more, gentlemen, we will get them." Although the run-up had been difficult, the meeting itself — while clearly carefully orchestrated by the elites of the settlement — was nevertheless a triumph for Riel and his policies. The settlers had not been carried away by Canadian generosity and sincerity when they were finally exposed to the Canadian "guarantees." They had not recoiled in horror at the discrepancy between local action and what the Queen would have preferred. And they had not demanded the instant release of all the political prisoners. Donald A. Smith clearly had little more power to negotiate an arrangement between the provisional government and Canada then the other two Canadian emissaries. But if the two sections of the settlement could agree on a position, he and the other commissioners could certainly take that back to Ottawa, where it would carry a considerable moral weight and be almost impossible for the Canadian government to ignore.

The Convention of Forty

The weather remained cold in January, as the settlement worked toward the meeting of the "Convention of Forty," as it often was called. The anglophone delegates were apportioned by committee. The subsequent election meetings in the various parishes often hedged the delegates with various instructions and conditions, but delegates were nevertheless chosen. In the midst of the elections, John Christian Schultz escaped from Fort Garry, perhaps using a knife and gimlet concealed in a pudding sent the Canadian leader by his wife. He left word with the guard to treat all the prisoners with rum at his expense, and the liquor passed through all the rooms in pails. It was the sort of performance to which Riel — who was not a drinker — most objected. When he learned of the escape of his arch-enemy he became quite incensed, marching to the cells and calling the prisoners "rascals and trash." When William Hallett answered that Riel was the rascal, the Métis leader responded by threatening, "Gentlemen, all who support that man will die in five minutes." The prisoners backed down, but Riel's use of death threats would increase over the next few weeks, suggesting that he was feeling the pressure of holding the rebellion together. Facing another public assembly, Riel was also acting as gaoler at Upper Fort Garry and as president of the provisional government. He certainly became fixated with recapturing Dr. Schultz, who remained successfully in hiding in the Scots area of Kildonan for several weeks.

Riel opened the first meeting of the convention of delegates at the courthouse at Upper Fort Garry on Wednesday 26 January 1870. This gathering, whatever the conditions of its election and convocation, was the closest thing to representative government that Red River had ever experienced, and it deserves to be better known. The meeting had been delayed by a heavy snowstorm, and as Riel announced the postponement, he commented to the anglophone delegates, "we have waited long for you to join us." When the meeting opened, Riel moved that Judge John Black be appointed chairman. William Coldwell was made English-language secretary, and Riel's old school chum Louis Schmidt was appointed French-language secretary. James Ross served as interpreter from French into English, and Riel himself did the interpreting from English into French. Like the officers of the convention, the delegates were a cross-section of the élite of the settlement, with mixed-bloods still under-represented but with the first aboriginal delegate, the Reverend Henry Cochrane, an Ojibwa clergyman, representing St. Peter's. After sorting out the disputed elections, Louis Riel placed in Thomas Bunn's hands a resolution with a request that Bunn move it. It read: "That notwithstanding the insults and sufferings borne by the people of the North-West heretofore, and the sufferings which they still endure, the loyalty of the people of the North-West toward the Crown of England remains the same: provided their rights, properties, usages and customs be respected — feeling assured that as British subjects, such rights, properties, usages and customs will be respected." The motion carried unanimously.

A committee was then chosen to prepare a Bill of Rights for the next day. The francophone delegates insisted that only "natives of the country" be allowed to sit on this committee, which ultimately was composed of Riel, Schmidt, and Charles Nolin on the French side, and James Ross, Dr. Curtis James Bird (who was not a mixed-blood but a full-blooded aboriginal) and Thomas Bunn on the English side. At this point, James Ross asked for the production of the governor-general's proclamation of 7 December. Had it been read, of course, it would have labelled the behaviour of all those who remained in attendance as openly rebellious. No reason for Ross's strategy was ever given. It was not dictated by his constituents. Fortunately for Riel, Ross found no support in the meeting for this demand, and dropped it for the moment.

The Committee on the Bill of Rights, chaired by James Ross, took almost two days to draft a document. According to Alexander Begg, the committee experienced considerable disagreement and had in the first instance not allowed enough time for the production of such a critical document. When Ross introduced it on 29 January, he noted that the committee had been much hurried and obliged "to present the document in very crude shape." The convention began sitting at mid-morning and continued meeting until late in the evening, by which point it had passed the first four clauses of the so-called "Bill of Rights." "Justitia" subsequently provided the *Globe* readership not only with the text of the articles, but with a gloss upon them which appeared to summarize the debate on the floor of the convention. The first four articles were quite different from the "List of Rights" agreed to by the meeting of the sections in early December, although some kinship between the two documents can be discerned. The crude presentation noted by the committee probably referred less to the composition of individual articles than to the failure to put the various items together in a well-arranged and logically-developed package. This may have been also the result of disagreement on the Committee as well as haste to get something to the convention. Nonetheless, even a quick glance at the draft demonstrated that the inhabitants of Red River, or at least their leaders, had some fairly sophisticated notions of what government was all about, far in advance of the original tutelage for the population assumed by the Canadian government. Although eight of the articles of the first Bill of Rights were in a general way repeated in the second Bill, the language had become less American and more acceptably British. And a number of items had disappeared.

Louis Riel v. Canada

Article 1 of the Committee's draft called for the continuation of existing import duties for three years, or until uninterrupted railway communication existed between Red River and either St. Paul or Lake Superior — a point already conceded by Macdonald. The rationale for this article, reported Justitia, revolved around the present heavy price of freight, and the market's inability to absorb higher costs in the form of higher duties.

Article 2 forbade direct taxation, except as imposed by the local legislature, for so long as the country remained a territory of Canada. Macdonald had in effect conceded this point as well, by stating the Canada would foot the bill for the territory. Because of its isolation and the absence of many amenities common further east, it was argued in the convention that Red River should not be taxed heavily, particularly since the people of Red River had no responsibility for Canadian levels of taxation.

Article 3 specified that while the country was a territory, all public expenses should be borne by the Dominion. This too had been conceded by Macdonald. The argument here was that such an assumption was merely an investment in the future on the part of the people of Canada. Article 4 called for the government of the territory by a lieutenant-governor from Canada and an elected legislature (by which the drafting committee seems to have meant a council rather than an assembly), with three of the heads of department nominated by the Canadian governor-general. According to Justitia, the convention allowed that Canada should have some political primacy while she was still footing the bill, but insisted that at least some of the officials of the territorial government should come from among the residents. The passage of these four clauses does not appear to have been at all contentious among the delegates. Moreover, three of them assumed that Red River would initially become only a territory of Canada, not a province. The same day that saw the beginning of debate over the Bill of Rights also saw the publication of another issue of the *New Nation*, one that was considerably less American annexationist in tone than the first issue. According to Alexander Begg, the newspaper carried considerable reportage on the convention, and was being distributed free of charge in the settlement.

The debate over the clauses of the Bill of Rights continued on Monday 31 January, with the convention convening at 1 p.m. Article 5 called for the admission of the country into Canada as a province as soon as population warranted. Article 6 insisted that the Dominion Parliament interfere in local affairs of the territory no more than it did elsewhere in Canada, while Article 7 called for the right of the territorial legislature to pass local laws by a two-thirds vote over the veto of the lieutenant-governor. This last article was a peculiarly American notion, which Justitia admitted was "not exactly in unison with the British or Canadian

Constitution." But, he argued, Red River would be the only territory in Canada and could be viewed as exceptional. Suspicion of lieutenant-governor McDougall was doubtless part of the background of this clause. Article 8 called for a homestead and pre-emption law, another distinctly American concept and one carried over from the earlier "List of Rights." The law was obviously desirable in a newly-settled country, but was regarded by Prime Minister Macdonald as unacceptable.

Articles 9 and 10 dealt with public expenditures. Article 9 insisted that $25,000 per year be appropriated for schools, roads, and bridges, while Article 10 said that all public buildings while the North-West remained a territory were the responsibility of the Dominion government. Justitia argued that the people of Red River were entitled to suggest how Canada spent the large sums she had already appropriated for the territory. Furthermore, he said, people in the settlement felt that much of the money already spent, such as on road construction, had been wasted. Article 11, the final article approved on 31 January, called for uninterrupted steam communication (i.e., a railroad) to Lake Superior within five years, and a rail connection to the American railhead as soon as it reached the international line. While one might quibble about the time-frame (as in British Columbia), Justitia was quite right in insisting on the absolute necessity of such communications. None of these clauses was particularly contentious, and they were passed relatively easily by the convention. According to Alexander Begg's journal, James Ross was visibly inebriated during the entire day's deliberations.

The convention reconvened about 10 a.m. on 1 February, striking its first contentious item on Article 12, which called for a "military force" — really some sort of police unit to maintain order in the country — composed of natives of the country serving for four-year periods. The article was struck down by a vote of 23 to 15. Many delegates opposed the expense, while others objected to taking up arms. On the other hand, it was argued that the importation of Canadian volunteers to do this job would be productive of trouble. Justitia called for a volunteer force raised from amongst the inhabitants, supplemented by a British regiment. Articles 13 and 14 were concerned with bilingualism in the legislature and courts. Article 13 called for the publication of all public documents and legislative acts in both languages, while Article 14 insisted that the judge of the Supreme Court speak both French and English. Justitia pointed out that these clauses were designed to encourage emigration from French Canada. They were also intended to help preserve the position of the francophone Métis in Red River. In any case, they were not at all contentious. Article 15 called for the swift conclusion of treaties between Canada and the several Indian tribes of the country. Article 16 specified that the settlement be represented in Parliament by one senator and three members, "until the population of this country entitles us to more." Delegates recognized that this specification would probably meet with resistance from the Dominion, which had refused to increase the representation from Prince Edward Island at the Quebec Conference, but still thought it worth including.

Article 17 called for respect for "all the properties, rights and privileges, as hitherto enjoyed by us," and for local customs, usages, and privileges to be under the control of the local legislature. Justitia thought that the Canadians had already guaranteed this clause, but saw no harm in reiterating the point. How it was interpreted would be critical, of course. Louis Riel had remained relatively quiet during most of the deliberation over these articles. He came to life on Article 17, however, and a debate between himself and James Ross occurred. Riel spoke of "halfbreed rights," while Ross objected to the combining of "halfbreeds" with Indians. This difference went to the heart of the Métis/mixed-blood disagreement. "The fact is," argued Ross, "we must take one side or the other — we must either be Indians and claim the privilege of Indians — certain reserves of land and annual compensation of blankets, powder and tobacco [laughter] — or else we must take the position of civilized men and claim rights accordingly. We cannot expect to enjoy the rights and privileges of both the Indian and White Man." Ross made clear he would be quite happy to be included under the "civilized men." The Canadian prime minister would have agreed with Ross. The Métis position, advocated by Riel, had long been that mixed-bloods shared in Aboriginal rights as well as in European ones, and were entitled especially to land on the strength of their Indian inheritance.

Article 18, which from our modern perspective might seem less important than the preceding article, was deferred until the following day because of its contentiousness. The convention spent most of 2 February debating Clause 18, on the issue of converting the two-mile haying privilege into simple ownership. What was at stake was not the haying privilege itself, but the whole concept of land ownership within the territory. The assembly finally passed by a vote of 21 to 18 an amended version of the hay privilege clause, which called for the local legislature to have full control over all lands within a radius from Upper Fort Garry equal to the distance of the American border from the fort, or roughly 60 miles. The clause in question was intended to prevent land speculation in the settlement and to discourage the cutting up of the property of settlers for railway construction. The vote was pretty much along sectional lines. According to Alexander Begg, McKenzie from Portage did not vote and Alfred H. Scott from Winnipeg joined the French majority. This voting pattern suggests that the French were slightly better disciplined than the English, but that both sides were fairly well organized throughout the debates. The Métis obviously thought the local legislature a better place to deal with such matters than leaving them in the hands of the Canadian government.

As time wore on, the convention was becoming increasingly raucous. The delegates found "refreshment" from their deliberations by stepping outside the courthouse into the open air. Here could be found the "bar," a snowbank into which a number of bottles of alcoholic beverages were placed. The delegates increasingly stepped out to take a nip. Nevertheless, in the afternoon of 2 February, they completed their discussion of the Bill of Rights. Article 19 specified the nature of citizenship in the territory. It enfranchised every "man in the country, except uncivilized and unsettled Indians," who was 21 years of age, as well as every British subject who was a householder of three years' residence. Non-British subjects (mainly Americans) could take an oath of allegiance. Justitia insisted that this clause proved where Red River allegiances lay. "British we are, and Canadians we meant to be, and every alien wishing to be a voter with us must first swear allegiance to the Crown." Article 20 declared that the territory should not be held liable either for the payment to the Hudson's Bay Company or the public debt of Canada at the time of entrance into Confederation.

With the Bill of Rights completed, representing what was agreed to be the minimal conditions for negotiation with the Canadians, a motion was made to call Donald A. Smith into the convention the next morning. At this point Louis Riel rose. He said that the Bill of Rights Committee had drawn up two lists, one involving admission as a territory and the other involving admission as a province. What he did not add was that the committee had apparently preferred the territorial list. But since the conditions of provincial status were laid down in the Confederation Act, Riel suggested, it might be well to consider this possibility. It would be better to discuss this matter before talking to Smith. James Ross tried to rush ahead, but the convention agreed with Riel. On the evening of 3 February, Riel visited Donald A. Smith and asked him whether the Canadian government would agree to receive Red River as a province. Smith waffled. He could not speak with certainty on the subject, he said, for the question had not arisen in Ottawa. Certainly the Canadian intention was that the North-West should initially be a territory, although it might become a province in a few years. Riel emphatically responded, "Then the Hudson's Bay Company is not yet safe," presumably a reference to the continuation of rebellion. Smith replied that such threats did not influence him in the slightest.

Although neither Riel nor Red River could know it at the time, on Friday 4 February, the Canadian cabinet met to discuss the possible lack of success of the missions sent to the settlement. The ministers knew full well that Messrs. Smith et al. could accomplish very little unless the settlers decided voluntarily to pack in their resistance, since the negotiators were hardly authorized to make any real concessions. The prospect of a military action was thus considered. As had always been the case,

Canada was really not very much interested in negotiating its way into Red River. So the cabinet did not talk about possible compromises or bargaining strategy. Instead, it went straight for the use of force. A joint Anglo-Canadian military contingent would be preferred, said Prime Minister Macdonald in a memorandum placed on the table at the opening of the meeting. Three good reasons existed for an expedition "undertaken, organized, commanded, and carried through with the authority of Her Majesty's Government." One was that such force would convince the United States of British commitment in North America. A second was that British regulars would be more intimidating than "untried" Canadian volunteers, who had hardly performed very well in the conflict with the Fenians. Finally, the Métis would be less hostile to "redcoats" than to volunteers from Canada. The British wanted to withdraw all troops from North America immediately, and convincing them to become involved would not be easy. No member of the cabinet questioned the use of force, however.

Thus, while the Canadians were contemplating the military invasion of Red River, the Convention of Forty was debating whether or not the settlement's annexation to Canada should come in the form of a territory or of a province. This debate once again demonstrated the political sophistication of those delegates. Provincial status was certainly Louis Riel's preference, which he apparently had not yet been able to push through the committee. Donald A. Smith wrote Sir John A. Macdonald on 1 February — immediately after the committee had reported to the convention — that "We have succeeded in getting expunged some of the most objectionable points in their demands." Since the most objectionable point would have been the demand for provincial status, this was presumably what Smith meant. In any case, Riel argued for provincial status strenuously at the convention on 4 February. He began by reading the British North America Act to show the powers conferred on provinces, paying particular attention to Article 5 about the management and sale of public lands, vested in the province. Riel granted that the North-West did not have the population of the present provinces, but pointed out that it had a much vaster territory. The grounds for entering as a province were that it would give the people of the country greater security for their rights and privileges by keeping the Canadians entirely out of local affairs, especially public lands and natural resources. The idea was obviously part of Riel's long-term suspicion of the Canadians, and his conviction that the less left to Canadian option the better. At one point in the debates he observed that Canada wanted the North-West "to raise money from it." Had he known about it, Riel would have seen the cabinet discussion of military invasion as yet another example of Canadian duplicity. James Ross spoke against provincial status, chiefly on the grounds that the other provinces had entered confederation with a full infrastructure, while Red River still needed one. Moreover, he added, the move was too sudden. From no self-government to full provincial status was too great a leap.

Chairman John Black intervened at this point, partly to complain about the agenda being reopened just at the point he had thought it concluded, but also to argue that immediate admission as a province was an "utterly hopeless" idea. His best point was that Red River could not afford the dignity of a province. "I must give it as my conscientious belief, that if this country can be admitted as a Territory on just and equitable principles, it is as much as we can look for." After a lunchtime adjournment, Riel attempted to continue the discussion, moving an amendment to that purpose. That amendment was carried, 20 yeas to 19 nays, which certainly suggested that provincial status had become something of a party issue. James Ross returned to the question. He pointed out that nobody in Red River held enough property to be appointed a senator. Moreover, the settlement would sacrifice the four representatives it was asking for as a territory, since its population at the 1871 census would only entitle it to one. Ross further insisted — quite mistakenly — that entrance as a province would subject Red River to federal qualifications for voters. His major argument was that as a territory, taxation would be lower. W.B. O'Donoghue spoke at some length, mainly to insist that special rules could be laid down for provincial as well as territorial entrance.

But Riel was not able to carry the convention with him. The English-speaking delegates (except for Alfred H. Scott) stood firm in opposition, and on this issue were joined by at least five francophones — apparently including Charles Nolin and Thomas Harrison from Oak Point, and George Klyne from Pointe à Grouette — in voting down the proposal. The French delegates who broke ranks had probably long been less radical than most of their Métis colleagues. They came from the more conservative districts north of the Assiniboine. The final vote on a motion to enter as a territory was carried, yeas 24, nays 15. The loss of this vote demonstrated that Riel was still having trouble keeping his own people together, as well as indicating the chasm between his own militancy and that of the anglophone mixed-bloods (and some of the Métis).

Riel had another radical proposal to make, which he insisted had to be discussed by the convention before it talked with Donald A. Smith. This one called for a declaration that the agreement between the British government and the Hudson's Bay Company was null and void. The point was not a silly one. Negotiations for the transfer of the territory, argued Riel, should be between the Parliament of Canada and the people of Red River, not between the HBC and the Canadians. His proposal would have had the effect of ending any payment of land or money to the HBC, while in effect transferring sovereignty to the people of the country. Smith believed that this attack on the Company was designed to put pressure on himself (as an employee of it). To some extent Riel was becoming increasingly convinced that the growing opposition to his leadership was being orchestrated by the HBC and that the Company should be brushed totally aside. In some ways this proposal was a logical extension of Riel's earlier refusal to take over the HBC administration of the settlement rather than declaring a provisional government. Riel spoke to his proposal on 5 February. He noted the way the HBC had acted toward earlier generations of residents. What really bothered him, of course, was that "A Company of strangers, living beyond the ocean, had the audacity to attempt to sell the people of the soil." His supporters cheered him as he called for cutting down Company influence. Chairman Black intervened to defend the Company, and the anglophone delegates — many of them former employees of the HBC — were no keener about this idea of Riel's than they were with provincial status.

The final vote was more or less a repeat of the one over provincial status. Only Alfred H. Scott, who had declared that he was soon leaving Red River, broke with the ranks of the anglophones, while Messrs. Nolin, Harrison, and Klyne all voted against Riel. Louis Riel was beside himself. He insisted, "The devil take it; we must win. The vote may go as it likes; but the measure, which has now been defeated, must be carried. It is a shame to have lost it; and it was a greater shame, because it was lost" — pointing his finger toward Nolin, Harrison, and Klyne — by those traitors." Nolin responded angrily in French, "I was not sent here, Mr. Riel, to vote at your dictation. I came here to vote according to my conscience. While there are some things for which we blame the Company, there is a good deal for which we must thank them. I do not exculpate the Company altogether; but I say that, in time of need, we have often been indebted to them for assistance and kindness."

Barely able to contain himself, Riel insisted that the proposal must be adopted and that "it will be carried at a subsequent stage." He warned that his friends on the provisional government would add it to the list on their own responsibility, and again turned on those who voted against him, saying, "Your influence, as public men, is finished in this country." Nolin angrily responded that Riel had failed to prevent his election, and that he would come back again. On this note of acrimony, the convention adjourned, its real accomplishments of achieving a common mixed-blood front somewhat tarnished by its final divisions. Most distressingly of all, Louis Riel had for the first time visibly lost his temper. On the earlier occasions when Riel had publicly acted in anger, such as outside the door of Dr. Schultz's house when he stamped on the lieutenant-governor's proclamation, there was some sense of stage management involved in the response. Here he appeared noticeably angry at not being able to have his own way, not very sensible behaviour for a man attempting to get people behind him.

It is difficult to determine how to interpret Riel's behaviour as the month of February continued. In many ways, his actions suggested a continual venting of anger, perhaps borne of the frustration of not being able to persuade people to do as he wanted. On 6 February a new version of the flag, larger than before, was hoisted at the fort. Then Riel moved against the various officials of the HBC under his control. He put the dying Governor McTavish under armed guard and threatened to shoot him before midnight. He searched out Dr. Cowan and gave him a tongue-lashing for his opposition to the Métis. He then demanded that Cowan swear allegiance to the provisional government or face death within three hours. Cowan responded that his allegiance was due only to Great Britain, and he was thrown into a cell with William Hallett (who had earlier upset Riel at the time of the Schultz escape and who was still in irons). Efforts by A.G.B. Bannatyne to assure himself that the McTavish family was safe were not only met with hostility, but Bannatyne was on 6 February himself detained as a prisoner. Since Bannatyne was among Riel's staunchest supporters among the anglophone merchants, this rupture was taken very seriously in the community. Riel's men and the Nolin brothers engaged in a scuffle in which guns were fired. Fortunately, both a pistol and a carbine misfired and nobody was hurt.

Dealing Again with Donald A. Smith

In this volatile atmosphere, the Convention of Forty reconvened to meet with Donald A. Smith. The anglophone delegates debated whether to attend such a meeting, but eventually decided to go. In his subsequent report to the Canadian authorities, Smith claimed that he had received a draft of the Bill of Rights and a series of questions about it at 11 a.m. on 7 February, and was given until 1 p.m. to prepare his reply. Smith complained that he was permitted no reference to any other documents and was carefully guarded while he wrote. Louis Riel and Ambroise Lépine appeared together just as Smith was finishing his response. It may be significant that Riel's companion and second-in-command in early February was now Lépine, while in early January (on the testimony of journalist Robert Cunningham) it had been W.B. O'Donoghue. Riel demanded that the answers to the questions posed to Smith must be "simply yes or no." Smith refused. At the subsequent convention meeting, Smith insisted that he had more power than de Salaberry or Thibault, but obviously not the power to negotiate, a point Riel kept driving ruthlessly home.

Riel was at his best this day, brutally exposing the weakness of Smith's position. At the start of the meeting, Riel maintained that he did not care "what Mr. Smith thinks, but what he can guarantee. I want some certainty, not merely an expression of opinion on what we desire. We are now in a position to make demands. How far is the Commissioner in a position to guarantee them on behalf of the Canadian government?" James Ross thought that Smith might be permitted to respond to the Bill of Rights, article by article. Riel disagreed. He wanted first to know whether Smith could, as commissioner, "guarantee one single article on the List?" Smith of course talked around the question, since both he and Riel knew that he had no powers to bind the Canadians. The commissioner's replies were masterpieces of official obfuscation, of diplomatic waffle-ese demonstrating that he would go a long way in the corridors of power. "I believe that the nature of my commission is such," said Smith, "that I can give assurances, full assurances, so far as any guarantee can be given that the Government of the Dominion would so place the right guarantee before Parliament that it be granted." Riel cut straight to the point, saying, "So you cannot guarantee us even a single article in that List?" The answer was obvious.

Eventually Riel stopped harassing the Canadian envoy. "You are embarrassed," he commented, "I see you are a gentleman and do not wish to press you." But the Métis leader's point had been made. "I see that the Canadian Government has not given you all the confidence which they ought to have put in your hands," he commented in one of his characteristic understatements. Riel was emphasizing two related points. One was that the Canadian government had once again demonstrated its inability — or refusal — to take Red River seriously. Secondly, nothing could be settled at this time. Therefore the provisional government could scarcely be allowed to wither away and the settlement give up its militancy. "We will hear your opinion," Riel told Smith, "although we are satisfied you cannot grant us, nor guarantee us anything, by the nature of your Commission."

Donald A. Smith proceeded to answer each article of the Bill of Rights *seriatum*. To some he offered "explicit assurances" while to others he talked about "deference" and "substantial justice." But he made no real commitments. Most of the convention seemed pleased enough with his responses, he later noted, although it must be emphasized that Louis Riel had eventually stopped embarrassing the Canadian commissioner with comments that exposed his lack of authority. Smith ended the discussion, he later reported to Ottawa, by inviting the convention "to send delegates, with a view of effecting a speedy transfer of the Territory to the Dominion." Perhaps this is what he meant to say. According to the *New Nation*, based on its shorthand reporter's notes, what he did say was that he was authorized "to offer a very cordial reception to the delegates who might be sent from this country to Canada," and that he was confident that the result would be "entirely satisfactory to the people of the North-West." A lot of work and effort went into getting Smith, on behalf of the Canadian government, to talk to the convention. And even so, nothing he said would have been binding, had he actually said anything.

With the invitation to the convention to send delegates to Ottawa, the delegates would have to rest content. As Riel knew only too well, its task had only just begun. Until a deal with Canada had been negotiated, somebody would have to mind the settlement. The members of the convention could not know that the Canadian government would later in the month regard the second List of Rights as "in the main satisfactory." The convention could only agree to meet the following day to consider a caretaker government and the selection of delegates.

When the convention again reassembled, it spent the morning discussing the question of negotiation. The result was a unanimous resolution, moved by James Ross and seconded by Louis Riel, that the invitation of the Canadian commissioners to confer with the Canadian government on the affairs of the country be accepted, and that such acceptance be communicated to the commissioners. Colonel de Salaberry had remained in Red River, reported Justitia, "to see if he can bring with him any dispatches of importance to the Council at Ottawa." Debate then turned to the question of "self government until word is received from Ottawa." Louis Riel insisted that a provisional government was necessary, pointing out that the Hudson's Bay Company was not administering justice and was, in Alexander Begg's words, "if not dead completely powerless." The anglophone delegates continued to worry about the legality of such a move, unwilling to label themselves openly as rebels against the Crown. They would have been much happier taking control of the Council of Assiniboia — in their minds still the duly constituted authority in Red River — and breathing life back into it.

Louis Riel argued for the continuity of the provisional government rather than for the continuity of the HBC authority. Riel insisted, "The Provisional Government is an actual fact. Why not recognize it? You have, in reality, practically recognized it by your acts in this Convention. It has accomplished some good. Help it do more." Someone suggested sending a delegation to Governor McTavish to ask about a provisional government. The result formed part of the testimony in the 1874 trial of Ambroise Lépine for the murder of Thomas Scott, as the court deliberated over the question of whether there was need for a *de facto* government. McTavish emphatically refused to turn over his authority to a provisional government, which would have made matters much more straightforward. But at the same time, from his sickbed he was reported as exclaiming irritably, "Form a Government, for God's sake, and restore peace and order in the Settlement." Given the rumours swirling outside Upper Fort Garry about violence and civil war, the delegates could hardly help but recognize this as sound advice.

-4-

The Portage Boys

The most serious threat to the peace of Red River came in February of 1870 from the settlement at Portage la Prairie, about 100 kilometres west of Winnipeg. Portage was on the Assiniboine River, with most of its population located between that river and Lake Manitoba. Founded in 1851 by the Anglican missionary William Cochrane, it was outside the formal bounds of the Municipal District of Assiniboia, and had never evolved into a fully integrated part of the Red River Settlement. Portage had become the home of incoming settlers from Canada, as well as a number of mixed-bloods and Métis, who had begun moving into the district in the early 1850s.

In 1867 one Thomas Spence, a Scottish-born Canadian recently arrived in the West, had — by his own testimony before a Parliamentary committee in 1874 — "organized a Provisional government over a part of the territory which was occupied by about four hundred people." Spence had then petitioned the imperial authorities for recognition as the "Republic of Manitobah." London replied that such proceedings were illegal, and the republic quickly collapsed. Subsequently, however, incomers from Canada had settled without permission on land around Poplar Point claimed by the aboriginals, who had to be persuaded to allow them to remain. The Canadian poet Charles Mair had visited the region west of Red River in 1868, and had raved in letters to the eastern press about its potential, writing "The country is great, inexhaustible, inconceivably rich. Farming here is a pleasure."

The Quarterly Court of Assiniboia had exercised a tenuous jurisdiction in Portage la Prairie in the late 1860s. In 1868 the court had conducted a murder trial involving one of the new Canadian settlers, Alex McLean, and a Métis named Francis Demarais. The deceased had been intoxicated and had threatened the McLean family, including Alex McLean's sister, at their farm. He had brandished a gun and even fired a shot before turning to flee the scene. Young McLean, who had been working nearby, arrived in time to see Demarais running away. He pulled out his revolver and shot Demarais in the back. McLean was defended by the American lawyer Enos Stutsman, who ran legal rings around Judge Black and easily obtained an acquittal from the jury. It was the first time a trained lawyer had ever worked in the Red River court. More important for our purposes were the revelations that the settlers in this region carried guns as they went about their work, and that a local Portage jury — composed entirely of Canadians — did not think that shooting a Métis in the back constituted murder.

In early 1870, several of the prisoners who had been captured at John Christian Schultz's house escaped from Upper Fort Garry and made their way to the "safe" refuge of Portage la Prairie, where the arm of the pro-visional government did not extend. The escapees included Thomas Scott, Charles Mair, and John Christian Schultz, who joined other Canadian refugees running from the troubles of Red River, including the surveyor Charles Arkoll Boulton, in a community inherently hostile to both Red River and to Louis Riel. Charles Mair found the Canadian surveyors holed up in a saloon run by an American named House. The new arrivals complained long and loud of their treatment while in cap-tivity, and with Scott apparently the loudest voice, succeeded in per-suading the young hot-bloods of the community that the remaining pris-oners deserved to be released, by force if necessary. Most of the Canadians in the settlement were unmarried young men in their twen-ties. They were restless, and had come to Red River in search of some kind of adventure. They were "the boys."

The prisoners at Upper Fort Garry were rapidly turning into a seri-ous problem for Riel and his government. Although a few had escaped and a handful had been released, most of those incarcerated resolutely refused to take any oath of loyalty to the government or to promise that they would not take up arms against it. Since they had been originally captured in an armed and fortified situation, it was only prudent not simply to turn them loose into the community. At the same time, they were expensive to feed and guard, and people in Red River and beyond were beginning to wonder why they were still being held.

Winding Up the Convention

With the question of the negotiations with Canada for the moment pretty well settled, Riel was able to turn his attention to the establishment of a revised provisional government which would include the anglophone mixed-bloods. At the meeting of the convention on 10 February, James Ross had spoken with passion about co-operation. "The fact is," Ross insisted, "we have no option in this matter. We must restore order, peace and quietness in the Settlement."

The same committee that had drafted the Bill of Rights prepared an outline for the new government. It was presented to the convention late on the evening of 10 February. A new council would consist of 24 members, 12 from each language group, and a president. Each section would choose its own members by its own means. Officers were recommended, with a preponderance of anglophones in the minor officers. James Ross would be judge, Henry McKenney would be sheriff, Dr. Curtis Bird would become coroner, A.G.B. Bannatyne would be postmaster, John Sutherland and Roger Goulet were to become collectors of customs, and Thomas Bunn would be secretary. On the francophone side, Louis Schmidt was to be sub-secretary, W.B. O'Donoghue would be treasurer, Ambroise Lépine would be adjutant general, and Louis Riel was to be named president of the council. The veto of the president could be overturned by a two-thirds vote. The committee recommended that William Dease be replaced as a justice of the peace, but that the other magistrates retain their posts. The committee also recommended that the General Quarterly Court carry on as before, with five petty courts located pretty much as they had been under the Hudson's Bay Company. There would thus be a considerable continuity between the old Council of Assiniboia and the new government, particularly in terms of the administration of justice.

One of the most important conditions the anglophone delegates had made in assenting to this co-operation was a promise from Louis Riel that he would release the prisoners being held at Upper Fort Garry. Governor McTavish, Dr. Cowan, and A.G.B. Bannatyne were to be released immediately, and the other prisoners would be freed over the next few days. Riel kept the first part of his promise immediately at the conclusion of the day's meeting. McTavish, Cowan, and Bannatyne were indeed released, and the men at the fort fired a salute to mark the occasion. The entire village of Winnipeg celebrated. Fireworks intended to greet Governor McDougall were set off, huge bonfires were lit, and guns were shot into the air. Alexander Begg reported, "A regular drunk commenced in which everyone seemed to join." The party went on until four in the morning. Louis Riel did not take part in the festivities, but according to Begg he did take "a good horn of brandy" with Bannatyne before actually releasing him. Over the next few days additional prisoners had been released, and Donald A. Smith reported to the Canadian prime minister that Dr. Cowan was informed in Smith's presence that the prisoners' rooms would shortly be returned to the Company. Riel added that he would have them thoroughly cleaned.

At its final session, the convention was told by Louis Riel that anyone was at liberty to shoot Dr. Schultz. The gathering then finally appointed its delegates to negotiate with Canada. The three men chosen were Father Noel Ritchot, Judge John Black, and Alfred H. Scott. Ritchot and Black were consensual choices, one from each language group. The choice of Scott was more problematic. Louis Riel refused to become a delegate. Scott was an anglophone American who had on several occasions voted in the convention with the Métis. While there might have been better candidates, Scott was not a bad compromise choice.

The same day that the convention concluded by choosing delegates to deal with Canada, the Canadian cabinet was meeting to deal with Red River. The cabinet agreed that delegates from Red River would be received. But several cabinet members, including the prime minister, were still not entirely happy about negotiating with the Métis, whom several continued to regard as shifty and not to be trusted. Moreover, the cabinet agreed it would not be pressured by threats to turn to the Americans. The minutes of this meeting noted, "But it is to be remembered that the Insurgent Leaders have already declared themselves in favor of annexation to the United States, and even if compelled by public opinion to acquiesce in the proposed mission of the Red River delegates to Ottawa, their good faith is more than doubtful." This complete misreading of the state of play in Red River came partly because of Donald Smith's report upon his arrival in the settlement, partly because the government, led by Sir John A. Macdonald, simply did not want to trust "half-breeds." As we have seen, Louis Riel and his followers had been working toward a mission to Ottawa for months. Should negotiations break down, as a number of the cabinet ministers obviously expected would be the case, it was agreed that Red River would have to be confronted immediately with a military force.

The resultant cabinet minutes recognized that any military expedition would have to be undertaken by the British, since Canada had "no authority beyond her own limits." The wisdom of refusing to take possession on 1 December now seemed vindicated. The cabinet thus asked the governor-general to inform the colonial secretary of the need for immediate action. The expedition should be dispatched as early as the opening of navigation in the spring permitted. Assuming that the Sault would open about 25 April, everything should be ready at Fort William by 1 May. The government did not seem to sense any incompatibility between its own refusal to be pressured by Red River threats of negotiations with the Americans, and the pressure the threat of a major military expedition would exert upon the delegates from Rupert's Land. Here, as almost everywhere else in the Red River business, Canada was not really willing to be reasonable and conciliatory, or to meet the Métis halfway. Mainly this was because the Canadians were quite annoyed that a handful of "half-breeds" could interrupt the inexorable destiny of Canada to possess the West.

On 12 February, Riel began releasing prisoners, as he had promised the convention he would do. He did his best to prevent them from becoming part of a potential armed opposition by insisting that they swear that they would keep the peace and abide by the laws of the country. Some of those being held agreed, but many of the young bucks refused to accept what they felt were illegitimate terms. A. W. Graham, in his diary, wrote that he and his fellows had been "offered our liberty by taking an oath of allegiance to Riel's government," and most had refused. Graham described the scene at the fort. The prisoners were held in a small room and then escorted upstairs one at a time to have an audience with Riel and W.B. O'Donoghue. Riel paced restlessly around the room, while O'Donoghue and a clerk sat behind a table and read the oath the prisoner was supposed to take. "I was a British subject on British soil and would take no oath to serve another government," Graham wrote angrily. He was sent back to his cell, as were a number of other recalcitrants. On this very day Anglican Bishop Robert Machray penned a gloomy letter to London complaining of the "hard and uncomfortable times in the land, where we never know what may be the calamity of tomorrow." Machray was no friend of the Métis, but he spent the winter counselling co-operation among his mixed-blood parishioners as an alternative to a blood bath. In his letter he added, "Sometimes there is hope of quiet settlement, and then the hope departs and the condition of things is only worse than before."

Little did he know just how accurate this observation was, for also on 12 February, the Portage boys began their march to Winnipeg. The Portage people did not know that Riel had promised to release all the prisoners and that their march was thus unnecessary. Word was sent to the Portage people to stop until the convention had finished its business, but apparently was not received.

The Portage "Invasion" and the Assemblage at Kildonan

The 60 young men who left the settlement in "high spirits" on a bitterly cold February day were led, after a fashion, by Charles Arkoll Boulton. A young Canadian who had served in the British Army in Gibraltar before joining John Dennis's survey crew, Boulton recognized the venture as the daft stunt it was. He claimed he learned of it only at the last minute, and reluctantly agreed to lead it to "endeavour to keep them to the legitimate object for which they had organized," as he put it in his memoirs. Most of the party departing Portage were not armed with guns or rifles, but only with oak clubs. They had little food and even less money, apparently expecting that they would be fed along their route by loyal supporters of Canada. Major Boulton's second-in-command was the mixed-blood William Gaddy. Although Thomas Scott was a part of this contingent, there is no evidence that he was one of its leaders. The party marched "merrily along the frozen snow" for about nine hours without rest, finally reaching Headingley, a settlement about 30 kilometres from Winnipeg. Boulton wrote that they were buoyed up by the thought of liberating their comrades, although one suspects that they were also fuelled by the liberal use of intoxicating substances. Along the route, the little army had captured several prisoners, one of them a supposed "spy," a Métis named Norbert Parisien. They had also added to their numbers at Poplar Point and High Bluff.

At Headingley, the young men were accommodated in the houses of some of the inhabitants for what was supposed to be a brief rest period. Their intention was to continue on and besiege Upper Fort Garry at dawn. A sudden snowstorm blew up, however, and the party was delayed for 48 hours by whiteout conditions. During the enforced stopover, a meeting was held at the house of John Taylor, an anglophone mixed-blood who had joined the expedition. At this gathering, Boulton had resigned as commander because he felt that many suspected he was not sufficiently keen about the enterprise. To his surprise, he was re-elected, having promised only to lead the men to their legitimate objective without undue risk to the party. For some reason, the snowstorm and the delay led Boulton to change the plan. Instead of immediately attacking Upper Fort Garry, the contingent would now march through the village of Winnipeg and head north to Kildonan Church, where they hoped to be joined by other "loyal" citizens.

Boulton's crew left Headingley at 8 p.m. on a fine moonlit night. They managed to pass by the walls of Upper Fort Garry early on the morning of 15 February. The guards at the fort fired an alarm, but did not follow it up. As evidence of the fecklessness with which this little army operated, having gotten by the fort without serious incident, they proceeded to stop in the village of Winnipeg at the house of a man known to be a relative of Louis Riel. They surrounded the house, while Boulton and Thomas Scott went inside to search in the hopes that they would be able to capture Riel. When it became clear the Métis leader was not inside, the party moved on. How much discomfort this little visit caused for the inhabitants of the house can only be imagined. While Boulton would insist that the visitors had withdrawn as soon as it was clear that Riel was not there, Louis Riel and others told a different story of armed searches. Riel would use this incident as evidence that the Portage Boys were interested in more than merely freeing the prisoners, as they always insisted. The army breakfasted noisily in Winnipeg. It was a small wonder that the Métis failed to catch up with them. At the house of William Dease, the Métis caught up with William Gaddy and a number of other mixed-bloods who were quite rightly suspected of stirring up trouble. Dease had escaped out the window, and most of those captured were soon released. Gaddy was held, however.

As the small army, by now about 100 strong, came close to Kildonan, it became increasingly clear to Boulton that it was not being greeted with approbation but rather with consternation. The people, he later wrote, felt that affairs were reaching a peaceful resolution, and "the appearance of another armed force on the scene cast all their hopes to the wind." Boulton rationalized away this reception by arguing that the Portage contingent had no idea of what was happening in Red River when it had set out, and that there were still prisoners to be released, as if this were sufficient reason for hare-brained schemes that might provoke civil war. His force pressed on to Kildonan Church, where it hoped to rendezvous with another armed party led by Dr. John Christian Schultz. According to one eyewitness, there was talk of capturing the Upper Fort, liberating the prisoners, and setting up a government with Donald A. Smith at its head.

The arrival of the motley crew from Portage stimulated another attempt to negotiate the release of the remaining prisoners with Louis Riel. This time the initiative was led by Miss Victoria MacVicar, a visitor from Fort William. "Vickie" MacVicar was spending the winter with relations at Red River. Her family was a prominent fur-trading one at the Lakehead. She was a vivacious young lady with a cousin, George MacVicar, among the prisoners. Vickie had visited the prisoners frequently over the weeks of incarceration, and had even smuggled letters into the fort. Now she enlisted the aid of A.G.B. Bannatyne — recently released from incarceration himself — by informing him that nearly 600 men were gathered at the Kildonan School House determined to attack Upper Fort Garry and release the prisoners. The two headed off to confront Riel, merely the latest of a long series of people asking Riel to release those he was holding.

When MacVicar and Bannatyne reached Upper Fort Garry, they discovered Louis Riel in the process of administering an oath to keep the peace to the prisoners. He was not having much success. Many of those being held had agreed to act in unison. The two visitors managed to persuade Robert Smith to sign, and gradually all the others fell into line. When Dr. James Lynch, who was being particularly recalcitrant, actually read the oath, he said he could sign. Riel refused to allow James

Farquharson to sign, saying that he had several times broken his oath already, and ordered the guards to push him out of the fort into the snow. During the oath signings, Riel had paced restlessly around the room. When the prisoners had finally all departed, Riel turned to Miss MacVicar and A.G.B. Bannatyne. What happened next was recorded by Alexander Begg in his journal, Begg doubtless having heard the story from his partner. Riel said, "I know there is something else behind this. Schultz will try and attack the Fort; but let him come; I hope he will." The two visitors replied that the anglophones were in arms only because the prisoners had not been released. Everyone would now disperse. "Well, well," said Riel, "This is the last thing I will grant to the other side." Having gotten all the prisoners at the Upper Fort freed, MacVicar and Bannatyne then had to go outside the fort to try to persuade a delegation from the gathering at Lower Fort Garry — consisting of Maurice Lowman, James Ross, and Colin Inkster — not to press their luck by demanding a general amnesty for all the Canadians, including Dr. John Schultz. Riel refused to receive this contingent, and told Ross that if "he would ask that again he would have him at once." Nevertheless, another crisis had seemingly been averted.

But as was the usual story in Red River that winter, to dodge one bullet only meant facing another. By the morning of 16 February, a large crowd of men were still gathered around the Presbyterian church in Kildonan, most of them milling about aimlessly. A few enthusiasts had raised over the schoolhouse a large red ensign bearing the British flag and the inscription "God Save the Queen," but most of the crowd was cold and hungry rather than militant. Many agreed with the statement of James McKay, who said, "I cannot take up arms against my own people." The clergy were counselling caution. One later correspondent to the *Globe* blamed the clergy for advocating "peace, peace, when there is no peace." The "Reverend Quartette," he insisted, had single-handedly defused the situation. Victoria MacVicar had been driven by sleigh from Winnipeg the previous evening with the news that the prisoners had now all been released. There were the 100 men from Portage, several hundred more from St. Andrew's and Mapleton, recruited by Dr. Schultz and marched to the rendezvous with the good doctor at their head, and a large contingent of Indians from the settlement and as far east as Lake of the Woods. The aboriginals were in full warpaint and regalia. Some estimates ran as high as 600 to 700 men in total gathered in Kildonan, badly armed and almost totally unprovisioned.

When word of the release of the prisoners was brought back to Kildonan, most of those gathered there rejoiced. A few of those who had assembled had already gone home, since there was little food and the cold was considerable. At this point, Norbert Parisien, one of those so-called "spies" captured by the Portage Boys on their march to Kildonan, escaped from Kildonan Church, where he was being held under guard. Parisien managed to seize a gun as he got away. He headed out onto the river, pursued by his captors, where he encountered young John Sutherland — the son of Hugh Sutherland, one of the Métis' strongest supporters among the mixed-bloods. The young Sutherland, a friend of Norbert, was on horseback. Perhaps fearing that the rider would try to stop him, Parisien fired several shots at Sutherland, who fell off his horse and was carried to the house of the Reverend John Black. Sutherland was mortally wounded and, despite the ministrations of Dr. Schultz and others, would soon die. The guards continued their pursuit of Parisien, caught him up, and administered to him a severe beating as they returned to the church. Parisien would live longer than Sutherland, but he too would die. The entire incident probably sobered the assembly. Charles Mair later recalled that he had expected the death of Sutherland to "fire the blood of every man," but it had done just the reverse. He found "an extraordinary scene, pitiful beyond description — exhibiting as it did a poltroonery on the part of the Kildonan people utterly astonishing."

After the shooting and recapture of Parisien, a council was held of the leading figures at Kildonan. It consisted of Schultz, Boulton, the Reverend John Black, Judge John Black, and Bishop Robert Machray, among others. The council had been called before the news of the release of the prisoners to draw up a list of demands. Its meeting had been put off by the excitement of the morning. Major Boulton wanted only a release of the prisoners, which Victoria MacVicar had already reported as achieved. Some of the others desired a change of government. The demands discussed included not only the liberation of all prisoners, but a guarantee that no more be taken; that all confiscated property be safely stored; that John Christian Schultz be granted his safety; and finally, according to a correspondent for the Montreal *Witness*, "that we form a Government of our own, allowing him [Riel] to carry on his without any interference, but letting it be understood that we countenanced him in no shape or manner." Many of the anglo mixed-bloods, along with Scots settlers and Canadians, continued to be unhappy about the provisional government, although how separating themselves from it would make them less rebellious was not entirely clear. The clergy, of course, opposed any untoward action. Men like Bishop Machray were simultaneously hostile to Riel and the Métis and to any attempt to supplant them, fearing that the result would be open civil war.

The eventual message to Riel from these divided counsels stated that the anglophones would not recognize the provisional government, and referred to the shooting of young Sutherland as a grievance. Thomas

Norquay, the messenger sent to Upper Fort Garry with this dispatch, was pre-emptorily thrown into a cell by Louis Riel, who ceremoniously tore up the letter into tiny pieces. The president of the provisional government told another visitor from Kildonan, who had come to the fort about the Parisien-Sutherland tragedy, "Go back to your people and tell them what you have seen." Riel insisted that Parisien had a perfect right to fire on anybody he thought was pursuing him, since he had been illegally detained in the first place. The death of Parisien would eventually become part of the package of Métis grievances against the anglophones, and would, by some, be set against the death of Thomas Scott in the balance sheet of atrocities committed by both sides over the winter of 1869-70. In Kildonan, young Sutherland's father publicly declared that no blood should be shed on his son's account. It would only make the grief of the parents harder to bear, he said, if through his son's death other innocent lives should be lost.

Riel eventually had second thoughts about his initial response to the message from Kildonan. He freed Thomas Norquay that same day and sent him back to Kildonan with a letter addressed to "Fellow Countrymen." Riel wrote, "for my part I understand that war horrible civil war is the destruction of this country." He added, "We are ready to meet any party. But peace our British rights we want before all." Riel emphasized that the prisoners were freed, and called upon the anglophones to help form the new provisional government. According to contemporary rumour, substantiated by later accounts of W.B. O'Donoghue and Charles Mair, Riel also sent verbal assurances via John "Flatboat" McLean that if the English disbanded and went peaceably home, they would not be bothered by his armed Métis. Exactly how far this offer extended was never clear. But peace might yet be possible. Alexander Begg was buoyed up at the thought of peaceful resolution, as well as by the news received this same day in the settlement that Bishop Taché would soon be back in Red River.

By the time Thomas Norquay had returned to Kildonan with Riel's reply, the assemblage had already decided to disperse. According to the correspondent in the *Witness*, many went home because they had nothing to eat and could see nothing being done. The Reverend Black had attempted to provide food from his own stocks, but the crowd was too large and there was no miracle of loaves and fishes. Others were unhappy with the prominence of Dr. John Christian Schultz in the gathering, regarding him as a Canadian troublemaker. "There was also no management in the affair," added the *Witness* writer despondently, "no provisions furnished, no leader to guide the men, and no order in the camp — just a mob of men gathered together, full of spirit, but without a plan to work by." Henry Prince and 50 of his Saulteaux agreed to remain at

Lower Fort Garry as guards. Most of the assembly melted away into the dark. The will to confront Riel and the Métis was no longer present.

The village of Winnipeg and Upper Fort Garry could not know immediately that the armed crowd at Kildonan had left. Alexander Begg's journal for 16 February recorded great activity in the village. Shopkeepers shuttered their windows and things of value (including books!) were hidden away. The Métis collected 62 kegs of gunpowder from Messrs. Bannatyne and Begg. Dr. Curtis Bird was sent to Kildonan to examine the mortally wounded Sutherland. He reported back that a conference was being held at Mr. Black's house but that Sutherland would not recover. The entire town was turned into an armed camp, preparing to resist a rumoured invasion of the people from Kildonan, led by the boys of Portage. The subsequent developments in Winnipeg have to be seen in the context of this situation.

Prisoners Again

Apparently oblivious to the panic they had caused in the village, the Portage Boys marched back toward Winnipeg, camping for the night outside Alfred Boyd's store in Point Douglas. Here, in the early morning of 17 February, the Portage party held a crucial council of war. It decided to return to Portage as a unit, which meant that it would have to march westward past Upper Fort Garry. Charles Boulton argued desperately for dispersal and a quiet return to the western community by individuals. He was fully aware that even if Riel had promised a safe conduct — and what that meant was never clear — to march an armed party under his nose was inviting trouble. In the context of the nervousness in Winnipeg and Upper Fort Garry, the decision was absurd. Certainly some of the sensible ones among the party, like John Garrioch, John Christian Schultz, and Charles Mair, had already left to make their own way. But as Sergeant-Major Michael Power, formerly of the Dragoon Guards, argued, "We had come down like brave men and that we should go back like brave men, in a body." This defiant argument, combined with an impatience to get home, prevailed over Boulton's objections.

Some of the group had heard — no one could say from whom — that Riel had sent a message that he would not take any more prisoners. Subsequent investigation by Donald A. Smith and Archdeacon John McLean reported that Riel's response to being informed that the party intended to march past the fort was simply, "Oh, that is good." In 1885, W.B. O'Donoghue wrote in the Toronto *Daily Mail* that Riel had verbally promised to allow the Canadians to return peaceably to their homes if

A young Louis Riel, probably on his arrival in Montréal to continue his studies at a collège classique in 1858.

Archives de la Société historique de Saint-Boniface – Musée de Saint-Boniface-0320

Louis Riel as a young man, at the time he started studying law before returning to Manitoba in 1868.

National Archives of Canada

Photograph of Louis Riel, circa early 1870s, by I Bennetto & Co., Winnipeg.

SHSB-843

Louis Riel, n.d.

Archives de la Société historique de Saint-Boniface – Musée de Saint-Boniface-1065

Some drawings depicting the execution of Thomas Scott feature Riel
delivering the *coup de grace*, which was false.

PAM

Riel, centre, with his provisional government in late 1869.

PAM

they disbanded, but this was in the context of the controversy over Riel's trial and execution; moreover, by this time, O'Donoghue had become a sworn enemy of Riel. Major Boulton claimed to be suspicious of any offers from Riel, but most of the others who doubted the Métis intentions had already voted with their feet and left the group.

Boulton later admitted that he knew better than to accept this decision of his party, but he insisted that he felt duty-bound to remain with his men. The group, now reduced from the original 100 to about 45, left Point Douglas about 9 a.m. Boulton intended to cross the open prairie through the snow, which was waist-deep, about one and one-half miles northwest of Upper Fort Garry. As the men departed Point Douglas, word came (false, as it turned out) that William Gaddy had been summarily executed at the fort. According to a later statement by Riel, Gaddy's execution for spying had been demanded on the spot by the Métis soldiers. He had been led to one of the bastions of the fort to be shot by Adjutant-General Ambroise Lépine and Elzéar Goulet. Instead, however, Gaddy was freed by his guards and told not to return to the settlement. He, at least, had sufficient sense to melt silently away. The Portage Boys did not.

In 1886, after the end of the second rebellion led by Riel in Saskatchewan, Charles Boulton hired a stenographer and sat down to compose his memoirs. Most of the best-selling book that resulted was taken up with Boulton's adventures as leader of a unit of mounted scouts in 1885, but he also told his story about his participation in events in Red River. In his memoirs, Boulton wrote that on 17 February his party set out single file across the open prairie to return to Portage la Prairie. The snow was waist-deep, so one man had to follow closely in his predecessor's footsteps, and progress was consequently slow. Alexander Begg, who claimed to be able to see what was going on from the village, insisted that there were men in carioles as well as on foot. In any event, the party was not likely to pass unnoticed by Upper Fort Garry. When the marchers got opposite the fort, a party of horsemen galloped out and rode toward the Portage group. They were followed about 200 yards behind by contingent of about 50 Métis on foot. When the horsemen were within 150 yards of the spread-out Portage Boys, Boulton's men attempted to form up a defence. Boulton shouted strict orders "that on no account should a shot be fired or any hostility provoked." The horsemen, headed by Ambroise Lépine and W.B. O'Donoghue, continued to approach. The Portagers sent one of their number to parley. He tried to explain that the marchers were returning quietly to their homes, but was apparently ignored. As the horsemen approached, O'Donoghue asked, "What party is this?" Boulton answered, "It is a party of men returning to the Portage." O'Donoghue continued, "Is Major Boulton here?" When Boulton acknowledged himself, O'Donoghue expressed pleasure and said he was sent by President Riel with an invitation to go to the fort to talk. Boulton said he preferred to continue on his way without interference.

After a brief tussle over a gun between Ambroise Lépine and a young Canadian, Boulton decided to surrender. He explained in his memoirs, "I was afraid that in the struggle the revolver would go off, which would be the sign for a massacre, from which there was no escape. We were not armed; we were up to our waists in snow; and in the presence of double our number, who were well armed, supported by a large force in the Fort near by, and who were excited over the events of the previous day." Full of forebodings, Boulton ordered his party to surrender and to march to the fort. As "Justitia," Alexander Begg wrote of this turn of events in the *Globe* with incredulity, asking, "When will complications cease?" He half-answered his own question, writing, "Only two days have elapsed since the release of the late prisoners, when another batch almost as numerous as the former are captured."

The major question, of course, was not why Boulton surrendered, but why his men were marching in broad daylight within sight of the fort in the first place. The Portage expedition was a disaster from beginning to end. It ought never to have begun, or if begun ought never to have been continued. "Justitia" offered his assessment in the *Globe*:

> In the face of Riel's guaranteeing the release of the late prisoners, and with the prospect of a speedy arrangement with the Dominion, held out by the commissioners from Canada, those who came down, and by the presence in a body armed and vowing vengeance on those in Fort Garry…fanned the flame of discontent among the English, until it burst out in a manner that will now sow seeds of discord to the future.

Charles Boulton appears to have been little but a dupe in the entire enterprise. His own explanation of his involvement, if accepted on face value, labels him as dense, weak, and insensitive, unable to consider the implications of his actions. Boulton should have exercised whatever authority he had to make these young Canadian hotheads behave sensibly, and under no circumstances should he have joined them. Participants in the operation insisted that there was really no leader. Alexander McPherson recalled that the Portage party "seemed to act spontaneously." Alexander Murray testified of the expedition that "there was not much commanding by any one."

The Threat to Major Boulton

Whatever his role in the expedition, Charles Boulton would pay a heavy price for it. Louis Riel focused a good deal of anger on the young Canadian militia officer. Why Riel behaved in this way is quite inexplicable. The potential armed challenge to his leadership and to the provisional government had been dissipated. Riel had managed to end the whole business on a positive note, calling for unity and for support of the provisional government. Perhaps the opportunity to capture the Portage men which dropped into his hands was too attractive to pass up, but there seemed little need for the behaviour which Charles Boulton described in his memoirs, most of which was corroborated by other witnesses.

Boulton was separated from his men and placed alone in a room next to them with his legs chained together. The room was without heat and extremely cold. Eventually Riel opened the door of the room and without entering said, "Major Boulton, you prepare to die tomorrow at twelve o'clock." Boulton answered, "Very well." Boulton managed to get some paper and wrote a note to Anglican Archdeacon John McLean asking him to visit. Riel came in the room to question him about the objectives of the Portage expedition, and especially its intentions in searching in Winnipeg for the Métis leader. Riel would return to this matter in his later confrontation with Thomas Scott, suggesting that it was of some considerable importance to him. Then Riel said he would allow McLean to come. The clergyman, in a "state of great excitement and anxiety," managed to obtain a 12-hour postponement of the execution. There had been no trial whatever. Boulton was persuaded that his guards bore him no ill will, and he insisted 15 years later that Riel's purpose in the execution was "to strike terror to the hearts of the people, and to more firmly fix himself as the autocrat of the country." It was certainly the case that in recent weeks the Métis leader had been constantly hurling death threats around the fort. Whether this one was more serious than the others, or was intended as a public bargaining ploy or a terrorizing gesture is not clear.

Boulton understandably had trouble sleeping on the night before his threatened execution. The room was cold and uncomfortable, and his guards were troublesome. One Métis, obviously agitated, came in regularly to wake him up and to pray with him. In early the morning this sentry — who Boulton later insisted was the father of Norbert Parisien, still alive but mortally hurt in Kildonan — was taken away in a state of mental breakdown. His replacement huddled more quietly in the corner, but about 3 p.m. made "a strange gurgling sound." Boulton glanced at the man only to discover that he had died. A squad was marched into the room and Riel himself held an inquest on the spot, concluding that the sentry had died of apoplexy. The Métis refused to allow a third sentry to be locked up with the prisoner. Riel subsequently offered to release Boulton if Messrs. Schultz and Mair would surrender themselves. The prisoner doubted that Shultz would make himself a "willing sacrifice."

After the event, Boulton learned that Riel was under pressure from many people to show mercy, although he kept up the death sentence threat all through 18 February. There were reports that Thomas Scott, John Taylor, and George Parker — other Portage men captured by Riel and also involved in the Winnipeg search party — had also been sentenced to death without any trial. The parents of the murdered John Sutherland pled for the lives of the condemned prisoners. Riel allegedly responded, "you have saved three lives — but Captain Boulton must suffer." Donald A. Smith later told Boulton that from the first news of the threat, "he knew he would have to give an equivalent in asking for [Boulton's] life." Smith obviously thought that the Riel's point in harassing Boulton was to gain some concession. Not until 10:30 p.m. on 18 February, however, could Archdeacon McLean inform the condemned man that he had been reprieved for a week. Boulton's life would be spared if Donald A. Smith could convince the anglophone parishes to elect delegates to meet with the Métis in the council of the provisional government.

Smith would report to Ottawa that Riel initially refused to yield on Boulton because the anglophone and Canadian settlers had laughed at the Métis. Peace would not come until an example of Métis firmness was made so that the opposition would know that they were serious. Boulton's execution was to be that example. Finally, at about 10 p.m., Riel agreed to spare the Canadian, saying to Smith, "Hitherto I have been deaf to all entreaties, and in granting you this man's life may I ask you a favour?" Smith replied, "Anything that in honour I can do." Riel went on, "Canada has disunited us, will you use your influence to reunite us[?] You can do so, and without this it must be war, bloody civil war." He insisted that the Métis only wanted their just rights as British subjects, needing the anglophones to join them to obtain these rights. "Then," said Smith, "I shall at once see them and induce them to go on with the election of delegates for that purpose." Riel replied, "If you can do this, war will be avoided; not only the lives but the liberty of all the prisoners will be secured, for on your success depend the lives of all the Canadians in the country."

Smith was absolutely scathing in his comments on the actions of the Portage Boys. "The rising was not only rash," he subsequently wrote to Joseph Howe, "but purposeless, as without its intervention, the prisoners would unquestionably have been released. The party was entirely unorganized, indifferently armed, unprovided with food even for one meal, and wholly incapable of coping with the French now re-united…. Under the circumstances it was not difficult to foresee that the issue could not be otherwise than disastrous to their cause. The attempt was, therefore, to be deplored, as it resulted in putting the whole Settlement at the feet of Riel."

Smith's promise to help bring the anglophones on line was doubtless more influential than the second visit to Riel of Miss Victoria MacVicar. She called on the Métis leader accompanied by a drunken James Ross. When she entered Riel's room she threw herself on her knees and cried, "Mercy! Mercy! Mercy!" Boulton fell asleep, exhausted by his ordeal. But he was soon awakened by Riel, carrying a lantern. According to Boulton in 1886, Riel said, "Major Boulton, I have come to see you. I have come to shake you by the hand, and to make a proposition to you. I perceive that you are a man of ability, that you are a leader. The English people, they have no leader. Will you join my government, and be their leader?" Boulton insisted that he found the proposal "serio-comic," as indeed it was, at the same time that it was quite sensible. He gathered himself and said he would consider the proposal if all the prisoners were freed. But he heard no more about it.

This incident with Boulton in many ways prefigures the later confrontation with Thomas Scott, a case in which Riel did not change his mind. Boulton's sentence of death without any legal process whatever — not the first such threat made under similar circumstances by Riel — suggests that Monsieur le President was not at this time concerned over legal niceties. He had the power and was prepared to use it. His conversation with Donald A. Smith further suggests that Riel knew perfectly well what he was doing, however erroneous his assessment of what the potential consequences might be.

Although Riel now turned from Boulton to a search for the two Canadians, Dr. John Christian Schultz and Charles Mair, both those men managed to get out of the settlement. Schultz headed south with Joseph Monkman on snowshoes on 21 February for the American railhead. Charles Mair left Red River by dog train at about the same time. Donald A. Smith, accompanied by Archdeacon McLean and Henry McDermott, honoured his promise by touring the anglophone parishes to advocate co-operation with the provisional government. These emissaries explained that the new government was "intended specially for effecting the transference of the country to Canada, and for ensuring safety of all life and property in the meantime." They wanted no conditional elections or candidates bound by instructions. Some local elections had already occurred before the general election date of 26 February.

On 23 February 1870, Prime Minister Macdonald wrote to his friend and former cabinet colleague, Sir John Rose, currently in England, on his meeting with Bishop Taché in Ottawa. The bishop had decided to leave the Vatican Council he had been attending and return to Red River. Taché had agreed that there should be no imperial commissioner appointed to negotiate with the provisional government, "believing, as indeed, we all do, that to send an overwashed Englishman, utterly ignorant of the country and full of crotchets, as all Englishmen are, would be a mistake." Although he did not say so in this letter, Taché was sent back to Red River to placate the Métis. What the informal understandings were between the prime minister and the bishop would subsequently become the subject of much controversy. What Macdonald did say was that he expected a delegation from Red River to come to Ottawa. It would probably include "the redoubtable Riel," who could surely be co-opted. "If we once get him here, as you must know pretty well by this time, he is a gone coon." There was no room in the cabinet for Riel, wrote the prime minister, but he could be made a senator for the Territory. Macdonald noted that he hoped to organize a mounted police force along the lines of the Irish constabulary, adding "These impulsive half-breeds have got spoilt by this *émeute*, and must be kept down by a strong hand until they are swamped by the influx of settlers." This single sentence made clear that the prime minister had not changed his stereotyped view of the Métis or his intention to overwhelm them with new immigrants. But the entire letter indicates that Canada would negotiate with the provisional government.

Back in Red River, where Riel seemed to be in the process of resolving most of his difficulties, Alexander Begg reported on 24 February that the president had been taken ill with "brain fever" at the house of Henry Coutu. He was quickly surrounded by priests and nuns. His mother was called in to nurse him. While Riel was still in bed, Joseph Howe cabled to Bishop Taché that the Bill of Rights had finally arrived in Ottawa. It was "in the main satisfactory but let the delegates come here and settle the details." Riel recovered quickly from his attack, whatever it was, and was back at work within a few days. There is a temptation to make a good deal out of this attack, never more specifically described than with a terse label. Riel was certainly a classic candidate for some sort of stress-related ailment, either physical or mental. He was full of restless nervous energy — many observers commented on his constant pacing, his inability to sit quietly while dealing with the many strands of his responsibilities — for which he had no observable outlet. But we simply do not have enough information about the nature of the illness to speculate.

When he did return to work, he found his problems had not really gone away. At least some of the anglophone parishes made clear that they had accepted the provisional government only because of Charles Boulton. Food, especially for his armed supporters, was becoming a bit of a concern. Riel seized the remaining stores, including the root cellars, at the fort. He ordered the systematic slaughter of Company cattle wintering on the plains. He sent messages to those Métis wintering on the plains to be prepared to sell their pemmican to the provisional government. He also invited the winterers to come and fight if needed in the spring. Riel recognized that his was still a government under military threat, from within the settlement, from the aboriginals on the plains, and certainly from the government of Canada.

Public opinion in Canada was harder to gauge than the attitude of the Canadian ministers. Editorial opinion in the eastern Canadian newspapers was in February less favourable to Riel and the uprising than it had been in November, but there was still some mixture of opinion. With the return to Canada of the ill-fated and unpopular William McDougall, the Toronto *Globe* returned to its more familiar stance of high-minded Canadianism, combined with an increasing hostility to Louis Riel. On 22 February, the *Globe* labelled Riel as "the great potentate of the North," but on 26 February, upon news of the incarceration of A.G.B. Bannatyne, Dr. Cowan, and Governor McTavish, the newspaper opined that "The whole thing looks like the mere waywardness of a passionate and weakminded upstart 'clothed with a little brief authority.'" This view echoed the earlier assessment of *Globe* reporter Robert Cunningham. A few days later, the prime minister was asked whether he really wanted "to hail Riel as the Emperor of the Nor'West?" On the other hand, the Montreal *Gazette* in a major editorial on 8 February was still blaming the Ontario people in Red River for their behaviour and the *Globe* for encouraging them.

In Quebec, as in Ontario, newspaper responses to Red River seemed to be more a party business than sectionally or racially motivated. Conservative papers supported the government and attacked the Métis. Opposition papers might be more favourably disposed to the aspirations of the people of Red River, but often found the question one of local self-determination rather than a part of a larger racial struggle. A statement attributed to John Bruce — "To us, Canada is just a foreign power" — was quoted by one newspaper in early February as evidence of the attitudes of the population in the settlement. At the same time, there was in Quebec over the late winter of 1870 increasing recognition of the possibility of a sectarian and racial approach to Red River. To a considerable extent, this was a reaction to the hostility to the Métis being exhibited in the Ontario press, where there was a strong undercurrent of criticism of the uprising as having been fomented by Catholic priests in order to produce a French Catholic province. But while some Quebec newspapers recognized the anti-clericalism of some of the Ontario attitudes, they did not draw up their wagons in defence of Louis Riel and the Métis. This pattern would soon be changed by the Scott affair, and especially by Ontario reactions to Scott's execution.

-5-

Exit Thomas Scott

D onald A. Smith and the Reverend John McLean had considerable success in persuading the anglophone communities to elect and send delegates to the council of the newly-organizing provisional government. At least some of the parishes made clear, however, that they had accepted the provisional government through extortion at the point of a gun. The people in Portage wrote Riel that they recognized the provisional government at the behest of Donald A. Smith, but had done so solely to save Charles Boulton's life. They would withdraw that support at the earliest opportunity. Other parishes suggested similar attitudes. At this stage in the rebellion, the Irish-born adventurer and Canadian loyalist, Thomas Scott, came front and centre.

Although Louis Riel could not at the time know it, the confrontation with and subsequent execution of Scott would become the controlling feature of the remainder of his life. It was Scott's execution that stood in the way of Riel's receiving an amnesty for his actions in Red River. The lack of an amnesty in turn led to his inability to establish himself in Manitoba, and to his eventual banishment from Canada. The banishment provided the context for whatever emotional and spiritual crisis he experienced beginning in 1875. The banishment would eventually lead to his decision to become an American citizen. Riel himself knew that Scott's death had been pivotal. He kept circling it in his writing, and a defence of his 1870 actions was among his last actions before his own execution.

Scott's execution, and especially the Ontario reactions to it, also became a critical turning point in Anglo-French relations in central Canada. Before Ontario's response to Scott's death, most French-Canadians had been prepared to interpret the Red River affair as a political matter. The Métis quest was for self-determination, and the struggle was not particularly a sectarian one. After the Ontario press was finished with its condemnations of Riel and the Métis for executing Scott, whom it presented as an Orange martyr and a sectarian figure, francophone Quebeckers found themselves inevitably rallying to defend Riel and to suspect the anglos of repressing the Métis because they were French-speaking Catholics. In some ways, the Scott affair became the first step on the long road to Quebec separatism.

Scott's Background

Thomas Scott had been born in Clandeboyne, County Down, around 1844. Lord Dufferin, governor-general of Canada in 1874, wrote that Scott "came of very decent people — his parents are at this moment tenant farmers on my estate in the neighbourhood of Clandeboye." Dufferin then added, "but he himself seems to have been a violent and boisterous man such as are often found in the North of Ireland." These two assertions need to be separated. Dufferin undoubtedly knew first-hand that the Scotts were his tenants, but the statement about violence and boisterousness is qualified with the give-away verb "seems," suggesting that the governor-general has extrapolated a stereotyped character from what he had heard about Scott rather than from personal knowledge. There was always a good deal of such extrapolation with Scott. In any event, Scott came to Canada in the early 1860s, probably to join his brother Hugh in Toronto.

One of the few surviving records of Scott's Ontario sojourn is a testimonial from one Captain Rowe, of Madoc, Ontario, of the Hastings Battalion of Rifles at Stirling. In a letter to the commanding officer after Scott's death, Rowe wrote: "I have to inform you that the unfortunate man, Scott, who has been murdered by that scoundrel, Riel, was for a time a member of my company, and did duty with the battalion at Sterling in 1868. He was a splendid fellow, whom you may possibly remember as the right-hand man of No. 4, and I have no hesitation in saying, the finest-looking man in the battalion. He was about six feet two inches in height, and twenty-five years of age. He was an Orangeman, loyal to the backbone, and a well-bred gentlemanly Irishman." The Reverend George Young, who attended Scott in his last hours, reprinted this testimonial in his 1897 memoir, noting that after the execution he had forwarded Scott's papers to his brother, Hugh. These papers included "many commendatory letters of introduction, with certificates of good character, from Sabbath-school teachers and the Presbyterian minister with whose church he had been connected in Ireland, as well as from employers whom he had served faithfully."

Among the material forwarded to Hugh Scott were savings of $103.50. Young also quoted from a journal kept by Scott in 1869. It noted that he and his brother had rowed on Belleville Bay, and wondered "where we shall both be ten years from today." Unfortunately, Young apparently did not copy the full texts of all the documents before returning them to the family, and could only refer to most of them in the most general of terms. Nevertheless, Young's evidence indicates that Scott had a Presbyterian upbringing and connection, as well as some education. The presence of substantial savings do not suggest a riotous lifestyle. Money may have played an important role in Scott's behaviour during his second imprisonment. According to Alexander Murray in his 1874 trial testimony, when he and Scott were taken prisoner in February, the two were searched and Murray had his pocket-book containing 60 pounds taken from him. Scott's was taken as well. According to Murray, Scott was demanding his pocket-book during the final contretemps with Riel.

As his militia commander suggested, Scott was physically a big man, standing about six foot two inches tall; a surviving photograph indicates that he was well-proportioned and muscular, obviously quite strong. Scott was unmarried and like many young men in his situation, in 1869 he decided to head west. He collected up his papers, doubtless including the introductions and testimonials later left by him with Reverend Young. According to an 1870 private letter of S.H. Harvard, reprinted by Young in 1897, he and Scott travelled from St. Cloud by coach in the summer of 1869. Since St. Cloud was the head of the railway at the time, Scott presumably had gotten there by train. Harvard described Scott as "a fine, tall, muscular youth of some twenty-four years of age," who "behaved properly" and whose bearing was characterized by "inoffensiveness" to "those with whom we came in contact." Harvard made such observations in full appreciation of Scott's execution. The two men shared a bed at a roadside inn outside Abercrombie. Scott told Harvard that he was heading toward the Cariboo to try his luck at the gold mines. If this story is accurate, his sojourn in Red River may have been intended to be brief.

The letter from Captain Rowe is one of the few first-hand pieces of evidence that Scott was not only a northern Irishman or Ulsterman, but "an Orangeman," a term used by contemporaries both to refer to all Protestant Ulstermen who were of anti-Catholic persuasion and especially to those who were actually members of the Orange Order founded in 1795 to defend the British sovereign and the Protestant religion. The 13 April issue of the Toronto *Globe* contained a notice which read: "Whereas Brother Thomas Scott, a member of our Order, was cruelly murdered by the enemies of our Queen, country and religion, therefore be it resolved that while we sympathise with the relatives of our deceased Brother, we, the members of L.O.L. No. 404 call upon the Government to avenge his death, pledging ourselves to assist in rescuing the Red River Territory from those who have turned it over to Popery, and bring to justice the murderers of our countrymen." Note that the Toronto Lodge does not claim Scott as a member of L.O.L No. 404, but only that Scott was "a member of our Order"; the local lodge to which Scott belonged never stepped forward, however, perhaps because it was in Ulster. It may be important that — although Canada learned of Scott's execution at the end of March — this evidence of his Orange connection did not appear until mid-April, after the return of Charles Mair to Ontario.

At the same time that the Orange Order claimed Scott, there is no evidence that he ever claimed the Orange Order. Despite the massive response of Orange Ontario to the death of a "brother," orchestrated by the Canada First movement, Scott left no record — even in the Métis-inspired accounts — of anti-Catholic sentiment. Even if Scott had been a fervent anti-Catholic, of course, there is no reason to regard him as any more a "bigot" than millions of other Americans, Canadians, and Britons who shared with him an antipathy to "Popery" in the 18th and 19th centuries. According to many scholars, extreme Protestant anti-Catholicism was part of the glue that held the "British nation" together in the early years of the 19th century. There was no reason to expect such sentiments to disappear by 1870. Whatever Scott's attitude toward Catholicism, as we shall see there is some evidence to support his brother's assertion that "where principle and loyalty to his Queen & country were at stake" he was "a thoroughly brave and loyal man." Loyalty to monarch was another Orange attribute, of course, perhaps as important as hostility to the Pope.

After his arrival in Red River, Scott worked on John Snow's road crew and, as we have seen, led a strike against Snow which resulted in conviction for aggravated assault in a Winnipeg court trial in November. Later stories of heavy drinking are not confirmed by the contemporary evidence. In the chief piece of evidence used by several biographers to substantiate the tales, Thomas is confused with Alfred Scott, who was a drinker. A few weeks after the assault trial, he was part of the Canadian contingent holed up in the house of Dr. John Christian Schultz, and he was in due course imprisoned at Upper Fort Garry. Persistent stories about some sort of early confrontation with Louis Riel exist which cannot be confirmed. What seems clear is that the 1885 account of he and Riel being in love with the same Métisse is a total fabrication.

Scott after his First Escape

S cott escaped from Upper Fort Garry on 9 January 1870. He became one of the Portage Boys, helped in the search of Henry Coutu's house on 14 February, and was recaptured outside Upper Fort Garry with the rest of the contingent on 17 February. The evidence on Scott's personality and behaviour is more than a bit contradictory, but most who knew him found him generally gentle and well-mannered. A minority of acquaintances found him to have a temper, and to be at times both outspoken and a bit foul-mouthed. There is little to support the notion that he was a leader of the Canadians or the Canadian Party in the settlement, however. He was too recent an arrival and too obscure in origins to have commanded much respect from his fellow Canadians, except perhaps as one of the louder and stronger of "the boys."

Scott was one of a handful of Canadians who spent two periods as a "guest" of the Métis at Upper Fort Garry. Until his escape, Scott kept out of trouble during his first confinement. Evidence for his behaviour during the second incarceration is both limited and confusing. There are two quite different versions of Scott's second captivity, one by most of his anglophone colleagues and clergymen, the other by his captors, especially Louis Riel. Two points stand out in the testimony of the anglophones. First, the time period between the capture of the prisoners and the court martial of Scott, especially after the time taken up with the threatened execution of Charles Boulton, was relatively short, less than two weeks. Secondly, none of the fellow prisoners or clergymen whose testimony has survived appear to have spent much time with Scott over the course of his captivity, and none, except Alexander Murray and George Sanderson (in a much later oral account) offered much account of his behaviour. Sanderson claimed that Scott had been continually offensive to everyone, including his fellow prisoners, but from what vantage point in Upper Fort Garry he had observed Scott is not clear. According to Alexander Murray, Scott was initially kept in a room in the same area as the other prisoners, but he was later put in a room on the opposite side. Certainly Scott ended up in solitary confinement. Murray added, "I heard that Scott had difficulties with the guards more than once, but never saw it." Few of the prisoners had actually seen any confrontations during the course of most of the confinement.

George Newcombe dated Scott's troubles from only the date before his execution. So did Alexander Murray, who offered a detailed account of Scott's last hours:

> I saw Riel, Lépine and O'Donoghue on the night previous to Scott being shot; They were in the guard-room; Riel came and asked me if I was a Canadian; I told him no! but I belonged to that party; I went back to my room; he followed me up and apparently looking [sic] in my room; I closed the door and said, "Boys, keep quiet, for Riel, O'Donoghue and Lépine are in the guard-room." I knelt on my knees and looked through the key-hole; I heard a knock on the door where Scott was confined; the door was opened slightly by one of the guard; Scott said, "I want

to get out"; the door was opened a second time; Riel stepped up to Scott, and Scott said he wished to be treated civil; Riel said he did not deserve to be treated civil and called him a dog; Scott asked for his book, I think a pocket-book; Riel said he hadn't it; the door was then shut; I understood it to be a call of nature.

Charles Boulton told a similar story in his memoirs. Although the events he described happened over a short time frame, there were several confrontations between Scott and his guards. About a fortnight after the capture, Boulton recognized Scott's voice in the guardroom, demanding his pocket-book. A considerable scuffle ensued and Scott was locked up in a room. Boulton investigated, and learned that Scott had just advised the prisoners to have nothing to do with Alfred H. Scott and others who had solicited their votes. The visit of Alfred H. Scott dates this confrontation in late February, and Boulton's story is in part confirmed by Riel himself. Later, Scott asked leave to go outside (presumably to the lavatory) and was refused, which led to another altercation. Riel and O'Donoghue visited Scott that same afternoon and evening, "and used violent language against Scott." According to Boulton, he did not manage to visit with Scott until the court-martial had been completed. "I found that similar questions had been put to him as had been put to me, and the same mode of passing sentence had been passed upon him as had passed upon me. I told Scott to be very careful what he said, as I felt sure that Riel meant mischief and would take his life if he could." By this point such advice was too late.

The evidence of the several Protestant clergymen who dealt with Scott was quite confusing. In the wake of the threatened execution of Charles Boulton, the Reverend John McLean told the court at the Lépine trial, he had spoken to the prisoners about the deal he and Donald A. Smith had made with Riel to save Boulton's life. He wanted to gain their consent, and admitted he did so by telling the prisoners "that I thought they were in dangers of their lives." But this warning was not particularly directed at Scott. McLean's recollections are quite compatible with those of Donald A. Smith, although not identical. Smith reported a meeting with Father Joseph-Jean-Marie Lestanc on 4 March, at which Lestanc had commented on the bad behaviour of the prisoners. According to Smith,

> I expressed much surprise at the information he gave me, as the prisoners, without exception, had promised to Archdeacon McLean and myself, that seeing theirhopeless condition they would endeavour to act so as to avoid giving offence to the guards, and we encouraged them to look forward to being speedily released,as fulfillment of the promise made by Mr. Riel.

Smith added that a prisoner named Parker had been described as quite obnoxious, but not one word had ever been said to him about Scott. This account certainly suggests that the prisoners had been difficult early in the confinement, if not later.

Reverend McLean also testified at the 1874 trial that he "saw Scott one day, found him handcuffed and his legs ironed; asked how he was and why he was there; he said he had some trouble with the guards; had some conversation with him about his spiritual wants and when I was coming away I asked permission to call upon him again, but that night he was brought up, and on the following day he was shot; I was totally ignorant of his danger; I learned afterwards that that was the last day of his life."

The Reverend George Young, Methodist missionary in Winnipeg, insisted in his 1874 trial testimony that he had no conversation with Thomas Scott before March 3, by which time the Canadian had been tried and was out of irons, but added that when he had visited Scott the previous Saturday — presumably without exchanging words worthy of the label "conversation" — Scott had been shackled. Young's account in 1897 in his memoirs was quite different: "On Sabbath, February 27, while visiting the various prisons, I was pained to learn that Scott had been sent into solitary confinement, and going at once to his room, found him in a most pitiable condition — a dirty and fireless room, a single blanket to rest on or wrap himself in, with manacles on both wrists and ankles. No marvel that he shivered and suffered under such circumstances. On my asking if he knew the reason of this increased severity, he assured me that he did not, and readily promised to carefully avoid, in action and utterance, whatever might be offensive to the guards."

The clerical accounts (and that of Alexander Murray) can be more or less reconciled by assuming that Scott's first serious confrontation with his guards (as reported by Murray and Boulton) had occurred on Saturday 26 February, and that Scott was in irons from at least Saturday to the following Thursday, when he was tried and then unshackled in preparation for his execution. But the chronology never entirely hangs together, suggesting that much of the evidence was generated well after the event.

The Métis perspective on Thomas Scott was very different. It is difficult to use the evidence of the trial of Scott by a Métis council on 3 March to ascertain exactly what Scott had done or why the Métis took it so seriously. The records of that trial were destroyed at the time, and there is only one eye-witness account. Ambroise Lépine's private secretary, Joseph Nolin, did offer a description of the trial in 1874 at his superior's trial for Scott's murder. Because it remains the only first-hand account, and because the secondary literature is so confused over details, Nolin's evidence (as written down by unofficial court reporters) must be quoted in full. He testified:

> Scott was tried on the evening of the third of March; at the council that tried him Lépine presided; the other members of the council were Janvier Richot, André Nault, Elzéar Goulet, Elzéar Lagemodière, Baptiste Lépine, and Joseph Delorme I was secretary of the council; Scott was not present at the beginning; some witnesses were examined to state what evil Scott had done; these witnesses were Riel, Ed Turner, and Joseph Delorme; don't recollect any other witnesses; do not recollect nature of the evidence; Scott was accused of having rebelled against the Provisional Government and having struck the captain of the guard; Riel made a speech, I think against Scott; after the evidence had been heard Scott was brought before the council; Riel asked me to read to Scott what had passed before the council; did not, as I had written nothing; Riel then explained the evidence to Scott, and asked him if he had any defence to offer? Scott said something but I forget what; Riel did not ask Scott whether hehad any witnesses; there was no written accusation against Scott; the work of the Council was done in about three hours; the Council sat about 7 o'clock; took some notes of the evidence; wrote them out regularly and gave them to the Adjutant General; Richot moved and Nault seconded that Scott deserved death; Lépine said he would have to be put to death — the majoritywant his death and he shall be put to death; that closed the business of the council; Riel explained to Scott his sentence; and asked him if he had any request to make or wanted to see a minister? I do not remember what answer Scott made; Riel said if the minister was at the Stone Fort he would send for him; Riel said he would send Scott up to his room, that his shackles would be taken off, and that he would have pen, ink, and paper to write what he wished to; Riel then told Scott he would be shot next day at 10 o'clock; I do not know what Scott said; he was then taken to his room; when the vote was taken Baptiste Lépine objected to taking the life of Scott; he said they had succeeded so far without shedding blood and he thought it better not to do so now; Ed Turner took Scott to his room; saw Lépine the next morning about 8 o'clock; Lépine told me to write a verbal report of the proceedings of the Council; Riel came to see the report and said it was not formal; Riel then dictated the report; it was made from notes of the evidence; don't remember what Riel changed; gave it to Lépine when written.

Louis Riel v. Canada

We will return to the trial procedures described by Nolin.

Nolin lists only two charges: Scott had "rebelled against" (perhaps we should read "opposed") the provisional government, and he had struck the captain of the guard. He elaborated on them later in his testimony, saying "Scott was accused of having taken up arms against the provisional government, after taking an oath not to fight against it; he was also accused of striking one of the guards, and Riel himself." On cross-examination, Nolin added, "The charge of striking Riel and the guard referred to the scuffle in the guard room," and that of taking up arms referred to his involvement with the Portage party. There is other evidence, however, which help us further to understand the charges.

One important witness was Donald A. Smith, the Canadian commissioner to Red River who was still at Upper Fort Garry at the time of Scott's incarceration. On 4 March, Smith was visited by the Reverend George Young about 11 a.m., and informed of the intended execution of Scott at noon. Young then went to plead with Riel, unsuccessfully, first for Scott's life and then for delay on the grounds that the young Irishman was not spiritually prepared to die. The minister sent a messenger to inform Smith of his failure. Smith, accompanied by Father Lestanc, then called on Riel himself. The Métis leader turned to Smith and said, "I will explain to you." In his subsequent report to Ottawa, Smith related what Riel had told him. Riel, wrote Smith,

> said in substance, that Scott had, throughout, been a most troublesome character, and had been ringleader in a rising against Snow, who had charge of a party employed by the Canadian Government during the preceding summer in road making, that he had risen against the Provisional Government in December last, that his life was then spared; that he had escaped and had been again taken in arms, and once more pardoned (referring, no doubt to the promise he had made to me that the lives of the prisoners were secured), but that he was incorrigible, and quite incapable of appreciating the clemency with which he had been treated; that he was rough and abusive to the guards and insulting to him (Riel), and that his example had been productive of the very worst effects on the other prisoners, who had become insubordinate to such an extent that it was difficult to withhold the guards from retaliating.

Riel further told Smith that Scott had admitted to him that he and the Portage party "intended to keep" Riel "as a hostage for the safety of the prisoners." Smith, who had never met Scott, responded that the worst case Riel had made out was that the Irishman was a "rash, thoughtless man, whom none could desire to have anything to do with." This statement represented Smith's summary of what Riel had told him, rather than his own assessment, although several biographers have written as though this was Smith's own assessment. The charges Riel raised against Scott, Smith suggested, did not deserve a death sentence. In this assessment it is difficult not to concur. The Snow affair was irrelevant, the searching of the Winnipeg house a natural by-product of the internal conflicts of the time, and Scott had never taken an oath of good conduct. Obviously prisoners should be well-behaved and docile, but prison authorities might well expect other behaviour, especially in the midst of a civil war. On the other hand, Riel did not here accuse Scott of breaking his oath, and the Canadian had certainly been a part of an armed party opposed to the provisional government.

At the end of this lengthy interview, which delayed the execution beyond its scheduled time, Donald Smith observed that the insurrection had to this point had been bloodless, and that bloodshed might make the negotiations with Canada more difficult. To this Riel replied, "We must make Canada respect us." Riel then offered one more example of Scott's offensive behaviour. When Alfred Scott, at Riel's behest, went to see the prisoners to ask for their vote in the upcoming Winnipeg election for councillor to the provisional government, it was Thomas Scott who had come forward to advise against such support, saying, "My boys, have nothing to do with those Americans." Riel and Smith then jousted about the American involvement in the uprising. Smith argued that Scott's comments were a trifling business, but Riel responded, "Do not attempt to prejudice us against Americans, for although we have not been with them they are with us, and have been better friends to us than Canadians." Nevertheless, why Riel thought Scott's comments and actions here were so offensive was not clear from the conversation as reported by Smith. Charles Mair, who was not imprisoned on the second go-round, reported an alternate version of this incident, based on a later account he received from Murdoch McLeod, who was there. According to McLeod, Scott had shouted, "Boys, you can do what you like, but I won't consent." He was thereupon "ironed with irons which had been taken off Boulton." In any event, Riel closed the discussion with Smith by observing, "I have done three good things since I have commenced. I have spared Boulton's life at your instance, and I do not regret it, for he is a fine fellow; I pardoned Gaddy, and he showed his gratitude by escaping out of the bastion — but I do not grudge him his miserable life; and now I shall shoot Scott."

The explanations given to Smith were quite compatible with Joseph Nolin's 1874 testimony about the charges. They were also more or less compatible with two subsequent statements released by friends of the provisional government immediately after the execution. The first appeared in the Red River newspaper controlled by Riel, the *New Nation*, dated the very day of Scott's demise. The *New Nation* described the deceased as "Private T. Scott," thus giving him (and the Portage Boys) formal military standing and turning the affair into a military one. It reported that from Scott's second capture, he was "very violent and abusive in his language and actions, annoying and insulting the guards and even threatening the President." The *New Nation* provided more details of Scott's threats against Riel: "He (Scott) vowed openly that if ever he got out he would shoot the President; and further stated that he was at the head of the party of the Portage people who, on their way to Kildonan, called at Coutu's house and searched it for the President, with the intention of shooting him." Donald Smith had reported Riel's assertion that Scott had admitted he would have held the President to ransom had he managed to capture him, but had not mentioned further threats of violence.

The second contemporary statement appeared in the Quebec clerical newspaper the *Courrier de Saint-Hyacinthe* the in March, and was translated and reprinted in the *Globe* on 7 April 1870. The correspondent began: "I send you the following details so that you may be able to use them in reply to the attacks which will doubtless be made." According to this account, Scott had "led the conspiracy against Mr. Snow," whose life had been saved by the Métis. When the Portage people "rose in insurrection against the Provisional Government, he was a strong partisan and entered a house in Winnipeg, where the President often passed the night, while others surrounded it, doubtless with the intention of killing Mr. Riel." Re-imprisoned, Scott had "insulted the President, attacked a captain and a soldier, his insolence was so great that one day Capt. Boulton asked to be admitted to his room so as to make him quiet." (According to Boulton, his only visit with Scott occurred after the sentence of death.) The *Courrier* letter maintained that Scott's behaviour had negatively affected the other prisoners. The execution was both to give an example and to "certainly prevent a great loss of life." The correspondent went on to claim that although Scott had been allowed to see a clergyman, he had told Reverend George Young "that he did not belong to any religion." Riel thereupon ordered all the soldiers in the fort to pray for Scott's change of heart. This letter was probably written by Father Lestanc, who according to the text had interceded for this unfortunate man "who had rebelled and taken up arms against an authority recognized by the two populations." The irony of a rebel government shooting a loyalist for rebellion appears to have escaped this correspondent.

We have now heard enough to recognize that whatever the reasons for Scott's execution, it was not really justified by his behaviour, at least as described by his enemies at the time. Before we turn to the complex question of why Thomas Scott was shot, there are two other matters to be explored. One is the nature of the legal procedure which convicted and sentenced Scott. The other is how Riel himself dealt with Scott's death in later years.

As we have already seen, Louis Riel was apparently prepared to shoot Major Boulton (or William Gaddy) without any trial at all. With Thomas Scott there was a legal procedure followed. It observed none of the normal rules of justice of either English or French non-military law, and was not even entirely recognizable as a summary court martial. Joseph Nolin was quite clear that Scott was not present for a most important part of the proceedings, the presentation of the evidence supporting the charges against him. Those charges and the evidence for them (emanating partly from Louis Riel) were subsequently summarized to Scott in English by Louis Riel. Scott was not condemned without being heard. He was offered an opportunity to respond to the charges, although not to examine the witnesses on whose testimony they were based. According to the Reverend Young in 1874, Scott said afterwards he had "objected to the trial as it was conducted in a language he did not understand, but was told it made no difference; he was a bad man and had to die." Scott's objection was only partially correct. While he was present before the tribunal, Scott was dealt with in English. But he was not present the entire time, and especially had not heard any of the testimony against him, much of which was in French. Scott certainly had no legal advice at any point and, according to subsequent reports, was quite stunned by the entire proceedings. He evidently was not present for the vote on his case, which was not unanimous. Indeed, the members of the tribunal were divided. Ambroise Lépine's brother was one of those who had opposed the death penalty, and the adjutant-general himself had broken the tie with his vote.

While the tribunal most resembles the sort of court used by the Métis on the buffalo hunt, those courts never dealt in capital cases. It certainly was not a court which was part of the normal administration of justice under the provisional government. On the other hand, although the court's composition and procedures were unusual, there was no hard and fast reason why Scott's court necessarily had to follow the rules of other jurisdictions or even of its own usual practices. Ambroise Lépine was the adjutant-general of the provisional government, charged with the administration of justice, and those involved could (and did) plead the need for emergency measures. The real issue, as we shall see later, revolved around whether the provisional government was a legitimate one, not whether the procedures employed in condemning Scott were legal.

As has already been noted, Louis Riel in the years after 1870 frequently replayed the execution of Thomas Scott in a series of writings and interviews, perhaps trying to justify Scott's death to himself rather more than to the outside world. What is noticeable in these revisitations is the extent to which Scott's character gets increasingly darker and his offenses more extreme.

Riel turned again to Scott in 1872, when he drafted "Mémoire ayant trait aux difficultés de la Rivière Rouge." In this document, Riel associated Scott with "Schultz et Co." Riel reported the searching of the house of Henri Coutu with the intention of capturing him, but did not here claim that Scott had threatened to shoot him. He noted the deaths of Sutherland and Parisien, but did not attribute blame to particular people for these occurrences. Scott was very violent in his second incarceration, wrote Riel, who concentrated on the Irishman's prison behaviour in this document. On the last day of February, Scott had really upset the guards, wrote Riel, beating on the "prison gates" and insulting them. The guards had taken him outside and were preparing to "sacrifice him" when a French councillor saved him. Although he does not say so, Riel may at this point have still been recovering from his illness. Riel quietened the guards a day later, but Scott continued to be offensive and the guards continued to demand a council of war, which they finally got on 3 March. Riel thus provided a label for the tribunal which had condemned Scott, calling it a "council of war" rather than a court martial. The impression Riel left in this document was that he had been pressured into acting against Scott by the insistent demands of his guards and Scott's refusal (or inability) to behave. The exact nature of Scott's offensive behaviour was not specified or described.

Riel and Ambroise Lépine presented a somewhat different argument in their famous memorial to Lieutenant-Governor Alexander Morris in January 1873, although the focus was still on Scott's prison behaviour. Scott and "Mr. [Murdoch] McLeod" had "beat their prison gates and insulted, and went so far as to strike their guards, inviting their fellow-prisoners also to insult them." Only a punishment could "restrain these excited men," and so, wrote Riel and Lépine, "we had recourse to the full authority of Government." Why Scott was chosen for exemplary punishment and McLeod allowed to remain free was not explained.

The same themes as in early documents reappeared in an 1874 account by Riel entitled "L'Amnistie. Mémoire sur les causes des troubles du Nord-Ouest et sur les negotiations qui ont amené leur reglement amiable," which he probably wrote while in exile in New York State. This document rehearsed the entire history of the rebellion from both Riel's and the Métis' perspective. Here Scott was described as "one of the most dangerous partisans of Dr. Schultz, McDougall, and Dennis," the first time Riel had promoted Scott to a leadership role among the Canadians. His involvement in the search for the President of the provisional government in Winnipeg was clear evidence that he was in arms against that authority. Once again imprisoned, he and fellow-prisoner Murdoch McLeod "forcèrent les portes de leur prison, se ruèrent sur les gardes, invitant leurs compagnons à faire comme eux." "Tous" wrote Riel, demanded that Scott be brought before the "conseil de guerre," and when the young Irishman persisted in his "mauvaise conduite," he was finally summoned, against a background of rising new troubles which were not specifically described. Scott was examined on "témoignages assermentés," was convicted, and was condemned to death. On 4 March the authority of the provisional government, which had the goodwill of the anglophone settlers, was used "to disarm our enemies."

"L'Amnistie" was subsequently published by *Le Nouveau Monde* of Montreal as a pamphlet early in 1874, and quickly drew a response — in the form of a lengthy letter published in various newspapers — written by Dr. James Spencer Lynch, one of the most extreme of the Canadian Party in Red River during the rebellion. Lynch had been taken prisoner at Dr. Schultz's house in 1869, and he played an active role in the anti-Métis and anti-provisional government campaign in Ontario in the spring of 1870. Lynch's letter objected to Riel's interpretation of the events of 1869-70 on a variety of fronts, including the condemnation of Thomas Scott. Lynch's principal complaint about the trial of Scott was that it had been quite improper, conducted as it was in French, a language that the accused did not understand. Lynch also criticized the manner and timing of the execution. Riel responded to Lynch's rambling critique with an equally rambling document that was printed in *Le Nouveau Monde* on 12 March 1874. Riel denied categorically that Scott's trial had been conducted in French, saying, "Durant le process, tout ce qui a été dit en français, a été traduit en anglais: et tout ce qui a été dit en anglais a été traduit en français." Given Joseph Nolin's subsequent detailed description under oath of the proceedings of the council of war, this denial seems a bit disingenuous.

In his response Riel also denied that Lynch had managed to rehabilitate "le caractère de Scott" by asserting that the Irishman was a decent man of steady habits. Riel's response was noteworthy for the introduction of a new level of attack on the integrity of Scott, bringing several new charges against him. "It is said" ("il est dit"), he wrote, that Scott had tracked down Norbert Parisien after the shooting of Hugh John Sutherland, attached a belt ("une ceinture") to his neck, and dragged him behind a horse for a quarter of a mile.

Scott was now well on his way to becoming "the bad man who had to die." That the young Irishman had sought to assassinate ('voulu assasiner") Mr. Snow in 1869 at Pointe de Chênes was an old accusation. What appeared now for the first time about the incident was the assertion that the community still recalled the disorders created by Scott and his companions during riotous evenings. While the men were away, the women and children guarded their doors and windows against the drunken Canadians. Riel closed his text: "Here is what the entire parish of Pointe de Chênes knows. Scott was reasonable? He was of regular habits? Let the reader decide."

Over the next few years, Riel returned more than once in his writings to the Scott incident, which he appeared to realize full well had involved a disastrous misjudgment. In one fragment of 1874-5, for example, he wrote, "Si j'ai mal fait de faire executer Th. Scott, ô Divin esprit, daignez me le fair connâitre parfaitement afin que je vous en demande pardon, que j'en implore contrition parfaite et que j'en fasse penitence; afin que j'en demande pardon aux homes; afin que j'avoue hautment cette faute, si je l'ai faite." But nothing new was said by Riel about Scott in these writings until — on a visit from Montana to Winnipeg in June 1883 — he gave an interview to a reporter from the *Winnipeg Daily Sun*. It is difficult to know what to make of this interview, which in its frankness was quite different from another Riel gave a reporter from the *Winnipeg Daily Times* only a day later. In the *Sun* interview, Riel categorically included the execution of Thomas Scott among those acts he would do again. He insisted that Archbishop Taché's presence would not have stopped the execution, "Because I was really the leader, and whenever I believe myself to be right no man has ever changed my opinion."

Riel insisted to the *Sun* that Scott was an important loyalist leader, "in influence and prominence" behind only Schultz, Dennis, and Boulton. Schultz and Dennis were beyond the reach of the government in 1870, Riel admitted. "They were more guilty, too," Riel opined, "although Scott was guilty enough." Riel told the *Sun* reporter that Scott came close to being killed by the Métis for trying to murder his guard. The Irishman had "seized a bayonet that was in the room and endeavoured to slay the guard by plunging it into him through an opening in the door of the guard room. He was always hot-headed and violent." As an example of one of Scott's "crazy acts," Riel repeated again the story of the dragging of Norbert Parisien with a horse, one end of a scarf tied around Parisien's neck and the other tied to the tail of the horse. This managed to make Scott an abuser of both man and horse. When Riel pleaded with Scott at Upper Fort Garry to be quiet, Scott had replied, "You owe me respect; I am loyal and you are rebels." From Scott's perspective, of course, this observation was indisputable. From Riel's, it was another illustration of Scott's insulting attitude.

According to a third-hand report reprinted in many Canadian newspapers in 1885, Riel purportedly told his confessor, Father Alexis André, shortly before his execution that he now saw the death of Scott as a "political mistake," but not a crime. Riel added that Sir John A. Macdonald was executing Louis Riel for the same reason that Riel had executed Scott, "because it is necessary for the country's good." He continued, "I admit Scott's shooting was mismanaged, but I commanded it because I thought it necessary. He tried to kill his guards. They came to me and said they could do nothing with him. The rebellion was on the eve of breaking out all over the country, but as soon as Scott was killed it subsided."

While we can never know whether Scott was the "decent man of steady habits" described by Dr. Lynch or the monster described by Louis Riel, one crucial point about Scott seems fairly certain. There is no contemporary evidence that Scott's membership in the Orange Order was public knowledge or widely known in Red River. The first reference to Scott as an Orangeman came in a dispatch from St. Paul reported in the *Globe* on 31 March, which argued that "Riel had him [Scott] shot because he was an Orangeman and obnoxious to the priesthood." By this time Charles Mair and other refugees had reached the Minnesota capital. Mair particularly had been friendly with Scott, and was probably the source of this information, which followed the interpretation of Scott's death he always favoured. Scott's Orange Lodge membership was subsequently established in the Ontario press in the journalistic reports of his death, aided and abetted by the publicity campaign of the Canada First contingent, which helped orchestrate a province-wide reaction to the execution. But none of the earlier Red River accounts of Scott mention the Orange Lodge. Begg's journal describes Scott as "one of the prisoners," while Donald A. Smith's report characterizes him only as a prisoner.

The *New Nation* account has Scott as one "who came here from Canada last summer," and none of the several newspaper letters which reported on his trial for aggravated assault mentioned the Orange Lodge business. The letter from Taché to Joseph Howe notes Scott as a prisoner "who was brought from Canada with Mr. Snow," and the *Courrier de St. Hyacine* the story makes him "an Upper Canadian" who claimed he belonged to no religion. A letter to the *Montreal Witness* from the settlement dated 26 March, which enclosed the *New Nation* account of Scott's "murder," did not mention the Orange Lodge. None of Louis Riel's earliest explanations of Scott's actions refer to Orangeism, and indeed, no contemporary testimony from the settlement (including that of Riel) offers either evidence of such membership or any examples of racial or religious slurs spoken by him. Before his death we have several examples of Scott using four-letter words, and he accused Riel of being a rebel, but there was no reference to bigotry. Among the documents left behind after his death there was no certificate of membership in the Orange Order. All the discussions of Scott's racial and religious attitudes are based on what was written about Scott in central Canada after his death.

On the other hand, if Scott was not an overt racial and religious bigot, neither were Louis Riel or the Métis. Religious and racial issues were simply not to the forefront of the confrontation between Scott and the Métis. Those were later additions, as Ontario and Quebec folded their longstanding hostilities into the situation. From Riel's perspective, Scott's execution was a political act, made necessary by the political context of events in Red River in early March 1870.

The Execution of Thomas Scott

Thomas Scott was executed by a Métis firing squad on 4 March 1870 at about one o'clock in the afternoon. The execution had been set for noon, but was almost an hour late because of last-minute attempts by Donald A. Smith to plead for Scott's life. Even before his execution, Scott's fate had begun to be shrouded in mystery and mythology. Scott was already well on his way to becoming the "Martyr of Red River," the innocent victim of the wrath of Louis Riel, and the controlling event in Riel's subsequent life. Eyewitnesses disagreed about almost every aspect of Scott's execution, from his last words and last actions, to the exact manner of his death. Reading the first-hand accounts is mainly an exercise that reminds us how fallible are the powers of human observation — and especially, human memory. More than 100 bystanders, apparently drawn by rapidly spreading rumours throughout the village of Winnipeg about the execution, were in place when Scott and the firing squad emerged from within the walls of Upper Fort Garry. These witnesses, as well as those *more* directly involved who were prepared to remember, could agree on little more than that Scott had been led out of the east-side gate at the fort and shot against the wall there. Beyond these two elementary facts, however, accounts varied widely.

Some reports had Scott already blindfolded, while others claimed he was blindfolded while standing against the wall. None of the accounts have his arms tied behind his back, although the several subsequent illustrations of the execution invariably contained this feature. Scott apparently prayed continually while in the open air. According to the Reverend George Young, who had ministered to him in his last hours, Scott had said on his way from his cell, "This is horrible! This is cold-blooded murder. Be sure to make a true statement." (But Young's first-hand account of Scott's death, published many years later in his memoirs, incorporated many details from Donald Smith's contemporary description in a published letter to Joseph Howe.) Outside the walls, Scott asked Reverend Young whether he should stand or kneel. He then knelt in the snow and prayed. Young asked, "Can you now trust in Christ for your salvation?" Scott answered, "I think I can."

According to most accounts, six men showing visible signs of intoxication then shot Scott with ordinary hunting weapons. The guns were presumably muskets, which were what the Métis usually used for hunting. They certainly were not sharp-shooting rifles. Reports of the number of shots fired varied. Several observers, including Young, agreed that the young man did not die after the initial volley. A number of witnesses claimed that Scott was dispatched on the spot by one of the firing squad who fired a revolver into his head. No medical authority pronounced him dead at the time, however. His body was then placed into a hastily carpentered box, described by one witness as "a large box made of rough boards," which was nailed shut and carried inside the fort.

Reverend Young attempted at the time to retrieve the body for burial. He was informed that if the Bishop of Rupert's Land would guarantee the body would be quietly buried without demonstration, the body would be turned over to him. The next day Young and Bishop Machray went to the fort for that purpose. Louis Riel now apologized to the clergymen for disappointing them, but the adjutant-general (Ambroise Lépine) was in charge of the disposition of the body, and he had decreed that it would be buried within the walls of the fort. Lépine never explained his decision, but presumably he wanted no martyr's shrines developing in the village of Winnipeg. Young continued to plead with Riel after the bishop had departed. He argued that Scott's mother was entitled to the comfort of knowing her son had received a Christian internment. He recalled that Riel seemed "much displeased with the remark that he [Scott] had a mother left to mourn over him."

In his journal, Alexander Begg noted of Scott's death that "A deep gloom has settled over the settlement on account of this deed." But Begg's entries for the next few days make quite clear that life in Red River did not come to a halt because of the execution. It would be more than a month before Canada's reaction to Scott's fate could be known in the settlement, and in the meantime, Riel and the provisional government got on with the process of administration of the territory. Quite a lot was going on. On 5 March, Louis Schmidt issued an order on behalf of the president that made the Town of Winnipeg the official capital of the "North West," establishing its boundaries, and calling for the election of two members to the provisional government that very day. Rumours of the impending arrival of Bishop Taché apparently circulated on the same winds as the news of the death of Scott. Some of these rumours indicated — quite erroneously — that England was sending commissioners to negotiate with the rebels. Leaders of the American party met in advance of the Winnipeg election in the evening, which chose Bob O'Lone and

Alfred H. Scott — both Yankees — as representatives to the provisional government. What Begg described as "the better class of Americans" apparently did not approve of the choice of a hotel-keeper and his bartender.

Some of the talk around Winnipeg in the days after the death of Scott suggested that Riel was not finished in dealing with opposition to the provisional government. Murdoch McLeod — the other troublesome prisoner along with Scott — was reported to have been put in irons. Further rumours suggested that he would soon be shot. Alexander Begg noted other arrests without comment. The *New Nation* appeared with a discreet account of Scott's death; Alexander Begg recorded that Riel had insisted on revisions before publication, but we have no idea what those revisions were about. What we do know is that Major Henry M. Robinson, the editor of the *New Nation*, told George Young on the evening of the execution that Scott was still alive five hours after the firing of the volley. Robinson later repeated this story to a reporter from Minnesota, and it subsequently appeared in the pages of the St. Paul *Daily Press*, where it was probably much embellished. In the American account, Robinson reported that Riel had shown him the box containing the body, and Robinson was horrified to hear a voice coming from it, exclaiming, "Oh, let me out of this! My God! How I suffer!" What we also know is that the settlement was openly gossiping about the gory details of Scott's continued sufferings after being shot.

Whatever the reasons for Louis Riel to authorize the execution of Scott, neither he nor anyone else in the settlement could have predicted the furore his death would cause in eastern Canada. In the end, Scott's seeming obscurity and expendability may have been central factors behind his death. Riel may well have miscalculated, assuming that Scott would not be much missed or mourned, and could be used to make some kind of point, either within the settlement or with the Canadians. If the decision to allow the execution to go ahead was a miscalculation, it was one of Riel's first. Unfortunately, it was also his worst.

-6-

Canada Reacts

Bishop Taché finally got back to Red River on 9 March 1870, the day of the first meeting of the council of the provisional government. The bishop was met by Riel and hastily sequestered from the public by a guard of 20 men. The president apparently wanted to hear Taché's report before releasing him into the settlement. Riel opened the meeting of the council of the provisional government (created on 10 February and called on 7 March) with a lengthy address, which was subsequently printed and distributed in the settlement. This meeting was attended by 19 of the 24 representatives elected. The Métis were present in greater numbers than the anglophones, but they had elected their members earlier as well. Riel observed with obvious pride "that the people generally now have, for the first time in the history of this land, a voice in the direction of public affairs." He hoped there would be no more disruptive public gatherings, pleading for unity and "a spirit of conciliation." Riel also noted that Bishop Taché had arrived, but made clear that he did not yet know whether he was "invested with full power to give us what we want."

Taché indeed had returned to the settlement as a Canadian emissary, but with no more power than the earlier representatives of Canada. He did bring word that the Canadian government thought it could work with the list of demands approved by the Convention of Forty, and two versions of offers of amnesty to the rebels, both apparently very limited. The first was contained in the proclamation issued by Governor-General Sir John Young in December 1869, which had never previously been published at Red River. This document commanded those in defiance of the law to disperse peaceably and return to their homes, promising that if the defiance ended, no legal proceedings would then be taken against any "parties implicated in these unfortunate breaches of the law." The proclamation did not specify a date by which dispersal had to occur, but now that the insurgents had finally received word of the order — and failed to obey it — the offer of amnesty it contained would presumably soon expire if it had not already done so.

A later letter from Prime Minister Macdonald carried by Taché made a different offer, stating: "If the Company's Government is restored not only will there be a general amnesty granted, but in case the Company should claim the payment for...stores, the Canadian Government will stand between the insurgents and all harm." Had the rebels taken over the Council of Assiniboia rather than establishing a new provisional government, or if the provisional government at this point had re-established itself as the Council of Assiniboia, this offer might well have been held to stand. But under the circumstances, the condition was not met. The bishop would later insist that he also carried unofficial assurances. He had specifically asked the prime minister whether his offer included unknown "blameworthy" acts perhaps not yet committed, and was assured that it did. But nothing of this sort was ever committed to paper, and the Council of Assiniboia was never restored. What was actually offered by Canada was hedged with conditions the resistance never met. Taché and Riel met at Upper Fort Garry on the day following the council meeting. They presumably discussed the Canadian "offers" and the Canadian position, but there is no record of this conference.

On Sunday 13 March, Taché preached at the cathedral to a crowded congregation. The Pope himself had told the bishop it was his duty to return to his people, Taché said. He described his journey home and his visit in Ottawa. Canada would treat the people of "this country" with justice, he added, and according to Alexander Begg he commended them "to use charity and forbearance to each other and to act in union together." The bishop often broke into tears in the course of his sermon, and his listeners (who included Louis Riel) responded in kind. At a subsequent meeting of the council of the provisional government on 15 March, Taché spoke again about unconditional amnesty, apparently suggesting that there was a Canadian commitment to one. At this meeting Taché did not refer specifically to the death of Thomas Scott, but merely alluded to "some circumstances to be regretted" in recent actions at the settlement. The bishop reported that the Canadian and imperial governments both condemned the actions of William McDougall and John Dennis. He read a telegram from Joseph Howe to himself saying that the government could negotiate on the basis of the Bill of Rights. Canada was awaiting the delegates from Red River, he said.

Louis Riel responded by stating that the Hudson's Bay Company would be allowed to resume its business dealings immediately, and, according to Alexander Begg, Riel also spoke of "conducting the Provisional Government on as near the footing of the later government as possible." Riel obviously had understood the condition for amnesty made by the prime minister in his letter to the bishop, and was doing his best to meet it without actually giving up the provisional government. A committee was subsequently formed to write a constitution for the provisional government. This concession by Riel would be somewhat lost in the later furore over the Scott execution. Riel also responded by continuing the process already begun of freeing some of the prisoners being held at Upper Fort Garry, and promising the release of the remainder shortly.

Most of the released prisoners and a number of other Canadians, including the wife of Reverend George Young and Victoria MacVicar, left the settlement in mid-March. Alexander Begg noted in his journal that many others were talking about leaving, including the American consul Oscar Malmros. The American was departing because his earlier reports from Red River were had been published by the U.S. Senate, a somewhat embarrassing circumstance, but also because it increasingly appeared that Canada had won the struggle for the settlement. A small and near-sighted man, Malmros subsequently got separated from his dog team on his way to St. Cloud. The party of Canadians in which A.W. Graham was travelling pulled Malmros out of a snowbank, gave him a shot of brandy, and left an axe handle protruding from the snow to mark where he was located. Certainly the road between Winnipeg and Grand Forks was crowded with travellers from Red River, many of them refugees, after the middle of March.

Preparing the Delegates to Ottawa

The settlement's delegates to Ottawa — Judge John Black, Mr. Alfred H. Scott, and Father Noel-Joseph Ritchot — did not immediately leave for Canada upon the arrival of Bishop Taché's news that they would be favourably received in the Canadian capital. Ostensibly they were waiting for better weather for the journey south to the American railhead at St. Cloud. Judge Black was particularly reluctant to depart too early — or, some said, at all. Winter journeys could be hazardous. The Canadian leaders John Christian Schultz and Charles Mair had both left the settlement in late February, by snowshoes and dogsled respectively, and both would have arduous journeys across the snowy wastes of the northern United States. Mair's party had dropped its dogs for horses at Grand Forks, but ended up leading the exhausted horses into Fort Abercrombie without snowshoes a month after leaving Portage. Schultz would later blame a lifetime of ill health partly on his trip across the plains in the winter of 1870. An equally important consideration as the weather was considerable last-minute jockeying behind the scenes over the credentials and final instructions to the delegates. As it would transpire, the delays would pitch the delegates into Ontario right at the height of the public reaction to the execution of Thomas Scott, which would work to their disadvantage.

Although the 20 articles of the Bill of Rights seemed fixed, a number of loose ends relating to the negotiations still remained to be sorted out. This was done by the executive of the provisional government, in effect Louis Riel and his lieutenants William O'Donoghue and Louis Schmidt, although Thomas Bunn, secretary of the council, was also present at the discussions and signed the final documents. Riel later claimed that the executive had to "work day and night in order to finish and enable the Commissioners to start at the time they did." Subsequently arguing pressures of time, Riel did not take any of this business to the full council of the provisional government.

One unsettled matter was the question of whom the delegates were representing. Their final commissions made clear that they were authorized by "the President of the Provisional Government of Assiniboia (formerly Rupert's Land and the North-West) in council." This phraseology managed to avoid the fact that the council had not actually been consulted in the drafting of the final instructions to the delegates. But it also represented a statement of the territorial jurisdiction of the provisional government which was more than a bit aggressive. In truth, the effective jurisdiction of the provisional government of Assiniboia extended no further than that of the old council of Assiniboia, a circle encompassing no more than 50 miles in all directions from the Forks. Had the government reassumed the powers of the old council, this would have still been its territory. Beyond its limits, the only legal authority in all of the North-West was exercised by officers of the Hudson's Bay Company, acting as magistrates. The provisional government could not really take over that authority, either *de facto* or *de jure*.

A second question related to the powers of the delegates. They were not authorized to bind the government they represented. Instead, all arrangements with Canada would have to be ratified by the provisional government. This was an interesting concept, for it apparently required that the Canadian government recognize the provisional government in order to complete the deal. As we shall see, Canada simply bypassed the provisional government in its dealings with the delegates and in its subsequent passage of enabling legislation.

A last question concerned the "final" version of the Bill of Rights carried by the delegates in their instructions. The whole matter of Bills of Rights has been a subject of considerable confusion for many years. As we have seen, there were a number of different versions of a bill of rights generated in Red River over the fall and winter of 1869-70. The first version, fairly brief and with no official standing, was sent by Walter Bown's brother to Prime Minister Macdonald in November. A second version was generated with the assistance of Americans, probably Enos Stutsman, in December of 1869, and was agreed to by the council of the two peoples in early December. A third version was produced by the Convention of Forty in February of 1870. This version was the one to which Donald A. Smith responded and which the government of Canada indicated to Bishop Taché could serve as a basis for negotiation. A fourth version, in the handwriting of Thomas Bunn, was in the hands of the Manitoba Historical and Scientific Society in 1890, and was reprinted by George Bryce, who numbered it as the "third" version because he was not aware of the one sent to the prime minister in November. It was the version printed in the settlement in French and dated 23 March 1870.

This fourth version was apparently the version which was intended to be given to the delegates to be taken to Ottawa. Although there were the same number of clauses in versions three to five, the "terms and conditions" were considerably different from one version to another. There was certainly a major difference from the list accepted by the Convention of Forty in February and the list printed in March. The changes were so substantial that this version could hardly be regarded as a revision or redrafting, but must rather be seen as an entirely new document.

We have no details about the writing of this version, which was in many ways the most radical of the bills of rights. Many of the changes in this printed bill of rights resulted from the insistence, in clause one, that the territories of Rupert's Land and North-West be admitted to confederation as the Province of Assiniboia. This alteration affected many of the clauses of the Convention of Forty's bill — particularly clauses one to seven, and nine and ten — which had been predicated on the understanding that admission would come as a territory, and created a number of new demands. The new province was to get two Senators and four members of the House of Commons, for example; be free of direct taxation from Ottawa for five years; and the local legislature would be paid 80 cents per head by the Canadian Government until the population reached 600,000. The revised draft also called for local control over all public lands in the North-West (as well as the right to annul all arrangements made with reference to these public lands), while the earlier February version wanted only lands around Fort Garry to a specified circumference equal to the distance of Fort Garry from the American border. This would have meant a circumference of about 60 miles. The new territory would be roughly the same size as Red River (or the Municipal District of Assiniboia) had been.

The new version called for on an engineering commission to explore the mineral wealth in the new province. Although the printed version wanted Indian treaties concluded quickly, it now insisted that the treaties required "the advice and co-operation of the Local Legislature of this Province." Several clauses editorialized on the recent troubles. Clause 17, for example, read:

> That whereas the French and English speaking people of Assiniboia are so equally divided as to numbers, yet so united in their interests, and so connected by commerce, family connections, and other political and social relations, that it has happily been found impossible to bring them into hostile collision, although repeated attempts have been made by designing strangers, for reasons known to themselves, to bring about so ruinous and disastrous an event. And whereas after all the trouble and apparent dissensions of the past, the result of misunderstanding among themselves, they have, as soon as the evil agencies referred to above were removed, become as united and friendly as ever; therefore as a means to strengthen this union and friendly feeling among all classes, we deem it expedient and advisable, that the Lieutenant-Governor, who may be appointed for the Province of Assiniboia, should be familiar with both the English and French languages.

Clause 19 argued that all debts contracted by the provisional government should be paid by the Dominion, "in consequence of the illegal and inconsiderate measures adopted by Canadian officials to bring about a civil war in our midst." A second part of this clause insisted that "none of the members of the Provisional Government, or any of those acting under them, be in any way held liable or responsible with regard to the movement or any of the actions which led to the present negotiations."

The insistence on provincial status returned to a clause advocated by Riel in the convention but defeated by the anglophone delegates, with the assistance of several Métis. Riel had said at the time that he would get his way, and apparently he had. But it would not be true to conclude that provincial status alone was the major change between the February and March versions. The size of the territory involved had also been greatly expanded. The new province of Assiniboia was to consist of all of Rupert's Land and the North-West Territories. Moreover, the powers of the local legislature were spelled out, protected, and extended much more clearly in the revisions. At the same time, despite the insistence on bilingualism in the legislature and the courts, there was no insistence on separate schools, and absolutely no mention was made of anything of a confessional or sectarian nature. Whatever the influences on this draft, they were not of a clerical variety. All of the commissioners were instructed to make the amnesty a *sine qua non* of the negotiations quite apart from clause 19, which meant that no further discussions could take place until the Canadians had conceded on this matter. Those responsible for the death of Thomas Scott obviously realized that they would have to be protected.

In 1889, Bishop Taché published another version (version five) of the bill of rights in the *Daily Free Press* of 27 December 1889, which he claimed was the version that accompanied the commission to the delegates dated 24 March 1870 and which was carried by them to be presented at Ottawa. This version is quite different from the version printed under date of 23 March 1870; the clauses are grouped and numbered differently. Constitutionally, the draft is less radical than version four, apart from its insistence on separate schools. Clause one specifies admission of "the territory of the Northwest" as a province, but does not name it nor list either Rupert's Land or the North-West specifically. It speaks of a local legislature with a "responsible ministry," and calls in clause seven for separate schools, with "the public money for schools…distributed among the different religious denominations in proportion to their respective populations according to the system of the Province of Quebec." The first version of Red River demands had spoken about bilingualism and the protection of the Catholic Church, but never about separate schools, and religious matters were never mentioned at all in versions two to four. A comparison of versions four and five indicates that while they have much in common, particularly in their second halves, they are really more different than the usual descriptions of them would suggest. The changes are more than simply the addition of a separate schools clause. Interestingly enough, both versions have the amnesty clause as number 19, which has caused endless confusion over which version was used in Ottawa.

In some ways, the fact that the final conditions carried by the delegates were substantially different from the earlier bill of rights passed by the Convention of Forty in February was not a problem. The earlier convention had no real standing, while the executive of the provisional government did, at least within the bounds of Red River. Moreover, the full council subsequently accepted the outcome of the negotiations. But it remained the case that there were two conflicting bills of rights generated for the delegates to be taken to Ottawa, one of which appears to have been ratified by the executive of the provisional government and the other generated apart from that ratification. Neither had been authorized by any full body representing "the people." Moreover, whichever version Canada was shown in Ottawa in April of 1870, the Dominion had previously accepted as a basis for negotiation a quite different set of demands than either of the ones carried to Ottawa by the delegates of the provisional government.

Louis Riel v. Canada

Once the delegation had departed for Ottawa, the whole business of negotiating with Canada was entirely out of Louis Riel's hands. Beyond the instructions to the delegates, which would to a considerable extent be ignored by all parties, he would have absolutely no input into the final outcome. Matters would turn out quite differently than he might have anticipated. In a sense, however, that negotiations were beyond his control freed Riel of one area of concern, liberating him to concentrate on building political institutions and running a country. The next six months would provide the only opportunity Louis Riel ever had in his life to be constructive and statesmanlike. But before we turn to examine his achievement, we must trace the steps of the Red River delegation to Canada.

The Delegates Travel to Ottawa

Father Noel-Joseph Ritchot left Red River on 26 March, accompanied by Colonel Charles de Salaberry, who was finally returning to Canada after having made little impact on events in the West. The priest carried among his documents an additional memorandum from Bishop Taché — quite apart from his formal instructions — which emphasized the need to reach agreement with Canada. Even an agreement *non parfait* was better than no agreement whatever, wrote the bishop. To a considerable extent, the fate of the settlement in the Canadian Confederation rested on Ritchot's shoulders, since he was the energy and the conscience of the delegation. Judge John Black was not eager to battle hard with the Canadians on political grounds, and he was ill as well. Alfred H. Scott was well-disposed toward the Métis, but in no way a prepossessing figure.

Ritchot was in his mid-forties in 1870. He had been born in Lower Canada and educated at the Collège d' L'Assomption. He arrived in Red River in 1862 and became priest in the parish of St. Norbert, which he served until his death. He was one of the few priests in the settlement in 1869 who was of French-Canadian background, and he was an active supporter of the resistance almost from the beginning. Ritchot was greatly admired in Red River for his intellectual powers, and they would certainly be put to the test in Ottawa. He was described by one British official in Ottawa as "a fine looking vigorous man, apparently about 40, with a great black beard. He does not speak English, but makes up for it by speaking French with a marvellous rapidity." Ritchot's weaknesses in English would prove something of a liability to the delegation, but his more important problem would be that, in the high-stakes game of poker he would have to play, he did not hold very good cards. Bishop Taché feared that Ritchot might prove too obstinate, but it was for his zealous stubbornness that Ritchot had been chosen by Louis Riel to carry the Métis struggle to Ottawa. Riel knew that Ritchot's sense of duty and his commitment to the Métis cause would not allow him to be steamrollered by the Canadians. Whether he could deal with Canadian guile and duplicity was another matter entirely.

On that very same day that Ritchot and de Salaberry left Red River, the *Globe* in Toronto carried on its front page the news of the Scott execution, having received word from Minnesota via the telegraph. The newspaper initially provided no details, and the death of Scott was not immediately a big issue in Ontario. The *Globe* on 29 March printed its first editorial on Scott's death. It called for Canada to take possession of the territory, and introduce a bill into Parliament "granting a liberal Constitution to the new Territory, granting representative institutions, and including such portions of the 'Bill of Rights' as are just and reasonable." Then, said the newspaper, that constitution "should be carried to Red River by a sufficient armed force to make resistance impossible."

No mention was made of the victim's Orangeism, at least in its early stages. It would soon become significant thanks to the deliberate orchestration of public sentiment by the leaders of the secret society called Canada First. Canada First had been founded in 1868 in Ottawa by five young bachelors — George Taylor Denison III, Henry J. Morgan, William Alexander Foster, Robert Grant Haliburton, and Charles Mair — who shared a number of common interests. Four of them were Upper Canadians (now Ontarians), and all were believers in the superiority of Anglo-Saxon Protestantism, as well as the inferiority of both French Canadians and indigenous peoples. Initially they had called themselves "the Apostles," after one of the secret societies at Cambridge University. Inspired by the death of D'Arcy McGee, who had been recently assassinated on the steps of the House of Commons, they agreed on the need to develop a true national spirit in Canada. Such a national development demanded the expansion of Canada as far west as British Columbia. The little group soon added John Christian Schultz to their ranks.

Canada First was the perfect embodiment of the values of Ontario imperialism, and George Denison III was the perfect embodiment of Canada First. Denison was a third-generation member of a prominent Upper Canadian family. His heroes were Napoleon, the Duke of Wellington, and Robert E. Lee. Like many others of his class and type, he had supported the Confederacy in the American Civil War, and his involvement with the South's Great Lakes raider *The Georgian* had forced him to declare insolvency and resign his militia commission in 1867. In later life, Denison would serve as a Toronto police magistrate, meting out justice in the form of heavy sentences to the wrongdoers who appeared before him. Denison was the author of numerous books, among which probably the most remarkable was *The Struggle for Imperial Unity: Recollections & Experiences*, published in 1909.

As Denison would later recall in his memoirs, the Canadian public had been markedly apathetic about the initial Canadian disaster at Red River. Most Canadians seemed to recognize that Canada had blundered badly, and deserved what it was getting. But the Scott "murder" and the impending return of Schultz and Mair to Ontario gave the Canada Firsters the opportunity "to draw attention to the matter, and by denouncing the murder of Scott, to arouse the indignation of the people, and foment a public opinion that would force the Government to send an armed expedition to restore order."

The arrival of the Canadian refugees in St. Paul at the end of March provided eastern Canada with its first detailed information about the Scott execution, and the subsequent appearance of these men in Ontario gave them an opportunity to embellish their stories with no fear of contradiction, there being none yet present from the Métis camp to offer an alternative interpretation of events. In his memoirs, Denison described in considerable detail — and with considerable relish — the hate campaign which Canada First aroused in Ontario in response to the death of Thomas Scott. What Denison did not inform his readers was that the early Canadian reaction to the death of Scott did not make anything of his Orange Lodge connection, but instead concentrated on the death of one loyal Canadian and the ill-treatment of others. Denison told a private meeting of Canada Firsters on 2 April "that there were only a few Ontario men, seventy in number, in that remote and inaccessible region, surrounded by half savages, besieged until supplies gave out." Any man who hesitated to welcome these men back home, he added, "is no true Canadian. I repudiate him as a countryman of mine." By this time, Charles Mair had left St. Paul by train, travelling east with Donald A. Smith. The two men discussed Red River on several occasions. Smith told Mair that he doubted the priests were seriously implicated in recent events, thus contradicting Mair's favourite thesis about the insurgency. At this point Smith also doubted that Scott's death was murder, although he would soon change his tune once he arrived in Ontario.

Since the government already had a military expedition in process, the main effect of the propaganda campaign was to inflame Ontario against Louis Riel and the Métis. While Canada First prepared incendiary editorials to plant in the newspapers ("It was like putting a match to tinder," George Denison later wrote), Messrs. Ritchot and de Salaberry were joined en route by Alfred H. Scott and later by Judge Black, who travelled in company with Charles Boulton. At Grand Forks, this party had overtaken J.A.N. Provencher, who had wintered at Pembina. Travel by this ill-assorted crew was done mainly at night because of the thawing roads. The delegates reached Fort Abercrombie on 1 April, where a fatigued Judge Black lagged behind while the remaining men took the stagecoach for St. Cloud and the railhead. While the provisional government's delegation was rattling along by stagecoach, Canada First was getting its campaign into high gear. The party from Red River arrived at St. Cloud on 6 April, almost immediately boarding the train for St. Paul.

On that same day, 6 April, Charles Mair, John Christian Schultz, and several other former Riel prisoners arrived in Toronto. Canada First was responsible for a monster rally on 7 April, originally called for the St. Lawrence Hall and later moved to the square in front of the City Hall. A crowd of at least 1,000 escorted Mair and Schultz to the Queen's Hotel, and another crowd of more than 10,000 forced the shift of venue to Market Square, where the speakers stood on the roof of the porch of the old City Hall. It was officially called by the mayor of Toronto, who welcomed the Canadian refugees home from Red River. There Mair, Schultz, James Lynch, and J. J. Setter, as well as several Ontario politicians, addressed the huge crowd. Mair insisted that the events in Red River "were not melodramatic." The speeches condemned Riel for cold-blooded murder and eulogized both the refugees, and especially Thomas Scott, for their loyalty and fortitude. Three resolutions were passed on this occasion. One welcomed the refugees and endorsed their "sacrifice" in resisting the usurpation of power by the "murderer Riel." The second advocated decisive measures to suppress the uprising, and the third declared that it would be "a gross injustice to the loyal inhabitants of Red River, humiliating to our national honour, and contrary to all British traditions for our Government to receive, negotiate, or treat with the emissaries of those who have robbed, imprisoned, and murdered loyal Canadians, whose only fault was zeal for British institutions, whose only crime was devotion to the old flag." One can sense the hand of Canada First in this rhetoric and in the lengthy story in the Toronto *Globe*. Whether the crowd actually heard any of the proceedings described in detail is doubtful, but it made good newspaper copy. Curiously enough, there was no mention of the Orange Lodge at any point in these proceedings. Ontario clearly did not require invocations of Irish sectarianism to get very angry about what had happened in Red River.

News of the gathering storm in Ontario was telegraphed west, and Father Ritchot avoided reporters in St. Paul only by declaring himself unable to speak English. At St. Paul, Judge Black and Charles Boulton took the train to Detroit, then on to Toronto. Father Ritchot and Alfred Scott were more prudent, boarding a train which proceeded via Buffalo to Ogdensburg, New York. There they were met on 11 April by Gilbert McMicken of the Dominion Police, who informed them he had been sent by the government to escort them to Ottawa. McMicken got Ritchot and Scott to the capital city without incident, and the priest was installed by 5 p.m. at the local Episcopal palace. That same day, the Canadian governor-general advised the British authorities that Canada was ready to accept the transfer of territory "if movement of troops settled."

While the delegates were travelling east from Minnesota by rail, Messrs. Mair, Schultz, and Denison were heading east from Toronto to Ottawa, where the Canadians from Red River would subsequently testify at a Senate hearing. Massive demonstrations of welcome were organized in towns like Cobourg, Belleville, and Prescott. "Public feeling was aroused," recorded George Denison many years later, "and we then knew that we would have Ontario at our backs." Scott's Orange background still had not become general public knowledge or a public issue at this point. Ontario was simply angry that one of its loyal sons (well, adopted sons, anyway) had been cruelly murdered by the half-savage Métis. The Canadian government was hardly pleased at this monkey wrench being thrown into the negotiations. Denison met with Sir John A. Macdonald and accused him of attempting to humiliate Canada First. Denison, with the assistance of another Canadian refugee from Red River, Dr. James Spencer Lynch, drafted a protest on behalf of the "loyal element of Fort Garry" against the reception of the delegates, while William Foster and others in Toronto were obtaining a warrant for the arrest of Ritchot and Alfred Scott on the charge of the murder of Thomas Scott. This warrant was forwarded to Ottawa, where it was mistakenly put into the hands of the Dominion government instead of the Ottawa police, which meant it was not acted upon.

Trying to Negotiate

On 12 April, Father Ritchot was introduced by Colonel de Salaberry to Sir George-Étienne Cartier, and the two men had a long discussion. Cartier, of course, was the leader of the French-Canadian "bleus" and Sir John A. Macdonald's trusted Quebec lieutenant. Like the prime minister, Cartier was a smooth talker. He was also an inveterate optimist. According to Ritchot, Cartier said the government regretted the death of Scott, "in that it had given ground for the agitation which it had produced in men's minds, but that it would not be a reason that the government should not profit by the means of pacification which it found in the persons of the delegates of the North West." The government expected that the agitation would soon go away, said Cartier, and begged for time to allow "minds to calm down." Meanwhile, Alfred Scott was arrested and jailed on the Toronto warrant at 10 p.m. on the evening of 12 April, and there was much talk of Ritchot's arrest as well. The following morning, the *Globe* printed the resolutions of Lodge 404 of the Orange Order (Toronto) relating to Thomas Scott, "cruelly murdered by the enemies of our Queen, country and religion." The resolutions called upon the government to "avenge his death" and rescue Red River "from those who have turned it over to Popery." This was the first introduction of ethnic and confessional issues into the Scott business. Accompanied by friends, on 13 April Ritchot made his way to the court-house, where the warrant was served upon him. Alfred Scott and Ritchot met at the police station, whence they were sent to their lodgings under armed guard.

On 14 April, Sir John A. Macdonald wrote to the Earl of Carnarvon that Thomas Scott's people were calling for retribution against Riel. "Indignation meetings" were being held all over Canada, reported Macdonald, and the government had been requested not to receive the delegates commissioned by Riel. Most of the Red River residents were loyal to Britain, insisted Macdonald, "though they would have preferred their present wild and semi barbarous life to the restraints of Civilization that will be forced on them by the Canadian Government and the new settlers." Matters were much complicated by the Scott incident, wrote the prime minister, which was a "barbarous murder" on the authority of a "sham Court" on "most frivolous pretexts." Macdonald still hoped that the military expedition being prepared — it still had not been agreed to by the British government — would be accepted not as a hostile force but as a friendly garrison.

Friendly was a relative matter, and behind the velvet glove was the iron fist. The prime minister subsequently complained to the governor-general that if the troops were not used "to force the people to unite with Canada," they were useless. The British may have wanted no part of a military expedition which would actually have to invade Red River, but "Why should we agree to pay for troops that may be ordered not to act when they get to Fort Garry?" At about the same time that the prime minister was writing to London, Judge Thomas Galt of the Ontario Court of Common Pleas was deciding that the Toronto police magistrate who had issued the warrant had no jurisdiction in the matter. The two arrested delegates were freed, only to be arrested again on a warrant sworn out in Ottawa by George Denison III. Ritchot and Scott again appeared in court, were referred to the police magistrate, and were released on bail until a hearing on 23 April. The British government found these legal actions most distressing, cabling the governor-general on 18 April: "Did Canadian gov't authorize arrest of delegates? Full information desired by telegraph."

On 20 April, Father Ritchot got tired of cooling his heels and decided to appeal to the Canadian governor-general. That evening, Sir John A. Macdonald answered questions in the House of Commons about the Red River affair. Macdonald denied that the government had received any official communication from anyone claiming to be a delegate. The opposition asked pointed questions about the implied recognition of the provisional government that would be involved in receiving the delegates formally, and Macdonald replied that the delegation "could have the credentials of representatives of the people." The Scott business was making the negotiations difficult to begin, argued the Dominion. The case against Ritchot and Alfred H. Scott was withdrawn at magistrates' court on 23 April. Outside the courthouse door, the two men from Red River were met by a large crowd of cheering French Canadians and Catholic Irish. The whole business was rapidly turning into a major sectional and sectarian issue.

That same day, the British colonial secretary cabled the Canadian governor-general that permission for the dispatch of British troops to Red River required that four conditions be met. They included the payment of the £300,000 to the Hudson's Bay Company and the completion of the transfer before 1 June. Most importantly of all, said the cable, "Canadian Gov't to accept decision of H. M.'s Gov't on disputed points of settlers' Bill of Rights." The British were actually prepared to make sure that the people of Red River got a square deal from the Canadian government. The Canadians had to complete the transfer (which meant satisfying Red River) before 1 June in order to get British co-operation in a military expedition. This should have been very useful to Father Ritchot and his fellow delegates, but was not, for several reasons. In the first place, in her infinite and inscrutable wisdom, Her Majesty (or her government) failed to inform the delegates of this condition before the negotiations began. In the second place, British representatives in Ottawa would ultimately cheat more than a bit in favour of the Canadians.

Negotiating

Discussions between the delegates began finally on 25 April. Once the negotiations began, they would not take long to complete. The Canadians had decided that they could concede on the matter of admitting a province by restricting its size rather severely. Judge Black, Alfred H. Scott, and Father Ritchot went to Sir George-Étienne Cartier's house to meet with that worthy and Prime Minister Sir John A. Macdonald. The talks were, in the parlance of the diplomatic community, "informal." The Canadians asked pointed questions about the various bills of rights passed by the settlement and, according to Ritchot's journal, asked for explanations of "the Bill of Rights already in their possession, work of the Assembly of Twenty-four sent by Hon. Wm. McDougall, then that of the Convention of Forty, then after all that we should compose a list we could finally present to them." Ritchot wrote in his journal that he had not "much taste" for this discussion. His concern may have been partly an uneasiness over the validity of the Bill of Rights which would serve as the basis for negotiation, but was also caused by a concern over the question of formal recognition of the delegation. Cartier disingenuously responded that the delegates were officially recognized, for Sir John had said so in Parliament. He offered to put the recognition in writing. Ritchot insisted that a general amnesty was a condition *sine qua non* of any settlement, and commented on the prospective Canadian military expedition.

The two sides met later in the day. The delegates were not in perfect harmony, with Judge Black far more amenable to the Canadian position than Scott and Ritchot. Prime Minister Macdonald tried to delay the making of a province and sought an elected interim government. When this position was rejected by Ritchot and Scott, Sir John A. floated a government of 26 members, six nominated by the government, and the remainder elected. Eventually the Canadians accepted the concept of a province and a responsible government of two chambers. Cartier emphasized that there would have to be several provinces in the North-West, although he was not specific about the sizes. Ritchot observed in his journal, "I made a pretense of not understanding. He often came back to the question."

On the following day, Secretary of State Joseph Howe provided a note which acknowledged the Red River emissaries, not as delegates from the provisional government but as "delegates from the North-West to the Government of the Dominion of Canada." The negotiators from Red River were given to understand that they were not being dealt with as representatives from the provisional government because the uproar over the execution of Scott made it impossible for Canada to negotiate with Riel's government. But in truth, if the furore over Scott had not occurred, the Canadians would have had to invent some other reason for not negotiating with Riel or the provisional government for fear of thereby recognizing it. Father Ritchot introduced the new Bill of Rights embodied in his instructions, which the Canadians reluctantly agreed to accept. Various clauses of the Bills of Rights were discussed, including the school system and the land question. Clause 19 (the amnesty clause) was mentioned. The Canadians claimed that amnesty was not "within their competence," but was a matter solely for the local government or for England. This argument was more than a bit specious, since responsible government was sufficiently advanced in Canada for the Canadian cabinet to expect the governor-general to issue an amnesty if it was officially requested. But the Canadians also said that settling the amnesty was easy. Ritchot replied, "Provided the matter is settled, it is all that matters to us."

On Wednesday 27 April, the third day of negotiations, the Canadians brought a draft of a bill, which was generally discussed. The clause in the Bill of Rights turning over control of the land and natural resources to the province had been lost. Judge Black was willing to accept Dominion control over land, but Ritchot was not. The Canadians claimed to be sympathetic to Ritchot, but pleaded "that to reach a settlement it is necessary to make some concessions." Ritchot agreed to accept Canada's offers, provided Judge Black could get them accepted by the people. Black admitted that he could not. "What should we do": asked the Canadian ministers. "Grant us control of our lands as per our instructions," answered Ritchot. "Impossible," said the ministers.

The general question of Métis rights was also contentious. The Canadians opened this discussion by observing that the settlers could not have both civilized government and "the privileges granted to Indians." This was the old line given to the Métis once again. Ritchot answered that it did not follow that because the settlers wishes to be treated equally they should lose their rights as descendants of Indians. In the end, the two parties rolled the twin questions of Crown lands and Métis rights into one package by discussing equivalencies to the Métis for the Crown lands, chiefly in the form of land grants to all inhabitants of Red River. The Canadians initially offered 100,000 acres to be granted to the children of the Métis, then increased the amount. Ritchot and Scott refused to concede on the amount of land involved on 27 April, but Prime Minister Macdonald obviously thought he had agreement on the principal of land compensation. He wrote to Sir John Young that evening, "We are nearly through our troubles with the delegates, and then we can take up the military matter."

Further discussions were postponed by another of Prime Minister Macdonald's "indispositions." Ritchot took the printed bill away to produce written comments about it, which have survived. Ritchot's "Remarks on Twenty-Six Clauses April 28 and 29, 1870" make clear that by this point the Canadian government knew what it wanted. The new province would be called Manitoba, and would be quite small in area, roughly 11,000 square miles, a limitation the priest appeared to accept readily. He was not happy with the education clause, which repeated the phraseology of section 93 of the British North America Act, but aimed his major criticisms at the article relating to the administration of Crown lands, which reserved all land not otherwise committed to the federal government. He also noted the need to settle article 19 (the amnesty question).

Ritchot's were not the only comments on the issues of the negotiations. Sir Clinton Murdoch, who was the special British envoy in Ottawa, sent to deal with the military expedition, wrote to London that many of the clauses of the Red River Bill of Rights were "inadmissable." He was especially concerned about the demands for control of Crown lands and for amnesty, but he felt that the Canadian government would manage to meet the British condition that its troops not be employed to force Canadian sovereignty upon the inhabitants of Red River. How he thought this could be done without conceding on the matter of amnesty — which was supposed to be the basis of all further negotiation — was not at all clear.

Sir John A. Macdonald's "indisposition" took him out of the negotiations at this critical stage. On 29 April the delegates met again at Sir George-Étienne Cartier's home. An arrangement was struck on the land question. Cartier agreed to propose to the government a grant of one million acres for the children of Métis. This arrangement contradicted the express demand of virtually every version of the Bill of Rights, including the one hammered out by the Convention of Forty and accepted by Donald A. Smith with the phrase, "full and substantial justice will be done in this matter." In part, this feat of legerdemain was possible because the Canadians and the British both refused to allow the Manitoba Act to be subject to confirmation by the provisional government. Officially the reason was that, as Sir Clinton Murdoch put it in a letter to Britain on 28 April, such confirmation "would have involved a recognition of Riel and his associates." The Canadians had always been very careful not to recognize the provisional government in any official documents, which made possible Canada's disassociation of itself from the acts of that government, including the execution of Thomas Scott. But unofficially, this refusal to allow Riel's government to agree to the Manitoba Act also made it possible to ignore the most important of the positive "rights" demanded by the settlement.

In the end, as historian Chester Martin pointed out as long ago as 1920, "Many of the terms of union were imposed upon the inhabitants of the new province not only without their consent, but even without their knowledge." In fairness to Canada, both the provisional government and the dominion played hard and loose with the consent of the people of Red River. But it is worth emphasizing that after all the trouble of the rebellion, the Canadians managed basically to have their own way. The concession of a special distribution of land to the Métis created an administrative monster that would go on for years. The Canadian insistence that the federal government, rather than the local one, controlled all public lands in the province also created a serious constitutional problem, because this insistence contravened section 92 of the British North America Act, which left the management of the public lands to the provinces. Canada would resolve this problem by having the British Parliament confirm the validity of the Manitoba Act. But all this was in the future. At the time, Ritchot and the delegates had come to terms on the land question, which left only the question of the amnesty on the table. Technically, none of the negotiations ought to have occurred without an agreement here, and certainly there ought to have been no done deal without one, but Cartier continued to insist that the delegates could be accommodated in this matter.

The Manitoba Act

S ir John A. Macdonald returned to the negotiating table on 2 May. Father Ritchot accepted an increased offer of 1,200,000 acres for the settlement of Métis claims and in place of local control of Crown lands, insisting that the lands could be taken anywhere in the province. That afternoon, Sir John A. sketched out the government's intentions for Red River in the House of Commons.

"Manitoba" had been selected as the name for the new province out of a number of "euphonious" Indian names. The chief alternative, Assiniboia, was rejected because of confusion with the river and the older District of Assiniboia. The new province would be small in area, but, Macdonald emphasized, the delegates had raised no objections about confining its boundaries to the old limits of the settlement. Macdonald stressed that in Manitoba there would be representative government, and there would be a reservation of lands to extinguish Métis claims comparable to the lands appropriated for the United Empire Loyalists. Manitoba would be entitled to four members of the House of Commons and two senators. The details of most matters, including constitutional ones, would be left to the local legislature. To ensure that law and order were respected in the new province, a mixed expedition of British regulars and Canadian militia would be sent there as soon as possible. The announcement of the expedition presumed that the delegates from Red River were satisfied with the terms of entrance. This was still not entirely the case, of course.

The Liberal Alexander Mackenzie poured considerable scorn on the size and population of the new province, which he said had a ludicrous look that might have come out of *Gulliver's Travels*. Mackenzie also complained that "half-breeds" were not entitled to land claims as if they were Indians. None of the divisions "which were for so many years disastrous in our own country" should be perpetuated in the new ones, he insisted. This insistence on homogeneity was not pursued very far, however. Mackenzie indicated that the opposition would concentrate much of their attack on the cost of administering a new province. The government deflected questions about compensation for the victims of the resistance. The printed bill was not actually available until the day after Macdonald's opening explanations. It was still being altered. On 3 May, Cartier asked the delegates whether it would be acceptable to allow Portage la Prairie within the boundaries of the new province, as had been suggested in the previous day's debate. They answered yes, providing grants and land reservations were increased. Nobody suggested consulting the people of Portage. Other changes were made on which the delegates were not consulted and with which they were less happy. But the opening debates left Macdonald sufficiently confident to write the governor-general on 4 May, "The Bill affecting Red River was received last night with great favour by the House, and will pass without any serious opposition."

While the Manitoba Act was being debated in the House of Commons, on 3 May the Red River delegates had a crucial meeting with Governor-General Sir John Young and the British envoy Clinton Murdoch. These two worthies were charged, on behalf of the British government, with making sure that the demands of the people of Red River were satisfied by the Canadian government. The imperial authorities had, after all, agreed to commit troops to Red River only on condition that the local inhabitants were contented with the transfer. According to Father Ritchot's testimony in 1874 before a parliamentary commission, on this occasion the governor-general had emphasized that if a satisfactory arrangement could not be reached with the Canadians, "I am ready to hear you and Sir Clinton Murdoch has to do you justice." The delegates responded that they had consented to the terms of the Manitoba bill, but were not satisfied that the amnesty question had been answered, because they had no written guarantee. Ritchot testified in 1874 that the governor-general then pointed to Murdoch and said, "He knows it is the intention of Her Majesty to declare a general amnesty in order to establish peace in the country. Besides, you have seen my proclamation, are you familiar with it?"

Ritchot did not point out that Sir John Young's proclamation had offered an amnesty in December if the insurgents immediately dispersed. He merely observed that the proclamation had only promised an amnesty, and what he wanted was the "promulgation of the actual amnesty promises." According to Ritchot, Murdoch emphasized, "You have nothing to fear, her Majesty wishes but one thing, and that is to pass the sponge over all that has happened in the North-West and establish peace." Ritchot said he would still like something in writing to show the people, to which Murdoch replied, "When you are treating with men such as those in whose presence you are today there is no necessity for written guarantees." He said in French, "tant mettre les points sur les I," adding, "You must leave us a certain latitude and you will gain by it." Ritchot responded, "Since there is nothing to fear I trust to your words." In their testimony in 1874, both Sir John Young and Sir Clinton Murdoch denied making such statements, and Murdoch could not even remember meeting with the Red River delegates. We shall return again to this matter.

Apart from the unresolved matter of the amnesty, even as the Manitoba bill was being debated in the House of Commons, Father Ritchot and the other delegates had begun complaining that the official language of the text was modifying the agreement the parties had reached. Ritchot was particularly concerned about the mechanism for distribution of the land promised the children of the Métis, now up to 1,400,000 acres. The delegates met with Cartier and Macdonald on this matter on 5 and 6 May. According to Ritchot's journal, the Canadian response was that assurance of the verbal understandings not reflected in the bill would be given the delegates before they went back to Red River. It would be impossible to "get the Bill passed if one changed its form, that they would have a bad enough time to get it passed just as it was, that in any case we had nothing to fear." Quebec members of Parliament also told Ritchot that "It was not prudent to touch the basis of the Bill," for any amendments could prove unfavourable to the people of Red River. Ritchot was not really in a strong position to raise serious objections, either about the amnesty or the alterations, since the alternative to a negotiated agreement appeared to be what would amount to an invasion of Red River with what might be great loss of life. He could not know that the British would not have co-operated militarily if the delegates had hung tough and refused to be satisfied. Nor could he know that the assurances of the two representatives of the British government, obviously working in tandem, would turn out to be so duplicitous.

At the same time, the provisional government's negotiators had been well and truly hoodwinked by Canada, aided and abetted by the confidential representatives of the British government. The delegates had been outmanoeuvred and lied to by Cartier and Macdonald. After all the disturbances, the only concession which Red River had actually gained over what it might otherwise have expected was immediate admission as a province. As we shall see, even that concession was hedged with conditions. It did not really include the introduction of responsible government. Manitoba certainly did not gain control of its natural resources, nor were the insurgents granted an amnesty.

On 6 May Prime Minister Macdonald collapsed with what was diag-nosed as an attack of gallstones, which meant that he was unable to shep-herd the Manitoba bill through its final reading. Despite his initial opti-mism, there was fierce criticism from Liberals and the Orange interests, now led by William McDougall. One of the strongest defenders of Red River, and, of course, the government, was Adams G. Archibald of Nova Scotia, who was especially unhappy that the settlement had been described as a "country of semi-savages," and the delegates as traitors or worse. In an impassioned speech on 7 May, Archibald emphasized that "we invite them to send delegates, and they send them on our invitation. The question is not whether the conduct of these people has been right or wrong. We want to know what it is they complain of, and they send these men to tell us." Any insults of the delegates were uncalled for, he maintained.

Sir George-Étienne Cartier admitted that there had been a "prospec-tive rebellion," but not against Canada, since Canadian authority did not exist in Red River. He advocated the drowning of the difficulties in "lib-eral measures," which included recognition of the halfbreed claims. He also insisted that the Convention of Forty in Red River would "contrast favourably" with the Quebec Conference of 1864. The opposition's objec-tion was to immediate provincial status, and when an amendment to substitute a territorial government was defeated by a vote of 95 to 35, the critics lost interest in the remaining details. The Manitoba Act was assent-ed to the governor-general on 12 May. The military expedition which had been in furious but informal organization for several months could now shift into high gear.

One of the greatest effects of the whole Red River business that cul-minated in the passage of the Manitoba Act was to be felt in Quebec. At the beginning of westward expansion, the province had assumed that the West was the natural hinterland of Ontario. To Quebeckers' surprise, it transpired that the West was not necessarily waiting to be settled by Ontarians. It already had a population, and much of that population was both French-speaking and Roman Catholic. Over the course of the Riel controversy, Quebec increasingly assumed the role of the protector of this oasis of French-Canadianism in the wilderness. Thus Quebec newspa-pers were pleased at the passage of the Manitoba Act, particularly at its language and religious clauses, but they were also poised and pre-pared to look out for the rights of the people of Manitoba as that tiny province entered Confederation. At the same time, Louis Riel had not yet become the symbol of the victimization of the Métis by the province of Ontario and its people. That role would develop for Riel only over the next few years.

Father Ritchot would spend several more weeks in Ottawa attempting unsuccessfully to get a commitment in writing on the amnesty that had been promised, but he eventually decided to return to Red River in early June without anything much on paper. All Ritchot had was a letter from Sir George-Étienne Cartier dated 23 May, which provided details on the verbal understanding on landholding. It continued by referring to the recent interview with the governor-general, "in which His Excellency was pleased to state that the liberal policy which the Government proposed to follow in relation to the persons for whom you are interesting yourself is correct and is that which ought to be adopted." A postscript authorized the use of this letter as "explanation" of Father Ritchot's negotiations. Ritchot reminded Cartier that the makeup of the committee for settling the 1,400,000 acres had not been clarified. Ritchot had initially been promised by Cartier and Macdonald that the Métis land would be distributed by the Manitoba legislature or by a special committee chosen by both parties. Canada had then changed the mechanism to the lieutenant-governor acting under instructions of the governor-general. When Ritchot complained, the Canadians promised an order in council allowing a committee to be named for distributing the land, but this had not happened. Cartier now added a second postscript promising that the distribution of land would "meet the wishes of the half-breed residents." Cartier insisted that this letter "contained the whole sense of the promise of amnesty as I had understood it at the moment." Ritchot was subsequently told by Cartier to "be quiet and not rack [his] head about anything; that the men with whom [he] was dealing knew something about business." Let Riel continue to govern and not make "des sottises," he wrote.

Back at the Settlement

In Red River, continuing to govern was exactly what Louis Riel was doing. One of the most neglected aspects of the entire Red River business and Riel's part in it has been the period between the departure of the delegates for the East in late March and the arrival of the Wolseley expedition in late August. Riel was not content to run a simple caretaker government. It was almost as if he wanted to prove that both he and the two communities of mixed-bloods were quite capable of governing themselves in approved democratic fashion. In this he was certainly encouraged by Bishop Taché. Even before the delegates had actually left Red River, Riel was busy setting constitutional matters in motion, tidying up from the winter, and even indulging in a bit of a celebration. A committee to write a new constitution for the provisional government was organized on 16 March. Most of the remaining prisoners, including

Charles Boulton, were released that same day. A good deal of attention was paid to dealing with potential dissent in the settlement, with a number of people temporarily imprisoned set free. The constitutional committee worked all day on St. Patrick's Day, 17 March, and a formal dinner was held that evening, with entertainment by the St. Boniface band. On the following day, Bishop Taché entertained at his palace at St. Boniface. There was another band concert, and a military drill by the boys of the college. Among the guests were Captain Boulton, A. G. B. Bannatyne, John McTavish and his wife, Alexander Begg and his wife, James Ross, William Coldwell, and others. Obviously no one at this gathering talked about Thomas Scott, who seems pretty well to have been forgotten, as Bishop Taché, on behalf of Messrs. Riel and Lépine, no doubt intended.

Riel stopped publication of the *New Nation* that same night, apparently over the newspaper's treatment of Bishop Taché's appearance at the council. Henry Robinson took this opportunity to resign as editor, and he was replaced soon afterward by Thomas Spence, the man from Portage who had organized the "Republic of Manitobah." This involvement of a leading Portage figure was a significant development, since it meant that at least some of the Portage group were willing to be more than merely sullen. The editorial policy of the newspaper, when it made its first appearance in early April, lost its annexationist edge. Spence printed a letter from Riel to Governor McTavish outlining the conditions under which the Hudson's Bay Company could resume in business, and the settlement expected the Company to be back in business within the week. Committees of the council appointed and set to work included not only the constitutional committee, but another to revise the old laws of the Council of Assiniboia and a third to deal with the hay privilege.

The provisional government did not forget that it was claiming to be the government of the entire North-West. On 7 April, Louis Schmidt sent a circular letter as "Assistant Secretary of State" to "the Settlers of the North and North-West," which was included in the mail packets to the posts and missions in the territories. The letter opened with a brief discussion of the troubles of the winter, noting the creation of a provisional government on 24 November. It spoke as though that government had continued in existence, and reported it "is today master of the situation, because all the peoples of the colony have felt the necessity of union and concord, because we have always asserted our British nationality, and because our army, although few in numbers, has always sufficed to hold high the noble standard of liberty and our native land." Schmidt could hardly help boasting, "We have to-day an undisputed hold over almost half a continent; the expulsion or annihilation of the invader has just restored our native land to its children." But the peoples of the North and

Louis Riel v. Canada

North-West had to help, by avoiding those who sought to take advantage of the disorders of the time. Pacifying the native peoples of the territories would take up much of the government's attention in the spring and summer of 1870. At about the same time as the dispatch of the circular letter, a regular police force of four men in Winnipeg replaced the armed Métis as the custodians of law and order in the village.

Two days later, on 9 April, Riel issued a proclamation to the people of the North-West. It reported that the assembly of representatives that had begun meeting on 9 March was working well together. It announced a pardon to those temporarily led astray, and offered amnesty to anyone who would submit to the government. The public highways were open, and the Hudson's Bay Company could resume business. The government was negotiating with Canada, said Riel, and it would guarantee resident rights and allow the population "a place in the Confederation equal to that of any other Province." Riel concluded by promising severity for any who challenged the government, while hoping that extreme measures would no longer occur. Unity was further encouraged by the appearance in the settlement of the Canadian government's publication of the *Correspondence and Papers Connected with the Recent Occurrences in the North-West Territories*, which doubtless made clear to all who read it that the Canadians were fools and responsible for the troubles.

Alexander Begg's journal also makes clear the extent to which the settlement was returning to normalcy in the spring of 1870. He reported that William McDougall's furniture looked good in Riel's apartment at Upper Fort Garry. The HBC was getting back in operation, Governor McTavish was well enough to appear outside, and a potential absconding debtor was arrested and brought before the authorities. Moreover, a good many Canadians and Americans were talking about leaving the settlement, which could hardly be considered a bad thing by the provisional government. On 20 April, Riel made a public statement by ordering the "Union Jack" raised at Upper Fort Garry. William O'Donoghue subsequently took it down, and he and Riel had a considerable argument over the flag. The Union Jack reappeared and O'Donoghue was told to go back to the States if he wanted. The president allowed the provisional flag hoisted underneath the Union Jack "as under the protection of it." According to Alexander Begg, this incident did much to reconcile the anglophone population to Riel and the provisional government. There were further ructions over the flags at the end of April, but Riel saw to it that the Union Jack was up on the flagpole for the meeting of what was described grandiloquently as "The Parliament of Red River." The settlement continued to remain quiet as news of the reactions to the death of Scott began to be received in early May. Perhaps the most significant result of the Ontario reaction was to make Canadians in Red River fearful of reprisal. Begg's journal was full of rumours of all sorts, few of which had any substance whatever.

On 17 May, the steamboat *International* left Red River carrying a large contingent of passengers. Among them were Governor William McTavish and his family. Their departure as much symbolized the end of the old regime in Red River as did the passage of new laws by the legislative assembly of the provisional government, which went into effect on 20 May. Shortly thereafter, word arrived from Pembina that most of the Bill of Rights had been enacted as the Manitoba Act. Not everyone was pleased with this news, for accompanying it came word of the military expedition, which according to Alexander Begg gave many Métis "a bad feeling." Continued accounts of the Ontario reaction to Thomas Scott and the vindictiveness of that province was equally disconcerting. Some information about the efforts of Charles Mair to organize armed parties of Ontario settlers to swamp the French may also have reached Red River. Certainly there were residual fears about the Indians as well. Both William McDougall and John Dennis had fished in the troubled waters of aboriginal grievances during their tenure in the West, and the natives were understandably uncertain about their treatment under the new Canadian government. The Saulteaux in the lower settlement — no friends of the provisional government — were clearly restive, and in early July they would invite other tribes outside the settlement to "consult" with them.

Captain Norbert Gay — rumoured to be a spy for Napoleon III — was drilling the Métis out on the prairies, and although everyone in the settlement was looking forward to the arrival of Father Ritchot with his report on the negotiations, there was a faction that thought the military expedition should be resisted. This group was probably led by William O'Donoghue. On 9 June, Bishop Taché wrote to Sir George-Étienne Cartier: "Some speak of raising a large force to meet and molest the coming troops at some difficult point on their way hither; and other plans, perhaps still more dangerous, are also afloat." According to a later memoir by Riel, Taché attempted to end the talk of resistance by promising that there would be a general amnesty before the lieutenant-governor arrived. Taché himself subsequently reported to Cartier, "I solemnly gave my word of honor, and promised even in the name of the Canadian government that the troops are sent on a mission of peace; that all the irregularities of the past will be overlooked or forgiven; that nobody will be annoyed for having been either leader or member of the Provisional Government, or for having acted under its guidance." Taché, of course, had no power to make such commitments.

As he travelled back to Red River, Father Ritchot understood that all was not well; he was no fool, and he knew waffle language when he heard it. He peppered Cartier with letters written from various points along his American route, worrying about the amnesty and about the treatment of the Métis by the military expedition on its way to the settlement. Ritchot got back to Winnipeg on 17 June aboard the steamer *International*. The priest assured Louis Riel that there would be an amnesty, although he had nothing in writing. Riel commented he "hoped it was so." On the following day, Ritchot met with the executive council of the provisional government. He had been promised a "full and complete amnesty" by the British representatives in Ottawa, he announced. It would arrive with the new lieutenant-governor. In the meantime, he noted that Sir George-Étienne Cartier requested that the Riel government remain in place until the new one had arrived. Ritchot then became ill, and did not immediately meet with the legislative assembly.

A week later, Father Ritchot repeated his report to a well-attended meeting of the legislative assembly of the provisional government. The settlement's delegate to Canada — the only one of the three who had returned to report to Red River — obviously thought it important that the people should approve his negotiations. He described his treatment by the Canadians, making light of the earlier problems in Ottawa and insisting that the government had privately if not publicly accepted the delegates as representing the provisional government. The terms presented by Red River which were rejected by the Canadians he explained as politically impossible, given the need for parliamentary support. Ritchot claimed that there had been the generation of a compromise list of rights acceptable to both sides. This invention explained the deviation of the final arrangements from the Convention of Forty's original resolutions without introducing the matter of the alterations made by the executive of the provisional government. Ritchot reported Cartier's request that the provisional government remain in place until it was replaced. Riel complained about the difficulty of maintaining order under such conditions, but said he would continue. In a later memoir written in 1874, Riel wrote that he knew that the formal date on which the territory would be transferred was 15 July, but that "From the 15th of July, 1870, until the 24th of the month August following we governed, in the interest of Canada, its Province of Manitoba and its territories of the North-West." Then Louis Schmidt moved acceptance of the Manitoba Act, which was carried unanimously. According to Alexander Begg, a messenger was sent to the newly-appointed lieutenant-governor, Adams G. Archibald, requesting him to come ahead of the incoming military expedition "to show that he does not come in at the point of the bayonet." Despite Ritchot's assurances, many in the settlement — including Louis Riel — remained uneasy about the future.

Waiting for Wolseley

A s for the expedition commanded by Colonel Garnet Wolseley, the first contingent of troops arrived at Port Arthur on 25 May, and preparations were begun to move the men by boat to Red River. By the end of June, advance parties had reached Lake Shebandowan and were working their way toward the Mattawan River. The last of 150 boats arrived at the lake on 6 July, having been tracked, hauled, carried, and portaged up the Kaministiquia River, 45 miles by water, 25 miles by land. From Lake Shebandowan, Colonel Wolseley issued a proclamation "To the Loyal Inhabitants of Manitoba," which he later described as having the purpose of "informing the people of the objects of the Expedition and calling upon loyal men to assist him in carrying it out." The proclamation insisted that the expedition's intentions were peaceful, its sole object to "secure Her Majesty's sovereign authority." Courts of law would be established to administer justice impartially to "all races and classes." Wolseley denied any religious or political partiality, insisting that private property would be respected and everything paid for. At the same time, the proclamation said nothing about an amnesty and pointedly asked the people of Red River to push ahead with the road to Lake of Woods, thus deliberately misleading the provisional government as to the route the expedition would follow into the settlement. The proclamation made clear that Canada was establishing a new authority, and not taking over from an existing one.

On 20 July, the steamer *International* docked at Fort Garry. A stranger was noticed by onlookers but he quickly disappeared. The stranger's luggage was confiscated. Rumour quickly spread that the stranger was Lieutenant William F. Butler of the 69th regiment, in Fort Garry in mufti to provide Wolseley with advance intelligence of the situation in the settlement. Butler had volunteered for this service. He had travelled west through the United States, and was heading to the East to join up with Wolseley. While he was visiting the Indian village, which was known to be hostile to Riel and the provisional government, he was invited to visit Upper Fort Garry. He replied that he refused to visit the fort while the "rebel flag" was flying. When Butler arrived at the fort, he subsequently reported in his book *The Great Lone Land* (1872), a tattered Union Jack and a well-kept "rebel flag" were both on the mast. Butler thus left the impression that he had forced Riel to drag out a Union Jack in order to meet the visitor's demand, while the truth was that both flags had been flying for months.

Butler was one of those supremely self-confident Englishmen so common in the later British Empire who were prepared single-handedly

— and armed with nothing but a swagger stick — to face down a horde of angry natives. One either admired their insouciance or hated them for their patronizing superiority — or both. His account of his subsequent interview with Louis Riel was well in the tradition established earlier by Robert Cunningham. Butler was ushered inside a house within the gates of the fort and asked if he would see Mr. Riel. "To call on him, certainly not." "But if he calls on you?" "Then I will see him." Thus the visitor had become the host, a not-so-subtle shift in relationship that Butler obviously found attractive. This sort of game should have alerted Riel to the true nature of the interview. Had the president any sense, he would have refused to play. In the room into which Butler was shown there was a small billiard table, and he started a game with the room's only occupant. Then, Butler wrote, there entered "a short stout man with a large head, a sallow, puffy face, a sharp, restless, intelligent eye, a square-cut massive forehead overhung by a mass of long and thickly clustering hair, and marked with well-cut eyebrow — altogether, a remarkable-looking face, all the more so, perhaps because it was to be seen in a land where such things are rare."

Riel was dressed in a black frock-coat, vest, and trousers, but this sober clerical costume was "marred," Butler thought, by a pair of Indian moccasins. The two men shook hands. Did Riel play billiards? "Never," was the reply. "Quite a loss, a capital game," said Butler. Riel retreated, saying, "I see I am intruding here." But he was brought back and left with Butler, who motioned him to be seated (again the visitor as host) and took a chair himself. According to Butler's account, Riel spoke with difficulty, dwelling long upon his words. He regretted that Butler had so mistrusted him as to prefer the lower fort and the English settlement. Butler said the rumours in the States were that Riel would resist the expedition. "Nothing was more false than these statements," Riel said, "I only wish to retain power until I can resign it to a proper Government. I have done everything for the sake of peace, and to prevent bloodshed amongst the people of this land." But, he added, "I will keep what is mine until the proper Government arrives."

Pacing incessantly about the room — a Riel characteristic when he became agitated — the president was surprised to learn that Butler was not coming from but going to the expedition, via the Winnipeg River and not the road from Lake of the Woods. Butler told him how big the force was, using its lower limits so "not to deter him from fighting if such was his intention." Like all the military men of the expedition, Butler was not so secretly spoiling for a fight. Riel did not once mention an amnesty or pardon, Butler noted. He strode about the room declaiming the advantages he had made for his country.

Riel always did have a tendency to lay on the rhetoric, even in face to face encounters where it was inappropriate, and it was one of those characteristics which led others to see him as being pompous and vainglorious. Like many, Butler thought he could see through the rhetoric. "Alas! For the vanity of man, it only made him appear ridiculous; the moccasins sadly marred the exhibition of presidential power…this picture of the black-coated Métis playing the part of Europe's great soldier in the garb of a priest and the shoes of a savage looked simply absurd." It apparently never occurred to Butler that he was one of those "overwashed Englishman, utterly ignorant of the country and full of crotchets, as all Englishmen are," that Prime Minister Macdonald had feared sending into Red River, or that his racism was only slightly suppressed. The Métis leader showed considerably more insight into the situation — and more tolerance — when he eventually remarked, "Had I been your enemy you would have known it before I heard you would not visit me, and although I felt humiliated, I came to see you to show my pacific intention." Then he darted out the door. Butler's subsequent account demonstrated that he had not learned very much truly useful about Riel from the encounter.

While Butler was departing Red River with his "intelligence" to rendezvous with Wolseley, Bishop Taché was back east, writing to Louis Riel from Hamilton that he was satisfied with the appointment of Adams Archibald of Nova Scotia as lieutenant-governor. Taché had suddenly headed back to central Canada in June, announcing his departure from the pulpit on 26 June. Although he did not say so, everyone in the settlement knew that he was worried about the takeover of the settlement. Taché and Archibald met informally with Sir George-Étienne Cartier at Niagara Falls. Taché was still anxious that Archibald arrive ahead of the troops and could enter the settlement under the auspices of the provisional government. Archibald said he intended to be in Red River before the expedition. The letter from Taché to Riel reporting this meeting was found by troops who ransacked Riel's house in late August, and was taken by Canada First as an example of the skulduggery engaged in by Sir George-Étienne Cartier and Taché to "condone Riel's crime." Although Canada First did not know of this correspondence in July, Robert Haliburton had inadvertently stumbled across Cartier, the bishop, and the new lieutenant-governor meeting together at the Falls. The Canada Firsters rightly assumed that some arrangement was being discussed, perhaps to scrap the military expedition entirely. The Canada Firsters hastily organized a hostile demonstration in Toronto to stiffen the backbone of the government. George Denison III and William Foster prepared a series of what Denison himself called "inflammatory placards" that were posted all over the city. They contained slogans such as, "Shall

French rebels rule our Dominion?"; "Orangemen! Is Brother Scott Forgotten Already?"; and "Will the Volunteers accept defeat at the hands of the Minister of Militia?"

What Cartier, Taché, and Archibald had discussed at Niagara Falls, according to the lieutenant-governor's testimony at the parliamentary enquiry of 1874, was the route that he should take into the settlement. The bishop wanted him to go overland from Lake of the Woods. Archibald agreed, so long as he was met at the Northwest Angle by a reception party from all sections of settlement, and not just the Métis as Taché had suggested. Archibald had indeed headed for the Northwest Angle after departing Ottawa on 8 August, but his guides at first had trouble finding it, then failed to find anyone waiting for him. Whether the provisional government ever sent a welcoming party is not known definitely, although it appears that none was dispatched. As a result, Archibald carried on via the Winnipeg River system, well behind the troops. Whether an earlier arrival would have made much difference is doubtful.

Meanwhile, another public meeting was held in Toronto on 22 July, calling on any proposal to recall the military expedition "a death-blow to our national honour." Another resolution called for punishment of the rebels. The next resolution — carried easily but not unanimously — declared that if the government recalled the volunteers, "it will then become the duty of the people of Ontario to organise a scheme of armed emigration in order that those Canadians who have been driven from their homes may be reinstated...and that we may never again see the flag of our ancestors trampled in the duty or a foreign emblem flaunting itself in any part of our broad Dominion." This was Charles Mair's colonization scheme with muscle. The final resolution called for the government "to strive in the infancy of our confederation to build up by every possible means a national sentiment such as will give a common end and aim to our actions; to make Canadians feel that they have a country which can avenge those of her sons who suffer and die for her, and to let our fellow Britons know that a Canadian shall not without protest be branded before the world, as the only subject whose allegiance brings with it no protection, whose patriotism wins no praise." This sort of Upper Canadian jingoism was Canada First's stock in trade. It was hardly a nationalism designed to appeal to everyone in Manitoba, however.

When Colonel Wolseley arrived at Fort Frances on 31 July, he met with a loyal mixed-blood from the settlement who brought letters from Bishop Machray and others about conditions at Red River. He described these accounts as interesting but melancholy. What these correspondents had to be depressed about is not at all clear. There was little evidence of despotism in the settlement, which was functioning more pacifically under provisional law than it would do for several years after the Canadian takeover. Certainly many were eager for the Canadians to arrive. Wolseley's summary of their message, however, was more than simply welcoming. It was, "Come as quickly as you can, for the aspect of affairs is serious and threatening." On 4 August, Butler arrived from the West. Wolseley reported that Butler "described the people as panic stricken — the English and French speaking population being afraid of one another, and both being in the direst dread of Indians." There was some truth about the panic in the settlement, but most of it was caused by uncertainty of the intention of the military expedition.

The intelligence Wolseley received at Fort Frances bore little relationship to what was really happening at Red River. Two factors seemed to be at work here. One was that the army had a vested interest in keeping the notion of resistance alive to justify its pressing forward in full battle readiness. A second factor was that the resident population at Red River was beginning to gear up for the expedition's arrival by employing the familiar tactic of turning on those who were about to be supplanted in power. One of the best ways to cover one's own collaborationism, of course, was by becoming a loud and vindictive loyalist. A lot of this behaviour would surface over the ensuing months.

By 22 August, Wolseley's flotilla was advancing down Lake Winnipeg toward the mouth of the Red River. When they reached it, the boats advanced in three lines, guns at the ready. It was hard to row against the current, and Lower Fort Garry was still a dozen miles away. The expedition reached the lower fort before breakfast the following morning, arriving in time for a huge repast that Donald A. Smith had ordered prepared for the officers. People on both river banks turned out — many of them Kildonan Scots — the men cheering, the women waving handkerchiefs, the bells of the churches all ringing, Indians discharging firearms. This welcome no doubt contributed to a warm feeling among the soldiers, especially the Canadian volunteers, that they were truly a part of a liberating army.

Colonel Wolseley observed in his subsequent account of this arrival: "The union-jack was hoisted by the servants of the Company — an emblem of nationality that none had dared to display for many months." Since that flag had flown — with place of honour above the flag of the provisional government — at Upper Fort Garry since mid-April, Wolseley was obviously badly informed. But it was exactly this sort of inaccurate mindset that would characterize both the arrival of Wolseley's force in Winnipeg itself and the subsequent Canadian occupation of its new province. Colonel Wolseley's orders insisted that he was engaged in "an errand of peace" and that his force should be free from "all sectional feelings." He was not ordered to use the expedition in a punitive manner. But Wolseley had bought into the Canada First view of the uprising, and he was unable to free himself from the view that the provisional government were rebels who deserved punishment, legal or not.

-7-

Her Majesty's Authority

Until the actual arrival of British and Canadian soldiers on 23 August 1870, Louis Riel had expected to hand over power to Lieutenant-Governor Adams G. Archibald, and then to lead his people into the transition to provincial status. It would not have been unreasonable for him to anticipate becoming provincial premier. Certainly, by the summer of 1870 he had eliminated all opposition to his predominance — whether from Canadians, Scottish settlers, mixed-bloods, or Métis — and consolidated his position.

Instead, from the first appearance of Colonel Wolseley, Riel and his lieutenants were on the run. Riel lived under the cloud of possible reprisals more from loyalists than from the long arm of Canadian law. Neither Colonel Wolseley nor Donald A. Smith would issue a warrant for Riel's arrest at the time of the arrival of the troops, although there is some dispute over whether Smith subsequently did issue a warrant. Certainly in 1873 a warrant was taken out for his arrest on the charge of the murder of Thomas Scott, at the same time that Ambroise Lépine was arrested. From late 1870 he was certainly a fugitive from bounty hunters, with a £20 reward for his capture offered by James Farquharson and later with a $5,000 price of his head voted by the legislature of the province of Ontario. The problem, of course, was the failure of Father Ritchot and the provisional government's delegates before the Canadian takeover to obtain an amnesty for Riel and his followers for deeds committed during the rebellion, and then the inability of Bishop Taché and others to convince the Canadian government to provide one later.

Wolseley Arrives

With the British regulars of the Wolseley expedition camped out in the rain a few miles from Upper Fort Garry, Louis Riel summoned his council on the evening of 23 August. Bishop Taché had arrived in the settlement by steamboat that very day, assuring all who met him that the mission of Wolseley was pacific in intention. He was certain that a deal had been worked out with George-Étienne Cartier and Adams G. Archibald, and was thus quite surprised to be told that the troops were coming up the Red River in full battle regalia. Despite Taché's optimism, Riel could now see that he would not be meeting Lieutenant-Governor Archibald for a symbolic transfer of authority from the provisional government to Canada. Playing the script out to its end, however, Riel told the councillors that it was their duty to maintain their positions until the troops took over. None of their men should go anywhere without orders, but he feared that the enemy would attempt assaults upon them.

Riel concluded by asking for four volunteers to accompany him on horseback to the expedition's encampment to reconnoitre the situation. Those who volunteered were Colonel Gay, Baptiste Nault, Francis St. Luc, and Pierre Champagne. They left "armed from head to foot" in a drenching downpour, the night so dark that visibility was almost zero. The horsemen reached the glimmers of the campfires and the sentry lines, scouted around, then turned back, re-entering the upper fort after midnight. Riel took off his wet overcoat and shoes, covered himself with two heavy blankets, and slept for less than an hour. Louis Schmidt was already at work packing up Riel's papers. Why this had not been done earlier is a bit of a mystery; the job was not completed and papers left behind became "incriminating evidence."

About 8 a.m., Riel was served a breakfast of cold meat and tea. Since he was hungry he ate, but because he was cold and tired, the food did not agree with him. He could not even drink his tea. Someone galloped up to the fort on horseback, shouting that Wolseley's troops were less than three miles away, and "you are going to be lynched." Riel ordered the fort evacuated, with himself and W. B. O'Donoghue the last to leave. They left the gates of the fort open behind them and crossed the river to the episcopal palace of Bishop Taché. There Riel explained to a surprised Taché that he had left the fort rather than "run the risk of being killed or murdered." Riel pointed out the obvious as the soldiers could be seen on the other side of the river overrunning the village. The good bishop had been deceived.

The incoming troops were slowed down by the weather on that fateful day, 24 August. The heavy rain made it impossible to march overland to Fort Garry in what Colonel Wolseley described as "all the pride, pomp, and circumstance of war. By daybreak the men were in the boats, rowing in three columns through the drenching downpour toward Upper Fort Garry. As they approached the Anglican cathedral, the Union Jack was run up the steeple and its bells began pealing. At about 8 a.m., at the time that Riel was trying to eat his breakfast, the troops landed on the west bank of the river, near Point Douglas, perhaps two miles from Upper Fort Garry.

Messengers from Winnipeg reported that Riel was still in the fort. The rumours spread that he would resist. "Riel is going to fight!" ran along the line. The troops slogged on through heavy mud, passing to the west of the village of Winnipeg. Skirmishers halted some people in buggies, who turned out to be councillors of the provisional government. They were allowed to continue unmolested. Because of the rain — and perhaps the threat of violence — there were no welcoming crowds from the village. Visibility was poor, but at any moment the troops expected gunfire. To their disappointment, they found the fort gates open and the fort empty. "By God! He's bolted!" was the cry.

"Personally," recorded Colonel Wolseley, "I was glad that Riel did not come out and surrender, as he at one time said he would, for I could not then have hanged him as I might have done had I taken him prisoner when in arms against his sovereign." Was Wolseley, in his obvious bellicosity, acting under orders from the government of Canada? We shall never know.

What followed was anticlimax. Those who entered Riel's house ransacked it from one end to the other, apparently searching for incriminating evidence and doubtless annoyed there would be no fighting. They found several letters from Bishop Taché, which would have to do. They also complained about the dirt and filth in the house. Other troops dragged out some of the cannons in the fort and fired a royal salute of 21 guns as the Union Jack was run up the flagpole. They and a tiny handful of Winnipeg residents, including J. J. Hargrave, gave three cheers for the Queen. According to the bard of the expedition: "No booming gun, no battle cry,/'Tis ended all and peacefully." William Butler went on to write of "that tempest in the teapot, the revolt of Red River," which found a "fitting conclusion in the President's untasted tea." Butler also pronounced an epitaph for Louis Riel when he wrote, "Vain, ignorant, and conceited though he was, he seemed to have been an implicit believer in his mission; nor can it be doubted that he possessed a fair share of courage too — courage not of the Red River type, which is a very peculiar one, but more in accordance with our European ideas of that virtue." Butler might well have been writing about an Ashanti chieftain.

The arrival of the troops was accompanied by a certain legal confusion. Wolseley's scenario had obviously been to enter the settlement — or at least Winnipeg — with guns blazing, beat back the rebellious enemy, and declare martial law. This design had been thwarted when the provisional government had stolen silently away. Sir George-Étienne Cartier's plan had been for Louis Riel, on behalf of the provisional government, to hand over authority to Adams G. Archibald, the incoming lieutenant-governor. This scheme had been thwarted both by the departure of Riel and the absence of Archibald, who would not arrive with civil authority for many more days. Wolseley insisted that there was no reason to proclaim martial law, but added that he had no civil authority to act. In the absence of the lieutenant-governor, the commander of the troops had no orders for governing. The inhabitants asked Wolseley to assume the position of provisional lieutenant-governor, which he refused to do. Wolseley found a legal solution of sorts when he maintained that the Hudson's Bay Company were de jure rulers of the country "until an official communication had been received announcing its transfer to the Dominion." Wolseley therefore recognized the senior officer of the HBC (Donald A. Smith, who had returned to Red River a few days earlier) as governor, "as if there had never been any rebellion whatever, and as if the rule of the Company had continued without a break." Smith reluctantly accepted this appointment, probably quite suspicious of its constitutional implications.

As with most "liberations," the "oppressed" quickly sought vengeance upon their oppressors. Somewhat to his surprise, Wolseley found the main function of his troops to be protecting the rebels from violent reprisals by those loyalists who claimed they had suffered over the previous winter. Keeping the peace would have been accomplished much more easily had the settlement been under martial law. The colonel set armed parties patrolling, but whisky was to be had everywhere, and the entire settlement went on a tear. Wolseley had commanded a teatotal expedition, with no drink except strong tea and weak beer, and the troops were understandably thirsty. According to Captain Butler, "The miserable-looking village produced, as if by magic, more saloons than any city of twice its size in the States could boast of. The vilest compounds of intoxicating liquors were sold indiscriminately to every one, and for a time it seemed as though the place had become a very Pandemonium." The Reverend George Young later reported, "It was most distressing for me to see, on that first night especially, so many of these men — soldiers, voyageurs and Indians — who had abstained from all intoxicants so advantageously to themselves and the entire force, now so crazed with the vile stuff they were buying at very high rates from these abominable rum-shops, as to be actually rolling and fighting in the miry mudholes of Winnipeg." When the volunteers arrived several days later, the streets of Winnipeg were — according to Sam Steele — "littered with bodies of drunken settlers, Indians, and one pet bear on the loose." It was hard to keep the loyalists and the former rebels apart. According to the *Telegraph's* reporter on 3 September, "I do not believe that any village was ever in so short a time so thoroughly demoralized as

Winnipeg, since our arrival — for Riel with all his faults — kept up an excellent police force."

Not everyone in Winnipeg was hostile to Louis Riel. The correspondent from the Montreal *Gazette* reported toward the end of August that the English-speaking inhabitants of Red River "maintain that but for Riel's command over his men, but for his strong personal influence and predilection for Canada and her institutions, the loss of life would, in all probability, have reached hundreds, massacre and assassinations would have done their bloody work, the Canadian expedition would certainly never have reached Fort Garry this year — and the second Lieutenant-Governor and his men would have fared very little better than the first in their attempt to enter the country." This journalist had obviously spoken to a different community than the Toronto correspondents.

On 28 August Wolseley issued an order to his troops, praising them for their performance. The expedition had demonstrated, he said, "that no extent of intervening wilderness, no matter how great may be its difficulties, whether by land or water, can enable men to commit murder or to reel against Her Majesty's authority with impunity." The commander (and his biographers) always treated Red River as another example of a place where rebellious natives had been summarily suppressed by British military might — and right. The Canadian Simon J. Dawson, who had organized the boats and the boat crews for Wolseley, complained bitterly of the commander's self-inflated approach. The rebels had not flown at his approach, like banditti, Dawson observed. "The people were quietly following their usual occupations," Dawson wrote, "and the insurgent leader who had remained in Fort Garry, with some thirty men, went leisurely out as the troops marched in. Peace reigned everywhere...." Moreover, Dawson insisted, the river highway which the troops had traversed had been used over the years by hundreds of men, women, and children, as well as by HBC boats, "some of them the most unwieldy tubs imaginable." It was no great feat to navigate it. While the expeditionary force headed west, Dawson noted, "two frail and poorly manned canoes, the one occupied by a very fat newspaper editor, and the other by a gentleman who had his wife with him, passed over all the rapids, portages and whirlpools of the Winnipeg without its occurring to their occupants that they were doing anything extraordinary."

The Fate of Riel

In the wake of the arrival of the troops, Riel soon headed for the United States, arriving after a difficult three-day journey in St. Joseph's in the Dakotah territory at the house of Father LeFloch.

A messenger sent back to Red River reported that he would remain with LeFloch until "matters are arranged." At this stage, Riel was not clear about the legal situation. Joseph Dubuc wrote in *La Minerve* on 27 August that there was constant talk about "issuing warrants against Riel and his colleagues," adding that the only solution was the arrival of the lieutenant-governor with an amnesty. "If there is no amnesty," warned Dubuc, "No one can foresee how things will turn out." Bishop Taché wrote in early September that the lieutenant-governor had not brought any amnesty with him and counselled patience. Word from Red River indicated that the Canadian volunteers had been abusing the Métis from their first arrival in the new province.

From the Métis perspective, the government's failure to honour its word was contemptible, while from any neutral observer's vantage point, Ottawa's behaviour could be best understood in the context of Machiavelli's "raison d'état." The evidence suggests that the government in face-to-face meetings had certainly led Father Ritchot and Bishop Taché to believe that there would be an amnesty. It is quite possible that these informal guarantees had initially been made in the spring of 1870 in the hopes that Ontario feelings about the execution of Thomas Scott would be soon forgotten. If so, Ottawa had reckoned without the deliberate maintenance of a high level of passion by Canada First, playing as it did upon a bedrock foundation of Orangeist hostility to francophones and Roman Catholics. According to Bishop Taché, Sir John A. Macdonald privately acknowledged the amnesty promise, but insisted, "No Government could stand on that question." In any case, the history of the tangled question of the amnesty is probably the best vehicle for understanding Louis Riel in the period from August of 1870 to 1875.

Bishop Taché and the Early Offers of Amnesty

As will be recalled, the first suggestion of an amnesty for the Red River insurgents had come in a letter from Canadian Governor-General Sir John Young to Hudson's Bay Company and Assiniboia Governor William McTavish on 4 December 1869, advising him that the transfer to Canada had not gone through, that he was still the Queen's representative in Red River, and that the inhabitants should deal with him. Young enclosed a proclamation dated 6 December stating that "certain misguided persons" had banded together to "forcibly, and with violence" prevent Her Majesty's subjects from entering the country. Her Majesty felt that such actions might be the product of misunderstanding, and through the governor-general would redress all well-founded grievances. The governor-general also had the exercise of all powers and authority in the support of order and the suppression of unlawful disturbances. Young assured the residents of Red River that civil and religious rights and privileges would be respected, property would be secured, and the country would be governed under British laws and the spirit of British justice, as in the past. He commanded those in defiance of the law to disperse peaceably and return to their homes. If there was immediate and peaceable obedience and dispersion, no legal proceedings would be taken against "any parties implicated in these unfortunate breaches of the law."

Obviously the parties had not dispersed. Moreover, there was a considerable question over whether the governor-general's letter and proclamation had ever reached their intended destination and had been "proclaimed." Copies of these documents were carried to Red River by the Canadian emissaries Father Jean-Baptiste Thibault and Colonel Charles de Salaberry. The rebels had seized all papers in the possession of these men upon their arrival in the settlement. Canada could not be sure whether anyone in Red River was aware of this proclamation. Ignorance of its existence would imply that those who had confronted Canada had not actually acted in deliberate defiance of the governor-general's authority. When Donald A. Smith finally, on 19 January 1870, met with the people of the settlement, he asked Father Thibault for copies of letters and documents which had been entrusted to him, including those from the government of Canada to Governor McTavish. Louis Riel protested, but the crowd cried, "We will hear it," and cheered. Objections to documents being withheld led the assembly to press for their production. Eventually they appeared, amidst many suspicions that Riel did not want the people to know what Canada had written. Perhaps he did not, although the documents were not very important. Riel had probably expected Canada to take the rebellion seriously but it did not do so. In the end, Riel conceded the point and personally seconded the demand to bring forward the missing material. In the end, however, the proclamation itself was apparently not produced and was never read.

While most of the manoeuvring over the document package that included the proclamation related to the settlement's knowledge of the continuation of authority to the Hudson's Bay Company, Bishop Taché saw the proclamation in a slightly different light. Taché had been shown the proclamation when he visited Ottawa on his way back to Red River from Rome, where he had been electing a pope. When he returned to the settlement on 9 March 1870, he brought what he regarded as two different versions of offers of amnesty. As well as the proclamation of Sir John Young, the bishop had a letter of 16 February 1870 from Prime Minister John A. Macdonald which stated, "If the Company's Government is restored not only will there be a general amnesty granted, but in case the Company should claim the payment for such stores, the Canadian Government will stand between the insurgents and all harm." Taché insisted that he had specifically asked the prime minister whether his promise of amnesty included unknown "blameworthy" acts perhaps not yet committed, and was assured that it did. But nothing of the sort was committed to paper, and in any case the provisional government had not restored the Company's government, although the anglophone mixed-bloods of the settlement had advocated this solution to the problem of legitimacy in November of 1869.

Even if the terms of the letter from Macdonald had not been met in particulars, Taché still felt that the terms of the 1869 proclamation were in the process of being honoured by the Métis. Taché wrote in 1874 of his meeting with the provisional government on 9 March, "I produced His Excellency's proclamation, inviting a delegation and promising an amnesty. I assured the insurgents and their leaders that their just reclamations would be listened to, and I shewed them the signature of our Gracious Sovereign, promising to give order that no legal proceedings would 'be taken against any' of them." The governor-general had not actually "invited" a delegation in so many words, but he had spoken of well-founded grievances and desires being brought to him personally. The bishop seemed to be stretching matters to interpret the selection of delegates as "immediate obedience and dispersion", but according to his own account he "transmitted the pledge of amnesty entrusted to me." When Taché on 9 June wrote to Canadian Secretary of State Joseph Howe that he had promised an amnesty for every breach of the law committed, including the death of Scott, Howe immediately replied that the Canadian government's position was that "the exercise of the prerogative of mercy rested solely with Her Majesty the Queen." It would be exercised upon advice of her Imperial ministers. Thus Howe wanted it clearly understood that "The responsibility of the assurance given by Your Lordship of a complete amnesty, cannot in any way attach itself to the Canadian Government." Moreover, he added, any amnesty would have been based on the governor-general's proclamation of 6 December, which he implied had not been obeyed.

In his summary of the amnesty question in 1875, Governor-General Lord Dufferin examined the Taché claim in some detail, and found it wanting. Taché did not have extensive powers, Dufferin opined, any more than those delegated to Messrs. Thibault, de Salaberry, and Smith. Moreover, "There is certainly no intimation in his instructions that he was authorized to promulgate a pardon in the Queen's name for a capital felony." Dufferin further maintained that the wording of the offer of amnesty of Sir John Young (by 1875 Lord Lisgar) made clear that it referred to "those minor political offences of which news had reached the ears of the Government when the document was framed." The promises conveyed by Sir John A. Macdonald based upon the proclamation could not be expanded "to condone such a savage murder as that of Scott's." Even more critically, said Dufferin, both offers of amnesty were based upon requirements that were not met by the insurgents. Even if Sir George-Étienne Cartier had sent a private letter of reassurance to Taché, "No private communication made by a single member of an Administration without the cognizance of his colleagues, can override an official despatch written in their name and on their behalf by the head of the Department specially responsible for the conduct of the business in hand." After all, concluded Dufferin, "Were such a view to prevail, every Government, and the Crown itself, would be at the mercy of any inconsiderate, rash or treacherous member of a ministry." Taché really had little answer to this analysis, except perhaps to plead inexperience in affairs of state. It is quite possible that the Macdonald government counted on this naiveté. It is also likely that Taché exceeded the authority intended to be given him by the Canadians in his eagerness to resolve the upheaval caused by the uprising.

The Delegates and the Canadian Government in April 1870

If it were possible to dismiss the amnesty promises of Bishop Taché as the misunderstandings of a neophyte negotiator, the claims of Father Noel Ritchot, one of the delegates of the provisional government who negotiated the agreement with the Canadian government in April of 1870, were only at first glance as easy to wave away. As Lord Dufferin noted in 1875, there was nothing in writing, and "so far as regards the individual statements of the personages concerned, there is unhappily a direct conflict of assertion." The question, according to Dufferin, boiled down to whether one believed Ritchot or the government. The problem with this approach, of course, is that it does not explain what happened. The delegates were sent east with instructions not to negotiate with the Canadians if a full amnesty was not the first item of agreement. The delegates did proceed to negotiate, and Ritchot (later backed by Alfred H. Scott) insisted that the government had made the necessary commitment, although never on paper. As Bishop Taché later cogently observed, "Negotiations are not entered upon with people, on the agreement with them, that they will be hanged afterwards.... It is impossible to dissemble that the negotiations spoken of would be unqualifiable and incomprehensible if not connected with, or justified by the amnesty it necessarily implies."

Louis Riel v. Canada

When the Red River delegates arrived in Ottawa, the Canadians set the tone for the discussions to follow by refusing to recognize them as representatives of the provisional government. Canada further constrained the negotiations by openly organizing a military expedition to Red River while talking with the delegates about a peaceful solution. As we have seen, Sir George-Étienne Cartier promised the delegates that their concerns about an amnesty would be looked after in order to negotiate, and the governor-general and the special envoy of the British government had made the further guarantees that were necessary in order to gain the delegates' full acceptance of the Manitoba Act. Nothing was put in writing. We must remember that what was at stake in these negotiations from the perspective of the Canadian government was both half a continent and the manifest destiny of the nation. Not only did the acquisition of the entire territory of the North-West depend on a satisfactory agreement with the delegates from Red River, but by this time the government of British Columbia had sent Canada exploratory messages about Confederation, which the Canadians had to defer until the Red River business had been settled.

Father Ritchot would spend the remainder of his stay in Ottawa attempting to get some written promises about amnesty, and was constantly fobbed off with oral assurances and complicated legal explanations of why nothing could be rendered in writing. At the time of the negotiations, however, the matter of Métis rights had seemed more contentious, and Ritchot devoted more energy to that question. Ritchot might have felt differently about the agreement he thought he had if he had seen the late April report to London of Sir Clifford Murdoch, the special British envoy in Ottawa. Murdoch wrote that many of the clauses of the Red River Bill of Rights were "inadmissable." He added, "The 19th condition [of the provisional government's bill of rights] would secure an indemnity to Riel and his abettors for the execution of Scott, and to all others for the plunder of the Hudson Bay Company's stores, and for other damages committed during the disturbances; concessions which this Government could not venture even if it had the power to grant, while the condition which, though not contained in the terms, was conveyed to Judge Black and the other delegates in writing, that whatever was agreed to here must be subject to confirmation by the Provisional Government, would have involved a recognition of the authority of Riel and his associates…. Under these circumstances there was no choice but to reject these terms."

Murdoch was particularly concerned about the demands for control of Crown lands and for amnesty, but he thought that the Canadian government would manage to meet the British condition that its troops not be employed to force Canadian sovereignty upon the inhabitants of Red River. How this could be done except through misleading the delegates of the provisional government is hard to imagine. Riel, Murdoch added, was expected to leave the territory in advance of the military expedition. This would be the Canadian government's preferred solution to the problem of Red River over the next few years. If Riel went into voluntary exile, all would eventually work out. Ritchot and the delegates thought they needed an agreement with Canada to avoid a hostile military invasion. They did not realize that the British government had insisted as a condition of participation in the expeditionary force that there be no coercion. Macdonald and Cartier needed an agreement with the delegates as badly as they needed one with Canada.

After some desultory moves to obtain a definitive amnesty over the weeks following the meeting with the British officials, Father Ritchot returned to the question on 24 May (the Queen's birthday) in a discussion with J.C. Taché, the bishop's brother and a minor Ottawa civil servant, who was acting as a messenger boy for the government. Taché brought word that Cartier and Sir John Young would agree to a petition to the monarch about the amnesty, although neither wished to be publicly associated with it. Ritchot initially refused to have anything to do with such a petition, but Taché cajoled him into the process by labelling it a charade necessary to avoid compromising the government. Look, said Taché, the government was even drafting the document and only a signature was required. The draft was brought back to Ritchot two days later, written only in his name, acting on behalf of his fellow delegates Black and Scott in response to an invitation of the governor-general to lay before him the wishes of the people of the North-West Territories. Ritchot altered a few sentences and signed the document.

The petition argued that owing to circumstances, the settlement was thrown into confusion and was without a regular government. The formation of "a sort of Provisional Government" was not intended to act in a hostile or insurrectionary manner toward the Queen, but was designed solely to provide for the local wants of the territory. During this period illegal acts had been committed by all parties, "each thinking they were in the right," which if brought before tribunals of justice might perpetuate feelings of vengeance and retard the progress of the new province. Therefore, the petitioners asked remission and forgiveness for "all acts partaken in of an illegal character" committed by anyone in the settlement, observing that they were so encouraged by the governor-general's proclamation of 6 December 1869. Ritchot subsequently had another interview with Cartier, who told him he "should be quiet and not bother [his] head about anything; that the men with whom [he] was dealing knew something about business." Provided one arrived at the right place, the minister claimed, the best route was the one "which would least run counter to the opinions of the people."

At this point Ritchot returned to Red River to explain to the provisional government about the agreement he had reached with Canada, including the amnesty. While he was in transit, on 8 June, a memorandum from Sir George-Étienne Cartier was sent to Lord Dufferin in support of his petition for the amnesty. In order to explain this somewhat "delicate and complicated" question, Cartier rehearsed the entire development of the resistance, employing most of the significant documents available to him. It may have been this memorandum which George Futvoye later testified in 1874 he had helped Cartier prepare. The shooting of Thomas Scott was the obstacle to an amnesty, wrote Cartier. There was no doubt that the execution of Scott was illegal, brutal, and an "act of excessive abuse of power," said Cartier, but he offered a number of points in mitigation. There was much hostility to the Canadians, who had behaved badly and were seen as invaders. The Hudson's Bay Company lacked any power, and the only rule depended on "the will and determination of the settlers themselves." Riel rejected appeals for Scott's life under the "delusive conviction" that he was saving the community from invasion and meeting the feelings of the majority. Cartier referred to the proceedings of an assembly in Toronto which talked of lynching Father Ritchot and Alfred H. Scott as evidence of the way in which the "feelings of the community" can be inflamed. Cartier did not advocate an amnesty which included the death of Thomas Scott, but one which covered all other acts and could be employed as part of the defence in a trial charging that offence.

Cartier then wrote a legal scenario. Riel could be indicted for high treason, levying of war, rebellion against the Crown, and murder, Cartier thought, but only before the ordinary tribunal and under the jury system now prevailing in the new province. The Manitoba Act did not alter the criminal laws and jury system, opined Sir George. Since nobody believed that Riel and his followers should be tried in Canada under the Canada Jurisdictions Act passed during the fur trade wars earlier in the century, it followed that they would be tried at Red River before a jury partly of their own people. They would claim in their defence that they did not levy war against the Queen, but acted "merely to effect the organization of some temporary local government to protect the lives and property of the settlers in the absence of any actual local government organized by Her Majesty, with a view to resist unauthorized invasions and attempts at war against them." The provisional government acted against many provocations according to the habits of the community. The murder of Scott was committed in the name of the *de facto* government to prevent invasion by the Canadians. Responsibility for Scott's death "would lie more on the illegal deeds and several unauthorized invasions of the

Canadians who, by their attempt at waging war against the settlers, provoked the regretted deed."

Since Riel and his colleagues could not be convicted of murder by a Red River jury, or by one in a neutral venue, argued Sir George-Étienne Cartier, it would produce a bad effect to exempt them from any amnesty. Therefore the best policy would be to "grant a general amnesty for any acts amounting to high treason, levying of war, rebellion and treasonable practices during the period mentioned in the petition of Father Ritchot." Such an amnesty would still leave Riel and his colleagues open to a charge of murder, but they could then plead not guilty and adopt as a line of defence that the deed had been perpetrated in the exercise of assumed and usurped political powers for which an amnesty had been granted. Cartier suggested extending the amnesty to those Canadians who participated in "unauthorized" proceedings, and advocated the exclusion of anyone who might resist the Queen's authority when the lieutenant-governor actually entered the province to take up his duties.

On 9 June 1870, Sir John Young forwarded Cartier's elaborate document and Ritchot's petition to Lord Granville in England with a covering note. The note said merely: "This document is entitled to all the consideration due to the writer's long experience and high political standing in British North America, but is not to be regarded as Minute of Council nor as the expression of the opinion of the united Cabinet." It is quite impossible to know whether this recommendation somehow meant that the governor-general was stabbing Cartier in the back by welching on a previous understanding between the two men. Certainly acquiring cabinet approval for any sort of amnesty, given the number of hostile ministers in the government, would have been quite impossible. As late as 1871, Joseph Howe was still arguing that "Murder is murder any where and [Riel's] taking of human life without any paramount necessity and in cold blood, is rarely pardoned without atonement by a civilized community." In any case, "Her Majesty" understandably paid no attention to Ritchot's petition or to Cartier's supporting letter. It was enough to know that an amnesty for the Red River insurgents was not Canadian government policy. The insurgents were, in a sense, trapped by the conventions of responsible government. The Canadians might insist to the Red River delegates that amnesty was the prerogative of the Queen, but the monarch was unlikely to act except upon recommendation of her Canadian ministers. The government was certainly not telling the entire truth when it told the delegates from Red River that an amnesty was the prerogative of the Queen alone, independent of the Canadian government. Sir George-Étienne Cartier's plans that Riel could hand over power to the new lieutenant-governor would prove as futile as his hopes for a petition to the Queen.

Louis Riel v. Canada

The Amnesty Question in the
New Province of Manitoba

Although Riel was a fugitive from justice from Wolseley's arrival, he did not instantly flee the country. Instead, he remained around St. Boniface for some days, and then for some months moved around southern Manitoba and the adjacent United States, occasionally re-emerging in St. Boniface. He made no effort to surrender to the authorities, and the authorities made no effort to try to arrest him. Ottawa, at this moment, did not want to arrest or try Riel, which might inflame Quebec opinion and might result in a court acquittal, which would inflame Ontario. Moreover, according to Lieutenant-Governor Archibald in 1874 testimony before a parliamentary enquiry, "The whole of the French half-breeds and a majority of the English regarded the leaders in these disturbances as patriots and heroes; and any Government which should attempt to treat them as criminals would be obliged to disregard the principles of responsible government." The cat-and-mouse game would continue for several years, with the wild card the reward on Riel's head, which might at any time attract a bounty hunter.

The absence of an amnesty was not a problem only for Riel, but for all the members of his provisional government who were still living in Manitoba. Colonel Wolseley had been ordered to make arrangements for the disposal of his forces over the winter, but was allowed to decide how best to do so. Wolseley chose to return to Canada almost immediately with all his regulars, leaving his raw volunteers, including a large contingent of young Ontarians anxious for vengeance for the death of Thomas Scott, in barracks in Winnipeg. He also decided to locate the Quebec Rifles (with a substantial number of francophones) at Lower Fort Garry amongst the anglophone mixed-bloods, and to place the Ontario Rifles at Upper Fort Garry, with their hostility to French-Canadians, close to the francophone areas of St. Boniface. This decision virtually guaranteed that there would be friction between the Métis and the soldiers. Many of those Métis most closely associated with Riel had joined him in temporary residence around the American border, and others had already begun moving farther west. Whether there was a deliberate "reign of terror" in Winnipeg over the autumn and winter of 1870-71 is difficult to determine, although many observers thought it to be the case. Such violence would not only mean reprisals against the Métis for their earlier behaviour, but would also drive away the possessors of the prime river lots on the Red and Assiniboine rivers. The *Manitoba News-Letter* on 20 September reported from White Horse Plains that "A good many of Riel's 'loyal men' are selling their claims dirt cheap and fleeing from the wrath to come," adding, "Why don't some of the new arrivals come into the locality and buy farms while the 'truly loyal' are scared?"

Lieutenant-Governor Adams G. Archibald was told upon his arrival in an address from the inhabitants of St. Norbert that "An essential feature is still wanting; we, nevertheless, expect it with confidence, seeing that it has been promised to us by men whose words were never spoken in vain." Archibald's position from the start was difficult. He knew perfectly well that commitments had been made, but he also knew that the government would not admit to them while feelings still ran high back home. He initially rationalized this dilemma by reporting to Ottawa that proclamation of an amnesty would not save Riel and his colleagues from the anger of the Ontario volunteers. Archibald also insisted that only a small band of bigoted and racist troublemakers stood in the way of the resumption of "good neighbourhood" among the people of Manitoba. This small minority "really talk and seem to feel as if the French half-breeds should be wiped off the face of the earth," he wrote. A series of incidents confirmed the hostility. Elzéar Goulet, a member of the provisional government and of the court that had sat on the Scott business, was chased by two soldiers and a civilian into the Red River, where he drowned. François Guillemette, who had fired his pistol into Scott's head, was mysteriously murdered near Pembina. Other Riel supporters, like André Nault and Thomas Spence, were severely beaten up.

On 17 September, Lieutenant-Governor Archibald issued a proclamation asserting that all the "faithful subjects" of the province would be protected "in the peaceful possession and enjoyment of their rights and property," adding, "No person or persons shall be allowed to take the law into his or their own hands, or proceed against any of our subjects in any other way than in due course of law." On that same day, a meeting of Métis was held at St. Norbert. Riel was in the chair. The gathering complained of the "perfidious treachery" of the Canadian government, the terrorism in Winnipeg, and agreed to send a petition to the president of the United States calling for his intervention with the Queen to investigate the Métis grievances. W.B. O'Donoghue wanted to go much further by demanding the American annexation of Manitoba. Riel objected, and the two exchanged angry words. O'Donoghue would subsequently carry a revised memorial to Washington, where he met with President Ulysses S. Grant in early January of 1871. The revision asked that the president do the investigation, and requested that the American government either annex Manitoba and the North-West or enable Red River to become independent. Despite the support of certain Minnesota annexationists, O'Donoghue was unable to convince the president that either annexation or independence were supported by a majority of the people. He was told to come back when annexation had more support.

Louis Riel v. Canada

On 18 September, Riel was among those who attended mass at St. Norbert. According to Marc Girard, a recently-arrived French-Canadian who had been appointed provincial treasurer and executive councillor by Archibald, Riel asked him on this occasion whether he was included in the recent proclamation. Girard answered yes, but advised Riel in the short run to leave the country because the military could not be counted on to enforce the peace. Archibald subsequently organized a mounted police force, a number of which were Métis, to keep maintain law and order, but this did not apparently offer any solace to Riel. Joseph Royal later testified that he had returned from Manitoba to Montreal at the end of September 1870, to be quizzed by Cartier about public sentiment. Cartier told Royal to inform Riel that "L'amnestie est une affaire décidé, c'est une affaire faite." Cartier then added, "Tell Riel also, to go away from the country for five or six years, so as to let the excitement pass away."

The excitement was not likely to pass away so long as the Ontarians continued to agitate about Thomas Scott. On 5 September a meeting of the "comrades and loyal friends of the late Thomas Scott, who was so barbarously murdered outside the walls of Fort Garry," was held. It determined to ask Donald A. Smith for Scott's remains, in order to provide a Christian burial. Smith declined to act, but the Reverend George Young would continue to press on this matter until he and others were finally allowed to exhume the grave in the courtyard of Upper Fort Garry in mid-October. Young's party found the top of the box about six feet underground, but when it was opened it was full of earth and shavings, with no body. The Ontarians were thus unable to mount a funeral which would undoubtedly have further stoked the flames of tension in the province.

In early November Sir John A. Macdonald wrote Archibald that the "public mind" in Ontario was still sensitive, especially about the "murder" of Thomas Scott. "Were it not for that unhappy event," he opined, "all parties would, I think, acquiese in the propriety of letting bygones be bygones, and an amnesty for the political offences would not be seriously objected to." Macdonald presumed in advance, of course, that the execution of Scott was not a political act, a quite different presumption than that of his old friend Sir George-Étienne Cartier. The prime minister liked Archibald's policy of accepting all the old rebels except Scott's executioners, and obviously shared with Cartier the hope that Riel and company would "submit to a voluntary exile." Cartier, of course, wanted Riel to pursue the strategy which Cartier himself (and others) had employed in the wake of the abortive rebellion of 1837. Exile without any actual criminal action being taken would eventually lead to public rehabilitation. This strategy had worked not only for Cartier, but for William Lyon

Mackenzie and Louis-Joseph Papineau, both of whom had eventually ended up back in the Canadian Parliament. The Canadian government did not ever have to produce a general amnesty *per se*, although many viewed the Rebellion Losses Bill of 1849 as a symbolic recognition of forgiveness.

The trouble with the Rebellion of 1837 model as an example of a course of behaviour for Louis Riel and his leading associates was that it did not really fit the situation of 1870. The insurgents of 1837 had actually rebelled against a government in power, behaviour that would be difficult to affix to the Red River situation. But more to the point, the earlier insurgents were never associated with particular criminal offences such as murder. To pursue the Cartier scenario into the 1870s, eventually memories would fade, but then what would happen? Even if the Red River rebels were simply quietly allowed to be ultimately rehabilitated without an amnesty, as had happened after 1837, the Scott death would still remain over the head of Riel and those associated with the Scott trial and execution. Any interested citizen could at anytime swear out a warrant for murder, and the justice system would be set in motion, as occurred in 1873 and 1874 with Ambroise Lépine and André Nault. Alternatively, when emotions had quietened down, the government could have issued a general amnesty which included Riel and associates like Lépine. But the Canadian government — including Sir George-Étienne Cartier — consistently argued throughout the entire affair that murder was not a crime that could ever be amnestied. From Riel's point of view, the best solution was probably not to wait for an eventual amnesty that might never come, but to follow instead the line of reasoning that Sir George-Étienne Cartier had advanced in June of 1870. Scott had been brutally killed, but no jury representative of Red River was likely to convict because of the mitigating circumstances. Had Riel stood trial and been acquitted in 1870, the government was off the hook, except for a responsibility to ensure that the Ontario racists were not allowed to make more trouble after the fact. Had Riel been convicted, as Lépine would be in 1874, such a conviction would merely force some sort of government resolution of the whole nasty problem. It may have been in the Canadian government's best interest not to try Louis Riel for the murder of Thomas Scott, but it was not in Louis Riel's best interest, whatever the politicians might say. There is no evidence that anyone ever gave Riel this advice. Certainly neither Bishop Taché nor Adams G. Archibald did.

Lieutenant-Governor Archibald wrote to Sir John A. Macdonald at the time of the elections to the first legislature in Manitoba: "I have striven to create the impression that if Riel wishes to shew himself a statesman, that the Good of his country is his governing motive and not pay and place, he has the opportunity to prove this now — and that his staying away from the country and taking no part in its politics at the first election will do more to give him that character than any exertions he could make within the country for the next ten years." In this letter, Archibald noted that Riel's public appearance would make it difficult "to restrain the passions of the people who suffered last year and who look upon these men as the authors of their wrongs." Riel went along with those who wanted him to keep a low profile in late 1870, when he refused many invitations to run in the elections, including one from a number of influential people in St. Vital. Those elections returned a number of members who had been associated with the rebellion and the provisional governments, who had run as men who had a "stake in the country." Most were favourably disposed to Riel and to a general amnesty, not least of all for themselves.

It is tempting to see some deliberate government policy in the generation of the conditions which seemingly made it absolutely necessary that Louis Riel not become involved in the politics of the province. Riel was, after all, the acknowledged leader of his people, who were clearly to be involved in a series of difficult situations as the transition from settlement to province were worked out. The Métis had done their best to protect their interests through their resistance or rebellion, and subsequently through the negotiations over the Manitoba Act. But everyone knew perfectly well that working out the Manitoba Act in practice was the important part. The Canadian government would argue, in effect, that Riel had disqualified himself from leading his people into the new era by his behaviour in the Scott affair. The legitimacy of that behaviour was certainly questionable. But all questions about that behaviour could have been overcome by either the declaration of a general amnesty or by a pardon. Such action would no more have redefined the past than the decision of the Canadian government to ask the imperial parliament to overcome the discrepancies between the Manitoba Act and the British North America Act by passing an imperial statute of validation. The Canadian government would have insisted that amnestying or pardoning Riel would have drawn the wrath of Ontario. But one might have thought that real statesmen would have bitten the bullet, rather than insisting that Riel alone had to exhibit statesmanlike qualities by hiding away. It cannot be proved that the Canadians deliberately forced Riel into hiding, although their policies certainly did. But his impotence at this time was certainly convenient, particularly given the problems over the constitutionality of the Manitoba Act itself.

When the results of the election were made public, about 100 Ontario volunteers rioted in the streets, breaking windows, invading a saloon to get liquor, and generally intimidating passersby. According to one correspondent in *Le Nouveau Monde*, the rioters had run through the streets crying "Death to the Pope! Death to Catholics! Death to the half-breeds!

Death to the priests!" The police had eventually suppressed the rioters, but the battalion took no disciplinary action against them. If this incident suggested that the soldiers who were supposed to be preserving the peace in the province were actually the very people who were the biggest threat to concord, further confirmation of such a suggestion was provided by another incident in mid-February of 1871. A large collection of volunteers forcibly freed one of their number from the police station, where he was being held on a gambling charge. In the ensuing effort of their officers to bring the rioters under control at Upper Fort Garry, a shot was fired which seriously wounded a soldier. There was little doubt that the officers had been unable to enforce discipline, and many called the affair a "mutiny."

Joseph Royal complained to the lieutenant-governor, asking "what protection can we hope for from a government whose soldiers are the first to make fun of the law and its authority?" The American consul, in his report on this affair, noted rumours that the Ontario troops were planning to expel the lieutenant-governor. He opined that Archibald might well find it necessary to "rely almost exclusively upon the supporters of the Provisional Government of last winter." Perhaps the fiercest condemnation of the activities of the soldiers would come not from newspapers in French Canada, but from *The Volunteer Review*, a journal devoted to Canadian military affairs. In a March 1871 editorial, the magazine pointed out that the Fort Garry incident had embodied the worst iniquity that could happen to a country, by putting its constitutional government at the mercy of its soldiers. *The Volunteer Review* blamed those who had incited the lawlessness, and those who defended them in the newspapers.

By the time of the "mutiny," Manitobans were aware that the Canadian government planned to disband the volunteers in May. In the wake of the Upper Fort Garry affair, a movement began to oppose the "recall" of the troops. The resolutions presented to the various meetings held on this question insisted that the real issue was "That the rebels of last winter have gained confidence from the fact that they remained unpunished — that warrants are refused for their apprehension — by the fact of the appointment of their chiefs and sympathizers to office and places of trust — and from their belief, openly expressed, of help to be afforded them from the Fenian element in the United States." The first anniversary of the death of Thomas Scott passed without serious incident, although "pictures of the murdering" were sold at the fort. These "pictures" were probably mass-produced copies of the drawing of the execution which had appeared in the *Canadian Illustrated News* on 23 April 1870. This drawing, which has become standard Canadian iconography, showed Riel himself administering the *coup de grace* with a pistol to a helpless Scott. In this illustration, Riel stands between the prone body of Scott and a hole in the ground, a coffin-like box behind him. A large crowd of onlookers are present, but about 50 feet away and clearly not connected with Riel, who alone is responsible for the deed. If this was the visual image Ontarians had of the death of Scott, it was small wonder that feelings ran so strongly against Riel.

As for Riel, he played no part in any of the events in Manitoba of this period. In February of 1871 he fell seriously ill in St. Joseph and was nursed again for several weeks by his mother. Some biographers are tempted to see portents of mental instability in what appears to be a physical ailment. We do have some clinical symptoms. Riel's temperature soared, and the joints of his arms and legs became swollen, red and painful. He may have become depressed, not unusual with such an illness. He may even have been concerned about assassination, but he was officially a fugitive on the run with a price on his head and men around him with instructions to kill him. It is hard to be paranoid when your enemies really are out to get you. George Stanley suggests that Riel's illness is somehow connected with hardships and fears of assassination, the strains and stresses of an uncertain future, the delays in the promulgation of the amnesty "until he could no longer bear the double burden of anxiety and misfortune. In February he fell ill, seriously ill." Stanley does not connect these two sentences, but their juxtaposition suggests a relationship. A germ or a virus is a more likely cause than emotional instability for this illness, however. In any event, Riel was weak for several months. When he got better, he decided to return to his home, and by early May he was back in his mother's house in St. Vital, entertaining visitors despite the risks of appearing publicly.

Bishop Taché returned to the amnesty in a letter to Cartier on 6 May 1871, just after Riel had returned to the province. Everyone had up to now been patient, said the bishop. But he found distressing various statements in parliament that assumed the courts of Manitoba had jurisdiction over the fugitives for actions committed by them before Canada had any official power in the region. This question of jurisdiction was a complicated one, and Taché's assumptions were not necessarily valid. Taché now began a double tactic that he would pursue for some years. First, he threatened to speak publicly about the promises that had been made to him. Secondly, he set the subsequent violence perpetrated by the soldiers against the actions of those "who, in order to protect themselves, had the misfortune to make one victim, the unfortunate Scott." The bishop's letter had no visible immediate effect.

At this point, the ongoing confrontation between the Métis and the Ontarians shifted from Winnipeg, where soldiers had fought with civilians, to the countryside, where new settlers confronted the old resi-

dents over the possession of land. In the spring of 1871, a number of settlers from Ontario had arrived in Manitoba expecting land to be available
for them. At least some of these arrivals had been sponsored by the
North-West Emigration Aid Society organized by Charles Mair. For a
variety of reasons, some dating back to the autumn of 1869, the surveys
in Manitoba upon which land granting was to be based were not completed. Recognizing the problem, the Canadian government had decided
on a temporary arrangement embodied in a memorandum dated 26 May
1871. This document stated that parties settled on land when the surveys
were finally made, "having settled upon and improved the same in good
faith as settlers under the land regulations" would be confirmed in possession under either pre-emption or homestead right. The newcomers
were obliged to settle in terms of the style of the survey to be adopted,
where the lines ran east-west and each quarter section was a half-mile
square. This temporary policy, of course, legitimized "squatting."

The immediate site of the conflict was the Riviére aux Ilets de Bois,
not far from the modern town of Carman, and now known as the Boyne
River (after the river in northern Ireland). The land along this river had
been used for many years by the Métis for pasturage and refuge from
floods, although they had not actually built homes there. Extremely
attractive land, incoming Ontarians had begun settling at Riviére aux
Ilets de Bois, probably advised to do so by people in Winnipeg. As the
new settlers began arriving in the province, the Métis had responded by
insisting that they be allowed to specify their 1,400,000 acre entitlement
in certain blocks, which would be closed to the newcomers. One of those
blocks would be at Riviére aux Ilets de Bois. As Lieutenant-Governor
Archibald pointed out in a letter to Ottawa in June, the Métis insisted that
they were to have first choice of lands, a claim founded not only on the
Manitoba Act but on a guarantee of Sir George-Étienne Cartier in his letter to Father Ritchot of 23 May 1870. He had received a letter from five
mixed-blood parishes, four of them francophone, raising the question.
The new arrivals from Ontario did not take the same view of the situation as the Métis. Nonetheless, Archibald had published an answering
letter in the *Manitoban* newspaper, which said that he would allow any
parish of "half-breeds" to choose a locality for their grant and support
their choice.

The confrontation was now set in motion. In the late spring of 1871,
a number of Ontario immigrants, including some disbanded volunteers,
established themselves at Riviére aux Ilets de Bois, knowing full well that
the Métis claimed it. According to Lieutenant-Governor Archibald, the
newcomers staked the ground, put up huts, and "declared they would
hold it against all comers." To make matters worse, they renamed the
river "the Boyne," thus invoking the spirit of Orangeism and angering

the Métis, who began organizing to drive off the new arrivals by force, if necessary. Archibald managed to intervene and warn the Métis "if they lifted a hand or struck a blow it was all over with them." The Métis backed down, and Archibald had demolished his own policy. What was being played out in miniature, of course, was exactly the scenario that had prompted the Métis to rise against Canada in 1869.

As matters turned out, Archibald's policy of permitting blocks or tracts of land to be reserved in advance by the Métis was countermanded by the government in Ottawa. Canada took the position that all lands not in actual occupation were open to everyone, but only after they had been properly surveyed. Joe Howe, secretary of state for the provinces, wrote a sharp letter to Archibald in November of 1871 that in terms of land policy, "Your answer to everybody is ['] I have nothing to do in the matter.' This is the view I take, and I would, if I were you leave the Land Department and the Dominion Government to carry out their policy without volunteering any interference." Such a statement was, of course, a logical concomitant of the dominion's insistence on its complete control of the land in the province. To allow the lieutenant-governor to make policy would be as bad as allowing the local legislature to do so. One might wish that in the process of asserting their control of the land, the Canadians had honoured the commitments they had made to the Métis in order to gain control of it in the first place. Joseph Howe certainly spelled out the government's policy plainly enough. The Canadian government would decide on the allocation and distribution of land to the Métis, but until this was done emigrants and volunteers had the right "to occupy and preempt vacant lands anywhere." Moreover, the allocation of land to the Métis would not be by blocks but by individual quarter sections. While all this manoeuvring was going on, of course, the Métis themselves were able to read the handwriting on the wall. Manitoba was to be for the Canadians, not for the Métis. Increasing numbers began to pack up and move further west. While his people were getting pushed around, where was Louis Riel? Father F.X. Kavanagh wrote in August from the White Horse Plains about "our phantom," the "stupid spectator of the violation of the rights of the Métis, who ought to be defending themselves, but who were, in effect, letting their enemies increase in number and in arrogance." Riel was in St. Vital, of course, still being "statesmanlike" by keeping out of politics.

At about the same time that the affair at Riviére aux Ilets de Bois was gathering momentum, W.B. O'Donoghue — having failed to convince the American president to support the annexation of Manitoba — was in New York trying to convince the Council of the Fenian Brotherhood to give its support to the Manitoba Métis. The Fenians were an organization of ex-Irishmen who had played an important, if inadvertent, role in the achievement of Canadian Confederation. As the troops from the American Civil War were demobilized, they were allowed to keep their arms. Many of the Irish among the soldiers joined the Fenian Brotherhood, which hoped to invade parts of British North America and hold them hostage for the independence of Ireland. The Fenians had been turned back in 1866 after a few minor border skirmishes. A number of leaders had been arrested and imprisoned, and the Brotherhood had retreated from active interventionism until there was more opportunity of success. O'Donoghue did succeed in gaining the support of General John O'Neill, a militant recently released from prison. O'Neill offered to resign from the council and not use Fenian resources in any western adventurism. In turn, the council agreed not to denounce a western raid. O'Neill and O'Donoghue knew that they could count on recruiting a military force of disbanded Irish veterans who would be laid off from railroad construction on the Northern Pacific Railway as the building season came to an end. The force would be led by experienced Fenian officers, including O'Neill, General J. J. Donnelly, and Colonel Thomas Curley, who still believed in the cause. The plotters also thought that if an invading force appeared in Manitoba, they could rely on the support of at least some of the Métis of the province, who were extremely unhappy about their treatment by the Canadian government. An agreement was signed among the conspirators to deliver the people of Manitoba from Canadian rule and establish a republican form of government, with W.B. O'Donoghue as president.

By the early autumn of 1871, the government in Manitoba was well aware of the Fenian plans. O'Donoghue and O'Neill were holding public meetings in St. Paul, one of which attended by Father Ritchot. Several Fenians visited Ritchot at his hotel, to be told that they would be resisted if they tried anything. Ritchot's report added substance to the rumours, and Lieutenant-Governor Archibald responded with expressions of serious concern for the safety of the province. It was true that he had virtually no military force at his disposal except a handful of policemen. It was also true that — as he pointed out to the prime minister — the Métis were extremely unhappy. Moreover, the head of the Canadian government's own Dominion Police (who was among other things the head of Canadian counter-intelligence) had been dispatched to Manitoba with inside information on the conspiracy, which suggested it did not have as yet large numbers but had to be taken as a real threat. But Archibald also knew that the Americans had full knowledge of the possibility of a Fenian attack, and were prepared to intervene if necessary. Archibald had even assured the Americans that there would be no objection to American troops crossing the border to deal with the situation.

At the same time, Archibald had to try to demonstrate to the Canadian government that its policy toward the Métis, especially its land policy, must be liberalized. The Fenian problem gave Archibald a chance to drive home the discontent of the Métis. The second issue was to be able to demonstrate to Ottawa that, despite their unhappiness, the Métis were still loyal to Canada. In this respect, a bonus might be an opportunity for Louis Riel to prove both his fealty and his ability to lead his people constructively.

Riel met with a number of his old associates from the provisional government on 28 September 1871. He was not in the chair but was one of the joint secretaries. He submitted five questions to the meeting. We cannot be certain of whether Riel knew the answers he wanted the meeting to give, or whether he was genuinely seeking advice. The latter is more likely than the former. The group began by discussing the question of whether the government was honouring its pledges to the Métis, and of course answered no. There was no general amnesty in view nor any sign of a land distribution. The next question was whether there were reasons for expecting them to be fulfilled in the future. The meeting deferred an answer on this point, arguing that a more definitive judgment "might exercise a wrong influence on the Métis." This was a position certainly more generous to Canada than it deserved. On the questions of whether O'Donoghue was coming and what would he do — the meeting concluded that the American was planning to attack the province. The final question, what should be done with regard to O'Donoghue and with regard to Canada, obviously provoked a lengthy discussion. The group concluded that they should reject any overtures from O'Donoghue, and attempt to bring the Métis to support the Manitoba Act and do no more than request loyally the fulfillment of the government's promises to them. Riel's minutes of the meeting do not record any of the actual debate. The group agreed that there would be frequent meetings, which could be called by any three members or even by a single member who had been contacted by O'Donoghue. That many of the natural leaders of the Métis should in 1871 be meeting privately — critics might even say conspiring privately — to deal with the impending Fenian crisis was one more of the inevitable consequences of the Canadian policy of refusing to provide closure for the chief members of the provisional government in 1869-70. On 2 October a messenger arrived from W.B. O'Donoghue inviting a number of Métis leaders, including Riel, to a meeting near Pembina.

Lieutenant-Governor Archibald consulted on 3 October with Gilbert McMicken, who had just arrived in Winnipeg. McMicken was taking the threat of invasion seriously, having heard in the United States that General O'Neill had 150 Springfield rifles and nearly 50 men. Archibald pointed out that he had no militia organization and that he had no idea what the Métis would do in the event of a Fenian invasion. Fathers

Ritchot and Dugas, with whom he had consulted, insisted that Louis Riel would not act unless there was an amnesty, more than a bit of an exaggeration. McMicken recommended a proclamation calling for loyal men to present themselves to defend the province, which would at least rally the "Ontario people" around the flag and the Queen. Gilbert McMicken reported to the prime minister on 4 October that the "English settlers" were indeed offering their services. Perhaps as many as 1,000 were available. In a private conversation that same day, Father Ritchot informed Archibald that the Métis, led by Louis Riel, would not only remain loyal but were prepared to repel the Fenians at the border. Archibald readily agreed to this support. Ritchot, in 1874 testimony to a parliamentary enquiry, said that he had pointed out Riel's difficult position if he appeared in public. Archibald had responded that this was a good time for Riel to demonstrate his loyalty. Ritchot said he would speak to Riel. On that same day, a meeting of the Métis leaders learned that most of their number had not responded to O'Donoghue's invitation, but that Baptiste Lépine and André Nault had gone to Pembina.

On 5 October, Father Ritchot wrote to the lieutenant-governor that Riel felt he could not expose himself publicly without some "assurance which will shelter him from any legal proceeding at least for the present." Archibald replied, testified Ritchot in 1874, by writing that Riel "need be under no apprehension that his liberty shall be interfered with in any way," adding that any co-operation from the Métis "cannot be looked upon otherwise than as entitling them to most favourable consideration." By this time O'Donoghue's force, reportedly 70 strong including 25 American mixed-bloods, had seized the Hudson's Bay Company post at North Pembina. By 6 October, the Manitoba authorities had managed to put a military force of 200 men en route for the border. The weather was wet and the irregulars had to struggle through heavy muck on their journey. Before they could arrive at Pembina, the American authorities had reacted. The arrival of a contingent of soldiers from Fort Pembina scattered the Fenians, but only a handful — including the leading officers and O'Donoghue — were captured. The prisoners were charged on 6 October with violations of section 6 of the 1818 Neutrality Laws of the United States, which defined as a criminal act any attempt "to retain another person to go beyond the limits of the United States with the intention to be enlisted into the service of either belligerent." Thanks to quick action by Enos Stutsman for the defence, the prisoners were all released within two days on legal technicalities. But Lieutenant-Governor Archibald was able to recall his men short of the border.

While the drama was being played out to the south, the Métis had organized militarily. The Métis leaders had met in St. Vital on the evening of 6 October. André Beauchemin, a member of the provincial legislature, was in the chair. Charles Nolin, who had been one of Riel's chief critics in 1870, was secretary. The chairman offered the meeting three alternatives: O'Donoghue, neutrality, or support for the government. The meeting, in a rare show of Métis unanimity and support for Louis Riel, declared "it is the wish that what Riel shall say shall govern." For his part, Riel observed that he feared divisions among his compatriots and the people. "I therefore pray you to unite, and since you show me such a great confidence, believe me, I am not changed. Do not side with injustice; but let us support unanimously the following motion: That it is just to make known to His Excellency the Lieutenant-Governor of Manitoba that the present meeting avails itself of the circumstances in which the country finds itself to affirm its attachment to the constitution which governs us." Seconded by Charles Nolin, the vote was unanimous. The following afternoon, at a further meeting at the house of André Nault in St. Vital, the "militia captains" of seven Métis parishes — Prairie de Cheval, St. Boniface, Pointe du Chênes, Ste. Agathe, Pointe Coupée, St. Norbert, and St. Vital — met to declare their support for the government. Some of these men had previously shown little enthusiasm for the government cause. Those leading the parish military organizations were the same men who had constituted the provisional government in 1869-70. Subsequent meetings were held at St. Boniface, St. Norbert, St. Agathe, White Horse Plains, and Pointe Coupée to indicate support for the government. By 7 October, Riel was able to write Archibald that the Métis were organizing militarily. "Your Excellency may rest assured that, without being enthusiastic, we have been devoted." The lieutenant-governor responded to indicate his gratitude.

Although the immediate crisis was over and while the Manitoba militia was marching back to Winnipeg, the lieutenant-governor was invited on 8 October to cross the Red River to Saint Boniface to review about 500 loyal Métis who were under arms. When Archibald appeared, the Métis fired a "feu de joie," which was observed by a crowd of Winnipeggers who had gathered on the west bank of the Red. Provincial treasurer Marc Girard introduced the lieutenant-governor to Louis Riel, whom he said was the individual "chosen as their chief for the occasion." The two men shook hands. Archibald also shook hands with Ambroise Lépine and Pierre Parenteau, who were introduced by name by Joseph Dubuc. Riel then made a short speech, declaring that "he was there with his friends to offer their services in defence of their country against all enemies." He asked Archibald to accept their services. The lieutenant-governor replied with thanks.

In this impromptu ceremony of about 15 minutes duration on the banks of the Red River, a symbolic reconciliation between the government of Manitoba and the province's Métis ought to have been achieved.

It was not. The problem was simple. When Archibald returned to Upper Fort Garry, his aide-de-camp ordered the barracks set up for occupation. Two of the officers of anglophone military units, Lieutenant E.H.G.G. Hay of St. Andrews and Captain Newcomb of Poplar Point, immediately informed the lieutenant-governor that if the barracks were being prepared to accommodate the men just reviewed, they and their men would immediately lay down their arms. These officers certainly suggested that the anglophones were not yet ready for reconciliation. Further evidence on this point was soon provided. When the military force sent to Pembina returned on 10 October, they quickly learned of the Métis response. According to Charles Napier Bell, writing years later, "a courier rode in and stated that French half-breeds in considerable numbers had ridden north on the east side of the river and were apparently making preparations to cross the Red River into the village of Winnipeg. The English-speaking soldiers clamoured to be led back to Winnipeg as they were much more suspicious and afraid of the French half-breeds than of the contemptible little Fenian force." Some of these men had been prisoners of Riel in 1869 and 1870, and more than 40 were recently arrived volunteers.

A day later, on 11 October, the Manitoba *Liberal* printed an editorial entitled "The Last Straw." It described Archibald's actions on 8 October as "the greatest blunder he ever did since he came here," and further characterized the whole occasion as "a trick on the part of the Riel faction to get pardoned". The *Liberal* returned to this theme in its next issue on 18 October. Here it raised all the bloody rags of the old hatreds. The place Archibald had met Riel was described as "within a gunshot of the spot where Thomas Scott was murdered," and "the Queen's representative shook hands with the murderer." Riel and his lieutenants were further labelled "the same who fled at the approach of the troops last year, and whom the gallant Wolseley characterized as banditti." The newspaper demanded Archibald's immediate recall. When "The Last Straw" was published in the *Globe* on 25 October, the Orange Lodges of the province responded with calls for action against Archibald.

The Canadian government itself soon reacted to Archibald's symbolic gesture. Joseph Howe was given the responsibility of educating Manitoba's lieutenant-governor on the realities of life. No amnesty had been promised, wrote Howe. Or at least, an amnesty "was never asked in any formal shape, and if it had it most certainly would have been refused by this government." Canada's secretary of state for the provinces acknowledged that most Quebec MPs might favour an amnesty, but added, "at no time, particularly after the murder of Scott, could this Government have entered upon such a step without throwing into opposition every supporter they have from Ontario." He continued by observing that the Macdonald government depended on the Orange Order for support. According to Howe's scenario, O'Donoghue was Riel's friend. He invaded the province, while Riel maintained a position of neutrality until word came that the invasion had failed. Only then did Riel declare his loyalty. All this would have been funny had Archibald simply ignored it. But for him to shake hands with Riel had endangered the government in Parliament and in the upcoming election.

It may well be that Archibald had attempted to use the Fenian business to produce a reconciliation in Manitoba. Certainly one was desperately needed. As he himself subsequently pointed out to Howe, there could be no responsible government in a province in which half the members of the legislature "were liable to be hanged or sent to the penitentiary." Not long after receiving Howe's lecture on political realities, Adams G. Archibald would resign as Lieutenant-Governor of Manitoba, observing in explanation to Governor-General Sir John Young that the "Ontario Policy" (the capitals were his) seemed to prefer "the punishment of past offences" to "the preservation of public peace."

As for Louis Riel, there was no amnesty, nor was there any chance of one from a Canadian government that felt it depended upon Orangeist support in Ontario for its very survival.

-8-

Amnesty Redux

The Fenian affair and its aftermath marked one period in the history of the efforts to obtain an amnesty for the Red River rebels. The press of events (and perhaps the taking some advantage of them by Sir Adams G. Archibald and Louis Riel) eventually had produced a wonderfully symbolic ceremony of reconciliation on the banks of the Red River, close to the main buildings of Métis Catholicism in Manitoba. Unfortunately, the reconciliation was only between the Manitoba government and the Métis. Ontario, the Orangemen, and a Canadian government that regarded itself as dependent on the Orange vote, chose not to take advantage of the opportunity. The main result of the ceremony was to press Ontario into fresh paroxysms of hatred, with Thomas Scott's death again resurrected as the centrepiece of the reaction. Instead of enabling the disagreements to be healed, the Fenian business had simply heightened them. Evidently there could be no amnesty under these conditions.

Government-sponsored Exile

Not surprisingly, the Fenian affair produced a subsequent fresh attempt by Cartier to get the Métis leader to accept voluntary exile. On Bishop Taché's visit to Montreal at the time of the Fenian crisis, he told Cartier that Riel could not leave his impoverished family. Sir George responded, "That is true. We will see about that." The two men agreed to settle the matter in Ottawa in December. Meanwhile, Lieutenant-Governor Archibald continued to maintain that Riel, Lépine, and O'Donoghue were "practically amnestied" but still could not appear in the settlement for fear of provoking "outrage." As if to prove his point, a band of masked men on 8 December 1871 broke into the home of Riel's mother in St. Vital, claiming they had a warrant for Riel's arrest. They searched the house and roughed up the family. That the intruders were masked says a good deal about their intentions.

Meanwhile, Bishop Taché and the prime minister had met in Ottawa about Riel. If Taché would advise Riel to leave the country, said Sir John A., "I will make his case mine, and I will carry the point." Taché promised to try to get Riel out of the settlement, and the two men agreed that the government would provide some compensation. On 27 December, Macdonald provided Taché with a sight draft on the Bank of Montreal for $1,000 for "the individual we have talked about." He instructed that the money was to be paid periodically rather than in a lump sum, and must last a year. After leaving Montreal in January of 1872, Taché received en route to Sarnia a letter from Cartier saying that Ambroise Lépine should also depart and that the money should be divided. When he returned to St. Boniface, the bishop spoke to both men. Lépine refused, on the grounds that he would not assist Ottawa to resolve its difficulties. For his part, Riel responded, "You know my disposition; I am sure I am killing myself in the estimation of my friends if I do leave, because they would say that I have been bought, and I am not in the market." Riel and Lépine were both in a difficult position, however. They were unable to support their families because they were still fugitives from justice, liable to seizure if they were to appear publicly. Thus both men subsequently agreed to leave, on the conditions that Taché provide them with a letter saying he had requested them to go, and that enough money was provided to look after their families in their absence.

Riel refused to accept any money from Taché. He insisted that the funds had to come from the Canadian government, adding that he and Lépine would "consider that we are going away on their behalf, and we would consider ourselves as under pay in their service." The two men requested $1,000 each, plus eight to 10 pounds sterling every month for their families. Taché objected to this amount as excessive. Riel responded acerbically that they knew that those on Canada's official business did not travel cheaply. In the end, Bishop Taché had to go to Lieutenant-Governor Archibald for financial assistance. Archibald himself had no funds available, and so he called upon Donald A. Smith (as representative of the HBC acting as bankers for the province) to furnish the money, on the understanding that it would eventually be reimbursed by Ottawa. Smith obliged, and the bishop gave Riel and Lépine $1,600 each, holding $1,000 back for their families. Although Sir John Macdonald and Sir George-Étienne Cartier acknowledged Smith's advance, it was never repaid, partly because the government went out of office over the Pacific Scandal, partly because Ottawa felt that Riel and Lépine had not fulfilled their end of the bargain. The Métis leaders were supposed to stay away until after the next round of elections, Archibald insisting that they not "hover on the frontier" and certainly ought not to stand for Parliament. The lieutenant-governor thought France the ideal place for exile, but Taché said there was not enough money.

The government had some reason in early 1872 for thinking that Louis Riel and Ambroise Lépine had been dealt with, at least for the next year or so. The two men left the province in February "for the good of the people," with two policemen escorting them to the border. Many regarded this solution as an acceptable one, since at this point the Archibald could not have arrested Riel and Lépine without provoking a civil war. But as Archibald had already written to Joseph Howe on 20 January, the question of the amnesty really transcended these two individuals. He complained that many members of the legislature and those who elected them still functioned "with ropes around their necks" because there had been no general pardon declared for the insurgents of 1869-70. Archibald exposed the ludicrous consequence of the absence, pointing out that his responsible ministry rested upon a majority in a House "of whose constituents more than half were liable to be hanged or sent to the penitentiary." Part of the problem, as Archibald subsequently noted in correspondence with Cartier, was that various Ontario bodies were offering large rewards — the Ontario legislature's figure was $5,000 — for the apprehension of "the so-called murderers" of Thomas Scott.

In the presence of Bishop Taché, Father Ritchot and Alfred H. Scott on 8 February 1872 signed a petition to the Queen rehearsing their mission as delegates to Ottawa in 1870 and their understanding of the agreement over a general amnesty. They laid much stress upon their meeting with the governor-general and his insistence on behalf of the British government (in return for the delegates' agreement to the terms of the Manitoba Act) that the guarantees made would be honoured. Two years later, the petitioners pointed out, nothing had been done. When this petition arrived on the governor-general's desk in Ottawa, Sir John A. Macdonald immediately wrote Lord Lisgar that no answer should be provided to this petition, because refusal of an amnesty would excite the Métis "to madness" and granting the amnesty "would excite the British settlers to the same extent." Macdonald added that most of the particulars of the petition needed to be denied and the statement of what had occurred "between themselves and Your Excellency is also altogether false and must be repudiated. I shall send you a draft of your reply in a day or two."

A few days later Lisgar forwarded the Ritchot-Scott petition to the Queen. He denied the petition's version of the meeting with himself and Sir Clinton Murdoch, saying that he had been on guard about the amnesty and had refused to make promises. At the same time, he admitted that he had realized that the amnesty was crucial to the Red River acceptance of the deal. To Sir George-Étienne Cartier, Lisgar wrote that he had at no point "given an assurance or promise of an amnesty to cover all offences committed during the insurrection." But he only denied his commitment, not any made by Sir Clinton Murdoch. For his part, Sir Clinton Murdoch could not remember much about the occasion, although he insisted he would have recollected any promises had they been made. Even if he and Murdoch had been clever enough with words at the time as to be able to testify subsequently that they had given no assurances — while at the time giving the impression to the delegates that they were committing the British government — the governor-general must have known that this was all only smoke and mirrors. Thanks to vehement and persistent denials from Lisgar and those others present at the interview of any promises, however, the Queen did not act on the petition, although the British government was still pursuing it in early 1873.

Riel Enters Politics

Meanwhile, affairs in Canada took yet another bizarre turn. In the August 1872 federal election, Sir George-Étienne Cartier was badly defeated in the riding of Montreal East, at least partly because of backlash against his behaviour in the Manitoba affair. In some respects the easiest solution for the government was to find him a constituency in Manitoba. The obvious one was Provencher, centred at St Boniface, which had a francophone population. There was one small hitch: Louis Riel was contesting the riding.

Riel had not been comfortable in exile. Despite living under another name, he feared for his life at the hands of some bounty hunter eager to gain the $5,000 which the Ontario legislature had offered on 8 March 1872 as a reward. There was some evidence that Riel's concerns were not mere paranoia. Two men had already sworn an affidavit in an American court that Dr. John Christian Schultz had offered them $1,000 from the Ontario reward to steal Riel's papers. Other private schemes had been set afoot as well, which Riel and Lépine would catalogue in a long letter to Alexander Morris early in 1873. Riel had used the time in St. Paul to write an historical account of the whole Red River business. It explained the execution of Scott as "necessary to intimidate the conspirators, isolate Schultz by silencing the dissensions among our own people which encouraged him, and to command the attention of Canada."

Homesick, fearful, and at loose ends, Riel was attracted by the idea of running for Parliament. In August of 1872 he was back in Manitoba on the hustings, thus reneging on the agreement he had made with

Bishop Taché and Lieutenant-Governor Archibald. It would appear that his candidacy was in part intended to provide a reason for his return from exile in St. Paul. It was probably also intended as a statement that he was no longer on the run and no longer prepared to listen to those who counselled him to hide patiently until the passage of time would allow him to be rehabilitated. He would probably have been much better advised to bring his problems to a head by surrendering himself and insisting that he be put on trial for the death of Scott. Confronting the criminal charge in the Manitoba courts was virtually the only option which had any chance of success. His decision to run for Parliament was approved by a few of his supporters, notably Father Ritchot and Joseph Dubuc, although not by Bishop Taché.

Initially, his opponent was Henry J. Clarke, Manitoba's attorney-general. An ambitious man, Clarke had difficulty in understanding why Riel should be running for public office at this time. The two candidates met on the same hustings in St. Norbert on 18 August 1872. Riel defended his candidacy against charges he was "returning to public life too soon" by saying that he was asking only to be heard. The federal Parliament would give him a platform to explain himself and fight for his people. Clarke ultimately would become so frustrated by the extent of the public support for Riel that he challenged his opponent to a duel with pistols.

Taché and Archibald (who was by now waiting to be replaced) saw the chance to elect Cartier as a way of binding him to the province and the amnesty. As for Sir John A. Macdonald, he had no objections to the arrangement of electing Cartier so long as Riel did not step down in Cartier's favour. Indeed, Macdonald may even have initiated the scheme. Macdonald thought there was no need for any deal, cabling Archibald "they could safely confide in promises which, being already made, can gain no strength in repetition." Exactly what these promises were was never clear, since the prime minister clearly had no intention of providing an amnesty for those responsible for the death of Thomas Scott. What transpired was the usual package of misunderstanding. On election day, both Clarke and Riel stepped down after being nominated. Cartier was elected by acclamation, with no visible strings attached to the event and no formal commitments on his part to anything. However, Riel, Lépine, Joseph Royal, and Joseph Dubuc sent Cartier a private telegram of congratulations that spoke of "reason to hope in the success of the cause trusted into your hands." Bishop Taché subsequently wrote the prime minister, "I hope we will be rewarded by the grant of the amnesty which alone can secure peace to this country."

As for Cartier, he was so ill at the time of the election that he never again attended a cabinet meeting, and sailed for London the following January searching for a medical miracle which did not happen. Although the Provencher election went off without incident, mobs destroyed the offices of both *Le Métis* and the *Manitoban*, evidence of the continued unruliness in the province.

In the aftermath of the Provencher affair, Lieutenant-Governor Archibald was replaced by Chief Justice Alexander Morris, who was less supportive of the Métis. Born in Scotland, and a law pupil of John A. Macdonald in Kingston, Morris had been an early supporter of Canadian expansionism and the annexation of Hudson's Bay Company territories. When he retired from federal politics in 1872 due to ill health, he specifically requested to be sent to Manitoba as a judge, where "the work would be light." He presided over the court for a few months, then acted briefly as administrator of Manitoba before becoming lieutenant-governor late in 1872. Fortunately for him, his health had improved in the western air.

In December of 1872 an unsuccessful attempt was made to arrest Louis Riel. As a result, he and Ambroise Lépine sent Lieutenant-Governor Morris a document which represented the fullest statement yet of the case to be made for the Métis and the amnesty. The two men depicted themselves as being held completely responsible by the Canadian government for the troubles of 1869-70, and sought to defend themselves against the charge. They went over the ground of the events preceding the execution of Scott, whose punishment was "long deserved and terrible." But it alone could "secure the triumph of peace and order which it was our duty to establish throughout the settlement." They then discussed the promises made to the Red River delegates by the Canadian government and British governments, and the wait at Fort Garry to turn over authority. Instead, Wolseley entered the province as an enemy, and his arrival was followed by the revival of animosities. They reminded Morris of their service at the time of the Fenian threat. The government at Ottawa, Riel and Lépine concluded, sought to isolate from the entire political situation one occurrence (the Scott execution) which was integral to it, in order to judge it "abstractedly from all the circumstances which have brought it about." Morris did not act on this statement, but simply forwarded it to Ottawa.

In the spring of 1873, the amnesty question again surfaced on the national level. Father Ritchot had signed yet another petition to the governor-general (by now Lord Dufferin). He took the petition to Ottawa and met with Dufferin, who was non-committal. After the meeting, Ritchot later testified, he had an interview with Sir Hector Langevin, who had succeeded Cartier as leader of the French-Canadian part of the government. Langevin said that no government could grant an amnesty, for it would not last five minutes if it took up the question, and "they were not bound to commit suicide." Ritchot answered, "we neither were obliged to commit suicide, and that we had trusted the promises which had been made would have been kept." Langevin cautioned about making waves, but Ritchot responded that the Métis had nothing to lose. Father Ritchot subsequently met with the prime minister, who showed him the letters from the British officials denying Ritchot's version of their meeting. According to Ritchot, the prime minister insisted that he had stated at the time that he would not deal at all with the delegates of the provisional government. Ritchot snapped back, "You did tell me that?" Macdonald replied, "No, I did not, but have told it to my friends."

The Macdonald government was on the ropes over the Pacific Scandal in June of 1873, when the prime minister wrote the lieutenant-governor that the time might be ripe for a general amnesty for all but the murderers of Thomas Scott. A general proclamation would isolate Riel and "drive him out of the country, which is a consummation devoutly to be wished." While Riel could be arrested and tried, Macdonald added, there was inherent in this strategy enormous potential for acquittal or a hung jury. A subsequent cabinet meeting discussed the amnesty question, reaffirming that the power of amnesty rested with the Queen and not the governor-general of Canada, since the "unfortunate occurrences" had taken place before Canada had any jurisdiction over the country. It recommended that the matter be brought before the British government. The prime minister later in 1874 while out of office told a parliamentary inquiry that he thought a complete amnesty might be possible, were it granted by the imperial government without any Canadian government responsibility. Unfortunately, the British refused to play the game.

On 24 July 1873, the Earl of Kimberly wrote to the Earl of Dufferin on the amnesty question. Kimberly insisted that the Dominion was wrong in its maintenance that the Queen and not the Canadian governor-general had the power of pardon in the Red River business. The Canadian courts had under earlier parliamentary legislation of 1803 concurrent jurisdiction with the HBC courts over crimes and offences committed in the territory of the company, and thus the governor-general could issue a proclamation of amnesty in this instance, so long as the pardon was not for a case of murder. Thus Dufferin could and should grant an amnesty for all offences committed in Red River except the murder of Thomas Scott. Sir John A. reported to Bishop Taché in August on this communication, adding, "This is not what you wish. I will go to England immediately after the Session, and I am sure they will settle the question of the amnesty." Taché's response was to write to Sir Hector Langevin about the interview, claiming that he had been used and was both a victim and tool of the administration. He trusted "that the Government will not compel me to reveal to the public all I know about the Manitoba question."

The death of Cartier in England reopened Provencher in mid-1873, and Riel would again be a candidate. The Canadian government in the persons of Langevin and Macdonald met with Taché on 22 August, pressing the bishop to force Riel to withdraw from the campaign. Taché refused, saying he had been deceived too often. Sir John A. promised to secure an amnesty; Taché insisted on something in writing. Macdonald refused, but Langevin made the pledge, offering to get the whole party in Lower Canada to resign in case Sir John A. did not follow through. Taché responded, "It is not your resignation I am working for, it is the accomplishment of the promise of the amnesty."

In the end, Ottawa dodged the bullet at this point when another warrant was issued (at the instigation of W.N. Farmer in Winnipeg before the magistrate John O'Donnell) for the arrest of Riel and Lépine. Farmer had been a fellow prisoner of Thomas Scott in Upper Fort Garry in February 1870, and O'Donnell had been one of the earlier Schultz prisoners. Both the Canadian and the Manitoba governments insisted that this warrant was a private initiative, detecting behind it the machinations of the Liberal Party and the Orange Order, but it certainly came at a convenient time. Forcing Riel to become a fugitive from justice was clearly in the best interests of the government, given his embarrassing political activity, while trying Ambroise Lépine would allow for a test of the various defences which Riel might be expected to employ in exculpation of his action. Even were Lépine acquitted, the case against Riel was not affected, and if he were convicted — who knew what might transpire? In any event, Lépine was seized by constables while playing with one of his children and was held for trial, while the rumour circulated that Riel had hid in a haystack to escape capture. Langevin wrote on 21 September to Taché on the Lépine arrest, claiming that it had been done without the knowledge of the government. The minister insisted that for Taché to expose his version of the amnesty would only "create national and religious difficulties which would benefit neither those whom you wish to protect in Manitoba nor our people in other parts of the Dominion." Lieutenant-Governor Morris forced Attorney-General Henry Clarke to declare under oath that he had not been involved in the Farmer warrant.

Louis Riel was forced into hiding. He published a letter objecting to Lépine's arrest in Le Métis on 20 September, insisting that it was a breach of faith by the government. His friends organized a protest meeting at St. Boniface two days later, which drafted resolutions and sent a group to discuss the matter with Lieutenant-Governor Morris and his cabinet. The meeting lasted for several hours, but came to no conclusions. The press in Quebec was upset with the arrest of Lépine, for it had increasingly over the years since 1870 come to take the Métis cause under its wing. The newspaper Franc-Parleur editorialized about the need for justice "to an insulted and betrayed people." Many newspapers in the province now took the line that there had been no rebellion, only a defence against improper aggression by Canada.

J. M. Bumsted

The Preliminary Hearing of Ambroise Lépine

As a legal question, the death of Thomas Scott was either incredibly simple or incredibly complex, depending on how one looked at it. There seemed little doubt that a prosecution could prove that Thomas Scott had been executed by firing squad on 4 March 1870. Whether that execution was murder, as William Farmer's information insisted, or even whether Manitoba courts had jurisdiction to try the case, were other matters entirely. Lépine was brought for preliminary examination before Mr. Justice Louis Bétournay at the Police Magistrate's court at Fort Garry on 23 September 1873. Bétournay was a former Lower Canadian attorney who had practised in a firm with Sir George-Étienne Cartier. Through Cartier's influence he had been appointed a judge of the Court of Queen's Bench of Manitoba in 1872. He had no knowledge of the common law before his appointment, but he was bilingual.

The examination was deferred for three days, and was subsequently opened by Bétournay on 26 September. None of the legal participants in the examination had been in Red River at the time of the death of Scott. Messrs. Cornish and Thibeaudeau appeared for the prosecution, and Messrs. Royal, Dubuc, and Girard for the defence. Francis Evans Cornish was an Upper Canadian Orangeman who was later awarded a share of the Ontario reward offered for the arrest of those responsible for the death of Scott. He was regarded as the ablest trial lawyer in the province. Prime Minister Macdonald correctly suspected that he was behind the Farmer initiative. W.B. Thibeaudeau was Cornish's law partner, and was with Cornish convicted in 1876 of stealing a poll-book from the home of the returning officer. Joseph Royal, founder of *Le Métis* in 1871, was a former law student in Cartier's firm. Joseph Dubuc was Royal's law partner and a Manitoba MLA. Marc-Amable Girard was another protégé of Cartier. The defence certainly consisted of the leading francophone lawyers of the province.

Joseph Dubuc, speaking in French, immediately raised the matter of jurisdiction, and the argument was repeated by Joseph Royal in English. The defence insisted that jurisdiction was a real issue, because the circumstances of Red River before Confederation were quite different from that of any other province. By imperial statute of 1803 and 1821, the courts of both Upper and Lower Canada had been given jurisdiction over criminal cases (including murder) in the territories of the Hudson's Bay Company. The imperial legislation had never been repealed, although Red River had subsequently gotten its own court in the Court of Quarterly Session. As Royal stated the claim, "From the time of the resignation of the Government of Assiniboia, in 1869, until Canada assumed the Courts by Act of Parliament in 1871, the jurisdiction in the North-West belonged to the Imperial Government." This argument, as we shall see, really rolled several issues together. In any event, since the offence before the court had a distinctly "political" aspect, Lépine's lawyers urged caution by the court. The defence apparently did not at this point raise the question of jurisdiction in the form that Lépine himself would subsequently do. It did not maintain that the provisional government had replaced a moribund Hudson's Bay Company as the *de facto* authority in Red River or that, by negotiating with the delegates of the provisional government, the Dominion had turned that *de facto* authority into a de jure one. Testimony before a parliamentary enquiry in 1874 (before the final trial but after the preliminary hearings) would demonstrate that while such a line of argument would be highly controversial, it might be quite sustainable. The defence appears to have relied instead on a line based chiefly on statutes.

The surviving reports of the hearings do not give a detailed statement of the defence argument at any point, although they are quite full for the Crown's reply. It is therefore not clear whether the argument of Thomas P. Foran in his *Trial of Ambrose Lépine at Winnipeg for the Wilful Murder of Thomas Scott: Question of Jurisdiction*, published in Montreal in 1874, was reflected in the defence case in the court. Foran pointed out that under Statutes 1-2 George IV, c. 66, and 22-23 Victoria, c. 26, "the courts to be established in the Indian Territories were not to have jurisdiction over offences punishable by death or transportation; and as these Acts contain the only authority to erect courts in those territories, it is clear that the Recorder's and other Courts established at Winnipeg and elsewhere since 1859, were not competent to try Lépine for the wilful murder of Scott." On the other hand, the Court of Quarterly Session had tried cases of murder whether it was entitled to or not, and had passed one sentence of execution that was carried out. Even these realities did not exhaust the complexities of the early history of criminal law and jurisdiction in the West, however.

Prosecutor Cornish insisted that this court could not decide jurisdiction, but merely whether there was sufficient evidence to send the prisoner to trial. He denied that the case had any political significance whatsoever, a position that the prosecution would adopt from beginning to end. The court decided that it could not determine the question of jurisdiction, but moved to an examination of witnesses, a process that took five days. At the conclusion of the testimony, on 9 October, the prisoner was permitted to read an address in French that denied the competency of the court to hear the accusation. The address went on to insist that the testimony just concluded demonstrated that it was "the political man that is aimed at in this prosecution, and not the pretended murderer."

The proceedings, continued Lépine, trampled upon the arrangements made in the spring of 1870 between Canada and the delegates of a provisional government supported by over three-quarters of the people of Red River. He further protested being singled out "to bear exclusively the responsibility of acts done by a Government acting in the plenitude of powers with which the people of a country had publicly and voluntarily invested it." Lépine was not complaining so much that Louis Riel was not in the dock with him, but that the entire provisional government was not there. He again declared that the accusation was not motivated by a spirit of justice, but by political passions and feelings. Lépine thus suggested a number of possible lines of defence, to which his counsel added the argument that it had not yet been proven that Scott was dead.

To the observer outside the system, legal proceedings often appear to take place in an isolated and insulated world of abstractions, in which technicalities often take the place of the quest for truth or justice. This is particularly true of many major criminal court cases of the past, where matters often turn on abstruse legal points and assumptions acceptable at the time that will no longer bear careful scrutiny. Such was certainly the case in the trial of Ambroise Lépine. The prosecution self-righteously insisted that "justice" demanded that Lépine be tried. Many observers at the time even insisted that the future of the rule of law in Manitoba hinged upon a successful completion of this case. Few in our own time familiar with the events that led up to Lépine's appearance in magistrate's court, however, would doubt that — as Lépine insisted from the first — this was indeed a very political trial, or to use the modern terminology, a "state trial."

Whether its political nature was sufficient to impeach the subsequent proceedings is another matter, and it is a fact that neither the prosecution nor the courts ever acknowledged the political nature of the case. Nevertheless, Ambroise Lépine was no ordinary murderer and this was no ordinary criminal trial. It was a showpiece trial in which the very legitimacy of the governments and courts of Canada and Manitoba, and the behaviour of their officials, had to be protected as much as Ambroise Lépine needed to be convicted. Given this reality, there could be no fair or just outcome arrived at through the judicial process. In some senses, the decision had been determined well in advance by the Canadian government's adamant and persistent refusal to admit publicly any legitimacy to the provisional government of Red River. The courts merely went through a charade of procedural fairness. In a series of decisions, they stripped the killing of Scott of all its historical context and mitigation. The defence was left with little to argue except that there was no body to prove Scott's death, a contention so manifestly weak as to be laughable.

The judicial process continued on 14 October with the decision of the magistrate's court. Mr. Justice Bétournay found that there was conclusive proof of the execution of Thomas Scott. He refused to recognize the existence of a "pretended government" or the arguments against his jurisdiction, reserving the latter decisions to a higher court. He totally ignored the arguments of the defence about the political nature of the trial. Finding a "made-out case," he committed the prisoner for trial before the next criminal assizes of oyer and terminer. Lépine was sent to the provincial penitentiary at Lower Fort Garry until the next step in the process.

While his former colleague languished in prison and Sir John A. Macdonald struggled mightily to remain in office, Louis Riel found himself elected by acclamation to Parliament for Provencher riding. He had not appeared at the nomination meeting on 13 October. No other candidates had come forward, although some rumours circulated that Attorney-General Clarke might declare himself. Men were prepared to arrest Riel if he appeared at the meeting, and the police were searching for him as well. Riel's supporters raised a fund to send him to Ottawa, and under a pseudonym he departed for the East on 21 October via the United States, accompanied to the border by a team of bodyguards, and on the American leg of the journey by a young Quebec journalist. In Ottawa, Riel was welcomed by Honoré Mercier and by Alphonse Desjardins, the proprietor of *Le Nouveau Monde*, which had taken up his cause almost from the beginning. Instead of taking his seat, however, Riel at the last moment slipped away to Montreal. He then took shelter with the Oblates at Plattsburg, just across the border on Lake Champlain.

On 5 November 1873, the Macdonald cabinet in Ottawa decided that it could not hope to win any majority vote in the House of Commons. Too many defections had occurred since the first charges of corruption in the choice of the Canadian Pacific Railway to build a transcontinental line across Canada. The defectors even included Donald A. Smith. Macdonald met with the governor-general and submitted resignations for himself and his colleagues, and announced this action in the House. Mr. Mackenzie, the leader of the opposition, was asked to form a new government.

Lépine and the Court of Queen's Bench

The Lépine legal process resumed a week after the government's resignation. An extra term of the Manitoba Court of Queen's Bench opened on Wednesday, 12 November, with Mr. Justice J. C. McKeagney on the bench. Like Bétournay, McKeagney was a political appointment of limited experience and capabilities, described by one contemporary as a "right-minded and conscientious non-entity — at best an old woman." He had been born in Ireland and called to the Nova Scotia bar in 1838. In 1867 he was elected an anti-confederate MP from Cape Breton despite private promises to support union. In 1872 he was rewarded by the Conservative government for contesting a federal seat in order to split the Catholic vote with a judicial appointment in Manitoba. McKeagney had no criminal law experience and his French was practically non-existent. Lieutenant-Governor Morris feared that assertive lawyers could easily "bully" him, as they did Bétournay.

On 15 November, a grand jury found against Lépine, charging him with the murder of Thomas Scott. The grand jury of 12 consisted of six men labelled "half-breeds" in the official record, only three of whom had French names. Whether the jury was linguistically balanced despite the imbalance of the names is not clear. The jury included W. A. Farmer, the individual who had laid the information which had begun the legal process. Farmer subsequently explained that the court had run short of jurors and had pressed him into service. This anomaly seemed to bother no-one and did not become a legal issue, although in a modern trial it would have impeached the entire proceedings.

Ambroise Lépine was arraigned under the indictment. His counsel wanted him to question the jurisdiction of the court rather than plead under it, while the prosecution wanted him to enter a plea before questioning the jurisdiction. With the consent of Attorney-General Henry J. Clarke — the man who had earlier challenged Louis Riel to a duel — Lépine was eventually allowed to put in a plea of "not guilty," subject to the plea of jurisdiction. This "concession" was granted, said the attorney-general, because "the prosecution was not one of vengeance but of justice," and it was important that the matter "be brought to an issue." This little legal tussle was symptomatic of many subsequent ones. The prosecution and court would ostentatiously bend over backwards in favour of the defendant on minor procedural points, insisting that such concessions demonstrated the concern for abstract justice in the proceedings.

Lépine's lawyers offered a simple argument on the larger question of jurisdiction. Mr. Royal maintained that since the territory including Red River had not been transferred to Canada until 23 June 1870, the Dominion had no power or right to delegate power to the province to try felonies committed before that period. The relevant jurisdiction in the interim was covered by imperial statute calling for trial in the courts of Upper and Lower Canada. He cited several unreported legal authorities, including a book written by Mr. Justice John Hamilton Gray of British Columbia, which dealt with the question. Considerable discussion ensued over whether this book was a proper "legal authority." Since it does not appear to have survived, it is impossible to test the prosecution's claim that it had been written as a partisan exercise by Gray before being appointed to the British Columbia bench. Again, the defence appears not to have introduced arguments about the provisional government and its interruption of legal continuity, or its implicit authorization of the execution of Scott. Nor did the defence point out the possibility that the Manitoba Act itself was quite unconstitutional, since it had ignored a key provision of the British North America Act in claiming federal control over all land in the province. While any possible unconstitutionality had been overcome by an imperial statute of validation in 1871, the need for such a statute suggests considerable legal complications in the 1869-70 period. It is possible that none of these matters were raised by the defence at this point in order to prevent them from being ruled upon judicially before the actual trial.

Because the status of the provisional government was not actually raised at this point, the Crown had an easier run at the jurisdiction question. It maintained that the Hudson's Bay Company had transferred all their rights and powers to Canada under an Imperial Act of Parliament passed in 1868. It then insisted that although English criminal law — as then in force in the two Canadas — had been extended to Hudson's Bay territory by imperial statute of 1803 and others, the imperial statutes of 1803, 1821, and 1859 had not removed the jurisdiction of the HBC, but merely provided a concurrent one involving the courts of the Canadas.

Given the complicated history rehearsed on the question of the law, the very force of Clarke's unqualified insistence on the court's power ought to have given McKeagney pause. Uncertainly over the law — particularly the concurrent jurisdictions — probably explains why the Canadian government did not immediately upon its takeover proclaim the criminal law of Canada in force throughout the West. What the attorney-general did not note in his arguments was the existence of a whole series of other facts that considerably muddied the waters of his categorical conclusion. The Council of Assiniboia, for example, had twice introduced the law of England into the settlement, in 1837 and again in 1864. The imperial government had never recognized the judicial authority of the Hudson's Bay Company, especially in capital cases, before the passage of the statute of 1868. That statute did not specifically extend HBC judicial authority to capital cases, which implied that Canada still had jurisdiction over trials for murder.

Furthermore, the Imperial Parliament had repealed the Canada Jurisdiction Act in 1872 by 35 and 36 Victoria, c. 63, which certainly indicated that this legislation had been in force in 1870. On the other hand, the Canadian government had insisted that the Wolseley Expedition be conducted under British authority and led by a British military force, because Canada had no standing in the West in 1870. In 1873 the Canadian government had by statute wiped out any problem for the North-West outside Manitoba by extending the whole of Canadian criminal law to the North-West Territories. Confusion over the law would subsequently lead the Manitoba legislature to enact 38 Victoria, c. 12, which declared English law as of 15 July 1870 to be and to have been in force in the province. This declaration would be legislatively endorsed by the Dominion Parliament in 51 Victoria, c. 33, s. 1. Retroactive legislation always suggests previous confusion. The only time that certainty ever existed about the state of the criminal law in Red River in 1870 was in the course of the trial of Ambroise Lépine.

Subsequent legal historians have been quite unable to come to a consensus on the question of whose law (and by implication, whose jurisdiction) would have applied to Red River in March of 1870, even if there had not in addition been the thorny question of whether the provisional government had effectively superseded the Hudson's Bay Company and its courts. The jurisdiction over any capital crime committed in Red River in the spring of 1870 would always had been contentious. What law and what legal procedures were in effect was almost impossible to determine. A variety of dates and sources could be advanced for a number of particular criminal laws. Moreover, while it was true that the Quarterly Court of Assiniboia had conducted trials in capital offences, it was equally true that its criminal proceedings in such trials had been quite idiosyncratic. The judge had often acted as prosecuting attorney, for example, and in the absence of trained lawyers the adversarial system had seldom been employed.

Mr. Justice McKeagney was understandably not eager to rule on the question of jurisdiction, although every step in the process which did not rule on this issue make it more difficult for the defence to win its arguments. He deferred an immediate decision, meanwhile allowing Lépine to be released on bail, on grounds that he had not run away before his arrest and was not likely to do so now.

Other Developments

With a new government in power in Ottawa, Bishop Taché attempted desperately to establish connections with and negotiate arrangements with the Liberals, but without much success. Former Lieutenant-Governor Adams G. Archibald opined late in 1873 that Riel was himself responsible for most of the difficulties involving the amnesty. "If only the unfortunate cause of all these troubles had the sense to see as others saw for him, that the true solution of the question both in his own interest, in the interest of his halfbreed friends, and of the Dominion was to keep himself in the background till the storm had blown over, all these difficulties would have vanished," Archibald wrote to Donald A. Smith. Riel was too impatient, unwilling to allow the passions of the moment to clear a bit. Archibald did not explain how he fit the arrest and trial of Ambroise Lépine into his scenario.

As for Lous Riel, he was by late 1873 in Plattsburg, New York. Here Riel found himself in more congenial surroundings. There was less fear of arrest or violence, and there was a nearby French-Canadian community at Keeseville, where he was warmly received by the family of the local curé, Father Fabien Barnabé. Riel suspected that Parliament would soon be dissolved and that there would be another election. He prepared yet another account of the resistance, which he took back with him to Montreal in early 1874. It would be published in *Le Métis* and as a separate pamphlet by *Le Nouveau Monde*. He himself entitled it "L'Amnistie. Mémoire sur les causes de Nord-Ouest et sur les négotiations qui ont amené leur règlement amiable." Again he insisted that Scott's death had been necessary and that the Canadian government had guaranteed the delegates of the provisional government an amnesty. This account provided further details of Thomas Scott's bad behaviour.

Before it was published, Riel had been elected to Parliament from Provencher riding for the second time. The Liberals were as desperate as the Conservatives had been to take Riel out of the spotlight and certainly to keep him out of the House of Commons. A.A. Dorion, the leading French-Canadian in the Mackenzie ministry, tried to persuade Riel through Lieutenant-Governor Morris and Bishop Taché not to become a candidate. The bishop refused to become involved. He pointed out to Dorion that there were others much closer geographically to Riel than he was. Moreover, Taché was tired of getting the runaround. He queried rhetorically, "What is to be offered to Mr. Riel as a recompense for the sacrifices which he is called upon to make?" His answer was: "Misery, exile, or a jail if he returns to his native land." There had been a formal opposition this time in the person of Joseph Hamelin, who had kept out of the resistance in 1869-70. But Riel was easily the victor. It was no clearer than earlier how he could exploit his position as a Member of Parliament, although this time he was apparently determined to take his seat.

While Riel waited for Parliament to be called, he was, as we have seen earlier, attacked in the English-speaking newspapers by Dr. Joseph Lynch, who responded to the pamphlet *L'Amnistie* by denying that Scott had received a fair trial. Riel had answered a bit disingenuously, but the exchange kept the whole controversy alive in the press. Moreover, instead of assisting the government, Bishop Taché decided to go public with his own account of the amnesty business, thus fulfilling threats he had been making for several years. Entitled *L'Amnistie*, Taché's pamphlet was published in Montreal toward the end of March, joining Riel's memoir and Lynch's critical letter in putting the issues of Red River before the public.

At the end of March, Riel had actually appeared before the clerk of the House of Commons with a fellow MP. The colleague asked that the two men be sworn in. The clerk routinely administered the oath of allegiance, and then presented a roll which was duly signed. Only did he realize whose name had been put on the rolls. Riel made a low bow, and left the building. But while this little escapade may have been great fun, it had no practical effect on anything, except to embarrass French-Canadian Liberals.

When the House of Commons actually met on 30 March, the question of the amnesty would be discussed on two separate occasions, the first at the very start of the session. Riel was not in attendance, but a motion for a general amnesty was presented by J.-A. Mousseau and Rodrigue Masson, both his supporters. It was defeated, and its only result was to lead Mackenzie Bowell, who was one of the leaders of the Ontario Orange Order, to propose a parliamentary committee to investigate the Red River affair. The next day Henry Clarke (whose presence in Ottawa has never quite been explained) exhibited the indictment against Riel for murder and called him a fugitive from justice. Mackenzie Bowell moved that Riel be ordered to attend the House on the following day. Despite great expectations and public interest — the governor-general's wife and a party of her friends attended hoping to see Riel take his seat — Riel did not turn up. He had left for Montreal shortly after signing the roll. A motion to adjourn for a week was passed.

Riel's behaviour in this whole parliamentary business can only be described as perplexing. The principal justification that would have been argued by Riel supporters for his elections to Parliament was that it raised consciousness for the Riel and the Métis cause, particularly in Quebec. Riel himself understood this point, writing Joseph Dubuc in March 1874 that "Our cause is shaking the Canadian Confederation from one end of the country to the other." By June of that year, A.A. Dorion wrote to Prime Minister Mackenzie that "The sympathy for Riel and his companions is getting stronger and stronger in Lower Canada and it will soon be a difficulty in the way of any Government."

We can to some extent understand Riel's reluctance to make an appearance in the House of Commons. After all, he would doubtless have been instantly arrested and would have joined Ambrose Lépine on trial for murder. But why then be present in Ottawa lurking about the House on two occasions? Did someone expect that he could invoke parliamentary privilege? Why actually sign the roll of the House and take the oath of allegiance? What was it he and his friends were hoping to accomplish through all these machinations? French Canada's Members of Parliament of both parties held a caucus supporting Riel during the adjournment, but what would they have done had he actually tried to take his seat? Riel may have provided some great guerrilla theatre in Ottawa, but did not really advance his cause. Many of his "friends" began to question the tactics of constant re-election, particularly given Riel's refusal to take his seat and make his case in person. Unfortunately, while support for Riel and the Métis was growing in Quebec, hostility was equally gaining strength in Ontario.

The House of Commons, after much debate, agreed to appoint a Select Committee "to enquire into the causes of the difficulties which existed in the North-West in 1869 and 1870, and into those which have retarded the granting of the amnesty announced in the Proclamation issued by the late Governor-General of Canada, Sir John Young…." This was a strange resolution, since it mentioned by name an offer of amnesty which no-one could possible believe could be honoured, but it got the committee in place. The establishment of the committee, of course, was a compromise that enabled the Liberals to get the Riel issue out of the House, at least for the moment. Young Wilfrid Laurier voted for it, for example, in order to avoid having to deal with Riel's expulsion.

The French-Canadian members hoped that no action would be taken on Riel until the committee had reported, but Mackenzie Bowell was relentless. He thereupon moved for Riel's expulsion from the House, on grounds that he was a fugitive from justice and had failed to obey an order to attend the House. The motion was seconded by one of Manitoba's own members, John Christian Schultz. Again Riel and the amnesty were debated. Again strong feelings were expressed. Again a vote on an amnesty was taken, but this time the Liberals from Quebec stood behind their prime minister, who had publicly called the death of Scott a crime against humanity and privately regretted that Manitoba had become a province. The Quebec press was very critical of the behaviour of its members in supporting "Anglo-Protestant fanaticism."

The Liberals' parliamentary committee to investigate the Red River affair began hearing testimony on 10 April 1874. Twenty-one witnesses were heard over the course of the hearings, which lasted until 21 May. Father Ritchot and Bishop Taché both got to tell their stories at great length, and Sir John A. Macdonald denied making any promises. The hearings were covered at great length by newspapers in both French and

English-speaking Canada, although the press often chose to emphasize different parts of the evidence. The *Globe* sought more to condemn Macdonald and Cartier for dealing with the Métis at all, for example than to acknowledge that commitments had been made. *Le Journal de Québec*, edited by Joseph Cauchon, editorialized about Bishop Taché, "that this man of superior worth, brought back from Rome to pacify the North-West, was shamefully deceived by a government that needed his services and his influence." What the hearings established conclusively was that there were no written promises to be honoured.

Any outside observer could only be amazed at how the Canadians had managed to keep the Red River delegates negotiating right through to their acceptance of the Manitoba Act without actually putting anything in writing, and while publicly maintaining that there could be no amnesty for murder. Obviously Father Ritchot did not read his daily newspaper. Macdonald and Cartier had the golden gift of gab, and the brazenness to lie afterwards about what they had done. Few who followed the testimony carefully could possibly doubt that the Canadian negotiators had promised orally a general amnesty as a condition of delegate agreement to the Manitoba Act, and the Quebec press pounced on the evidence that the Métis had been "gulled and bamboozled mercilessly and unceasingly." The committee's report was noncommittal. Parliament now had the evidence, and could "consider whether under the circumstances stated, any other steps shall be taken."

Although the tide of politics in Manitoba seemed to be turning toward the Métis in the late spring and early summer of 1874 — a provincial government led by Henry Clarke had been replaced by one headed by Marc Girard — Riel could not yet go home. The problem was the impending trial of Ambroise Lépine. Mr. Justice McKeagney had again deferred a decision on the jurisdiction question in February, regarding himself as "not competent or justified of deciding a question of such great importance without a full bench." The chief justiceship had not been filled since Morris had moved to the lieutenant-governor's chair. McKeagney reported that if the post remained vacant, he and Bétournay would have to have the case reargued and would make a decision.

The attorney-general tried to browbeat McKeagney into giving "a decision on a question so simple as that of your own jurisdiction as a judge of the Court," openly charging him with shirking his duty and casting doubts on his competence. But McKeagney refused to be budged. Contemporaries regarded McKeagney's position as one of weakness and lack of confidence, but those qualities were undoubtedly combined with his realization that this decision was not so "simple" as the attorney-general wanted to make it. By the June 1874 session of the court, Chief Justice

Edmund Burke Wood had taken his place on the bench Sir George-Étienne Cartier had earlier insisted that those involved in the death of Thomas Scott could never be successfully convicted in a Manitoba court. That insistence was about to be put to the test. The defendant was not Louis Riel, but Ambroise Lépine would serve well enough in his place.

Chief Justice Wood Rules on Jurisdiction

C hief Justice Edmund Burke Wood had only one arm as a result of a shooting accident, and he compensated for his handicap with an attitude of total assurance and self-confidence. Born in Upper Canada, he had graduated from Oberlin College in Ohio in 1848, being called to the Canadian bar in 1854. He was the leading Reformer in the Ontario cabinet in 1867. The *Globe* described Wood as a leading paid agent of the Grand Trunk Railway. Prime Minister Alexander Mackenzie had passed him over for the new Liberal cabinet, but had rewarded him with the Manitoba appointment. Wood was, Mackenzie reported to the province's lieutenant-governor, "perhaps too impulsive for a judge, but that is a good quality in a new country." Soon after his arrival in Manitoba, he told the St. Andrew's Society that, "Here we wanted no race, nationality, church, sect or religion to be dominant or in the ascendant; but we wanted all to be British subjects; all to be Canadians, all to be Manitobans, whatever his origin, language, race or pedigree." Canada First could not have objected to these sentiments.

Wood heard rehearsals of the arguments of the defence and prosecution on the jurisdiction question, and then proceeded to read a lengthy opinion obviously prepared in advance. He began by outlining the imperial legislation in some detail. He then observed that the court of Rupert's Land had tried civil and criminal cases (including capital offences) for 30 years without having its jurisdiction questioned by the imperial government. Indeed this court was — he insisted — fully recognized in the last clause of the Rupert's Land Act of 1868, which continued its powers until otherwise enacted by the Parliament of Canada. Despite the imperial legislation, the Canadian courts had only a concurrent rather than an exclusive jurisdiction.

Wood further ruled that the offence at issue had been committed on 4 March 1870 under the jurisdiction of the General Court of the Hudson's Bay Company, which continued in authority until 15 July 1870 (the date of the transfer of the territory to Canada) and then onward until the organization of the Supreme Court of Manitoba. The Manitoba Act of 1871 specifically stated in section 6, c. 14, that no person would be liable to any punishment or penalty for any act done before its passage that he would not have been liable to under the laws in force at the time the act was passed. Wood further denied that confederation had swept away the concurrent jurisdiction of the Canadian courts and returned jurisdiction to the imperial parliament, calling the arguments based on the British North America Act "strained." Without at any time considering the question of the status of the provisional government and its effect on continuity, the chief justice saw no interruption of jurisdiction to prevent the Manitoba Court of Queen's Bench from hearing the case. Having resolved the jurisdiction question to his satisfaction, Mr. Justice Wood then allowed the prisoner to plead "Not Guilty," and bound him over for trial in October 1874.

Wood had offered a plausible interpretation of the complex written record, as plausible as any other that could be advanced. It was an interpretation, however, which did not take into account the possibility of an interruption of continuity by the proclamation of William McDougall or through the subsequent seizure of power by the provisional government. This further suggested that Wood was not prepared to entertain seriously any contextual arguments in the death of Scott, either before, during, or after the fact. The death of Scott would be considered purely abstractly, in splendid isolation from all that went on around it. Such an approach would, of course, be devastating to the defence.

-9-

Amnesty Resolved

Despite considerable private doubts by some of his more prominent supporters, Louis Riel once again stood for Parliament from Provencher riding in the federal election of September, 1874. Once again he was unopposed, and once again he was elected. Riel now saw his candidacy as a national matter, throwing down the gauntlet to Ontario Orangeism on behalf of French-Canadian Catholicism everywhere in the Dominion. The strategy was clearly designed to identify the cause of the Métis in Manitoba with French Canada. Riel also now understood that he need not try to take up his seat for this strategy to be effective.

The Trial of Ambroise Lépine

Shortly after Riel's fourth election to Parliament, Ambroise Lépine was finally brought for trial before the Manitoba Court of Queen's Bench. The trial was one of the first major events in the new courthouse recently constructed in Winnipeg on the west side of Main Street between the present-day Bannatyne and William Avenues. By this point, Joseph Dubuc had become attorney-general, and obviously could not prosecute the case because of his previous involvement with the defence. The prosecution was thus again headed by the Orangeman, Francis Cornish. Dubuc remained a less active member of a defence team that had been augmented by the arrival from Montreal of Joseph-Adolphe Chapleau, one of French Canada's leading Conservative politicians and its most celebrated trial lawyer. Chapleau had a reputation for defending in murder cases and winning most of them. Over the years he would win 21 of 22 murder trials, losing only in Manitoba. Chapleau had volunteered for this service and paid his own expenses. In some ways his presence — which could not very well be rejected — may have been a hindrance rather than a help. The local defence team was not very enthusiastic about the hot-shot lawyer from the big city taking over the case. Chapleau's courtroom style was overblown and very rhetorical. He expected to win by wowing the jury, especially the francophones, with his oratory. Moreover, he would later claim that deep in his heart he knew in 1874 that Lépine and Riel were murderers.

Our knowledge of this trial and its preliminaries is based on unofficial court reports. Two such reports exist, one in a publication entitled *Preliminary Investigation and Trial of Ambroise D. Lépine for the Murder of Thomas Scott, Being a full report of the proceedings in this case before the Magistrates' Court and the several Courts of Queen's Bench in the Province of Manitoba* (Montreal, 1874), which was based on the court reports of various reporters for eastern Canadian newspapers, and one in Winnipeg's *Free Press*, which was based on the work of local reporters. The two sets of reports have much in common, because the various participants distributed their set speeches in advance to the press, but also because the local and visiting reporters often pooled their resources. But the two sets of reports are not identical. Most of those writing about the trial, mainly because of its obvious connection with Louis Riel, have used the Montreal publication rather than the *Free Press* accounts, although the latter contains some significant material not repeated in the Montreal version. In addition to the published accounts, the trial notes of Judge Edmund Burke Wood also survive, in the Provincial Archives of Manitoba. These provide over 160 pages of crabbed judge's notes, written on the go and often illegible to anyone but the note-taker (and perhaps even to him). The notes are of the testimony itself rather than about Wood's larger strategy or interior thinking, but they do demonstrate that he paid attention during the trial.

As in most such controversial cases, the makeup of the trial jury would be absolutely critical. Sir George-Étienne Cartier had doubted that any of those involved in the death of Scott could be convicted by a jury of Red River residents, at least if the convention (which was subsequently translated into the law) of composing the juries half of anglophones and half of francophones was observed. Given the importance of jury selection, the surviving court records are quite unsatisfactory on this point. We do know that four prospective jurors were challenged by the Crown, and "about sixteen" by the defence. We do not know whether the 16 challenges exhausted the defence's allotment, or how long the jury panel list was at the outset. The defence would subsequently complain about list manipulation. In any event, a jury was eventually empanelled, consisting of six anglophones and six francophones. How many of these were mixed-bloods is not clear, however.

In his opening remarks to the jury, Crown Prosecutor Cornish made clear the prosecution strategy of concentrating strictly on the deed. It was "foul murder," announced Cornish, and if Lépine was found fully implicated, he was guilty. Over the next 13 days of the trial, a battery of witnesses appeared on the stand to be questioned by the prosecution and the defence. This testimony provides us with as much evidence taken under oath as we will ever have on the events surrounding the death of Thomas Scott. Some of the witnesses would contradict their testimony in later oral reminiscences, but that is probably par for the course. More importantly, almost without exception, the prosecution brought to the stand only Métis who were regarded as "loyal" to the new government. It called no "hostile witnesses" who were known still to be Riel supporters. The prosecution's witnesses, therefore, included few individuals close to the centre of events in 1870. The star witnesses were Joseph Nolin, who was present at the trial of Scott, and John Bruce, who had been the early president of the provisional government.

According to the testimony, Scott was tried in French on the evening of 3 March, with Lépine presiding. Several witnesses testified that there had been rumours of Scott's execution circulating around Upper Fort Garry for weeks before that date. The chief witnesses at the trial of Scott had been Louis Riel and Joseph Delorme; no witnesses were called on Scott's behalf, and he himself was not heard in his own defence. The Canadian was accused of having rebelled against the provisional government and striking both the president of the provisional government and his guards. There was no written record of the Scott tribunal available, although one had been kept, and the only witness who testified to the events of that tribunal was Joseph Nolin, who had been Riel's private secretary in 1870 but had subsequently broken with Riel. In his prosecution summation at the conclusion of Lépine's trial, Francis Cornish insisted that one charge had been that Scott had broken his oath to the provisional government, an oath he had never taken. Joseph Nolin had testified under cross examination that this breaking of an oath was part of the charge of rebelling against the provisional government, but it was never clear whether the tribunal had held the oath important, and the defence did not pursue the matter. Certainly Scott had been involved in armed opposition to the government. The hearing of Scott lasted less than three hours and ended with Janvier Richot moving and André Nault seconding a motion for execution. Only Baptiste Lépine objected to the death penalty, on grounds that the resistance had been without bloodshed to this point. The testimony never established clearly exactly what Scott had done to deserve death. By Anglo-Canadian standards, he had been obviously condemned by a kangaroo court without due process.

In retrospect, Lépine's defence appeared curiously weak. Why this should be the case is not entirely clear. We do know that Joseph Royal was not happy with Chapleau's arrival to lead the defence. We also know that Royal managed to sabotage the defence through his summation to the jury, which was supposed to be in English and merely a preparation for Chapleau's major effort. Instead, Royal spoke in English for four hours, running over the dinner recess and not ending until 11:00 p.m. Royal did not address any of the contextual questions, but rehearsed the testimony in enormous detail to demonstrate the contradictions and discrepancies. Royal made much of the inability of the prosecution to prove that Lépine had actually been present at the execution. It was a very boring speech which must have struck many jurors as irrelevant. George Stanley in his biography of Riel claims Royal's relatively lack of familiarity with English may account for the speech's flatness. In any event, Chapleau had to follow with another two and one half hours of oration in French, in the early hours of the morning. Joseph Dubuc reported, "Il s'éleve aux plus hautes rétions d'eloquence, et prononce un des plus beaux discours de sa vie." However brilliant was Chapleau's oratory, it probably fell fairly flat on the ears of exhausted jurors.

Certainly Chapleau's strategy throughout the trial and in his summation seemed ineffectual. Indeed, Chapleau did not call many witnesses for the defence at all. Perhaps many individuals he might have questioned felt too implicated in the crime being addressed to risk a court appearance. Louis Riel did not testify, and Lépine himself did not take the stand or utter a single word in his defence. In fairness to Chapleau, he could not properly demonstrate that the delegates in 1870 had been officially recognized and had been promised a full amnesty. Both Archbishop Taché and Father Ritchot, who were called as witnesses — Taché making a dramatic appearance on a stretcher — were fully prepared to recite chapter and verse on the dealings they had conducted with Ottawa and how they had been misled by cunning Canadians. They had certainly done so in their appearance before the select committee of parliament earlier in the year.

In terms of all the evidence of Canadian "bamboozling," Chapleau and the defence had been stymied by the Chief Justice, who had made quite clear that he would accept no evidence of unrecorded conversations with third-parties or hearsay evidence, but only documents, orders in council, or acts of parliament. This ruling was patently partisan and could hardly in any case be seriously and systematically followed. The judge had allowed John Bruce to introduce all sorts of hearsay evidence about earlier threats against Scott and the disposition of the body. Chapleau had objected to this testimony at the time, but was over-ruled. Many witnesses reported what they had heard rather than what they had seen and were apparently not challenged. In any event, Chapleau did ask Father Ritchot whether he had anything in writing on the amnesty agreement with Canada, and dropped the line of questioning when

Ritchot said he did not. Whether the defence would have been allowed to introduce the testimony given before the parliamentary enquiry — which certainly had been published and was a document — was never tested, and should have been, at least to provide grounds for appeal.

Equally to the point, Chapleau did not bring out very well the important distinction between a legitimate government and a *de facto* one. Chapleau's defence was clearly dependent on the argument that the provisional government was a *de facto* one, for the Métis tribunal that condemned Scott derived its legitimacy from this point, but he did not establish the point very well. For example, he did not ask the witnesses — both his own and the prosecution's — whether they believed that the provisional government was indeed the one in power and whether they willingly obeyed it, whatever its legal standing might have been. Nor did the defence try to make the point that there was no hard and fixed requirement, given the unusual circumstances of the time, that Scott's tribunal be bound by any of the rules of Anglo-Saxon justice. Some judicious questions of Joseph Nolin might have been extremely useful in this regard. Perhaps the limited spectrum of witnesses told against the defence, or perhaps, as George Stanley has speculated, both Chapleau's and Royal's limited command of English may have told against them, particularly in cross-examination of anglophone witnesses. This trial was conducted principally in English, except for some closing speeches, with an unknown but substantial amount of simultaneous translation.

In his summation for the prosecution, Frank Cornish began by dismissing the defence's contextual argument, which he construed as being that the killing of Scott "was the act of a regular government, duly empowered and acting under the constitutional authorities of the country." This was the definition of a legitimate government, not a *de facto* one. Deliberately obfuscating the normal distinctions between *de facto* and de jure governments, in his next sentence Cornish asked rhetorically, "When did that government become *de facto* and who gave it that authority?" He went on to assert that the provisional government "was only a government of physical power and that this was used to enforce its will," as if a government of such physical power could not be a *de facto* one — or indeed that a *de facto* government could exist without physical power. Cornish had managed to sneak legitimacy into the definition of *de facto*, and the jury was never disabused of the point.

Cornish quickly disposed of defence arguments that the absence of a body left the question of whether Scott was dead in a reasonable doubt. One suspects that the jury was pretty certain that Scott had been killed, whether or not the body could actually be produced. Defence suggestions that he might still be alive somewhere were far-fetched. The defence insistence on the importance of the absence of the body probably was a negative influence with the jury, since it detracted from more important arguments and suggested a state of desperation. Cornish maintained that "It is a principal of British law that all persons who participate in the taking away of life deliberately and without authority are guilty of wilful murder." He compared the opportunities for defence afforded Lépine with those denied to "poor Scott," and made much of Lépine's refusal to give up the body for burial. "To refuse the clay of Poor Scott, the last rites of the Christian Church, was an act which must impress upon your minds the character of the prisoner at the bar." The evidence of Father Ritchot merely proved, said Cornish, "that there were others behind the scenes, misguiding and misleading those whom they should have been teaching and instructing." Cornish concluded by insisting that while "the so-called Provisional Government was not legal, or lawful" (not really the issue), this entire line of argument was a red herring. All that really mattered were the "immediate facts of the murder of poor Scott."

The summation of Cornish was followed by an address to the jury in French by junior counsel Stewart Macdonald. This address answered what the prosecution described as the principal "three objections" of the defence. It was Macdonald's job not only to refute these objections, but to establish in the minds of the jury that these did indeed represent the defence's case. Not surprisingly, Macdonald concentrated on the arguments relating to the absence of a body. He insisted that Scott had to be dead, that his body had been secreted by the guilty parties, and that Scott had been condemned to death by a an illegitimate and uncivilized court in a mock trial. Macdonald was particularly eloquent on the nature of the process that had found Scott guilty. As he put it:

> Riel was the accuser, the chief witness, the prosecutor and the judge, and it was at his request that poor Scott was sentenced whilst he was denied the right of presence at the tribunal which ordered his death in twelve short hours. Of whom did this so-called Court Martial consist? Why, gentlemen, it was composed of seven men who had been duped by Riel to imagine themselves a court of justice, and of this would-be court the prisoner at the bar was the leading spirit. Was it civilized justice when Scott was refused the evidence against him made known to him in his own language before he was sentenced? Was it the acts of righteous judges to refuse his petition in this respect, or was it the act of men who had coolly and deliberately planned the death of a man of whose fearless character they stood in awe?

For the reader re-examining the trial reports more than a century later, the prosecution was well ahead on points before the Chief Justice's charge to the jury. Contemporaries regarded that charge as brilliant, and the assessment has been repeated over the years. The *Free Press* wrote at the time, "For five hours yesterday, interrupted only by the intermission of an hour for recess, Chief Justice Wood marshalled legal fact after legal fact, and in one of the ablest charges, if not the ablest, ever given to a jury in Canada, expounded the law clearly, powerfully and exhaustively, so that a child might have understood him." Such an assessment is quite correct, particularly if we understand that its brilliance was in directing the jury to an inexorable verdict of guilty, both by the charge's interpretation of the law and by its shaping of the events of 1869-70. Wood would go a long way toward the successful disproving of Cartier's earlier dictum about the difficulty of trying the killers of Scott before a Manitoba jury. It *was* possible to get a conviction, especially if the arguments were artfully presented. Part of the reason for the length of time it took to deliver the charge was that it was translated, sentence by sentence, to the jury by the clerk of the court.

We too can admire the chief justice's achievement, so long as no modern reader is left believing that either Wood's charge or the jury's verdict necessarily represent some mysterious arrival at the "truth" in the Scott case or some glorious vindication of the doctrine of "fairness." At the outset of his charge, Wood insisted on the usual distinction between fact and law, repeating the old maxim that "the jury are responsible to the facts and the judge to the law." But he did not leave all "the facts" to the jury's discretion. Instead, Wood confidently interpreted most of "the facts," a procedure that not surprisingly worked to the great disadvantage of Ambroise Lépine.

Wood spent much time going over the events of 1869-70 with the jury. His interpretation was to emphasize the arbitrary behaviour of the Métis and the various governments in the settlement. The narrative was not objectively presented. Wood took various side-swipes at Riel and the Métis leaders in the process, under the thin disguise of rhetorical questions to the jury. He then began expressing opinions on the question of the government's status, observing "If only one of their acts was in accordance with British law and organization I fail to see it." He subsequently proceeded to rule the entire *de facto* argument out of court, insisting that "no organization can be set up as a justification for an act not sanctioned by British laws. Besides being a *de facto* Government it must be a Government de jure that has a legal basis." He continued, "The settlement of Red River or Rupert's Land was under the protection of the laws of Great Britain, and the constitution and the laws cannot tolerate any organization that has not its sanction and its authority, but any revolt or organization of that kind cannot be set up as a justification for the [exercise] of sovereignty." Only the Queen in council could recognize the court that had tried Scott.

Portrait of Louis Riel by the
illustrator Henri Julien, n.d.

SHSB-518

Photo of Louis Riel published in
Father Morice's *Histoire de l'Église
catholique dans l'Ouest canadien*,
Montréal, 1912, volume II.

Louis Riel in 1885, drawn by the
surveyor P. H. Dumais.

SHSB-511

This image appeared in Quebec
newspapers after Riel's execution.

SHSB-512

Heroic depiction of Riel rallying his Métis followers at Batoche.

PAM

Riel in the dock during his trial for treason at Regina, 1885.

PAM

Wood further insisted that although the defendant could not use the status of the court and the provisional government as an argument in exculpation, this did not really matter. He instructed the jury to look only at the fact of the killing. "I repeat, then, gentlemen, that all that has been [said], whatever opinion you may form in respect of that organization, whether you say it was a one man power or whether it was a definite Government or not, whatever you may call it, I repeat in so far as you or I am concerned, it can have no influence or weight in determining this question whatever." This instruction left the defence with little to rely upon other than the absence of the body, an argument which was hardly very convincing.

The jury retired at 4:30 p.m. on 2 November. The defence was apparently confident of at least a hung jury. Indeed, over-confidence was probably one of its biggest liabilities in arguing the case. Anticipating a lengthy deliberation, the defence counsel went out for dinner, and were therefore not present when the jury returned just two and one half hours later. The verdict was guilty, but with a recommendation for mercy. At this distance, it is quite impossible to interpret what the jury meant to accomplish by such a recommendation. The most likely explanation is that the jury, impressed by the judge's instructions, had agreed that Lépine was guilty, but still thought that there were extenuating circumstances, and was trying to tell this to the court. Eleven years later a jury would deliver a similar verdict in Louis Riel's treason trial, and comments of jurymen outside the courtroom suggested that this was the jury's thinking in 1885. What neither jury seemed to understand was that recommendations for mercy were less effective in highly politicized state trials than they might have been in ordinary capital cases. If the jurors wanted to mitigate, they would have to vote not guilty.

Justice Wood allowed the verdict to be delivered without the defence lawyers in attendance, which was certainly showed an absence of judicial courtesy to the francophone team. Lépine's lawyers heard the verdict delivered at their dinner party by a messenger. "Une cartouche de dynamite explosant au milieu de mous n'eut pas produit un effet plus saisissant," later recalled Joseph Dubuc of the occasion. "Tous se levérent le table absourdid." The defence would have been better advised, of course, to have prepared for this eventuality, particularly given the nature of Judge Wood's summation.

After some objection by the defence team, the Chief Justice pronounced sentence. He rejected the recommendation for mercy because, as he put it to Lépine, "You did not spare poor Scott." In approved Victorian fashion, Wood's words in sentencing left the spectators in the courtroom in tears. He did defer the execution long enough for the entire court proceedings to be transmitted to Ottawa and laid before the governor-general in council. This was not a part of the appeal process. The law obliged him to do this in cases where the death sentence was imposed. Canada did not yet have a Supreme Court, and any appeal would have to go to the British government.

Despite the earlier arguments of Sir George-Étienne Cartier that those involved in Scott's death could never be successfully tried in a Manitoba Court, Ambroise Lépine was there prosecuted and found guilty of the murder of Thomas Scott. The conviction followed a trial in which the presiding judge had managed to insist upon the entire Ontario interpretation of Scott's death, rejecting any notion of diminished responsibility because Lépine was acting on behalf of a *de facto* government and ruling out of court any mitigation because of unwritten promises made to the provisional government by Canada.

In Manitoba, there were several curious aftermaths to the Lépine trial. In the first place, the Crown, apparently flushed by its success, brought similar charges against André Nault and Elzéar Lagimodière, both of whom had been part of the tribunal which had condemned Scott. We do not have detailed transcripts of these trials, both of which resulted in hung juries, the outcome that the defence had confidently anticipated in the trial of Lépine. In the second place, although Louis Riel was never brought to trial in the Scott matter, on 10 February 1875, the *Free Press* reported in its column on routine matters in the Court of Queen's Bench, that final writs of exigent (a writ of exigent commanded the sheriff to summon the defendant to appear before the court on pain of outlawry) were read by the sheriff in the cases of Louis Riel and W.B. O'Donoghue, and they were declared returned. Outlawry was an obsolete English legal procedure for dealing with known criminals who could not be captured, in order either to bring them to trial or to convict them without trial; it had apparently been employed in dealing with culprits like Robin Hood. Almost by definition, most of those declared outlaws were or would become folk heroes.

By this action Riel and O'Donoghue were in effect convicted in absentia of Scott's murder without a trial, and each man became a "fugitive from justice." The Liberal government in Ottawa would soon use this declaration of outlawry of Riel as a reason for expelling him from the House of Commons.

The British Response to the Lépine Case

As we have seen, while the Lépine case was working its way through the Manitoba court system, Louis Riel had several times been elected to the Canadian Parliament, and had on one occasion actually managed to sign the official roll before he was expelled. These activities provided little but minor annoyances to those in power. It was the sentencing of Ambroise Lépine that finally provoked Governor-General Lord Dufferin into action. On 10 December 1874, he transmitted a large file on the amnesty question to the Colonial Secretary Lord Carnarvon in England, requesting that the imperial government settle the embarrassing issues still outstanding from the Red River uprising of 1869-70. Dufferin rehearsed the Canadian government's version of the amnesty, insisting that Taché, Ritchot, and Alfred H. Scott had all been told repeatedly that the Canadian government had no power to grant an amnesty and thus no Canadian official could promise one.

The governor-general went on to discuss the various grounds on which the amnesty was claimed. He insisted that early proclamations of pardons were all conditional, and predated Scott's execution. He denied that authorizations had been made to Archbishop Taché in early 1870. As far as promises made in connection with the negotiations between Ottawa and the delegates, Dufferin saw only "a direct conflict of assertion." He noted that Lisgar, Murdoch, and Sir John A. were "perfectly in accord as to what passed." He further hypothesized that Father Ritchot had not understood English very well at the interview with Lord Lisgar. As for Cartier, whatever he said was because of his "naturally sanguine temperament," which led him to believe he would eventually be able to obtain immunity for those involved. But in any case, Cartier's "casual conversations and private letters" could not possibly bind the government. So far so good. From Dufferin's narrow and strictly legal standpoint, whatever members of the Canadian government had led the delegates of the provisional government and the friends of Riel to believe about an amnesty were irrelevant. As for the meeting with Lord Lisgar and Sir Clinton Murdoch, Dufferin obviously preferred the "perfect accord" of Lisgar, Murdoch, and Sir John A. Macdonald to the assertions of Father Ritchot and Alfred H. Scott, despite the fact that the logic of their situation made it impossible for Ritchot and Scott to accept anything less than a British guarantee of an amnesty.

Explaining away the argument that Scott had been executed by a *de facto* government acting legally if ill-advisedly was no more difficult. Whether or not Riel's government had thought it had legitimately succeeded the HBC was irrelevant, the governor-general insisted. Quoting Chief Justice Wood in the Lépine court decision, Dufferin maintained "It is not possible for any lawful executive authority to spring into existence within Her Majesty's Dominions, unless it emanate from Herself." Since the Queen had not approved Riel's government, it was illegal and rebellious and so were its actions. Dufferin personally had the most problem with the final argument for amnesty he discussed: the acts and declarations of lieutenant-governor Archibald at the time of the Fenian crisis. To what extent was the Crown committed by its lieutenant-governor, he asked, especially since he was never disavowed or repudiated by anybody in authority? He himself would subsequently have pursued as a felon an individual he had previously invited to save the province, he asserted. Nevertheless, Dufferin did admit that Riel was regarded by many as a patriot who had been promised a pardon, and even Ontario had come to recognize the impossibility of a death sentence for those responsible for Scott's death. The governor-general was prepared to commute Lépine's sentence under his own responsibility, he concluded.

Two anonymous memoranda were attached to Dufferin's letter. One, entitled "Memorandum on Report of the Select Committee to Enquire into the Causes of the Difficulties in the North-West Territory in 1869-70," rehearsed the evidence placed before the select committee, arguing that the government had certainly made promises about an amnesty. The Dominion did not actually promise to grant an amnesty, it insisted, "but to secure it. This promise implies, that they would use every means in their power to obtain it." The Canadian government could not claim its obligations discharged until those promises were fulfilled. The other memorandum was entitled simply "NORTH-WEST QUESTION." It argued that promises of an amnesty had been conveyed to the insurgents. Furthermore, "The leaders of the insurgents have executed their share of the agreement, and that which was the consequence of the promise of amnesty, and the Government have taken advantage of that promise and of its results." The likelihood is that these opinions came from French-Canadian civil servants.

A few days later, on 18 December 1874, Louis Riel was in Washington, D.C., visiting Edmund Mallet, an American acquaintance of French-Canadian origins. Why Riel was in Washington is not clear, although he had perhaps some idea of seeking American assistance for the Métis. If so, no record has been left of his efforts. Riel did know of the sentence of death passed upon Ambroise Lépine, and probably suspected that this would provoke a final denouement on the amnesty business, although he was not aware of the official actions being taken by Lord Dufferin. In any event, as he himself would later write, on that day, "While I was seated on the top of a mountain near Washington…the same spirit who showed himself to Moses in the midst of the burning cloud appeared to me in the same manner. I was stupefied. I was confused. He said to me, 'Rise up, Louis David Riel, you have a mission to fulfil.' Stretching out my arms and bowing my head, I received this heavenly message."

This was the first unequivocal example of a vision that Riel has discussed in writing. It would have much consequence in the future. In the meantime, Riel went to visit Worcester, Massachusetts, where a substantial French-Canadian community existed. He spoke at a protest meeting called to support an amnesty for himself and Lépine. He told the gathering that "The sound of Lépine's and Nault's chains have aroused the sympathies of every French Canadian and every Catholic," adding, "The amnesty will be granted to us." He also invited his audience to emigrate to Canada, to help "assure the victory of the French-Canadian nationality in the vast territory of the North-West."

Less than a month after receiving Lord Dufferin's letter, Lord Carnarvon replied. He agreed the question of the amnesty required immediate disposition, and approved of a course of action by Dufferin apart from his ministers. The British government had always maintained that the governor-general had the right to act in such a situation. He also agreed with Dufferin's analysis of the arguments about government commitment to an amnesty. Archbishop Taché should have understood that the Crown could not delegate to Dufferin an unlimited power to pardon. The idea that there was a *de facto* government independent of Her Majesty was "unworthy of discussion." As for Archibald's actions, lieutenant-governors did not hold commissions from the Crown but were merely colonial administrative staff. But Carnarvon admitted the service rendered by the offenders was considerable. The question was not one of amnesty, he argued, but the extent of the just and reasonable punishment, given subsequent good service to the State. Lépine's sentence should be commuted, but it should be made clear that his offence was considerable. Riel must be treated the same way. Any liberation of these men after sentence should be predicated on a "total exclusion from any participation in political or parliamentary life."

On 20 January 1875, Lord Dufferin cabled Lord Carnarvon that he had commuted Ambroise Lépine's sentence to two years imprisonment and perpetual forfeiture of his political rights. The next day, on 11 February 1875, the Liberal government of Alexander Mackenzie finally dealt with the issue legislatively, introducing a motion, after considerable debate, granting a full amnesty to all involved in the Red River uprising, except Louis Riel, Ambroise Lépine, and W.B. O'Donoghue.

The Parliamentary Debate of 1875

The parliamentary debate of February 1875 was, of course, a highly partisan business. The Liberal government used the occasion to be critical of the previous administration, and the previous administration was forced to defend itself from accusations of impropriety and bad judgment. At the same time, the debates offer some interesting commentary, both on the subject of the negotiations with Canada and, by implication, on the recent conviction of Ambroise Lépine. Although the debate tells us much about politics in Canada in 1875, it also tells us much about Canadian attitudes toward Red River and Louis Riel. The leading political figures in the 1875 Parliament — Alexander Mackenzie, Sir John A. Macdonald, and Edward Blake — all had their say, as well as a number of less well-known figures and some who were yet to become well-known, such as Mackenzie Bowell and Wilfrid Laurier.

Prime Minister Alexander Mackenzie opened the final debate. A stereotypically dour Scot, Mackenzie was also a man of probity and honour. Perhaps most importantly, he was not a lawyer and took a common-sense approach to the complex legal issues of Riel and Red River. He insisted that his government was prepared to act on the Red River matter although it bore no responsibility for the events that had led to it, which he described as "an exceptional state of affairs — one that perhaps might not arise again in the lifetime of any of the members." He also maintained that he had sympathy with the people of the North-West Territory in their resistance to Canada, so long as that resistance was peaceful. Despite the violence, however, Mackenzie argued that the previous government had agreed to deal with the "insurrectionary party of Manitoba." Not only did the government thus recognize the provisional government, but also Louis Riel as its head. Mackenzie cited Archbishop Taché's testimony of his meeting with Sir George-Étienne Cartier in June, in which Cartier told the archbishop to tell Riel to continue to govern and be at the head of his people when the representative of Her Majesty arrived.

The prime minister had several obstacles to overcome in his argument. One was the assertions of the imperial statesmen that no *de facto* government could possibly exist in Her Majesty's territories without her consent. Mackenzie dealt at length with these constitutional technicalities about which Chief Justice Wood had made so much in his charge to the Lépine jury. He asserted that there had been a recognition of a *de facto* government. He admitted that "technically, perhaps constitutionally," there could be no such recognition of such a government within the British Empire. But nonetheless the government exercised authority and was the *de facto* government, "although legally and constitutionally they had no right to appear there in that character." It is worth noting that unlike Chief Justice Wood, Mackenzie had no hesitation to employ the documents generated in the parliamentary enquiry. He insisted that while it may have been technically true that there was no proof of an absolute promise of amnesty, "It was a mere evasion of the truth, to say no promise was made in any quarter than an amnesty was to be given." The prime minister added that evidence on this point was so abundant that he would be able to read extracts from it. Although Mackenzie did not make the point, these were extracts that Chief Justice Wood had not heard in his court.

Another problem faced by the prime minister were the specific denials of the British representatives that they had made any promises. Mackenzie proceeded to read copiously from the enquiry testimony of Taché and Ritchot as to the oral promises made by members of the government. He emphasized that "It was not a stray expression, not a mere remembrance of words cropped in conversations and successive and continuous interviews, it was the sole subject of discussion; that there was no possibility of being mistaken, and that the evidence showed conclusively that those people were led to believe that what they asked would undoubtedly be granted." The prime minister discussed the money given Riel and Lépine to leave the country. He added that it would be difficult to bring the two men to trial "without placing the minister of justice [who was Sir John A. Macdonald] in the dock along with them," although Chief Justice Wood had managed to do so.

In the matter of the Fenian business, Mackenzie took a similar line. Whether it was "really the law or not, whether it was to be understood as the law of nations or not; as the law of Great Britain or not; as a matter that binds the Crown or does not bind the Crown technically," there could be no doubt that the government had accepted services of Riel and the Métis. Under ordinary constitutional law, said the prime minister, when a government accepted the services of parties and asked them to risk their lives, that this acted as "a condonation of the offences of all such persons." It did not matter whether Lieutenant-Governor Archibald had misconstrued the danger or not.

The prime minister's interpretation of the events of the past did not go completely unchallenged, of course. The Orange leader Mackenzie Bowell, who was also a Conservative, immediately rose to declare his astonishment at both the resolutions and the line of argument used to defend them. He insisted that the prime minister's speech had been motivated by partisan politics. He denied that Mackenzie had given a "fair résumé" of the evidence, although most of his examples were from recent negotiations and statements rather than from the earlier ones. Bowell was also able to quote from the late imperial correspondence, particularly Lord Dufferin's letter, to demonstrate that Taché had exceeded his authority in making promises about an amnesty, although the prime minister's arguments did not really rely on this part of the archbishop's testimony. Bowell laid heavy emphasis on all the denials by Sir John A. Macdonald, Sir George-Étienne Cartier, Sir John Young, and Sir Clinton Murdoch, especially Murdoch. How could one prefer the evidence "of a gentleman with a very imperfect knowledge of the

English language, the language in which the interview had taken place, against that of the Governor-General and Sir Clinton Murdoch, and the deductions drawn from the whole evidence by the Governor-General and by Lord Carnarvon?"

Sir John A. Macdonald began his speech by insisting that the key question was whether the Crown of England was pledged to an amnesty. If the Crown was pledged, he said, the pledge must be honoured, regardless of the heinousness of the crime. Macdonald refused to accept Mackenzie's distinction between technical senses and actual ones involving the honour of the Crown. He also disagreed that the people of Red River were entitled to be upset about the Canadian takeover. He stood by every action of his government, even the thousand dollar promise to Riel and Lépine to leave the country. All were essential to acquire the western extension of territory. He admitted that the Scott murder complicated matters, and insisted that the present government had stimulated antagonism to Red River for partisan purposes.

Mackenzie, said Sir John, had gone around the country "holding his [Sir John's] Government responsible for the failure to arrest and punish the murderers of Scott, charged with a dereliction of duty, charged with soiling their hands and dipping them in the blood of Scott." His triumph was now, proclaimed the former prime minister. The very men who had so maligned and attempted to ruin him "were now bringing into this House a resolution that he [Sir John] would never have dared to propose in this House." Macdonald complained that he was being blamed for Mackenzie's inability to carry out on his own earlier promises to see Louis Riel hanged. He disparaged the banishment as any sort of punishment, claiming that sending the culprits to the United States for five years was no great hardship. Moreover, he insisted that the prerogative of mercy was the Crown's, and not Parliament's. Most of Macdonald's lengthy speech was devoted to insisting that the government had done what was necessary to acquire the North-West.

Despite his earlier support for Canada First (and its campaign against Louis Riel) and his constant battle with Alexander Mackenzie for dominance in the Liberal Party, Edward Blake supported the resolution for amnesty. He began by observing that Sir John A. Macdonald had ranged far beyond what was relevant to the question before the House. He understood the need for the former prime minister to defend his government, but the question was not whether Macdonald had acted for the best but what he had done and what were its consequences. With his usual incisiveness, Blake said that there were three classes of people who needed to vote against the resolution. One class were those who believed that the Crown was pledged to absolute amnesty, for this resolution imposed conditions. Another included those who did not believe that the Crown was pledged to anything. The third class composed those who thought that the Imperial government should act.

Blake himself insisted that the present resolution was the only practical one. None of the facts stated in the resolution had been really disputed. The government had not mentioned any of the disputed material, including Father Ritchot's conversation with Sir Clinton Murdoch and Lord Lisgar. It had been established in the parliamentary enquiry that the persons implicated in these troubles were absolutely convinced that a general amnesty had been promised, "and that conviction tended to facilitate the acquisition of the territory by Canada. Of that there could be no doubt." He approved avoiding the disputed points. Taché may or may not have been authorized to offer an amnesty, but he thought he was authorized, and the Canadian government did not publicly disavow the promise. The resolutions granted most people involved an absolute amnesty, and said to three or three people that there would be a large measure of relief, but that a sense of the horror of the crime committed was being conveyed.

Not until very late in the debate were any voices heard from French Canada. The main speaker from Quebec was Joseph-Alfred Mousseau, a Conservative from the Bagot riding. A nationalist, Mousseau had been a supporter of Riel for some years and had advocated his elections to the House of Commons. He saw the troubles in the North-West as standing in the way of the building up of the nation as an equitable union. Those in Quebec, said Mousseau, were convinced that the trouble had begun when a young people had been denied the rights, privileges, and immunities allowed to every province in the dominion. They thought Riel was being denied an amnesty because he belonged to the minority. Mousseau emphasized that there was no authority in Red River against which to rebel in 1869-70, and thought that this fact had been forgotten in the recent harsh words by the governor-general and Lord Carnarvon. He added that although Joseph Howe told Bishop Taché that he had exceeded his instructions in promising an amnesty upon his return to Red River, Howe did not withdraw the offer.

The Quebec MP made much of the question of what happened when ambassadors exceeded their powers, as Taché had apparently done, and concluded that the government was responsible for such transactions. He insisted that Lépine had been convicted only because of a "packed jury" and "a strong charge from a partial judge," since subsequent trials for the same offence had not resulted in verdicts. Louis Riel had suffered deeply for his part in the Scott business, spending five years as a fugitive apart from his family. Mousseau noted that eight Catholic bishops had transmitted a petition calling for an amnesty to reconcile the French minority of Quebec and of Manitoba. The death of Scott was not a crime, but "the act of a Government organizing an administration for the affairs of the country, and was at most only what others called an error of judgment." Mousseau concluded by moving an amendment that a full amnesty be granted to all persons connected with the North-West troubles, and for all acts committed. The amendment was supported by the Conservatives F.-L.-G Baby and Louis-François-Roderick Masson, both long-time defenders of Louis Riel.

A young Wilfrid Laurier rose immediately to answer Mousseau. He objected to introducing sectional antagonisms into the business at hand. Laurier insisted that he personally supported a full amnesty, but "the Imperial Government said that a complete amnesty was out of the question, and therefore nothing more need be said on that point." He was surprised that Mr. Mousseau was asking for something which the colonial secretary had declared impossible. This declaration was the main reason Quebec Liberals supported the resolution, said Laurier. Amor de Cosmos from British Columbia agreed that he would have preferred a total amnesty, and had voted for one in 1874, but would accept the present resolution as the best available. He did not claim that the problem was the imperial government, however, but that the difficulty with complete amnesty was that it could neither carry the House nor be accepted in the country. Several other speakers agreed with de Cosmos.

The vote on the amendment drew the support of only 23 MPs, all Conservatives from Quebec. No Liberals voted for it. One more minor amendment was attempted, and then the House divided on the main resolution, which was carried 126 to 50. The loss of the amendment for a complete amnesty disguised the amount of support in the House for an amnesty; all but one of those who had supported Mr. Mousseau were to be found in the negative. In reality, therefore, the support for at least this amnesty arrangement was 149 to 28. Unfortunately, the only amendments actually proposed to the House sought to extend the resolution, and so we have no way of knowing how much hard core opposition there was to any amnesty. Whether either Riel or Lépine would have found any consolation in these facts is another matter. What is clear is that the resolution carried so easily because it did not wipe the slate clean, but "punished" the two leading rebels for the murder of Scott. For Riel and Lépine, the amnesty would apply only after a period of banishment for five years from Her Majesty's Dominions. As a final closure to the Red River business, the parliamentary resolution was hardly satisfactory to anyone. But it did grant full pardons to a good many inhabitants of Manitoba, freeing them from possible prosecution for earlier "criminal" activity and officially rehabilitating them after the rebellion.

A Postscript

The parliamentary vote on the amnesty was not quite the last word on that subject. Ambroise Lépine rejected the amnesty offer because of its condition of exile, and he served out the remainder of his sentence for Scott's murder in the penitentiary, being released on 26 October 1876. He apparently continued to live without his political rights until his death in 1923. As for Louis Riel, he was still a Member of Parliament from Provencher in February of 1874. The House of Commons debated his membership later that month. On 22 February the prime minister laid the record of Riel's outlawry in Manitoba upon the table of the House of Commons. Three days later, Mackenzie opened the debate by observing that a judgment of outlawry had been entered against Riel, and without entering into the question of the legality of the legal process in Canada and following an earlier English precedent, he therefore moved that the record be read. This motion was carried, and the prime minister then moved: "That it appears by the said record that Louis Riel, a member of this House, has been adjudged an outlaw for felony." The House debated briefly whether the Louis Riel outlawed in Manitoba was the same individual who was a member of Parliament.

At this point, the Hon. J. H. Cameron moved to the real question at hand, which was whether a judgment of outlawry was constitutionally legal in Canada. Cameron emphasized that he wanted to expel Riel from Parliament, but felt it was important to do so properly. Cameron rehearsed the complex and lengthy proceedings by which outlawry could in English law be declared, insisting that it was essential that everything be done properly and in the exact order and giving the requisite amount of time between steps. The result, after all, was that an individual declared outlaw was liable to immediate execution without further proceeding. Therefore, as a form of protection of the individual, the law had to be extremely strictly observed, and any minute deviation was fatal to the process, for courts over the centuries had reversed the judgment for the smallest defects. Cameron argued that the process with Riel had many defects, but on its very face was flawed because he was outlawed on the same day he was required to appear in court. No individual who had the entire day to appear could possibly be outlawed until the following day, insisted Mr. Cameron, who pointed out a whole series of defects in the procedure. In short, there was some considerable doubt expressed about legality of the declaration of outlawry, but very little about the desirability of expulsion.

Toward the end of the debate, Sir John A. Macdonald offered a scathing judgment on what appeared to be the government strategy, claiming "There was no legal man in the House who would venture to say that the judgment of outlawry, as declared in these documents [of the Manitoba Court of Queen's Bench], would be sustained where British law existed, yet the House was told that for Parliamentary purpose this rotten, illegal paper must be accepted as correct." The vote, on 24 February, was 141 to 16 in favour of expulsion, although some members made clear that they did not agree that Riel had been adjudged an outlaw. While Riel had been expelled, chiefly on the grounds that he was an outlaw, it remained quite unclear what other effect the judgment of outlawry would have upon him. A number of lawyers in the House had insisted that the judgment would not stand up in court, although what court would overturn this action of the Manitoba Court of Queen's Bench? None of the lawyers had commented upon the timing of the parliamentary resolutions, although it would appear that because the amnesty was condition upon five years of exile, up until the end of the period of exile, Riel would still be regarded in Canada as a fugitive from justice and under sentence as an outlaw. Unlike Lépine, however, Riel tacitly accepted the conditional amnesty and began a five-year period of exile. He did not give up his political rights, however, and he did not always remain out of the country either.

It was entirely typical of Riel's complex life that even his expulsion from the Canadian House of Commons in 1875 should be accompanied by a considerable debate over the legality of the motion. It was Riel's fate to become involved in a long series of complicated legal issues, and his "outlawry" was simply one more of them.

-10-

Banishment and Regeneration

On 25 April 1875, the condition of five years' banishment from Her Majesty's Dominions took effect against Louis Riel. By this time, Riel had already been on the run for nearly five years, living mainly in the homes of friends and accommodating priests in the United States, and occasionally venturing to Quebec or Manitoba, obviously with some trepidation. He had no gainful employment, was never able to collect a salary for his parliamentary activities, and was constantly worried about money. Some funds came from the sale of land, but he was probably mainly supported by Bishop Taché, perhaps with laundered government money designed to keep him away from home — and by the charity of friends.

Riel's sentence was in some ways harsh — too long a period to meet with equanimity, too short a time to decide to put behind him thoughts of an eventual normal life among his own people, or even a life of leadership among the Métis. In any event, Riel might have done what thousands of other exiles before and since have done, by finding somewhere to settle in for the duration and making the best of it, perhaps among congenial fellow refugees. The United States certainly had a number of communities of political refugees in its larger eastern cities to which he might have attached himself. It also had a number of Franco-American communities which were sympathetic to him. Riel might also have joined many European exiles in Paris, which was the home of many more displaced people than the United States. He talked about Europe in the autumn of 1875, but apparently never seriously considered it, probably partly because of the cost and partly because he was quintessentially North American. Alternatively, Riel might have determined to break totally with his past, and again like thousands of exiles before and since, opted to begin a new life in the United States. In the short run, he did not decide firmly on either of these choices, and found himself almost inadvertently overcome by a third possibility, the result of his religious visions.

Riel was not able to stick singlemindedly to any of his options for very long, and they appeared and disappeared from his life over the next few years. Part of him wanted to start afresh in the free air of the United States — holding a steady job, having a wife and family, becoming a moral influence on his community. We might call this the "responsible" or "sensible" Riel. It was mainly in this context that American citizenship became so symbolically important. Another part of him, however, wanted to complete the liberation of his people he had begun in 1869. We might call this the "radical" Riel. To this end he attempted a variety of strategies, which over time became less extreme and more ameliorative, but they all started from an American base. In this context, his American exile was practically useful. First he tried to organize in the United States a military invasion of Manitoba, then he attempted to create an international alliance between First Nations and Métis peoples, and finally he turned to seek the gradual improvement of the living standards and morals of his people in the United States. This last effort nudged him back into the "responsible" mode. Yet another quite distinct and powerful part of Riel, ever since his vision on the mountaintop late in 1874, wanted to become the prophet of a new messianic movement. We might call this the "prophetic" Riel. As we shall see, this part of his ambitions and personality became intimately connected with what some people thought was mental instability or madness. After years of suppression, this aim finally emerged fully triumphant in 1884 and led straight to his final confrontation with Canada.

These contradictory aspirations often warred with one another in Riel's life, with first one then another coming to the fore. Occasionally elements of all three aspirations would fit together to form a new pattern, making Riel's life during the years 1875 to 1884 often seem quite kaleidoscopic. Our inability to date precisely most of the private writings of Riel in these years undoubtedly contributes to the sense of constantly shifting and recurring inconsistency in his behaviour.

The Invasion of Manitoba

Riel's first response to exile was an effort to restore his position in Manitoba by military force. His correspondence in 1875 contained a number of veiled references to these plots and plans. In October he went to Indianapolis, Indiana to consult with Senator Oliver P. Morton about his plan, which he presented in skeletal form without an elaboration of all its details. He blamed both the lack of detailed explication and his weaknesses in English with the lack of enthusiasm evidenced by the American politician. During his meeting with Morton, who was partially paralysed from a stroke, and according to Riel's own subsequent account, he prayed for the healing of one of Morton's legs. The reason for concentrating on one leg was so that Morton would know who to be grateful to for any restoration.

The "plan" Riel presented to Morton was undoubtedly the same scheme which appeared in a "memoir" (or memorial) to President Ulysses S. Grant written around the same time, but probably never communicated to the American leader, at least not in this form. Between 10 and 15 December, Riel did meet with Grant, but there is no record of their conversation. Riel opened this memorial by reminding Grant of their previous audience in late 1874, where he had first introduced his idea. He had interpreted the president's response at that time as potentially favourable, although it was probably much the same as Grant had offered the Métis in 1871 — come back and see me when you have more support. Now Riel again outlined the grievances of the Métis against the Canadian government accumulated since 1870. According to the memorial, Canada had not fulfilled its promises, and the Métis had exhausted all peaceable means of redress. In order to force Canada to complete its treaty agreements with the Métis, Riel had a six-point programme, headed by "rescuing" the government of Manitoba and the North-West from Canadian hands, setting up a new government under British auspices, and inviting from the United States "all the French Canadian and Irish American citizens who would be willing to share our fortune." He envisioned the French in Manitoba and the Catholic Irish in a province farther west. The new government would be funded by bonds sold in private markets.

While the presentation of grievances was quite lucid and credible, Riel's calculations of potential support verge on the incredible. "In all, I have in Manitoba and North-West," he wrote, "about 68,000 souls to support my policy. The Canadian government have not more than 10,000 souls, to resist my forces." He anticipated total armed backing from all the mixed-bloods, from three to four thousand "adventurers who are against Canada to a man," and the "favourable dispositions" of 38,000 aboriginal inhabitants of the region. He discounted 3,000 of the pro-Canadians as Mennonites who would not fight. As for the new Mounted Police, they "can hardly take care of their horses." These were the calculations of an impotent rebel leader indulging his fondest fantasies. Riel clearly saw himself in 1875 as British (he talked about England rather than Britain), and the United States government chiefly as a supporter of an independent Métis state.

The Mad Business

Sometime in early December of 1875, Riel had a powerful experience of mystical illumination in St. Patrick's Church in Washington. The usual date given is 8 December, the fifth anniversary of the proclamation of the provisional government of Red River. Riel's most detailed account of this experience is available only through the later writings of one of his critics eager to demonstrate his insanity, and its reliability cannot be tested. In his autobiographical notes written in the Regina prison, Riel recorded that he "receives the Holy Spirit at the Gloria in Excelsis during high Mass at St. Patrick's Church in Washington. And then God anointed him with His divine gifts and fruits of His Spirit, as prophet of the New World." About the same time he also had an encounter with a virgin who has "sometimes stood over my desk." She would later appear with a child, supposedly the baby Jesus. By 16 December 1875, his friend Edmund Mallet had removed Riel from Washington to Worcester, Massachusetts, explaining that Riel had a bout of insanity in the nation's capital.

Even a well-adjusted and perfectly normal person has ups and downs, periods of exaltation and periods of anxiety. A life without emotional variation would be genuinely abnormal. We are told that the mass killer "Son of Sam" had no emotional life. Although some biographers have hunted diligently in Riel's previous history for suggestions of emotional problems or even madness, none of these early symptoms is very well documented, and little detailed clinical evidence is presented. Not only is much apocryphal material employed, but in some biographies conversations are invented and every bit of emotional difficulty is overinterpreted. Most of the evidence for a supposed 1864 bout of depression, for example, is based on comments written by Riel's uncle John Lee after Riel's execution in 1885. Lee wrote in 1886 that after the death of Louis's father, "I perceived then that this profound sorrow was affecting his brain and that he was delirious. This was obvious in his exaggerations and religious eccentricities, for he threw himself into excesses of piety and spoke in language on religious matters which I found unreasonable. My wife noticed the same thing and mentioned it to me. Afterwards he remained very melancholic. I observed that to last about a year and a half, after which he became his own self again." One might well expect a young man to be thrown off stride by the unexpected death of a beloved parent, especially when he was having romantic difficulties at the same time. If Riel exhibited excessive piety and language — and Lee does not give us examples or explain what he regards as "excessive" — it must be remembered that he was a devout young man whose training and instincts would lead him to turn to his religion to help him deal with his problems. Even if John Lee truly believed the later Riel to be insane and transferred the diagnosis to the earlier period, there is really nothing described here that passes beyond the bounds of impassioned adolescent behaviour.

The next major bout of illness for Riel came in late February of 1870. He fell seriously ill. His mother was summoned, and the reported diagnosis was "brain fever," with no further clinical symptoms offered. The term comes from Alexander Begg's diary, and it conjures up images of fevered ravings, but we know little about the illness. This illness was very brief, and was probably a virus. It was true that this was a complex period in Riel's life, and that it was followed quite promptly by the great miscalculation of his life with Thomas Scott. But beyond the series of threats which Riel had issued to many of his prisoners before finally following through with Thomas Scott, there is no evidence of mental unbalance in his behaviour. Again, however, some biographers would like to make much of this illness.

In February of 1871, Riel fell seriously ill in St. Joseph and was nursed again for several weeks by his mother. This illness apparently led his loved ones to fear for his life. Once again biographers are tempted to see portents in what appears on limited evidence to be a physical ailment. We do have some clinical symptoms. Riel's temperature soared, and the joints of his arms and legs became swollen, red, and painful. He may have become depressed, not unusual with such an illness. He may have even been concerned about assassination, but he was officially on the run and men were lurking around with ambitions to kill him. It is hard to be paranoid when your enemies really are out to get you. George Stanley suggests that Riel's illness was somehow connected with hardships and fears of assassination, the strains of an uncertain future, the delays in the promulgation of the amnesty "until he could no longer bear the double burden of anxiety and misfortune." In a lovely example of the legerdemain possible in writing about these matters, Stanley's next sentence is "In February he fell ill, seriously ill." Stanley does not explicitly link these two sentences but merely juxtaposes them. Many readers will assume the connection, however. A germ or virus seems a more likely cause than emotional instability for this illness.

Through all the problems of the next few years, Riel was constantly complaining of "anxiety" and difficulties in sleeping. But on the whole, he does not appear to have suffered any serious illness in this trying period, surely a tribute to his inherent emotional stability. Nor was any of his behaviour during a complex set of political manoeuvrings in any way aberrant. By January of 1874, Riel was tired. A meeting with Bishop Bourget revitalized him, but it is hard to find anything abnormal here. A year and a half later, not long after the expulsion from the House of

Commons, Bourget sent a sympathetic letter of support for Riel which was full of vague generalizations about faith and spirituality. That such vagueness struck a respondent chord suggests that Riel's religious state had not yet achieved much focus.

And so Riel's behaviour in 1875 appears to have had few documentable antecedents. Before we examine this behaviour more closely, a few words about the profound sea change in our understanding and interpretation of insanity which has occurred since 1875 are perhaps in order. In 1875, most Canadians would have recognized three types of mental illness: congenital or traumatic mental deficiency, raving mania, or irrational belief and action. The society in general was a good deal more tolerant of aberrant behaviour than we are today. Professional experts for dealing with madness were almost non-existent in Canada. They consisted of a handful of men who ran the asylums and an equally small handful of doctors who were either trained in a new speciality called neurology, which was concerned with nervous conditions, or who called themselves "alienists." The asylum doctors tended to be much more repressive and conservative in their views than the neurologists and alienists, who wanted to place more emphasis on understanding the emotions. The asylum doctors were keepers of the insane, often more interested in restraint than rehabilitation.

Everybody could agree that madness was a disease of the brain, with a specific set of causes. Dr. Henry Howard, who admitted Louis Riel to Longue Point asylum in 1876, defined insanity as "a physical disease caused by a pathological change in the sensory nerves and the organ of consciousness." Heredity was important. Although the experts did understand that absolute irrationality did not necessarily mean madness, and rationality did not necessarily mean sanity, this was often forgotten. Medical views of insanity tended to be very mechanistic and the doctors treated religious impulses basically as delusions. If one were more than conventionally religious, it was probably a good thing to stay away from the madness experts. The American psychologist William James would not deliver or publish his seminal *The Varieties of Religious Experience: A Study in Human Nature: Being the Gifford Lectures on Natural Religion Delivered in Edinburgh in 1901-1902* until early in the new century. Nobody in 1875 doubted that there was an objective state called "madness" or "insanity" or that it could be readily identified. Explaining its causes or treating it was a bit trickier.

Whether insanity has an "objective reality" is now a question which has been hotly debated in the scholarly literature over the past generation. The leading critic of the reality of insanity has been Thomas Szasz, who in a whole series of books, such as *The Myth of Mental Illness* (1972), has argued essentially that madness is an invention or construction of society and its agent, psychiatry, for essentially repressive purposes. Unable to deal tolerantly and openly with the various symptoms of irrationality, it has chosen instead to allow those who exhibit the symptoms to be labelled, treated, and institutionalized. Even if one does not take such a cynical view of the modern psychiatrist and the modern mental institution, there is plenty of evidence that the medical profession cannot agree on either the diagnosis or the treatment of mental illness. Moreover, in recent years the whole scientific basis of the psychiatric enterprise as exemplified by Sigmund Freud has come under heavy attack. The assurance of the 19th century that there was a reality called insanity and that it could be understood scientifically can really no longer be safely maintained or sustained.

The identification of insanity is now often understood as particularly difficult in the case of those whose symptoms have a religious dimension. What one made of extreme religious experiences in the 19th century to a large extent depended upon context. Joseph Smith could uncover the golden tablets of the book of Mormon with the aid of an angel and become the spiritual leader of a large community of Americans. Mary Baker Eddy could discover with God's aid that most illness was in the mind, and become the head of another major church in the United States. Within the Roman Catholic Church, spiritual visitations were an everyday occurrence in convents and monasteries across the continent. Riel's sister Sara had religious experiences as a nun that might have seen her institutionalized in secular life. The behaviour of many people at outdoor camp meetings of Protestant evangelists would have been regarded as quite aberrant if witnessed on the street. Madness takes on a different meaning when it is inspired by or closely associated with religious revelation or — as Roman Catholic spokesmen might put it — the quest for "heroic sanctity." "One half of the Christian world," wrote William Cowper in 1766 of his own religious experiences — "would call this madness, fanaticism and folly: but are not these things warranted by the word of God?" It was, and is, a good question.

How severely Riel was afflicted over the ensuing few months after his removal from Washington in late 1875 depends on the witness and the period of observation, since the affliction was intermittent. Ferdinand Gagnon thought him quite sensible. Father Jean Baptiste Primeau wrote that Riel wanted to proclaim in Worcester the message "he would soon have to proclaim throughout the world," and broke down in tears when told this was impossible. John Wesley might have responded the same way to similar information. Riel was moved from Worcester to Suncook, New Hampshire, on Christmas Eve, a journey described ten years later by Ferdinand Gagnon for his newspaper *Le Travailleur*. According to the reporter, on this train ride, Riel imagined himself part of a holy trinity that included the Count de Chambord and Don Carlos of Spain, and he snorted like a bull until silenced by Father Primeau with "a severe look."

In January 1876 he was taken to Keeseville, New York, where he disturbed the Barnabé household by remaining awake all night, pacing up and down, crying and howling. On the night his uncle John Lee stayed in Keeseville he roared for hours like a bull. John Lee took Riel back to Montreal on the train, where he shouted at the passengers, "Keep still. Do not laugh. I beg you. I am a prophet." At Lee's house in St. Jean Baptiste, he tore his clothes and bedclothes, denied that he was ill, and shouted in a loud voice that he was a prophet. He insisted, "No, I'm not crazy! Never say I'm crazy! I have a mission to perform and I am a prophet. You should say that you don't understand. I am sent by God." In all of Riel's unusual behaviour, he was clearly acting on the basis of what he thought was divine revelation. Even the Catholic Church would allow that conventional definitions of insanity and sanctity are not necessarily incompatible.

Did Riel need to be institutionalized? Had he been at home with his mother and family in Manitoba, the answer is no. He doubtless could have been shepherded through this period with love and tolerance. He was not a danger to anyone except perhaps himself, and it does not appear he would really have done himself any harm. On the one occasion when he lashed out at an individual, it was at a nun at the asylum who tried to take away a book in which his sister had written his name. He did sometimes struggle with the guards who tried to restrain him. One wonders whether he ever remembered Thomas Scott on any of these occasions. But before his commitment he had not been in a comfortable place surrounded by those he loved. He was far from home and a transient exile, being looked after mainly by priests and their households. The priests tried to be sympathetic, but were not accustomed to dealing with such strong religious feelings and expressions. Even in the asylums Riel had most of his trouble with the priests, not surprising given their orthodox views and his insistence on prophecy. At one point, having been barred from the chapel for excessive behaviour, he wrote to the chaplain at Beauport: "I forbade you orally this morning, and I forbid you this afternoon in writing, to say or sing the holy mass, claiming the right to command 'in the name of the Holy Spirit, because the divine spirit has consecrated me sovereign pontiff, His prophet and priest-king, by descending upon me; and because the bishop of Montreal, bishop of apostolic, Catholic, and Roman ordination, has endowed me with total jurisdiction in pronouncing over me the following words: 'Therefore be blessed by God and men.'" This missive was signed "Louis 'David' Riel. By grace of Jesus Christ Prophet, Infallible Pontiff, and Priest-King."

When in early March of 1876 Riel was admitted to the Hospital of St. Jean de Dieu at Longue Point, he was listed as patient number 565, "Louis R. David." The pseudonym was necessary, of course, because technically Riel was still in exile, although a fair number of people, including Sir Wilfrid Laurier, were eventually aware of his situation. The welcoming Dr. Henry Howard could see little initial sign of abnormality, but in Longue Point Riel wrote letters full of religious ramblings. He later recorded that what others saw as insanity was really "continual commitment with God." Dr. Henry Howard, who has left us an account of Riel's stay at Longue Point, accepted him as a patient because "I believed him to be guilty of the murder he was accused of, [that of Thomas Scott] and I believed every murderer to be either insane or a fool." Howard was in many ways a typical asylum superintendent in Canada. Trained in Dublin and London, he specialized in ophthalmology upon his immigration to Canada in 1842. Despite an absence of professional credentials in the field, he was appointed medical superintendent of the asylum at Saint-Jean, Quebec in 1862, and apparently acquired his expertise with the insane on the job. Howard was unusual, however, in his conviction that all serious criminals were not responsible for their actions because of moral derangement. He was not called to testify in Riel's trial in 1885. Although Howard did believe in rehabilitation, most of the problems Riel experienced at Longue Point were because he was being forcibly detained, a familiar cycle for those institutionalized at this period. He broke ornaments and candles on the altar in the chapel, ran through the corridors naked, and struggled with his guards. When forbidden to attend Mass because of his excesses, he went on a three-day hunger strike. He spent much of his time restrained in a strait jacket.

Not surprisingly, Dr. Howard eventually sent Riel on to The St. Michel-Archange Asylum at Beauport, where he continued to behave abnormally for some months. Beauport had a much lower record of "cures" than Longue Point, because it was run on a lower budget and paid less attention to rehabilitation. The admitting doctor at Beauport filled out a medical history which noted the absence of physical symptoms and added that psychological symptoms consisted chiefly of a tendency to become 'furieux" when thwarted in his role as a prophet. Much of Riel's time at Beauport was spent writing about and describing his visions and revelations. At one point he met Sir Wilfrid Laurier, who found him sensible until religion came up. Then, wrote Laurier, "Riel's deep-set eyes lit up, and he launched into an excited and humbled harangue, boasting vaguely of the great mission for the further revelation of God's will which a heavenly vision had urged him to undertake."

Somewhere in the course of his days at Beauport, Riel apparently learned how to hide the symptoms he was experiencing and to present to the world the behaviour it desired. He gradually ceased to struggle against confinement and he became increasingly less confined. Eventually he was even allowed outside the asylum for brief periods if accompanied. He restricted his prophetism to his private writings, which persuaded one clerical observer by February 1877 to observe that "He is beginning to forget his role as prophet. He hardly prophesies any more." Father J. B. Bolduc, the asylum chaplain, subsequently reported to Archbishop Taché, "He isn't pope any longer. He went to communion yesterday." Both these reports speak to what it was about Riel that bothered people, especially the clerics. By early January of 1878 Riel himself was able to observe to one of the doctors that "I had come believe myself a prophet or something similar," adding, "However, one day, tired of remonstrances and objections I asked myself if perhaps I was wrong and everyone else was right. From that moment light dawned in my mind." He did not actually stop believing he was a prophet, however, but had merely learned to keep quiet about it in public.

Riel learned about the need for external conformity sufficiently to be discharged from confinement and released back into the world. That his doctors had some inkling of what had happened is demonstrated by the comment of one of them that he was cured — "more or less." Having once been institutionalized, however, he would always carry with him the stigma of having been crazy. One observer in October 1878 reported that "His mind shows the most perfect lucidity, the greatest ability. One could truthfully say that he never had a breakdown, if one never knew anything of his past." But people did know Riel's history. In January of 1879 Riel met in Manitoba with old friend Joseph Dubuc, who asked him whether he had truly been mentally ill. Riel answered that he had been merely pretending to be mad in order to find sanctuary from two governments that sought his death. Dubuc later reported to Taché on this conversation, adding, "When I heard him express these ideas in an inspired and prophetic tone of voice, I understood that he was still a bit touched in the head."

Much ink has been spent in attempting to diagnose Louis Riel's mental condition. Most medical opinion has held that he suffered from some sort of megalomania which gave him delusions of grandeur and spiritual revelations. An alternate answer seems simple and straightforward enough, however. Riel had experienced visions and believed that he was a special prophet of God. As Dr. Augustus Jukes observed at Riel's trial in 1885, "There are men who have held very remarkable views with respect to religion and who have always been declared to be insane until they gathered together great numbers of followers and became leaders of a new sect, then they became great prophets and great men." Riel did not manage to found a sect before his death, but this failure does not affect the overall conclusion. Given his spiritual state, the question of whether or not he was mad is totally irrelevant. Religious visionaries have never been bound by the normal rules. If they were, the lives of Jesus or St. Paul (to mention only a few of those who were God's prophets) would have been far different. This position has been accepted by several scholars specializing in Riel studies in recent years, most notably Thomas Flanagan and Gilles Martel.

The Evelina Interlude

Upon his discharge from Beauport, Riel headed almost immediately for Keeseville, New York, and began the first of two different attempts to "go straight" — that is, to become a conventional individual eschewing his own self-conception as a Man of Destiny. In Keeseville he borrowed money from his friend Father Fabien Barnabé and rented a small holding which he intended to farm. Riel expressed his thinking at this time in his poem "L'Ésprit immonde est un colosse." In part, he wrote: "Lord, calm in me the political spirit, give me stability." That stability, he prayed, would come through farming, the rural environment, and through the love of a good woman.

Riel had the woman in the person of "Evelina, ma trés aimable blonde." Riel had probably begun courting Marie-Elizabeth-Evelina Barnabé, Father Barnabé's consumptive sister, before he was whisked away to Montreal at the end of 1875. Born in L'Assomption, Quebec, Evelina (as she was usually called) kept house for her brother in Keeseville, New York, in the mid-1870s. According to biographer Maggie Siggins, she was blonde, blue-eyed, slight of build, and a first-rate musician who played the organ in her brother's church. Riel's poetry written about Evelina suggests a real but ambivalent passion. Evelina was "ma soeur" in his verse and she signed her letters to him, "votre petite soeur," an interesting juxtaposition of roles. He and Evelina became secretly engaged; her mother did not approve of Louis.

Partly because of the maternal objections, but mostly at Evelina's behest, Riel felt it important to be able to support her before asking her to marry him. Thus Riel headed for New York City, never to see Evelina again, although the two corresponded for some months until May 1879. She certainly expected him to make something of himself, and in one of her last letters doubted that she had the qualities he wanted in a wife. She was right, apparently, although she wrote that her problem was that she was humble and not very courageous, "not suited to the high position that I should have to occupy if you are successful." When Riel went to New York City at the end of the 1878 harvest, he was looking for a job and also pursuing more schemes for the invasion of Manitoba with the Fenians. Riel got so far as to place a classified ad in a New York newspaper, but could find no occupation or career which seemed to suit him. It was probably at this point that he wrote his poem "Dans la grande république." This poem began, "Dans la grande république/ Je viens faire un peu d'argent," and ended several of its stanzas, "Ça je suis canadien." It spoke of being "deadly serious about comfort and gain," not normally a Riel characteristic. Evelina's letters to Riel in New York are very supportive, especially of his attempts to become a Métis leader. We do not know very much about Evelina, but her surviving correspondence suggests that she was intelligent and stubborn. Despite her comments, perhaps she intimidated Louis. Evelina herself may have appreciated this fact.

In late 1878 Riel travelled west to pursue an employment opportunity with a Catholic colonization agency headed by Bishop John Ireland of Minneapolis. When Ireland spurned him, he drifted back to St. Joseph, North Dakota, near the Manitoba border. While residing there he refused to permit his friends to pursue the question of a pardon. "I don't care about it," he wrote. "I do not even wish to take advantage of it to return to Manitoba. I want to stay here, on the frontier, a living and perpetual protest against England for its ill-intentioned proceedings against me." At this point, Riel obviously saw himself as an outcast from English injustice rather than as that new man, an American. In the summer of 1879, Riel joined the Métis buffalo hunt as it travelled west in search of the diminished herds. By December of that year, he could write his brother from Fort Assiniboine that the buffalo hunters had elected him chief of the camp, the most prestigious leadership position they could confer. Although he did not say so, he had stopped writing to Evelina.

Organizing the Métis and Native Peoples

During his first months in Montana, in late 1879, Riel entertained notions of organizing some sort of radical political movement among the Métis and the First Nations of the region. We do not know a great deal about these efforts, and much of the evidence is suspect, for it comes from accounts after Riel's surrender and execution. Nevertheless, according to later statements by several different individuals, Riel — while he was staying at the Milk River over the winter of 1879-80 — met with a number of aboriginal leaders in an attempt to forge an alliance. Superintendent James J. Walsh of the North West Mounted

Police later recalled visiting Chief Red Stone of the Assiniboine, who had in his possession a document jointly signed by himself and Riel proclaiming they would protect the lands that belonged to them.

Chief Crowfoot, after the 1885 uprising, told a journalist that in the spring of 1880 he and some Cree leaders met with the Métis leader. Riel "wanted me to join with all the Sioux, and Crees, and half-breeds," Crowfoot recalled. "The idea was to have a general uprising and capture the North-West, and hold it for the Indian race and the Métis." At this meeting, Riel seized Chief Little Pine's copy of Treaty No. 6 and theatrically trampled it under his foot, much as he had done with Lieutenant-Governor McDougall's proclamation ten years earlier. Crowfoot's interpreter, Jean L'Heureux, who had been supplying information to the Canadian government throughout the 1880s, reported to Sir John A. Macdonald in 1886 that "The practical plan was to take opportunity of some horse difficulties of the Police with the halfbreeds; attack and take possession of Wood Mountain Fort; they were then to make for Fort Walsh, and from the last place, make for Battleford. The Blackfeet were to take possession of [RCMP Commissioner] Macleod. After that last exploit, Riel was to proclaim a provisional government." In the autumn of 1880, Heureux informed Lieutenant-Governor Dewdney that Riel was agitating halfbreed conspiracies with the Indians. His "modest motto" was "That the N.W.T. is the natural property of the Indian and Half-breed, ought to be set apart for their exclusive use, ruled & governed by them alone." Most of the chiefs treated Riel with downright suspicion. Big Bear told him bluntly, "We should not fight the Queen with guns. We should fight her with her own laws."

As he was about to be executed in November of 1885, the aboriginal extremist Wandering Spirit gave a "jailhouse interview" to two Canadian journalists. In it he said:

> Four years ago, we were camped on the Missouri River in the Long Knives' land. Big Bear was there, Imasees, Four Sky Thunder and other chiefs of the band. Riel was there, trading whisky to the Indians. He gave us liquor and said he would make war on this country. He asked us to join him in wiping out the Canadians. The government had treated him badly. He would demand much money from them. If they would not give, he would spill blood, plenty of Canadian blood.

It is hard to decide what to make of this testimony. It is in the nature of "death-bed" statements, and much of it is confirmed by other accounts. What is new here are the statements that Riel was dealing in whisky and that he was distributing liquor to the Indians in order to win their allegiance. The latter piece of information is quite credible, since liquor was one of the basic components of gift exchange on the western frontier, as it had been since the 17th century. It would be hard to attempt to win over the First Nations without distributing it. The former comment, that he was "trading whisky to the Indians," is in a somewhat different category. Wandering Spirit might have meant "distributing whisky to the Indians," which is a bit different than trading in it. In any event, attempting to demonize Riel on the basis of one phrase, possibly badly translated, as one recent author has done, seems to be going a bit far. Riel was not necessarily corrupting aboriginals the length and breadth of Montana.

The major surviving evidence in Riel's writings of his meetings with aboriginals at this time is a document "L'avenir des chefs Métis-Canadiens-français dans les États-unis," which was written about this time. This memorandum is little more than a series of catalogued descriptions of the various Indian tribes that frequented the Milk River region over the winter of 1879-80 in the vicinity of the Métis buffalo hunters' encampment. In the later part of the winter of 1880, Riel wrote to the American commander at Fort Assiniboine in very humble terms to thank him for allowing the Métis hunters to winter on the Indian reservation at Milk River and reporting that those who had not yet left the site would soon do so. Riel would travel aimlessly with this group of hunters — a motley collection of Métis, aboriginals, and rough types — for the next couple of years.

Settling Down, Part II

On 17 May 1880, Riel declared his intention to become an American citizen and renounce his allegiance to Queen Victoria. He would later write in a poem, "The United States sheltered me/The English didn't care/What they owe me they will pay/I am a citizen." His five-year sentence of banishment had ended only a few weeks before his declaration. In his final speech to the jury at his 1885 trial in Regina, Riel explained the timing of his declaration:

> Did I take my American paper, put my papers of American naturalization during my five years' banishment? No, I did not want to give to the States a citizen of banishment, but when my banishment had expired, when an officer at Battleford — somewhere on this side of the line, in Benton — invited me to come to the North-West I said: No, I will go to an American court, I will declare my intention, now that I am free to go back, and choose another land. It sored my heart…but I felt that in coming back to this country [Canada] I could not reenter it without

protesting against all the injustice which I had been suffering, and in doing it I was renewing a struggle which I had not been able to continue as a sound man, as I thought I was, I thought it better to begin a career on the other side of the line.

This strategy had been quite sensible and obviously carefully thought out. Riel saw the question of citizenship as important, particularly as a symbolic act in his own life.

For the time being, instead of forging Métis-aboriginal alliances to invade Canada, Riel turned instead to ameliorating the conditions of his people in Montana. On 6 August 1880 he took the first step in his new policy by drafting a petition addressed to Colonel Nelson A. Miles at Fort Keogh on behalf of the Métis of Montana. The petition was a modest one. It asked the American government "to set apart a portion of land as a special reservation in this territory for the half-breeds," from which liquor would be excluded. It also requested money for education, agricultural equipment, seed, and livestock. The petition did not talk about the Métis' share of aboriginal rights, but pointed out that "as halfbreeds we stand between the civilized and uncivilized man, and are closely related with the several tribes of the northwest." This suggested that the Métis had some influence with the Indians, which the American government might find useful. Miles liked the idea, but United States Indian Agent A. R. Keller dismissed it out of hand, noting that although the Métis dressed "like Americans" they were "British subjects, possessing however the habits customs and manners of the aboriginees in the main, but with superior intelligence and cunning which render them dangerous." For Keller, the Métis would "certainly be an undesirable class of population to encourage to settle in this Territory." As Thomas Flanagan has pointed out, many of the Métis who signed this petition had actually been born in the United States or had been resident there for many years.

From the time of the 1880 petition to his departure for Saskatchewan in 1884, Riel concentrated his public life on improving the situation of the Montana Métis. He tried chiefly for self-reform, criticizing the people for their alcoholic consumption and neglect of the Sabbath. Sometime in early 1881 Riel met a young Métisse woman. Her name was Marguerite Monet Bellehumeur. Her father, Jean Monet Bellehumeur, was a native of Quebec who had married Marie Malaterre, probably in Red River. Marguerite had been born in St. François Xavier on 15 January 1861. She was a very pretty young woman. Her only photograph shows off her oval face (but does not suggest a dark skin) and her black hair, with fashionable ringlets in the front and what looks like a pony-tail behind. Although illiterate, she spoke Cree, French, and English. Riel fell in love with the quiet young Métisse, and married her (with her father's permission) on 28 April 1881 according to the fashion of the country; their marriage was solemnized by Father Joseph Damiani on 6 March 1882.

Marguerite bore Riel two children — Jean and Marie Angélique — and lost one in pregnancy while Riel was in prison in 1885. Marguerite was apparently passive and submissive, and she supported her husband without question. The marriage to Marguerite is one of the many mysterious parts of Riel's private life. She was quite different in background from his two earlier known female loves, both of whom had been of French-Canadian origins. Riel married Marguerite while still formally (if secretly) engaged to Evelina Barnabé; at least, he had never officially broken off their understanding.

Riel also became involved in Montana politics, supporting the Republicans rather than the Democrats. In this period the Republicans tended to be the radicals and the Democrats the backroom boys committed to the status quo. We do not know what Riel made of the label put on the Republican faction opposed to President James Garfield in 1881. It was the "halfbreeds." There was some controversy over his activities, chiefly charges that he had sought votes from Métis who were not American citizens. In fact, as he would later demonstrate in court, the Métis in question were born in the United States. He also served briefly as a deputy marshall. In late 1882 Riel wrote a letter to the editor of the Helena *Daily Herald*, which was printed on 18 December of that year. In it he denied that he had been a rebel, but was rather the leader of a political movement resisting an armed annexation of his country. Both American public opinion and the administration at Washington had supported his movement, Riel claimed. He also denied that he was a renegade. He had been banished, but he could have returned to Manitoba in 1880. "Notwithstanding the invitations of my friends and even some of my former enemies, I have freely determined not to re-enter my Province, because the British rule does not suit me, and I have chosen this country as my adopted land." On 16 March 1883 Louis David Riel became an American citizen in an open session of the U.S. District Court of the Third Judicial District of the Territory of Montana, again renouncing his allegiance to Queen Victoria in the process. It is perhaps worth noting that he used his "prophetic" name in his citizenship ceremony.

A few weeks before the final citizenship ceremony, in February 1883, Evelina Barnabé unexpectedly reappeared in Riel's life. She wrote her fiancé a letter, having read a story about him in an American newspaper. She tried to get his address from his sister Henriette, then wrote to him in Montana. Her letter noted that she had been ill, perhaps with the tuberculosis that would eventually kill her, and it assumed they were still engaged. Riel understandably had much trouble in answering her letter, which begged him to write the truth and added, "If you do not do so you will bring on yourself the greatest curses God can utter, for having destroyed forever the future of one who has only one regret if such as the case, of having known and loved you." How could he answer this command, with all its deliberate invocation of guilt? Riel's response, which was never completed and survives in several drafts in his papers, was of course pretty lame, although it offers some hints toward the motives for the abandonment of Evelina. He suggested that he was not happy about keeping their engagement secret and feared that she was ashamed of the relationship. He mentioned her insistence that she could not marry him until he had provided a proper home for her. We will never know the entire answer, however, although it would appear that Evelina had set her expectation level too high.

Shortly after the shock of hearing from Evelina, Riel got his first regular job in his entire life, apart from heading the provisional government for nine months from late 1869 to 1870. He was now nearly 40 years of age, and he had never been permanently employed, had never received a regular salary — and, of course, had never been subjected to the tedium of the daily routine of work. He was employed at the Jesuit's St. Peter's Mission on the Sun River, teaching young Métis. Teaching was rewarding, but the routine was more than a bit of a shock. He found, as he reported to his employers in June of 1884, "My health suffers from the fatiguing regularity of having to look after children from six in the morning until eight at night, on Sunday as well as on the days of the week." But this remark, it should be noted, came after he already knew that there was a life of adventure looming before him.

In June of 1883, Riel visited Manitoba on business. He wrote to announce his presence to American consul in Winnipeg, James Wickes Taylor, whom he had known in 1870. Riel noted that he had become an "American citizen in good faith, honestly, only to better my personal condition and standing in the world; and not to create any difficulty." He added, "My title as American citizen invites me now to take a particular pride in what you and our American government have done here to keep the right of nations on its fundamental grounds and to secure the great principle of equality of races, before law and government, thereby advancing the interests, the cause of humanity." A few days later he forwarded to Taylor formal documentation to prove "that I am an American citizen, that I owe no allegiance whatever to British authorities and that I belong to the independent U.S. people." He did hope for American protection in the event of threats of assassination. Riel subsequently gave a lengthy interview to a journalist from the Winnipeg Daily Sun. He admitted that he had run into political controversy in Montana, and insisted that he had come to Pembina to obtain the naturalization papers of some men with whom he had been involved politically. He did not further discuss the citizenship question, but he did assert that "The best lands of Canada, so far as climate is concerned, are not so good as the worst lands of the Western States." Of this visit Louis later wrote his brother, "L'an dernier personne ne voulait de mois dans les cercles politiques influents du Manitoba."

In his entire Montana period, Riel gave no outward evidence of instability (mental or otherwise), religious mania, or even discontent. He wrote a good deal of poetry, both political and religious. He continued to be interested in his people, the Métis or "halfbreeds," as he himself referred to the mixed-bloods of Dakota and Montana. His writing about the "American Halfbreed Question" was judicious and balanced. He wrote mainly in English, a language Riel used for business but not for passionate matters.

The Invitation

In March of 1884, Gabriel Dumont, the leader of the South Branch Métis community in the Qu'Appelle Valley of Saskatchewan, called a meeting of his people to report his inability to convince the Canadian government to respond to their needs. At the top of his list of grievances was a failure to get the government to fit their river lots into the square survey system it was employing. But there were other problems as well. Dumont concluded, "And let me tell you, my friends, that's not the end of it. The government will never give us anything! They stole our land with promises and now when they've got control, they're laughing at us…. We'll never get anything from them, until we take matters into our own hands and force the government to give us justice."

Dumont observed that the only person who might be able to gain the government's attention was Louis Riel. After some discussion and some reservations expressed about forcing the government's hand, the meeting decided to invite Riel to help them, but only after they had gained more support from the larger Métis community. A gathering of several hundred people — including a number of anglophone mixed-bloods elected a committee to decide on a course of action. Within minutes of deliberation, the committee reported "that a delegation be named and ready to leave in fifteen days to go to Louis Riel and that the public be asked to bear the cost of the expenses." Dumont and James Isbister (a leading mixed-blood) were initially selected. The delegation did not leave immediately, and over time it added additional names to its number. Rumours at the time, later repeated by Conservative Prime Minister Macdonald in Parliament, suggested that the return of Riel was financed by Prince Albert Liberals.

By May of 1884, several letters were written to Louis Riel in Montana about the delegation and its mission. Both were signed only with initials. One, addressed to "Dear Cousin," reported that the English were "the hottest in your favor," adding "it may be said that the part of the N.W. which we inhabit is Manitoba before the trouble, with this difference that there are more people, that they understand better and that they are more decided." This writer also observed, "You have no idea how great your influence is, even amongst the Indians," and spoke of "the closest union" existing "between the French and the English and the Indians." The other letter, from "T.L.," observed that "None of us feels capable of undertaking so great a protestation against a despotic authority." Both of these letters considerably overstated the support a movement of protest might expect to receive from the anglophones and from the First Nations. There was an opposition, led by Bishop Vidal Grandin and Father Alexis André, which insisted that sending for Riel was a great blunder. The good fathers were fearful of violence, but they also suspected Riel's prophetic tendencies, which were well-known among the western priests of the Church. On 19 May, a delegation of Gabriel Dumont, Michel Dumas, Moise Ouellette, and James Isbister left for Montana. While Riel awaited its arrival, he began to prepare a paper comparing the Canadian and American governments, but he never got beyond the opening sentence.

The Saskatchewan delegation turned up at St. Peter's Mission on the evening of 4 June. Riel was at Mass, but the newcomers waited patiently for his return. Riel asked for a day to think about their request, and then returned with a written reply. He agreed to return to Canada, partly to make his own claims upon Canada, partly to assist his people to obtain their rights. He would spend the summer in Saskatchewan, he wrote, and then return to continue to lead the Montana halfbreeds. A few days later, Riel and his family left for Saskatchewan. Virtually his last act before departing American soil was to tell a newspaper editor in Sun River (a former member of the Wolseley Expedition of 1870) that he was "an American citizen, and…he considers the land over which the stars and stripes wave his home, and now only goes to assist his people as much as lays in his power, and after which be it much or little, he will return to Montana." Little did he realize how quickly and massively his plans would change.

-11-

The North-West
Rebellion, 1884-85

In the late spring of 1884, as Louis Riel and his family made their way from St. Peter's, Montana, to the Qu'Appelle Valley in Saskatchewan, Riel doubtless devoted a good deal of time to trying to sort out what he knew about the situation into which he had been invited. The political problem was, of course, more complex than he initially imagined, and it would only be exaggerated by his presence. Riel had heard a good deal about Métis grievances over the years, however, and he understood that conditions in the North-West were in some ways related to the insurgency which he had led in Red River in 1869-70, but he had little real understanding of the evolving situation.

The Governance of the
North-West Territories

Although the Métis had forced the Canadian government to grant Red River provincial status in 1870, the remainder of the North-West continued to be treated as a colony by the Canadians, who had no real plan for its governance. Most of the population consisted of a handful of Hudson's Bay Company traders, some mixed-bloods and perhaps 25,000 First Nations people. Initially, the lieutenant-governor of Manitoba also governed the North-West Territories. What sort of council he would have to assist him was another matter. For two years, Lieutenant-Governor Archibald administered the region without any council at all, looking after all the details of Indian affairs personally, including the negotiation of the first two treaties with the natives. When a council was finally created, late in 1872, it consisted mainly of Manitobans. Prime Minister Macdonald actually had to fend off eastern criticism that it was not sufficiently representative of Ontario — the

Ontario party, he wrote one correspondent, "seem to think that the whole of the North West was made for that Province alone"

By and large, appointments to the council over its lifetime represented both the francophone element and the immigrants from Ontario, but few were residents of the territory itself. Despite having appointed the council, Ottawa refused to allow it much power. Nevertheless, the North-West Council produced at least one landmark piece of legislation, "An Act respecting the Administration of Justice and for the Establishing of a Police Force in the North-West Territories," which created the force which later became the Royal Canadian Mounted Police. Under Lieutenant-Governor Alexander Morris, more Indian treaties were negotiated, including the notorious Treaty No. 6, and the government experimented with various forms of local administration of Indian affairs.

Under the government in Ottawa led by Alexander Mackenzie from 1873-78, little attention was given to governance of the North-West. An act in 1875 was quickly followed by amendments in 1876, chiefly because of sloppy draftsmanship. The territory continued to be governed by the lieutenant-governor and appointed council, although provision was made that in any area of not more than 1,000 square miles containing 1,000 adults (not aliens or Indians), an electoral district could be established to return a member to the council. Despite this supposedly liberal feature, most of the administration of the territory under the Mackenzie government continued to emphasize top-down government and an absence of any policy toward moving the territory from colonial to provincial status. At the same time, the Métis inhabitants of the territory had moved quite apart from Ottawa to establish local government upon highly democratic principles. In October of 1876 Canada established Battleford as the new capital, but it was almost a year until a new lieutenant-governor was appointed and moved there. This was David Laird, a Prince Edward Islander with little administrative experience, who found himself facing a substantial amount of popular unrest from new settlers, apart from the Métis. The immigrants appeared literally to move with their newspapers — edited by experienced journalists — which soon began publishing editorials complaining about the treatment afforded the territory by Ottawa. Most of the complaints were about the limitations on the establishment of municipal and school district organizations.

Canada resolved most of its immediate problems in 1878 by extending the boundary of Manitoba to incorporate most the settlements. Ottawa did not worry much about representative government since it was footing most of the expenses of government in its annual parliamentary appropriation, and would do so until 1891. Unfortunately, although those appropriations may have been adequate for what needed to be done in the territory, David Laird failed to spend it all. Payments for First Nations under various treaties negotiated were usually cheese-paring, while the needs increased in the early 1880s as the buffalo disappeared; there was little money for public improvements; and only half of a teacher's salary was supplied from the territorial government. The whole flow of European settlement was gradually increased by the movement west of the Canadian Pacific Railway, and more newspapers were founded with even louder complaints about Canadian inaction.

Grievances in the North-West

The general unhappiness was shared by the three main population groups in the North-West, the Métis, the First Nations, and the Europeans, although each group had its own specific litany of complaints.

The Métis

The complaints of the Métis in the North-West had their origins in the development of Manitoba under the Manitoba Act. The Métis insisted that they had been systematically dispossessed of land guaranteed them in 1870. There was probably no deliberate conspiracy to dispossess, but rather a considerable difficulty in working out the details of the provisions of the Manitoba Act in a way satisfactory to all the interests represented in the Canadian government — and equally satisfactory to all the interests in Manitoba itself. The advantage of the Métis, as we have already seen, was seldom really considered. The Canadians had made concessions to the Red River delegates mainly to meet the British insistence that the people of the settlement had to be satisfied. The commitments were made with little thought to their subsequent implementation, and with considerable confusion over what the government thought it had promised, and what the delegates — especially Father Noel Ritchot — thought had been accepted. Beyond this confusion were several unsettled points about the granting procedure for the "Métis Lands." Father Ritchot and his constituents wanted block grants along the riverfronts that would keep their linguistic and confessional rights intact. Most Métis were not interested in what Lieutenant-Governor Archibald described as "mixed communities." The Canadian government certainly had no interest in promoting blocks of settlements of Métis; it wanted Métis land distributed in small parcels on an individual basis.

The establishment of Manitoba was followed by a protracted period of government wrangling over the distribution of Métis land. Canada did not want to end up with much of the best land in its new province committed to the old residents in advance of settlement, a result that would hardly satisfy the Ontario expansionists. The Dominion would have preferred the Métis sorted out and the land surveyed before settlement from the East began, but the difficulties of working out administrative details meant that substantial numbers of settlers had arrived with the land business still unresolved and surveys still not completed. As with the amnesty, it proved impossible to satisfy both the Métis and the new arrivals simultaneously, leading to the temptation to defer a decision. When new Dominion land agent Gilbert McMicken proposed a new initiative in early 1872, (it called for a new census, the drawing of quarter sections randomly from all 408 Manitoba townships, and the issuance of scrip as evidence of land rights) the plan was leaked to Bishop Taché, who protested it.

The distribution of Métis land in the province remained unimplemented at the end of 1872, although the *Manitoban* reported that speculators were already active in buying rights to scrip and claimed that one individual already held rights to 40,000 acres in the town of Winnipeg. As a result, the Manitoba legislature attempted to pass a bill preventing heads of families from selling their children's allotments, but was told by Ottawa that such legislation would be unconstitutional. In response, a Canadian order-in-council of 3 April 1873 excluded heads of families from involvement in the allotments. The fall of the Macdonald government in November of 1873 provided another setback to resolution of the land business. It would take many months for the Liberal government of Alexander Mackenzie to get on top of the issues, and when it did, it felt no particular sense of obligation to the Métis.

Not surprisingly, while all the changes in Métis land policy were occurring, large numbers of Manitoba Métis had picked up their property and headed farther west, re-establishing themselves on apparently uncontested ground in the North-West Territories. Some of these migrants may have been attempting to escape the pressure of the Canadian newcomers into the province, others to attempt to follow their traditional way of life of hunting the buffalo, while still others were fleeing bad harvests and epidemic disease of the early 1870s. Most of this departing contingent were among the poorer and least agriculturally-oriented Métis, and they tended to cluster around the buffalo-robe hunters of the Saskatchewan region. But all the migrants felt a sense of grievance against the Canadian government for its failure to honour its commitments to the Métis.

In April of 1875, the Mackenzie cabinet issued another order-in-council, establishing a commission to enumerate the population of the province as of 1870, a process upon which land claims would be based. The commission compiled its lists, and a lottery for land began on 30 October 1876 that was not finished until 1880. The process was a slow one, hampered by continued political dissension and bureaucratic stubbornness. Demands for information from the proposed recipients about their allotments led, in 1877, to the production by Ottawa of lists of prospective allotments, which were greatly prized by "claim-runners." How many of the patents were actually collected by speculators is the subject of considerable scholarly debate, as is the extent to which the continued delays forced the Métis out of the province. Late applicants continued to appear after the original acreage was all distributed. An order of council on 20 April 1885 allowed until 1 May 1886 as a deadline for proving claims, but in practice they were honoured with scrip for much longer. While the final distribution of Métis land may have complied with the wording of section 31 of the Manitoba Act, it hardly accorded with the agreement Father Ritchot thought he had negotiated in 1870.

Another exodus of Métis from Manitoba occurred after 1879. This was composed of river-lot owners, many of whom sold out to incoming settlers for decent prices. These farmers appear to have decided that they should take advantage of the returns they could get for their land, and move elsewhere. Some may have despaired of the future of the province for francophone Catholics of mixed-blood background, but not all who left were francophone Catholics. A number were anglophone mixed-bloods.

Those who went to Saskatchewan swelled the Métis population at places like Qu'Appelle, Batoche, and Duke Lake. French, Scottish, and English mixed-bloods in the region demanded grants similar to those given under the Manitoba Act. Government surveyors caused uncertainty and fear, as they had done in Red River a decade earlier, partly by being too slow about surveying and partly by not being flexible enough about meshing the traditional river lots of the Métis with the square survey system they were introducing.

Métis fears were increased by the activities of land colonization companies, operating under the patronage of the Canadian government. The Prince Albert Colonization Company, for example, had been founded by Mackenzie Bowell and had been granted — while Bowell was still in the Canadian cabinet in 1883 — a grant of a township in habited by a large number of Métis. The mixed-bloods already had a sense of grievance against Canada for the failure of its promises, and had come to appreciate what Riel had achieved. Canada had honoured neither major concession — the amnesty and land rights — wrested from it by the Métis uprising in 1870, at least not in a form acceptable to the Métis, but this was hardly Riel's fault. The poorer Métis left first, but the more prosperous "old settlers" clung precariously to a share of power until the end of the 1870s, when they were finally swamped by settlers from Ontario. Some of these Métis were suffering as much as the First Nations from the abrupt departure of the buffalo and the need to find new ways of earning a livelihood. As the Hudson's Bay Company factor Lawrence Clarke pointed out in 1884 of the many Métis who were hunters and freighters: "There is not sufficient overland freighting going on in the country to afford labor to a third of their number, hence they are getting poorer year by year." Many of these people were the basis of Louis Riel's support after 1884, for they were his natural constituency.

The First Nations

Canada had acknowledged the aboriginal rights of the First Nations living in the North-West and negotiated treaties that extinguished native rights to the land in exchange for reserves, often on the most marginal and least attractive land. These treaties not only freed land for settlement, but enabled the Canadian government to continue to pursue its pre-Confederation policies with the Indians, which had been to settle them on the land as farmers. The treaty negotiations were complex and difficult. In 1876, for example, the Indians of central Saskatchewan gathered at Fort Carlton to consider the terms of the government's Treaty No. 6. The Plains Cree Chief Poundmaker objected to the government's offer, arguing that Canada needed to do more than simply provide the natives with small plots of land, livestock, and farming implements and then expect them to become good farmers. He wanted government training and further assistance, particularly after the buffalo disappeared. This objection was regarded by Lieutenant-Governor Alexander Morris, who had presented the terms for the treaty, as an example of pure greed on the part of the Indians. It was pushed aside. Poundmaker nevertheless signed the treaty. Another important Plains Cree chief, Big Bear, refused to sign for six years. But on 8 December, 1882, he signed when his people were starving and desperately needed food.

Administration of the Indian treaties and of Dominion Indian policy in the West left a good deal to be desired. The First Nations were obviously caught in an inexorable process that was going to change forever their traditional way of life. The buffalo were rapidly disappearing, the victims of overhunting and the arrival of new agricultural settlers. Epidemic disease was still rampant. Most native leaders saw the handwriting on the wall clearly enough. They did not get enough help from the Department of Indian Affairs, however. The government expected the Indians to be able to become self-sufficient virtually overnight. Under the Mackenzie Liberals, Canada did not provide enough money for Indian assistance. It did not supply the new reserves with enough food to prevent starvation and disease, and when the natives slaughtered their livestock for something to eat, the Indian agents criticized them.

The reserve land tended to be marginal, the assistance supplied was inadequate, and the attitude of many of the government's Indian agents was unsympathetic. The Assistant Commissioner of Indian Affairs, Hayter Reed, insisted that the native people should not get government assistance unless they were aged or were prepared to work for it. He calculated how much land could be cultivated by one yoke of oxen, and Indians who fell short of the amount could expect little sympathy. He was a confrontationist rather than a negotiator. The Canadian government's position was that too much assistance would permanently cripple the First Nations. By the early 1880s, the North-West was a virtual powder keg of aboriginal discontent. Cree leaders in what is now Alberta sent a letter to Sir John A. Macdonald (who was Minister of the Interior and head of Indian Affairs as well as prime minister) complaining of destitution and noting that the creed of the Indian was: "If we must die by violence let us do it quickly." The winter of 1883-84 was particularly harsh and severe. Many were starving. Some Indian agents wrote to Ottawa, but nothing was done.

In June of 1884, during the time when Louis Riel and his family were on the road to Saskatchewan, Big Bear and his followers, with many other Indians, travelled to Poundmaker's reserve. More than 2,000 Cree gathered for a council and a ritual Thirst Dance. A confrontation ensued between an Indian administrator and some of the aboriginals and blows were struck. The situation was allowed to escalate, with attempts made to arrest the main culprits, and eventually a general melee developed which ended in arrests.

The Indian agents advocated a more generous policy in the distribution of rations, but the officials in the Indian Department refused to yield. They wanted troublemakers like Poundmaker arrested at the first opportunity. Many thought that an open war might actually be beneficial, for it would bring repression and keep the aboriginals in their place. A number of the most militant First Nations leaders were familiar with Louis Riel. They had rejected his leadership in 1880, but seemed more willing to listen now.

The European Settlers

By the early 1880s, the Europeans in the North-West were becoming as restive as the aboriginals and the Métis, although for quite distinct reasons. Their concerns were much more political, much more related to the

Canadian government's insistence on keeping the territory in colonial tutelage, without any observable policy for the transition from colony to provincial status. Most of the new settlers were both British subjects and of anglo-Canadian background. The birthplaces of the North-West population in 1885 — apart from the native-born — showed 7,158 born in the British Isles, 8,823 born in Ontario, 1,340 born in Quebec, 895 born in the Maritimes, 3,114 born in Manitoba, 1,007 born in the United States, and 562 born in Europe. As the crusading newspaper editor of the Regina Leader, Nicholas Flood Davin, put it early in 1885 of this population, "Were they — an immigration d'élite — a select immigration — the flower of the old pioneers of Canada — to remain 'disestablished and disendowed' and outside the pall of the Constitution?" The settlers had many grievances, all of which were constantly reiterated in a number of outspoken newspapers published in the territory. In March of 1883, the Qu'Appelle Settlers' Rights Association had passed resolutions calling for parliamentary representation, land law reform, proper legislation for settlers, and government assistance for immigrants. In December of that year, a Manitoba and North-West Farmers' Union was organized in Winnipeg. A motion for repeal of the British North America Act and the formation of a "new confederacy of the North-West Provinces and British Columbia" was only barely rejected by the assembly. The convention did pass a "Bill of Rights" — the invocation of 1870 was deliberate although the demands were not — which called for an end to the withholding of land to actual settlers, an end to the protective tariff, an end to the CPR monopoly, an end to the elevator monopoly, and further construction of railway branch lines.

The western settlers were sufficiently angry by 1884 to be willing to entertain introducing Louis Riel into the equation. Even before the invitation to Riel, the *Edmonton Bulletin* and *The Prince Albert Times* in February 1884 carried an editorial by Frank Oliver, which replied to advice from an Ontario newspaper to stop threatening rebellion:

> If it was not by — not threatening, but actual — rebellion and appeals to the British government for justice that the people of Ontario gained the rights they enjoy today and freed themselves from a condition precisely similar to that into which the North-West is being rapidly forced, how was it? Was it not by armed rebellion coupled with murder, that Manitoba attained the rights she enjoys today from the very men who now hold the reins of power at Ottawa. If history is to be taken as a guide, what could be plainer than that Without rebellion the people of the North West need expect nothing, while with rebellion successful or otherwise they may reasonably expect to get their rights.

There are two interesting features of this editorial. One is that the reference to Manitoba still considered the death of Thomas Scott as "murder." Many of these settlers were Ontarians, the very people who had led the protests against Louis Riel in 1870. The second point is that Oliver did not think that the rebellion had to succeed, merely to be undertaken. From the perspective of the European settlers, Louis Riel could serve either as a catalyst to shake up the dormant politicians of Ottawa, or as the sacrificial martyr/leader of a failed rebellion that had made its point simply by existing. In either case, Riel was totally expendable. Many contemporaries insisted that the Métis had been drawn by the white settlers into their resistance, for reasons apart from the interests of the Métis.

All these interest groups had in common an abiding anger with the government of Canada, as well as a sense of misery brought about both by bad weather in the early 1880s — a combination of frosts and droughts — and by the collapse of a land boom that depopulated many homesteads. Partisan politics entered into the equation as well. But from the standpoint of Louis Riel, on his way to assume leadership of the protest movement of the people of the North-West, the situation was mainly pregnant with potential misunderstanding. Riel did not appreciate how different conditions were in 1884 than they had been in 1869, or how limited was the ultimate support for him of all except a hard core of Métis. And most of the supporters saw Riel as the man who had orchestrated a successful political uprising in 1869-70, not as the prophet who was bringing the "Massinahican" with him and who intended to institute a religious reform movement in the Canadian North-West.

The Massinahican

Over the years of his residence in Montana, Louis Riel had written a book. He called it the Massinahican, which in Cree means "the book," with particular reference to the Bible. This book was apparently not finished until early in 1884, when Riel wrote his brother that he wanted to come to Manitoba and present the manuscript to Bishop Taché, saying, "Monsigneur, here is what I have written. I wanted to publish it without speaking to anyone, but I decided I would rather show it first to your Grace." Had it been completed in June of 1883, Riel presumably would have shown it to Taché on his visit to Winnipeg at that time. Unfortunately, the manuscript has not survived in its entirety, but only in bits and pieces in Riel's papers. Thanks to the work of Gilles Martel and Thomas Flanagan, however, we have a reasonably good idea of what the manuscript probably contained. Basically, it was to be the foundation of Riel's prophetic teachings, the equivalent of Joseph Smith's

Book of Mormon or Mary Baker Eddy's *Science and Health with Key to the Scriptures* or Emanuel Swedenborg's *Opera Philosophica et Mineralia* or William Blake's *Book of Thel*.

Like many other religious teachers transcribing personal visions and revelations, Riel combined philosophy, science, metaphysics, and theology in his writings. Flanagan speculates that Riel was directly affected by American theosophy, which included Swedenborg as one of its spiritual antecedents; but whatever the intellectual influence, the *Massinahican* was intended to be both a book of revelation and the presentation of a total integrated system of religion. It was meant to accompany Riel's intention to reorganize the entire Church of the New World in accordance with his revelation about the papacy being transferred from Rome to Montreal and put under the supervision of Bishop Bourget of Montreal. Not for nothing did he label himself the "Prophet of the New World." Riel did not think of himself as a priest, but rather as a prophet whose teaching depended upon divine revelation. "I am," he wrote to Bishop Bourget in 1876 from Longue Point, "in direct communication with my creator."

Riel's religious beliefs and his religious system had a number of important characteristics. One was an outgrowth of his conviction that it was his mission to found a new church: "église, catholique, apostolique et vitale des Montagnes Lumineuses." This new church would represent a success in his life which he felt he had not otherwise achieved. Riel was hardly an exclusionist about this church, but it was plainly meant to appeal particularly to what he regarded as his own people — the Métis and First Nations of the West. The Métis in particular were God's chosen people. Riel saw the origins of the Métis and the Indians, at least mythologically, in the Egyptians and the Jews, both of which had travelled to America.

Not surprisingly, Riel based his moral teachings on his own version of the Mosaic Law. Like other North American prophets of the 19th century — such as Joseph Smith, with whom Riel had much more in common than he would have recognized — Riel's code recognized the institution of polygamy for males. His new religion contained echoes not only of the Book of Mormon, but of Millerite numerology and theosophy. Whether Riel was familiar with these religions in any detail or simply shared with their founders in the general religious atmosphere of the 19th century is not entirely clear. Many commentators have pointed out the similarities between Riel's thinking and that of a number of founders of so-called "cargo cults," native reform movements influenced by Christianity as well as a reaction against it. Riel's religion was also fundamentally antinomian, since it was based entirely on his direct communication with God. Whether Riel would have allowed an equal privilege to members of his church is another matter, however. He almost certainly regarded his teaching as comparable to that of Moses or other prophets, which means that once it was revealed it became set in stone. Finally, Riel was a universalist, since he believed that all humankind could be saved.

If seen in a comparative sense, Riel's religion assumes some interesting features. One of the most important is in the tension in his beliefs between traditional Catholicism and the reformism inherent in his visions. Like many reformers, Riel insisted that he was retaining the essence of Catholicism, and in his personal devotions he was extremely pious and conventional. The priests, of course, perceived matters differently. They saw a heretic who might be forgiven only because he was mad. For the missionaries with whom Riel dealt after returning to Saskatchewan, the conviction that he was crazy was the only way of making sense of both his behaviour and his thinking. But significantly, Riel's revision of traditional Catholic teaching took quite a different form from native revisionism in Central and South America, which tended to merge pre-Christian mythology and ritual with Catholic orthodoxy. The results of this merger included an enhanced role for the Virgin Mary, who assumed characteristics of various pre-Christian goddesses, and the elaboration of Catholic ritual. Riel's religion had no overtones of Mariology or pre-Christian paganism. Instead, most of its overtones were North American, particularly of North American extreme Protestant sectarianism. At least at the beginning of his Saskatchewan sojourn, Riel kept his religious beliefs fairly well submerged. Publicly, he was merely an orthodox if really intense Catholic.

In Saskatchewan

Louis Riel and his family were greeted with much enthusiasm when they finally arrived at Batoche. He rejected an attempt by old friend Louis Schmidt to join him, saying that Schmidt could be more valuable as a contributor to the French-language press than as an agitator. Instead, he accepted the offer of William Henry Jackson to become Riel's private secretary. Jackson was a young member of a prominent settler family that was highly critical of the Canadian government and had been involved in the organization of an opposition movement in the region. He had been educated in classics at the University of Toronto. Jackson would serve as the equivalent of W.B. Donoghue in 1884 and 1885, often sounding a more radical note than his chief. Certainly Riel's first speeches to his supporters were measured and moderate. Riel returned to his constant theme from the earlier rebellion in Red River and emphasized the need for unity. Later in July he spoke by invitation to an audience composed mainly of white settlers. Again, unity and non-violence were his principal themes. One former member of the Wolseley expedition tried to protest against Riel, but he was tossed out of the meeting. He would protest in the local newspaper about the irony of the present support for the man who had murdered Thomas Scott. For the moment, at least, the European settlers seemed the most enthusiastic of Riel's supporters.

The enthusiasm of the settlers and the unity of the protest movement began to dissipate almost immediately. The problem was that the protest was trying to be too many things to too many people, and some of its constituency was fundamentally incompatible. It might be possible, as William Henry Jackson attempted to do in a manifesto issued on 28 July, to convince the Europeans that "Riel has been painted in blacker colours than he deserves," and to describe "the remedy to the root of the evil to be provincial status with full control over our resources and internal administration, and power to send a just number of representatives to the federal legislature." But Riel was already meeting with Big Bear and other First Nations chiefs, and would offer help to the Indians in satisfying their grievances as well. This inclusion of the aboriginals frightened many people, including most representatives of the federal government in Saskatchewan, who started worrying about a bloodbath. Some of the government officials even blamed the growing First Nations unity on Riel, although in retrospect it is clear that the natives had their own issues and their own movement. Talk of an Indian uprising also frightened the Catholic clergy, especially when Riel combined support of the aboriginals with talk of a new church. In one exchange with Father Alexis André in mid-August, the missionary complained of Riel's conviction of a "divine mission" and called him a "veritable fanatic."

On 5 September, Riel and the Métis leaders met at St. Laurent with Bishop Vital Grandin and Amédée Forget, the clerk of the North-West Council, who had accompanied the bishop on his ecclesiastical rounds. Forget suggested that Riel might be appointed to the territorial council, an idea that Riel angrily rejected. Riel and his companions complained that the clergy were not sufficiently supportive of the Métis cause, while Grandin replied that the clergy had never really been informed of what the cause was. Riel subsequently wrote to Grandin that what was wanted was responsible government, guarantees for pre-survey squatters, a Métis land distribution of 240 acres per head as in Manitoba, and government assistance. This document dropped a request for proper rations for the First Nations from an earlier draft. At one point, Riel also advanced a fantastic scheme to set aside millions of acres for the half-breeds, using the proceeds of the sale of these lands to provide for schools, orphanages and hospitals for his people.

Louis Riel v. Canada

The Métis leaders and the bishop agreed to heal their breach with the establishment of a national Métis association under the patronage of St. Joseph. But the Métis continued to be persuaded that the Church was not behind them, and the clergy in their turn worried about Riel, who was described in early September by one cleric as "a Joshua, a prophet, even as a saint" in the eyes of his people. Bishop Grandin agreed with this assessment, writing that for the Métis, Riel "was a saint; I would say rather a kind of God." When Riel spoke at the inauguration of the Union Métisse St. Joseph on 24 September from the steps of the church in St. Laurent, he called for unity and gave no evidence of any religious unorthodoxy, but the clergy still saw him as a loose cannon.

In Ottawa, Sir John A. Macdonald met the news of Riel's return calmly. "The news from the north-west," he wrote the Governor-General Lord Lansdowne in early August of 1884, "is a little disquieting." The prime minister blamed the trouble not on government policy (or lack of it), but on the weather and crop failures. He did not think there would be any trouble from the First Nations unless the Métis rose in arms. Nor did he anticipate a revolt from the European element, which was plotting conspiracies rather than acting. "My experience of the Fenian business," he wrote another correspondent, "has taught me that one should never disbelieve the evidence of plots or intended raids, merely because they are foolish and certain to fail."

Only the Métis were really dangerous, he thought, and even with them, the government was attempting to work out compromises on the land business. On the other hand, the government had no intention of another issue of scrip. "The scrip is sold for a song to the sharks and spent in whiskey," he told Lord Lansdowne, "and this we desire above all things to avoid." But always an alert politician, Macdonald sensed in Louis Riel's moderation an opportunity for negotiation. "There is, I think, nothing to be feared from Riel. In his answer to the invitation sent to him, which was a temperate and unobjectionable paper, he spoke of some claims he had against the government. I presume these refer to his land claims which he forfeited on conviction and banishment. I think we shall deal liberally with him and make him a good subject again." As usual, Macdonald assumed that his opponent could be easily bought. As for the Métis, the "true policy," the prime minister told the governor-general, "is rather to encourage them to specify their grievances in memorials and to send them with or without delegations to Ottawa."

Indeed, Louis Riel's movement was moderate and ought to have been capable of being negotiated through to some acceptable understanding. The only constitutional point it demanded that had not been asked by many others, including the territorial council itself, was a vague "separate federation of our own in direct competition with the Crown." The land demands given to Bishop Grandin in early September were in the prime minister's hands in less than two weeks, and while they had been dismissed out of hand, Macdonald had already promised the North-West Council in July that the Minister of the Interior would "take into his serious consideration the claims of the Half Breeds at Prince Albert and elsewhere in the North-West Territories." The officials in the North-West explained to the prime minister what was needed: employment to provide some income (Lieutenant-Governor Dewdney insisted that work "would circulate a little money among them & the want of it is the secret of their uneasiness") and to resolve the land question. "If the Half-breed question is arranged this winter," Dewdney wrote Macdonald on 19 September, "it will settle the whole business; if not, a good force in the North will be necessary." But Dewdney did not follow up on this prediction, and the government in Ottawa continued to do nothing. The prime minister at one point insisted that "no amount of concession will prevent…people from grumbling and agitating."

Riel and William Henry Jackson spent the autumn of 1884 preparing a petition to the Canadian government in Ottawa. It was an omnibus document with something in it for everyone, addressed to the Hon. Joseph-Adolphe Chapleau, the Secretary of State for the Dominion of Canada and the man who had defended Ambroise Lépine so unsuccessfully in 1874. The petition started with a request for more food for the First Nations. It then demanded 240 acres of land per Métis, as in Manitoba. It asked for confirmation of titles for old settlers and squatters, dealt with all of the political concerns of the local population — responsible government, representation in Parliament, control of natural resources, tariff reduction, the vote by ballot — and suggested that the people of the North-West be allowed to send delegates to Ottawa with a bill of rights to serve as the basis for negotiations for entry as a province. In a covering letter, Jackson described the petition as "an extremely moderate one," and suggested that it ought to have been directed to England and not to Canada, which had ignored previous petitions. Chapleau acknowledged receipt of this petition, and at this point, it could have been argued that Riel had done the job he had been summoned from Montana to execute. Unfortunately, there was little evidence that Riel thought he was done. Instead, just the reverse was the case. Riel became even more involved in his mission and in his ongoing disputes with the Catholic clergy.

Part of the trouble was initiated by Father Vital Fourmond, who petitioned the Canadian government for a subsidy for the Catholic school at St. Laurent. Louis Riel recognized perfectly well that this introduction of sectarianism was dangerous to the larger North-West movement. He disassociated himself from it at a public meeting and indicated his support for both Catholic and Protestant schools. He subsequently used the Fourmond petition as evidence of the attitude of the clergy, and engaged in several confrontations with them. In these confrontations, more and more of his unorthodox religious ideas came to the fore. He talked with anger and passion about his vocation as a reformer and about the need for both political and spiritual reform. Such talk only confirmed the suspicions of the missionary priests. Riel was a madman, and worse still, he was a heretic. Father Valentin Vegreville wrote Bishop Taché in mid-December: "The present movement is none other than that of 1870; to establish an independent nation of which L. Riel will be the royal autocrat, with his own religion of which he will be the supreme pontiff; and to attain this end all means are justified." Father Alexis André would later write:

> Our people considered him a hero and identified in him the qualities that distinguish a genius and all the virtues which characterize a saint. But under his mask hid a diabolical pride and an immeasurable ambition. At the bottom of his heart was a secret hatred for all authority except, to be sure, his own.... I had terrible struggles with him, and I aroused his anger so much that he lost all control of himself; he became in those moments truly a maniac, twisting himself into conto tions in a rage that rendered him unrecognizable.

Riel became so extreme that Louis Schmidt felt obliged to reassure the priests: "For my part, I do not think that Riel is crazy, but I do think that he is too enthusiastic and too confident in his star. He relies on the fact that he has always been looked upon as a man to be feared; and if he uses only commonplace methods to make himself understood, he thinks he may thereby lose his prestige and appear as an ordinary individual." To what extent such a view was a defence of Riel is another matter. In early January of 1885, Superintendent Leif Crozier of the Mounted Police reported to Lieutenant-Governor Dewdney that Riel had begun to appear publicly as a religious reformer.

Riel's Compensation Requests

Father André attempted to encourage Riel to return to Montana by arranging for a representative of the government (D.H. MacDowall, a member of the Territorial Council) to meet with him and hear his requests for compensation. They were considerable. Riel spoke at one point of $100,000, at another of $35,000 promised him by Prime Minister Macdonald. The priest thought the demands excessive, but wrote, "I think it is really the duty of the government to get Riel out of mischief as soon as possible." MacDowall wrote to Lieutenant-Governor Edgar Dewdney, "If red tape can be abolished for one month, I can tell you how to settle the whole of this half-breed row at the expense of some $6,000." MacDowall's account of his four-hour interview with Riel in late December was on the prime minister's desk in Ottawa in January of 1885. Riel was at this point thinking about again becoming "respectable" and looking properly after his family. His claims for compensation were not entirely unreasonable. He had never been paid for governing Manitoba until the arrival of Wolseley. He had not received his 240 acres of land. He had been effectively prevented from working by the actions of the Canadian government.

"My name is Riel and I want material," he told MacDowall. "I suppose," reported the councillor somewhat testily, that this "was a pun." "He then proceeded to state," MacDowall continued, "that if the government would consider his personal claims against them and pay him a certain amount in settlement of these claims, he would arrange to make his illiterate and unreasoning followers well satisfied with almost any settlement of their claims for land grants that the government might be willing to make, and also that he would leave the north-west never to return." In many respects, this report was a turning point in the 1885 Rebellion. According to MacDowall, "Riel made it distinctly understood that 'self' was his main object, and he was willing to make the claims of his followers totally subservient to his own interests." There is no detailed independent account of this conversation, and MacDowall may have overinterpreted it. Father André would later testify that Riel had said, "If I am satisfied the half-breeds will be," but that is quite different from MacDowall's account of Riel's cynical attitude.

In any event, it does not really matter what Riel actually meant. What matters is what the government would make of this report. It is doubtful if Riel appreciated that there were spies everywhere, and that virtually every word he uttered was reported to Ottawa, often within hours. While Riel was behaving as an altruistic leader of his people, he had to be taken seriously, but as a man who "came in for the purpose of attempting to extract money from the public purse" — as Sir John A. later told the House of Commons — he need not be taken seriously at all. Macdonald wrote to Lieutenant-Governor Dewdney in February that "We have no money to give Riel. He has a right to remain in Canada and if he conspires we must punish him. That's all." Nor did his movement have to be attended to with any real haste. MacDowall's report made it possible for Sir John A. Macdonald to turn to the more pressing business on his agenda, which was dealing with another financial crisis involving the Canadian Pacific Railway.

Riel's interview and the seeming exposure of his true motivations made it possible for the Canadian government to continue to obfuscate on the problems of the North-West. Ottawa's response was only to recommend a commission to enumerate the Métis in the North-West, not to investigate the grievances or to deal with Riel's personal demands for compensation. On 24 February, a public meeting at Batoche was held to deal with the government response. Riel declared that he was returning to Montana. The Métis responded by shouting, "No! No!" Riel asked, "But the consequences?" The answer was loud and clear: "We will accept them." Several observers thought the whole business represented a brilliant piece of orchestration, but regardless, Louis Riel was staying to see the agitation to its conclusion. Soon after this meeting, W. H. Jackson announced that he was leaving his position at the Settlers' Union to devote his time to spiritual matters. He would be replaced in March by Phillippe Garnot, whose later memoir emphasized the extent to which Riel was becoming influenced by his religious experiences. It may have been those religious experiences that brought Riel out of his apparent selfish phase.

Strategy Changes

On 1 March, from the steps of the St. Laurent church, Riel told his followers that there would be a change in strategy. The reason for this is not entirely clear, but we know that a few days later he travelled to Prince Albert to ask Father André's permission to declare a provisional government. André refused, and Charles Nolin persuaded Riel to hold a nine-day novena to pray for guidance, beginning on 10 March. Everyone breathed a sigh of relief, but it would appear that Riel was now firmly associated with the more militant Métis, led by Gabriel Dumont. Members of the Mounted Police began to warn the authorities that the Métis were arming and that a rebellion was likely "to break out any moment." On 18 March, Riel and a party of horsemen set off for Batoche. Along the way he met Dr. John Willoughby, a Saskatoon doctor who later reported on their conversation. He could wait no longer, said Riel. "The time has come now," he insisted, "to rule this country or perish in the attempt."

Outside Batoche, Riel had a confrontation with the priest at St. Anthony's Church, accusing him of being a Protestant for denying the Métis the use of the building for a meeting. Riel then shouted, "Rome is fallen," and held his meeting, which talked about the provisional government. At Batoche, Riel and some of his men strode into the Walters and Baker store. Riel announced, "Well, Mr. Walters, it has commenced.'" "What has commenced?" asked Walters. "Oh, this movement for the rights of the country," was the reply. The visitors then helped themselves to food and ammunition. Riel and Dumont ordered men to cut the telegraph line to Prince Albert. Riel and W. H. Jackson, who had recently declared himself a convert to Catholicism, proceeded on to St. Laurent, where Jackson was to be baptized. There he told Father Fourmond that a provisional government had been established. "Old Rome has fallen," said Riel, "There is a new Pope in the person of Mgr. Bourget. You will be the first priest of the new order, and henceforth you will obey me." Fourmond refused, but did baptize Jackson.

The Exovedate

A large number of Métis were assembled at Batoche by 19 March. In front of a screaming crowd, Riel and Dumont announced the creation of the provisional government. As each man was chosen, the crowd shouted its approval. The council of the new government was given by Riel a new name — the "Exovedate," a Latin word meaning "picked from the flock." Dumont became "Adjutant-General of the Métis nation" and "head of the army," both positions which had been held by Ambroise Lépine in 1870. Riel himself wanted only to serve as a prophet. Somewhere in the midst of these events, William Henry Jackson, who had been chosen secretary of the "Provisional Government of the Saskatchewan" became so obviously unbalanced that he was replaced. It may have been in some attempt to gain clerical support that Riel arrested Charles Nolin — in 1885, as in 1870, his principal critic. There was a brief trial in which Riel accused Nolin of treason. According to Philippe Garnot, Riel "said that an example was necessary and that it was essential that Nolin should be condemned to death." Here was the old 1870 business repeating itself again. Nolin was properly impressed, and agreed to support Riel, however reluctantly. But if the Métis leader hoped by this action to intimidate the clergy, he failed dismally. Riel insisted that he would force Sir John A. Macdonald to his knees. Gabriel Dumont began to prepare his army. Riel now advocated the seizure of Fort Carlton, and the Exovedate voted in favour. The fort had by this point been reinforced. It would not leave its doors open to the Métis as had Upper Fort Garry in 1869.

On 21 March, two anglophones, Thomas McKay and Hillyard Mitchell, were sent by Superintendent Crozier, who was busily strengthening Fort Carlton, to talk with Riel. The plan seemed to be to buy some time. The emissaries commented that it was dangerous to resort to arms. Riel answered again that the time had come. He attacked McKay for being a mixed-blood who was not helping his people, and shouted at

Louis Riel v. Canada

McKay, "You don't know what we are after — it is blood, blood, we want blood; it is a war of extermination, everybody that is against us is to be driven out of the country. There are two curses in this country — the Government and the Hudson's Bay Company." He agreed to send two men with a message for Superintendent Crozier at Fort Carlton, now manned by a force of Mounted Police and volunteers from Prince Albert. The letter demanded the surrender unconditionally of Fort Carlton, or the fort would be attacked on the following day. Once open violence had begun, wrote Riel, "a war of extermination" would be begun "upon all those who have shown themselves hostile to our rights." In a postscript to the messengers, Riel presented the formula which Crozier was to use in surrendering: "Because I love my neighbour as myself, for the sake of God, and to prevent bloodshed, and principally the war of extermination which threatens the country, I agree to the above conditions of surrender."

All this excitement galvanized the whole countryside into action. The anglophone mixed-bloods between St. Laurent and Prince Albert hurriedly met, and sent a delegation to Riel. They refused to join the Métis and expressed a desire to remain neutral. Riel sent an answer back, which listed the ways the government had dealt with the mixed-bloods and calling for unity among the half-breeds. The mixed-bloods met again. While circumstances had changed to the point where 1870 could not be replayed in 1885, the anglophone mixed-bloods behaved much as in Red River earlier. They wanted to remain neutral, but indicated their sympathy and understanding for their Métis cousins, however much they disapproved of the "resort to arms." Riel wrote another pleading letter. Only a strong union between the English and French-speaking half-breeds would "guarantee that there would be no bloodshed." The mixed-bloods met for a third time. They still preferred neutrality, but their spokesman — ironically named Thomas Scott — wrote that "the voice of every man was with you, and we have taken steps which I think will have a tendency to stop bloodshed and hasten a treaty."

The following day, at a large gathering, 455 signatures were collected subscribing to a document which called on the government to deal with the grievances of the population of the North-West as the only alternative to war. It was probably too late for petitions, and the actions of the anglophone mixed-blood community only hastened the coming confrontation. It is difficult to know how best to act in such volatile and potentially revolutionary situations as the mixed-bloods found themselves in March 1885. But as one student leader at Berkeley put it succinctly about fence-sitters almost one hundred years later: "If you're not part of the solution, you're part of the problem." If the mixed-bloods intended to be part of the solution, they had to do better than simply to propose another petition to the Canadian government. This action virtually assured that there would be violence. Worse still, the delays while the mixed-blood communities negotiated enabled Superintendent Crozier to prepare properly for an attack.

While the Métis had been negotiating with the anglophone mixed-bloods during the period 21 to 24 March, the Canadian government had moved itself into action. Having managed to waste the winter without acting either on Riel's compensation or the Métis grievances, Sir John A. Macdonald found it much easier to begin an armed response. He ordered reinforcements for the Mounted Police on 19 March, and four days later, ordered Major-General Frederick Middleton, the commander of the Canadian militia, to Winnipeg with instructions to mobilize militia units. Before Middleton had actually arrived by an American train in the Manitoba capital, having travelled incognito through the United States because the rail line was not finished north of Lake Superior, the first advance unit of the 90th Regiment, the Royal Winnipeg Rifles, had left by a special train for Troy (now Qu'Appelle). The men were housed in the immigration sheds, with 18 inches of snow on the ground.

Duck Lake

On 25 March, Gabriel Dumont goaded Louis Riel into allowing him to take 30 men to raid the stores of the opposition in Duck Lake. The Métis took supplies from Hillyard Mitchell's store successfully. At dawn the following day, the Métis learned that Superintendent Crozier had sent a contingent of 15 police and seven volunteers (under Thomas McKay) to retrieve some goods from Mitchell's store. Dumont and his men rode off to intercept the police party. A confrontation ensued in which insults were exchanged but nobody was hurt. The police retreated without firing a shot, but before the Métis were able to unsaddle their horses back at Duck Lake, they were facing another armed contingent, this one consisting of 56 Mounted Police and 43 volunteers from Prince Albert. Dumont's party of horsemen was reinforced by the arrival of Louis Riel and nearly 300 Métis, as well as some Cree Indians, who were attracted to Duck Lake by news of the earlier encounter. As was often the case in these accidental confrontations, nobody was certain who fired the first shot. But Gabriel Dumont's elder brother probably went forward with an Indian chief to have a parley. The Indian reached for the gun of one of those they were meeting, and Crozier gave the order to fire. Isidore Dumont fell dead, and the battle began. Thirty minutes of gunfire exchanges followed, during which lives were lost on both sides.

Louis Riel v. Canada

The Métis, who outnumbered Crozier's men, forced them to retreat. Gabriel Dumont later recalled this confrontation in vivid detail:

> They had to go through a clearing so I lay in wait for them, saying to my men: "Courage, I'm going to make the red coats jump in their carts with some rifle shots." And then I laughed, not because I took any pleasure in killing but to give courage to my men.

> Since I was eager to knock off some of the red coats, I never thought to keep under cover and a shot came and gashed the top of my head, where a deep scar can still be seen. I fell down on the ground and my horse, which was also wounded, went right over me as it tried to get away…. When Joseph Delorme saw me fall again, he cried out that I was killed. I said to him, "Courage! As long as you haven't lost your head, you're not dead!…

> While we were fighting, Riel was on horseback, exposed to the gunfire, and with no weapon but the crucifix which he held in his hand.

Dumont shouted to his men to "follow them and finish them off," but Riel begged that no more be killed, "saying enough blood has already been shed." The police left unmolested with their own dead but left the volunteer dead on the field. Back at Duck Lake, Riel called on the Métis to thank God "who gave you so valorous a leader." He and a somewhat recovered Dumont agreed to allow men from the fort to collect under a safe conduct the bodies of the volunteers, which were stored in an empty house until they were recovered by men from Prince Albert. While the bodies were being laid out, Riel talked to a wounded prisoner. He said the country belonged to the Métis and First Nations, and he discussed the "new church" which he was founding, evidence that his role as a prophet was constantly on his mind. Among the wounded were relatives of a number of Canadian politicians, including Francis Hincks, Joseph Howe, and Alexander Mackenzie.

The victory at Duck Lake led the Mounties to decide to abandon Fort Carlton, which would have been difficult to defend. The occupants departed on the night of 27 March, leaving behind a smouldering fire in the walls. Gabriel Dumont wanted to ambush the retreating column. "We could have killed a lot of them," recalled Dumont later, "but Riel, who was always restraining us, formally opposed the idea."

Over the course of time, Dumont managed to develop an interpretation of the Rebellion in which his good ideas for aggressive tactics were reined in by a far more pacific Riel, with the result an inevitable defeat. There are several problems with this interpretation. One difficulty with the Dumont interpretation is the implicit notion put forward by Dumont

260

that if he had been solely in charge, the war against Canada would have been fought much more successfully. Perhaps the Métis might have succeeded in killing more Mounties or even militiamen, thus giving a better account of themselves, but this is different from an eventual victory. A Métis military triumph was most unlikely, given the comparative numbers. Dumont had no more than a few hundred soldiers, while Canada could have poured large numbers of troops into the region. There is absolutely no evidence that Canada would ever have agreed to deal with the insurgents; too much national honour was at stake. All the evidence instead suggests that Canadians would volunteer in substantial numbers to put down the Métis uprising. Moreover, the Métis were good buffalo hunters and some of them were experienced in fighting against the Sioux and other First Nations, but they were not disciplined soldiers. The decision not to oppose the Wolseley Expedition with arms in 1870 had probably been the right one.

Another difficulty with Dumont's version of events is that there is evidence against much of it. The records of the Exovedate indicate that most strategic military decisions were taken collectively. Dumont would later insist that he wanted to attack at Fort Carlton and Prince Albert from the beginning, but had been opposed by Riel. The council minutes indicate that there was unanimity on a defensive position from the outset. After Riel had issued the ultimatum to Crozier on 21 March, the council had been reluctant even to occupy Duck Lake. On 24 March, when the council divided six to six on taking over Duck Lake, it was Riel who broke the tie by voting in favour. Dumont was restrained by his colleagues as much or more by Louis Riel, who seems by and large in military matters to have reflected the opinions of the majority.

On 27 March, Riel took advantage of an offer by a prisoner to convey a message to Superintendent Crozier (offering a safe conduct in order to recover the dead bodies of the volunteers). The letter began: "A calamity has fallen upon the country yesterday. You are responsible for it before God and men. Your men cannot claim that their intentions were peaceable, since they were bringing along cannon. And they fired many shots first." It continued by offering the victory "to the Almighty." The letter was signed by Riel as "Exoveed" and by the "representatives of the French Half-breeds." Through William Jackson's brother, Riel also wrote to "the people of Prince Albert," calling for a meeting of delegates to "discuss the conditions of our entering into confederation as a province." As more than one biographer has noted, Riel seemed to be permanently caught in an 1870 time warp, thinking that what had worked in Red River could be replicated here. Thomas Jackson never delivered the letter and told Riel's trial that it had been destroyed. Jackson tried to retrieve his brother from Riel's custody, but Riel refused to release him.

Louis Riel v. Canada

On 27 March, General Middleton arrived in Winnipeg at 7 a.m., and was greeted by news of the action at Duck Lake. He inspected the remaining units of the 90th Regiment, which had been formed in 1882 by veterans of the Wolseley Expedition of 1870 who had remained in Manitoba. "He seemed very much dissatisfied with the accoutrement," wrote the Manitoba *Free Press*, "and the fact that some of the privates wore overshoes, while others wore long boots and many without the other necessary equipment displeased the general considerably." Middleton had only been a few months in Canada, and he didn't seem to understand how equipment worked in the Canadian militia — each man supplied his own footwear. Later that afternoon, the 90th marched out of its drill hall, the regimental band playing "The Girl I Left Behind Me," and departed on the 6 p.m. train for Troy. One Winnipeg reporter observed, "Seldom has a military force been sent out so poorly equipped, I do not envy General Middleton his task." The troops were no better trained than equipped. Urban types, most of the men had never fired a rifle or any weapon whatsoever. But there were few short-term alternatives to the Royal Winnipeg Rifles, the only organized militia unit west of The Lakehead.

In any event, Riel and the Exovedate, meeting at Duck Lake, voted on 31 March (on a motion made by Dumont) to pull back to Batoche. That same day, the Exovedate also voted:

> That the Canadian half-breed Exovedate acknowledges Louis David Riel as a prophet in the service of Jesus Christ and Son of God and only Redeemer of the world; a prophet at the feet of Mary Immaculate, under the visible and most consoling safeguard of St. Joseph, the beloved patron of the half-breeds — the patron of the universal Church; as a prophet, the humble imitator in many things of St. John the Baptist, the glorious patron of the French Canadians and the French Canadian half-breeds.

The vote was unanimous, although Moise Ouellette declared "if after a time his views changed, he would record his vote." Riel wrote in his journal praying to "Jesus, Mary, Joseph and John the Baptist" to change the heart of Ouellette so that he would "embrace entirely the celestial reforms of Divine Worship and reject all those things that the religion of Rome has inculcated in the hearts of all the nations of the globe."

News of Duck Lake travelled swiftly across the North-West, and encouraged a number of First Nations groups led by the more militant chiefs to mount their own actions. Battleford was pillaged by aboriginals from Poundmaker's and Little Pine's reserve, and Big Bear's people, led by Wandering Spirit, killed an Indian agent and two priests at Frog Lake. In early April, Riel wrote letters to all the Indians and Métis living in Saskatchewan, asking them to seize stores and ammunition and come join the Exovedate at Batoche, where preparations were ongoing to meet another attack from the government forces. It must be emphasized that the Indians had their own agenda, and while they may have been influenced to action by the success at Duck Lake, Louis Riel had not really incited them to rebellion.

The Canadian Advance

General Middleton was a fat and fussy British officer of the old school, understandably suspicious of the inexperienced militia under his command. He made them take daily target and rifle practice with their short five-grooved Snider-Enfield rifles. The general's prohibition on alcoholic beverages led to a number of letters back to Winnipeg requesting carefully-wrapped parcels of "medicine." The prime minister's son, Hugh John Macdonald, gave full instructions on packaging to his wife. A contingent of volunteer scouts arrived, recruited by Major Charles Boulton in western Manitoba, and on 6 April, with the Scouts leading the way, the first contingent of Canadian soldiers headed toward Batoche. The column consisted of the men of the 90th, the Winnipeg Field Battery, 120 wagons, and a small number of Winnipeg cavalry. The pace at first was slow, only about 20 miles per day. A reporter for the Winnipeg *Sun* wrote of a scarcity of blankets and the need for the troops to sleep in their tents "spoon fashion, resting on one side until their lower limbs on the frozen ground get too numb and then, on signal, they all roll over with due regard for the distribution of the scanty blankets."

Middleton was pleased at the health of his men, which he attributed to liberal use of hot tea and the even freer use of tobacco. He described his troops as garbed "in the regular British uniform, supplemented with snow boots, fur caps and gloves, and most of them with hideous red comforters around their necks." The men of the 90th were not dressed in red coats, but in the dark green jackets traditional with rifle regiments. The militia marched through the Salt Plains, living on pork and hardtack, a diet which led Major Lawrence Buchan to produce the regimental marching song, "Pork, Beans and Hardtack." The little army paused on 17 April at Clark's Crossing, on the South Saskatchewan, to wait for the arrival of the 10th Grenadiers and an artillery battery from the East. Another similar contingent commanded by Major-General T.B. Strange was to march from Calgary to Edmonton and then to tackle Big Bear from the rear. When Middleton captured Batoche, the two forces would join to face Poundmaker.

Fish Creek

At this point, having been joined by the 10th Grenadiers, Middleton determined to split his little army of 800 men on either side of the river as they headed toward Batoche. The left force was commanded by Gilbert John Elliot, Lord Melgund, the military secretary to the Canadian governor-general, who had begun the campaign as an observer but had been appointed by Middleton as chief of staff. The plan was to catch the Métis in a pincer movement. The general was still expecting more reinforcements, but at the moment he had about 400 men on either side of the Saskatchewan. The contingent under his command had to pass through a ravine past Dumont's Crossing. In the ravine, the Métis under Gabriel Dumont had dug in. The battle of Fish Creek (as the Canadians called it) was about to begin.

While the Canadian militia marched, Louis Riel had been busy attempting to rally his people. It was not easy. Numbers of Métis quietly stole away in the night. Riel cajoled some, threatened others, and spent a good deal of his time with the Exovedate organizing the new church. The names of the week were altered, and the signs of the zodiac were given new meaning. But mostly, Riel prayed, wrote down his visions in his journal, and reported some of them to his followers. He seemed to have a constant barrage of visitations. Both his secretary, Philippe Garnot, and his old friend Louis Schmidt, were convinced that Riel was manipulating the prophecies in order to stir up support among the superstitious Métis. There is no particular reason to be skeptical, however, given the lengthy persistence of Riel's spiritual experiences and what he had made of them over the years.

Gabriel Dumont advocated a strategy of guerilla harassment against the soldiers. Riel and the Exovedate did not agree. It instructed Dumont and his men to wait to strike, trusting in "Our Lady, the Blessed Virgin Mary," for success over General Middleton. Dumont later wrote, "I yielded to Riel's judgment, although I was convinced that, from a humane standpoint, mine was the better plan; but I had confidence in his faith and his prayers, and that God would listen to him."

On 21 April, Riel recorded, "I have seen the giant — he is coming. It is Goliath. I pray to intercept the communications of the enemies…. Strike them with stupefaction. Stagger them when the right takes place so that when they hear the thunder they will know the Almighty is preparing to inflict retribution upon them." Finally, Dumont could wait no longer. He said he would deal with Middleton's men as "we would buffalo." "All right!" answered Riel, "Do as you wish." But Riel was still not happy, because his visions pointed in other ways than Dumont's plan.

In the end, Dumont sent Riel and a small detachment back to Batoche to attend to a rumour that the Mounted Police were coming. While the day-long skirmish occurred — and those in Batoche could hear the gunfire — Louis Riel prayed with his arms held over his head. When he tired, two Métis held them up for him. With a small force of about 130 men, badly armed, Dumont confronted the Canadians on the morning of 24 April. The first contact was between Boulton's Scouts and advance scouts from the Métis. At first the buffalo hunters did well. Dumont had instructed his men to steal away as their ammunition ran out, and by noon there were perhaps only 60 Métis left in the coulee. Both sides were reinforced, but at the end of the day both withdrew from the field of battle. The miracle that Riel had prayed for seemed to have occurred. Middleton was stopped, the Canadian casualties much heavier than those of the Métis. The Métis had experienced four dead and two wounded, while the Canadians counted 10 dead and 40 wounded. Dumont knew full well that he had been outnumbered, while Middleton was still not certain how many Métis were in the field, or how his green troops (although now baptized under fire) would respond to more heavy casualties. Gabriel Dumont would later attribute his success to Louis Riel's prayers. It was as good an explanation as any.

The next day, Middleton ordered the dead buried on the field of battle, and waited 12 days for more reinforcements, including Captain A. L. Howard from Connecticut with the new Canadian secret weapon, the Gatling gun, which was reputed to be able to fire 1000 bullets a minute. While the Canadians paused, the Exovedate debated a motion "that the Lord's Day be replaced by the seventh day of the week as revealed by the Holy Ghost." The motion was carried by majority, but not unanimous vote. So too was a subsequent motion to change the date of Easter. As Riel began gradually to begin to reform the church, numbers of Métis fell away from supporting him, and the clergy became openly hostile. The priests at Batoche (who were being held in semi-captivity) denounced the latest revisions by the Exovedate and threatened excommunication. Riel replied by insisting that he represented the Holy Ghost, who would reform Christ's church. In a subsequent confrontation with Father Fourmond on 4 May, Riel answered a statement about rendering unto Caesar with the retort, "Yes render to God, glory, honour and adoration, but to the tyrants of the world, render that which is due them. Sling back their authority, which they have usurped, in their teeth, tumble them from power, that is what God orders." He then continued with a tirade about the "sacred…cause ordained and directed by God, the cause of your native land…." Gabriel Dumont advocated confronting the enemy outside of Batoche, but Riel insisted that his visions told him the battle must be fought there. Dumont acquiesced.

Eventually the paddlewheel steamer *Northcote* arrived with Canadian reinforcements. General Middleton equipped it with cannon and sent it downstream to Batoche. Unfortunately for the general, sniper fire from the shore knocked out the wheelhouse, and a cable set up by Gabriel Dumont took out the smokestacks. The steamer retired for repairs, and Middleton would have to fight a traditional land battle rather than the first naval engagement on the Prairies. By 9 May, General Middleton had around 900 men: 262 Royal Grenadiers from Ontario, 275 Royal Winnipeg Rifles, 116 from the Midland (Ontario) Battalion, and 100 mounted scouts, half under the command of Major Boulton and the remainder from Qu'Appelle under Captain Jack French. He had four field pieces and the Gatling gun. Gabriel Dumont had no more than 200 men, many of them aged, ill-armed, and short of ammunition, plus an unknown number of Indians.

Batoche: The Final Battle

For the first three days of the assault of Batoche, Gabriel Dumont shuffled his forces about the area to make it appear that they were more numerous than was the case. He apparently convinced Middleton and Lord Melgund that the Métis army was formidable, especially defending its home territory and loved ones. Melgund set off on 9 May and returned to Ottawa, presumably to plead for more reinforcements. There was much speculation on his mission. One story was that he was summoned home by a pregnant wife. A number of reporters were with the Canadians, ready to speculate on the mission and to dispatch news of a victory to the telegraph line.

Middleton settled in for a siege. He ordered his men to "peg away" at the enemy whenever possible, knowing that he had far more ammunition than Gabriel Dumont at his disposal. Many of the soldiers were becoming highly critical of Middleton for his caution. One trooper reported that the young militiamen "wanted to charge and being young and inexperienced soldiers could not understand why they should not charge." On the evening of 11 May, Middleton had dinner with his officers, and announced his battle plan, which would go into effect the next morning. He would use the Scouts and a contingent of newly-arrived Land Surveyors to head across the fields to draw the enemy's attention, and then the infantry would assault the Métis positions in and around the village.

The general's plans did not go quite as planned on 12 May. The Scouts did their feint, but for some reason, the infantry, under the command of Lieutenant-Colonel Bowen van Straubenzie, did not advance.

Middleton rode off to see what had gone wrong, and was met by two men from Batoche with a message from Louis Riel. The message threatened to kill the captives held by the Métis if "you massacre our families." Middleton penned a swift reply, which assumed that Riel was concerned about the artillery barrage: "Mr. Riel, I am anxious to avoid killing women and children and have done my best to avoid doing so. Put your women and children in one place, and let us know where it is, and no shot shall be fired on them. I trust to your honour not to put men with them." Riel now sent a second note, saying that he would inform Middleton later about the location of the women and children. On the outside of the envelope he wrote at the last moment, "I do not like war, and if you do not retreat and refuse an interview, the question remains the same as regards the prisoners." The general had failed to react to the first clumsy offer to negotiate, perhaps because he did not understand it, perhaps because he did not wish to do so. By the time the second note reached him, it was too late. Middleton had finally met with van Straubenzie. Words were exchanged, and the general ended the discussion by heading for lunch.

At this point, the Canadian officers acted to resolve the whole business. Apparently operating in concert, they ordered a charge. With the Gatling gun rattling away, the soldiers quickly overran the village, leaving many of the Métis forces still out on the perimeters. The prisoners were released. One soldier from the 90th wrote home, "In the last house we found the body of a nice little girl, about 14 years old. She had been killed by a shell and was dressed for burial. So I lifted the poor little thing into the coffin, and covered it up and put it to one side to keep it from being knocked about." The Canadians had five killed and 25 wounded, while the numbers of Métis casualties was unknown. Most of the Métis, including Gabriel Dumont and Louis Riel, got away, at least in the short run. Old Joseph Ouellette, aged 93, refused to join the leaders. His last words to Dumont were, "Just one more Englishman."

When Riel met up with Gabriel Dumont (for the last time) outside the village, Riel asked, "What are we going to do?" "We are defeated," Dumont told him. "We shall perish. But you must have known, when we took up arms, that we would be beaten. So, they will destroy us!" Dumont helped Riel find shelter for his wife and two children, and then headed for the American border, the traditional refuge for Canadians whose rebellions had failed. As for Riel, he responded to General Middleton's offer of protection — presumably from the wrath of the militiamen — by giving himself up to a small troop of scouts looking for him and other Metis leaders on the 15th of May. One eye-witness account, written up by a correspondent for the *Times of London*, suggests Riel was attempting to slip away, but regardless Riel was brought before Middleton and the two men exchanged courteous words.

Captain Hugh John Macdonald, son of the prime minister, wrote to his wife just after the battle that "had our fellows taken [Riel], he'd have been brought in in a coffin, and there'd be no thoughts of a trial." Hugh John, of course, had been wounded in the rear end earlier in the campaign, and was not feeling very well disposed to the Métis.

Later, Middleton put Riel in the custody of Captain George Young of the Winnipeg Field Battery, who had been a captive of Riel in 1869 and was the son of the Methodist minister who had pleaded for Thomas Scott's life in 1870. Young then escorted Riel on board the steamship *Northcote* for Regina, which they reached on 23 May. The two men discussed religion and theology, and Young reported that he had been overmatched.

The Canadian forces still had some mopping up operations to carry out against the First Nations, including the capture of those responsible for the slaughter at Frog Lake. But with Riel's surrender, the Métis phase of the Rebellion of 1885 was over.

-12-

The Trial

L ouis Riel was the first and only individual in Canada ever tried for high treason. His trial was a highly dramatic one, conducted in an atmosphere of party and racial hostility.

The setting of a courtroom is by its very nature conducive to the unfolding of a real-life theatrical event, but Riel's trial contained all of the fundamental elements of great tragedy, particularly in the situation in which he eventually found himself. Riel faced the dilemma of having to choose between surrendering his honour and his self-esteem in order to save his life by allowing his attorneys to plead insanity, or remaining true to his own perception of himself by convincing the jury that he was not mad in the slightest. As is often the case in fiction but seldom in real life, this basic quandary involved a variety of subtle shadings of meaning and interpretation, particularly in terms of his own character and behaviour. Louis Riel was no simple victim of his own decision.

Long before the North-West Rebellion burst into open violence in March of 1885, it had become a partisan issue right across Canada. The Canadian government, Conservative politicians, and the Conservative press were all convinced that there was no legitimate reason for any course of violence by the inhabitants of the western territory, while the Liberals were equally convinced that the unrest had been brought about by both government policies and government inaction. Once the shooting had begun, most Canadians in the East from both parties — and their newspapers — initially condemned the violence, although some sympathizers of the Métis argued that the government could have done more. A public meeting supportive of Riel was held in Montreal on 31 March 1885, and as events developed there was increasing support for the Métis. Even before Batoche, many French-Canadians had begun to rally to the their defence. Arthur Turcotte, MP for Trois Rivières, moved in the Commons on 13 April that a resolution that emphasized "this uprising is more the result of a momentary dispute than of conscious and premeditated disloyalty." The Turcotte resolution was later debated in the Quebec Legislative Assembly, which defeated it on 20 April by a vote of 41 to 15. A public meeting on 23 April 1885 organized by Club National was attended by about 2,000 people where speakers denounced the government. *La Patrie* told its readers on 15 May, "With Sir John it is war to the bitter end; it is blood and pillage and national desolation and persecution and reprisals, and finally the complete annihilation of our brothers in the Northwest."

While there was some support for the Métis, there was not as much popular sentiment favourable to Louis Riel. Virtually all editorial opinion wanted Riel's head. The Montreal *Gazette* was typical in declaring on 14 May that "the blood of a hundred loyal Canadians calls for vengeance," and a few days later insisted that "simple justice demands that the arch mover in the rebellion shall suffer the penalty of his crime and that right speedily." While there was some mention of Riel's mental state in the press coverage, his "madness" was not yet a serious issue. Most newspapers were more eager to bridge the chasm between Ontario and Quebec than to be concerned about the legal treatment of Louis Riel and the other rebels.

As for Riel, he could easily have escaped across the border, but he had given himself up to General Middleton, apparently in the hopes that he could employ the subsequent trial to publicize the complaints of the Métis and to justify his own behaviour.

Originally, Captain George Young had been ordered to escort Riel to Winnipeg for trial, but while en route the destination was changed to Regina, where the prisoner was put into a small cell in the NWMP barracks and shackled with a 20-pound ball and chain attached to his leg. His jailer, Inspector R. Burton Deane of the Mounties, decided that Riel would be allowed visitors only with the approval of the prime minister and prevented from having access to any newspapers. He was held without legal advice or assistance until mid-June. Sir Wilfrid Laurier would complain about this treatment. While it was certainly harsh, rumours flew around the West all spring and summer about attempts to break Riel out of jail, and the government was taking no chances. Riel had no money to employ legal counsel and no opportunity to hire any while held in shackles. Eventually, a Riel Defence Committee was organized after a public meeting in St. Roche on 5 July 1885. More than 5,000 Riel supporters in Quebec City decided to raise a public subscription on his behalf, to ensure a fair trial. This committee hired the lawyers François Lemieux, Charles Fitzpatrick, and James N. Greenshields, and sent them west to serve as Riel's legal counsel. Riel himself was not entirely happy with this action. He wrote to the secretary of the defence committee that he wanted a trial "on the merit of my actions" and "before the Supreme

Court." He also complained that the lawyers chosen were too visibly Liberals; he would have preferred a defence team better balanced ethnically and politically.

From the beginning, the Canadian government had two fundamental ambitions with regard to Louis Riel. One was to see that his trial was regarded as "fair." The second was to see that he was found guilty and duly punished. In order to achieve these goals it made legal decisions which were perfectly appropriate at the time but which reflected the need to stack the odds against the defendant. At the same time, it should be emphasized that the Crown was under no particular obligation to bend over backwards for the Métis leader. The Crown was obliged, by 18th century statutes, to respect his civil rights and give him a fair trial, but it was not required to presume him innocent until proven guilty. Indeed, given the Canadian adversarial system of justice, it was in many ways the Crown's job in the trial to do everything it could to prove him guilty. It thus hired a team of distinguished eastern lawyers to handle the prosecution. Such considerations applied mainly to Riel, because he was perceived as a national figure who would serve as a lightning rod for public opinion in Quebec and Ontario. The remaining rebels and the First Nations involved in the uprising would be treated far more summarily. The government apparently intended to deal fairly gently with the other Métis involved in the uprising, putting upon Riel the full responsibility for the rebellion. This was, of course, quite the reverse of government response to the rebellions of 1837 and 1838, when the ringleaders escaped scot-free and the rank-and-file bore the weight of the exaction of justice. Henry J. Clarke wrote the prime minister in 1886, in the course of requesting a judicial appointment, that he had written a number of the depositions of witnesses at Riel's trial, "placing…all the responsibility of the Rebellion on Riel and others, and all condemning him without stint." On the other hand, the government intended to deal with the First Nations insurgents without mercy, but quite apart from the uprising, for they were "murderers" rather than rebels.

The trial of Louis Riel opened at 11 a.m. in a small courtroom in Regina. Riel was brought in by the RNWP dressed in a Mountie uniform, to guard against rescue or assassination. The trial was from the outset intended as a "show trial" or "state trial" in the traditional sense of the term. As Mr. James Greenshields for the defence stated early in the proceedings, "This being a state trial, and the public at large being interested, and the case having gone so prominently before the public, as well as the events preceding the rebellion, that the public naturally expected that a fair trial should be given." Here there are a number of interesting themes to be explored. We now know considerably more about the trial, the history of Canadian law, and the mad business than contemporaries did in the 19th century. Nevertheless, there is no possibility of a definitive statement on the topic. The subject remains controversial, with a number of major points based on irreconcilable assumptions about the nature of fairness, and others which are simply shrouded in mystery and uncertainty. We do not know, for example, why Riel's conviction was never appealed to the Supreme Court of Canada, or exactly what orders the defence team was acting under. We do have a complete trial transcript, which begins when the trial opened 11 a.m. on 20 July 1885. I have quoted from the transcript liberally in the discussion that follows, since many of the accounts which attempt to summarize complex testimony succinctly do so inaccurately or misleadingly.

By the time the preliminaries had been dealt with and the trial actually begun, it was 28 July. On 24 July, William Henry Jackson had been put on trial for his part in the rebellion. The charge was treason-felony rather than high treason. Jackson declared himself willing to share in Riel's fate. The defence argued insanity and the Crown did not much protest. Only three witnesses were called, all of whom testified that Jackson was indisputably mad, and the jury found him "not guilty on the ground of insanity." Like Riel subsequently, Jackson insisted that he was not insane, but he could not find anyone to believe him.

Preliminary Jousting

The Question of Venue

Louis Riel's destination out of Batoche was changed from Winnipeg to Regina because it was decided by the Crown that any trial of any rebel in Manitoba might produce a "miscarriage of justice." Such miscarriage was at least as likely to result from juries favourable to the prisoners as from any hostility to them. Given the fact that the defence would rely on a plea of insanity, the remoteness of Regina may have made it more difficult to obtain expert medical testimony. Some authorities have argued that the law after 1880 provided for capital trials in the North-West Territories, and therefore the case had to be tried there. Did the government have to try in the North-West Territories? The answer to this question appears to be no. The 1873 North-West Territories Act specified Manitoba as the venue for capital trials, but although this provision was dropped in the 1880 amended act which created a local court system, it was not expressly appealed. The question of a Manitoba trial was never raised in the courts, since the government did not bring the trials to Manitoba or attempt to do so, and the defence did not argue for such a move.

Perhaps a better question might be: could the government have moved the venue elsewhere on the grounds that the accused could not receive a fair trial in the North-West Territories? The court's ultimate refusal to change the venue did not necessarily depend on its total inability to do so. There may have been political reasons for not changing the venue, but these are different from legal ones. Riel's lawyers argued for a venue in Ontario or British Columbia on technical grounds, rather than directly on the point of unfairness or injustice. Their first point was that the composition of a jury in the North-West Territories was different than elsewhere, to the defendant's disadvantage. A North-West Territories jury consisted of only six jurors, rather than the normal 12. Not only did this deny the accused the usual safeguard of the usual sort of jury trial, as guaranteed as long ago as Magna Carta in 1212, it also obviously reduced the possibility of hung juries. Six jurors were more likely to agree than 12. The Crown pointed out that smaller juries were employed in other Canadian jurisdictions, such as New Brunswick, but the defence riposted that New Brunswickers had a chance to vote for the legislators that had decided on these rules.

Secondly, Riel's lawyers argued that prior imperial legislation, never repealed, denied Canada the right to conduct trials for capital offences in the North-West Territories. The second argument was probably never very useful, since for any court to concede this jurisdictional question would have been to create chaos in the system of justice as practised in the West since 1870. The Manitoba court in 1874 had decided against similar sorts of arguments on behalf of Ambroise Lépine, and just previous to the Riel trial, a murderer named John Connor had been tried in Regina, convicted, and summarily executed. On the other hand, while the jury system of the North-West Territories may have been legally defensible, the government need not have rested content with it. The jury of six was chosen from the neighbourhood of the location of the trial, and was composed entirely of jurors of British Protestant background, most of whom apparently understood no French, a language in which many of the witnesses testified. The jury selection went fairly swiftly, with the defence using five challenges and the Crown one. The defence later grumbled about the jury selection, but did not act upon the complaints in any way. One of the reasons the government may have preferred Regina as a venue (not to Winnipeg but to Ontario or British Columbia) was because the surrounding population might be less sympathetic to Riel, but local attitudes probably could not have been made the basis for a change of venue.

It is not known if there was some reason the defence did not argue these questions explicitly in terms of fairness and justice — rather than solely on technicalities. Whether the court properly understood that

Louis Riel v. Canada

what Riel's lawyers were trying to claim was that he could not get a fair trial in Regina — if that was what they were claiming — is not entirely clear. But Hugh Richardson, the stipendiary magistrate selected to try the case, was able to be obtuse about the matter because of the way the objections were phrased.

Richardson was not a tenured judge but served at the pleasure of the government. Richardson did not speak French. One MP pointed out in subsequent Commons debate in 1886 that "It was an unhappy choice to select, of the three or four judges, the person who filled the position of the political adviser, the political law officer, to the Government in the Territories to be the judge in this particular trial." This was particularly true since one of the underlying complaints of the rebellion was about the administration of justice, or the lack of administration of justice. Richardson was receiving a salary as legal advisor to the lieutenant-governor. He was a lawyer with limited trial experience and a very limited imagination who was not likely to have independent views. He had a strong dislike of the Métis, but his racial attitudes would probably not have disqualified him in the eyes of either the Crown or the legal system. Hugh Richardson — unimaginative, weak, inexperienced, prejudiced — was the perfect instrument for a government looking to convict and execute Louis Riel.

The Charges

Two separate issues arose over the charges. First, there was the statute under which the charges against Riel were laid, and second, there were the charges themselves. The Canadian government had a choice of three statutes under which it might lay charges against Riel. It chose to proceed under the 1352 Statute of Treasons, 25 Edward III, stat. 5, c. 2. This statute called for execution as the only possible outcome of a guilty verdict. Actually, it called for the convicted traitor to be hanged, drawn, and quartered, although the drawing and quartering had fallen into disuse in the 19th century. Written hundreds of years before the establishment of the British Empire, its language might have been regarded as anachronistic, since it spoke — for example — of the accused levying "War against the Lord the King in his realm." Nevertheless, the 1352 statute remained until well into the 19th century the standard statute under which the Canadian authorities laid general (or high) treason charges, both during the War of 1812 and the rebellions of 1837 and 1838. It was also the major treason statute in force in the North-West Territories in 1885.

One of the important features of the development of treason law under the 1352 statute was the doctrine of local allegiance. According to

Matthew Hale's The History of the Pleas of the Crown (1736), "If an alien the subject of a foreign prince in amity with the king, live here and enjoy the benefit of the king's protection and commit a treason, he shall be judged and executed, as a traitor, for he owes a local allegiance." As for foreign aliens who had originally been born British subjects, Blackstone had made the definitive traditional statement: "Natural Allegiance is therefore a debt of gratitude, which cannot be forfeited, cancelled or altered by any time, place, or circumstance." England had amended this categorical ruling by section 6 of the Naturalization Act of 1870, 33 Victoria, c. 14, which declared that when any British subject became naturalized in some other state, he would be "deemed to have ceased to be a British subject and be regarded as an alien." This legislation was virtually cloned by the Canadian Parliament in its Naturalization Act of 1881, 44 Victoria, c. 13, although the Canadian legislation allowed British subjects naturalized in a foreign state to continue to be British subjects, providing they had declared the same and taken an oath of allegiance within two years after the passage of the act. There is some question as to whether the Naturalization Act of 1881, declared in force on 4 July 1883, extended to the North-West Territories. If it did not, this provided another illustration of the failure of the Canadian government to extend the protection of all its laws to citizens of the North-West Territories. If it did extend to the North-West Territories, Riel could not be charged with high treason as a British subject. The need felt by the Crown to avoid any slip-ups on this point led to the duplication of charges noted below.

The Crown could have proceeded against Riel under two other statutes. The Fenian Act of 1866 declared that it was treasonable for an alien of a nation at peace with Canada to levy war against Canada. Proceeding under this statute might have required the government to prove that Riel was an alien, which the government at the trial stated was "a responsibility the Crown did not choose to assume." The Crown could also have proceeded under the 1868 Canadian treason-felony statute, 31 Victoria, c 69, formally entitled, "An Act for the Better Security of the Crown and of the Government," as it did in the cases of all other parties tried for treason in 1885. The chief difference between this statute and the high treason one was that 31 Victoria, c. 69 did not insist on a mandatory death penalty upon conviction. This treason-felony statute was often regarded as being milder than the high treason one, but since juries often refused to convict if death was the only sentencing option, this is not necessarily the case. Contemporaries were themselves often confused about which statute Riel was being tried under. At least one of Riel's own attorneys began the trial under the impression that the 1868 statute was the operative one, and in the 1886 House of Commons debates over the trial, Sir Hector Langevin specifically if mistakenly defended the government's use of the treason-felony statute.

The question of citizenship was taken into account by the prosecution and was discussed by the lawyers during the opening defence challenges against the proceedings of the court. The information against Riel consisted of six charges. In the first three he was charged with "being a subject of our Lady the Queen, not regarding the duty of his allegiance, nor having the fear of God in his heart…." The second three charges repeated the substance of the first three, but described the defendant as "living within the Dominion of Canada and under the protection of our Sovereign Lady the Queen, not regarding the duty of his allegiance, nor having the fear of God in his heart…." In short, Riel was charged both with being a subject of the Queen and with being a resident of Canada living under her protection. This was to cover any possible confusion over Riel's citizenship. The defence attempted halfheartedly to demur to the indictment because of the duplication of the charges. The Crown maintained in rebuttal that "In three counts we have charged him as a British subject and having violated his natural allegiance, and in three counts we have charged him with having acted contrary to his local allegiance," adding, "It is quite sufficient that a man may live in a country to be guilty of treason." It has been since argued that the charges based on Riel as a British subject should have been dismissed, since it was never proven that he was a British subject. The matter of Riel's citizenship was never proven in court, another instance of shortcomings by the defence, which should have insisted on the proof. But he was still liable as an American citizen. The defence obviously did not regard this demurrer very seriously. The omnibus charges were never unpacked by the judge and may well have perplexed the jury. But from the very beginning of the trial, the main line of defence was to be the plea of insanity.

The Defence Request for Time to Prepare

One of the most important parts of the preliminary efforts of Riel's defence team was to request more time for preparation. The defence pointed out that the prisoner had been arraigned and asked to proceed immediately with his defence. The defence not only wanted an adjournment, but it wanted the court to provide financial assistance in bringing witnesses to Regina for trial, and it wanted documents produced. The witnesses it sought to call fell basically in four categories: first, the Métis who had invited Riel to Saskatchewan in 1884, many of whom were now in political asylum in the United States; second, the members of the Exovedate in custody; third, medical men to testify to the state of Riel's mind; and finally, a number of government officials who had custody of many documents in the matter. The documents fell into three types: first, Riel's own papers seized at Batoche; secondly, the various petitions and applications to the government for redress of grievances; and finally, the documentary evidence as to Riel's citizenship. The areas to be covered by these witnesses and documents suggest the four lines of defence that Riel's lawyers initially had in mind. They were planning to argue that Riel was invited to the North-West for peaceful purposes, that the "agitation in the North-West Territories was constitutional and for the rights of the people," and that any rebellion had been unpremeditated; that the rebellion had been made by the Exovedate rather than by Riel, who "did not participate in any engagement or commit or countenance any overt act of treason"; that Riel had a history of insanity; and that the Rebellion had been at least partly justified by the absence of government policy for the region.

The Crown opposed delay for a number of reasons. If the defence had tipped its hand by its requests, the Crown indicated its strategy by the nature of its opposition. It stated the obvious ones in the court. It would be quite impossible to get Métis in exile in the States to testify. Riel's history of prior medical troubles was irrelevant to his state of mind at the time of the uprising. Documents petitioning for redress on constitutional grounds were not evidence "to form a justification for armed rebellion," and were regarded by the Crown as "utterly inadmissible" in any case. The Crown was particularly perturbed at the defence application for an order to produce all papers found in the hands of Riel at Batoche, since (as Mr. Robinson argued) many of them implicated others. Unstated was the fact that Crown strategy called for placing as much of the blame as possible upon Riel's own shoulders, which would allow the government to treat leniently many of his followers. The Crown grudgingly offered a week's postponement, and Mr. Fitzpatrick for the defence readily agreed — so readily that it seems likely that a deal had been worked out privately on the matter. This incident probably was the turning point in the trial. The Crown had certainly exposed its hand by announcing that it would oppose any attempt to introduce evidence of the previous attempts of the people of the territory to get grievances answered as a justification for the rebellion. The defence had backed off this line at the first sign of Crown assertiveness, which meant that Justice Richardson did not have to rule on the admissibility of the documents. More and continued pressure on all the points in the defence case was what was required, not least to force Richardson into rulings that could be challenged on appeal. The Manitoba court which heard the initial appeal at least suggested that it would have liked to have heard more about the documents.

Louis Riel v. Canada

A Preliminary Hearing?

The question of a preliminary hearing came up in two forms, one contemporary and one long after the fact. Contemporaries were well aware that in the North-West Territories there was no provision for grand juries. This meant that there was no preliminary investigation before a grand jury, and there was no bill of indictment. The information in the case was laid in the city of Hamilton, Ontario, and Riel was not informed of the charges against him. Riel's lawyers made little of the absence of a grand jury (which the American consul in Winnipeg thought was important), but subsequent critics of the fairness of Riel's trial certainly did so.

The question of a pretrial hearing was not the same thing as a preliminary investigation by a grand jury. It was not raised in 1885 but was first suggested by the Canadian psychiatrist R. E. Turner at a symposium held in Vancouver in 1964. Turner argued that "It is a matter of law and procedure at the outset of a trial to consider whether accused is fit to stand trial." He pointed to chapter 29, section 101 of the 1869 criminal code of Canada, which provided: "If any person indicted for any offence be found insane, and upon arraignment be so found by a jury empanelled for that purpose, so that such person cannot be tried upon such indictment, or of, upon the trial of any person so indicted, such person appears to the jury charged with the indictment to be insane, the Court, before whom such person is brought to be arraigned, or is tried as aforesaid, may direct such finding to be recorded, and thereupon may order such person to be kept in strict custody until the pleasure of the Lieutenant-Governor be known." This point was reiterated by L. H. Thomas in his 1977 article on the Riel trial, which argued that Riel was not given a fair hearing.

Thomas Flanagan has insisted that the reason there was no such hearing in Riel's case was because Canadian rules of criminal procedure had to be specifically extended by statute to the North-West Territories, and chapter 29, section 102, had not been so extended. Apart from the obvious observation that this failure to provide the territories with the full measure of the Canadian criminal code suggests a neglect of the region by the Canadian government and a reason for changing the venue, there is also the question of whether the absence of statutory enactment really means that a pretrial hearing was "legally dubious, if not impossible," as Flanagan contends. Who know what the court might have accepted? Flanagan himself argues that the way the Crown dealt with the lack of pretrial process for Riel's secretary William Henry Jackson was to try him and to allow the jury to find him not guilty by reason of insanity. We do not know why the Crown so dealt with Jackson.

What a pretrial hearing would have done was to put the spotlight straight on the question of whether Riel was responsible for his actions. Had the government chosen to avoid hearing days of testimony and to permit Riel to plead insanity, it might well have chosen this option. On the other hand, it seems unlikely that the medical experts would have agreed at this point any more than they did in the trial itself on the matter of responsibility.

The Prosecution Case

In his opening address to the jury on 28 July 1885, Mr. Britton Osler for the Crown dealt briefly with the charges and the reasons for them, rehearsed the Crown's version of the sequence of events that had led to bloodshed, and insisted that Riel had ordered his men to fire on the police at Duck Lake, which was his first act of treason. Osler was noted for the tenacity of his prosecutions and his insistence on categorical answers from witnesses — which was another way of saying that he was a bullying prosecutor — as well as for his familiarity with medical detail. This was the case that first provided him with national exposure. Osler made much of Riel's invitations to the aboriginals, especially Poundmaker. He emphasized that Riel was basically trying to extract money from the government. He interpreted Riel's religious beliefs as put forward because the church to which he belonged opposed him. 'The prophet of the Saskatchewan' was the cry under which his poor dupes, and many of them should have known better, were supposed to rally, intending by combining religious power to follow on the North Saskatchewan, the methods of eastern leaders." Not wrongs and grievances, but the "personal ambition and vanity" of Louis Riel were responsible for the uprising in the North-West.

The Crown then proceeded to call 15 witnesses in rapid succession. The questions put to them were crafted to elicit responses which directly associated Riel with the various acts of violence and which generally sought to blacken his character. Cross-examination by Riel's attorneys was for the most part brief and perfunctory, directed mainly at attempting to elicit evidence of Riel's irrationality. Some witnesses were not cross-examined at all. Finally, on 29 July, in the midst of a lengthy testimony by Charles Nolin, Riel could keep silent no longer. Nolin had under cross-examination testified that Riel had visions, revelations, and "inspirations that worked through every part of his body." But he also talked of the demand for $35,000, and the way in which he said Riel had manipulated the Métis. Almost every answer he gave maliciously twisted Riel's behaviour against him. He had then described the visit of an RNWP officer to Batoche in the winter of 1885, with the vaguest hint of something improper between Mrs. Riel, Mrs. Dumont, and the officer. Riel interjected, "Your Honor, would you permit me a little while — " The judge told Riel he would have his opportunity to speak in due course. Riel persisted. "If there was any way, by legal procedure, that I should be allowed to say a word, I wish you would allow me before this prisoner [the word used by Riel] leaves the box."

The judge attempted to tell Riel to suggest any questions to his counsel, and Mr. Fitzpatrick for the defence team declared that the prisoner should be instructed to work through his attorneys and "he must not be allowed to interfere." In the course of a subsequent exchange between Judge Richardson, the prisoner, and both the Crown and the defence, it became clear that Riel substantially disagreed with the conduct of the proceedings by his lawyers, who in turn felt that he was "obstructing the proper management of this case." Riel's complaint was twofold. First, his lawyers were attempting to demonstrate that he was insane, and secondly, his lawyers were not asking the right questions of the witnesses because they were not sufficiently acquainted with the context. His lawyers came from a far province, he said, and had only recently taken on the case. "They have to put questions to men with whom they are not acquainted, on circumstances which they don't know, and although I am willing to give them all of the information that I can, they cannot follow the thread of all the questions that could be put to the witnesses. They lose more than three-quarters of the good opportunities of making good answers." The judge again insisted that Riel would have an opportunity to speak at the proper time, to which he responded, "The witnesses are passing and the opportunities." He continued that he already had 200 questions which had not been asked by his counsel.

The court took a break while Riel consulted with his lawyers. The lawyers returned from this consultation to insist, as they had previously, that all questions should be put to witnesses through counsel. If Riel insisted upon asking questions of the witnesses, the defence team threatened to withdraw. The Crown, obviously well pleased at the evidence of disagreement in the ranks of the defence, was happy to allow matters to take whatever turn they might. As for Judge Richardson, he was initially quite prepared to allow Riel to take part in his own defence, although he warned the prisoner that his lawyers had threatened to resign if he interfered. Richardson also appeared willing to give Riel considerable leeway, saying at one point, "If this were a criminal case, I should not hesitate, but this is beyond the ordinary run of cases that I have had to do with in my whole career." But Riel's lawyers were absolutely adamant that he should not interfere. Riel admitted he was caught in a dilemma, saying, "while I wish to retain them, I cannot abandon my dignity." He recognized that without the lawyers (and behind them the eastern friends and supporters who had hired them) he was at the absolute mercy of the court. He saw the alternatives as being self-defence or "the animal life of an asylum" which did not "carry with it the moral existence of an intellectual being." He maintained, however, that he had the constitutional right to self-defence. At this point, Judge Richardson was handed another "authority," which he claimed held that a court refusal to allow the defendant to cross-examine did not violate the constitutional right of defence by himself. That authority was not specified by name in the transcript. Richardson therefore ruled that Riel was totally in his counsel's hands. One observer, a former magistrate, wrote to Bishop Taché of his empathy and agreement with Riel at this point, adding that "I had not been quite in sympathy with the style or mode of the defence."

The examination of Nolin continued, closing with Nolin's statement that "If the prisoner had not made himself appear as a prophet, he would never have succeeded in bringing the halfbreeds with him." Here was a perfect opportunity for the defence to begin to explore the implications of Riel's religious visions and teachings, but Mr. Lemieux, on re-cross-examination, indicated by his line of questioning that he really was interested only in the effect on the clergy of Riel's "making himself out as a priest," in itself a misapprehension of the prisoner's religious beliefs. Riel tried again to put a question and was again refused. Whether the question would have more adequately brought out his religious position cannot be known, since he refused to allow his lawyers to ask it and the court refused to allow him to ask it. At this point, Crown attorney Robinson summarized the situation: "I understand the prisoner to say that he declines to make his choice between allowing his counsel to examine witnesses and joining him in examination, that he wishes then to examine him, and that he wishes to ask himself directly such questions as he desired; and I understand counsel to say that they cannot accept the responsibility of conducting his case if he insists upon that." To this statement the defence counsel agreed, "Yes, that's it." Several more witnesses appeared after this interchange, and Riel's lawyers continued to fail to take full advantage of their testimony, particularly with regard to his religious beliefs. Riel now remained silent.

The Insanity Plea and the McNaghten Rules

Before turning to the defence proceedings, in which Riel's lawyers would attempt to advance a plea of insanity, we need to examine the background of this plea in some detail. Before the Riel trial, there had been no serious attempt in Canada to produce legislation defining the meaning of insanity in the context of the criminal act. The first point that has to be emphasized is that there was a considerable difference between the medical definition of insanity and the legal test applied in this case, which was governed by application of the so-called McNaghten rules formulated by the House of Lords in 1843. In that year, one Daniel McNaghten, who had shot to death Sir Robert Peel's secretary under the mistaken impression that he was Peel himself, was acquitted by a jury after a brilliant defence by Alexander Cockburn. The defence attorney had persuaded the court that it should allow medical evidence that a person of otherwise sound mind could harbour a delusion that carried him beyond self-control, even though he knew the difference between right and wrong. The acquittal, which included a lifetime sentence to mental institutions, was heavily criticized by Queen and country alike. The upshot was the tendering of a series of hypothetical questions to a panel of common law judges relating generally to the insanity defence, and especially to the question of responsibility. The answers were deliberately intended to deal with the McNaghten defence of "partial insanity."

In their responses, the judges developed what was always regarded as the key "McNaghten Rule," which was that "at the time of the committing of the act, the party accused was labouring under such a defect of reason, from disease of the mind, as not to know the nature and quality of the act he was doing, or if he did know it, that he did not know he was doing what was wrong." In answer to another question about the use of testimony of medical experts who had never seen the prisoner before the trial, but who were present for the whole trial and the examination of witnesses, the answer was basically that such testimony was at the discretion of the judge. This opened the door for expert witnesses to be asked hypothetical questions. Many lawyers, judges, and medical men recognized almost from the outset of the formulation of the McNaghten rules that there were problems with them. There were a variety of reasons why a defendant might not be responsible for the action or actions for which he was being tried, and as one American jurist argued in 1871, it was impossible for a court to "lay down an abstract general proposition, which may be given to the jury in all cases, by which they are to determine whether the prisoner had capacity to entertain criminal intent." This judge went on to insist that the McNaghten formula attempted to apply "a rule of law wherewith to solve a question of fact.... No formal rule can be applied in settling questions which have relation to liberty and life, merely because it will lessen the labor of the court or jury."

These questions — both of the test of responsibility and whether it could be set down in advance by the court or had to be decided by the jury itself — had been discussed at great length in the 1881 American trial of the assassin of President James Garfield, one Daniel Guiteau. The

Americans in 1881 had also clearly recognized the important distinction between medical diagnoses of insanity and the application of the McNaghten rules. Guiteau was a lawyer himself who understood the difference between insanity "as a medical man would judge" and "legal insanity," which was "irresponsibility...an act without malice." Guiteau's trial was another "state trial" in which the prosecution was determined to get a conviction in order to execute the prisoner and thus answer public demand for his death. Not long after its completion, however, many people began to argue that the trial (and the jury) had ignored much testimony that Guiteau was insane. By 1885 the Guiteau trial was generally regarded in the United States as having been an appalling travesty of justice. Canada might have learned something from this, but apparently did not.

Many people in psychiatry had also by 1885 come to regard the McNaghten test as irrelevant. No formal rule of law could measure true responsibility given the complexities of the mind. The English authority John Buckmill in 1854 had pointed out that the law did not provide for degrees of responsibility, although there were gradations. The question was not whether one knew something to be correct, but whether one could manage to conform to such knowledge. Control rather than understanding was the key.

The most commonly used British textbook on medical jurisprudence, by Wharton and Stille, emphasized that: "Any species of insane delusion exempts from punishment the perpetrator of an act committed under its delusion," and further commented of the lack of responsibility involved in "insanity accompanied by delusions of such a character that the patient believes he is authorised by superior power to dispense with the law of the land...." In such a case, the authors observed, "it is clear that their objects are not responsible to the ordinary process of penal justice. Yet to such patients the 'right and 'wrong' test might pronounce sane. In such cases this test cannot be exclusively applied." Judge Richardson was obviously not one who shared in any of the soul-searching on the McNaghten rule, however. He charged the jury in the exact words of McNaghten and informed them that this was indeed the law. Richardson was clearly acting within what he regarded as the bounds of Canadian law in so informing the jury. The real question at Louis Riel's trial was whether anyone in the courtroom, particularly among those involved in the defence, understood the complexities of the question at issue. Curiously enough, it has been subsequently argued that the McNaghten rules should not have been applied in this trial in the first place, since they were a part of the common law and the common law had never been extended to the North-West Territories. Canada extended the common law to the Territories only a year later.

The whole question of insanity is complicated by the continuing major disagreement between Riel and his lawyers over the insanity plea, to which Riel was unalterably opposed. It is not clear whether Riel understood the distinction between insanity and legal insanity, but from his perspective, it did not matter. Whether he was medically insane or legally insane, he would end up living an "animal life in an asylum." In the course of the trial, as we have seen, Riel made clear that he did not agree with his lawyers, and they did their best to silence him. The lawyers insisted that they took instructions not from Riel but from unnamed "others," probably some Liberal brain trust back east, perhaps the Riel Defence Committee in Ottawa. The reliance on the insanity plea meant several things: first, that the defence spent much of its time in examination and cross-examination trying to establish that Riel was and had long been mentally unbalanced, and second, that the defence did not work as hard as they might have to establish an alternate line of defence.

Moreover, it seems fairly apparent that the defence was somewhat confused on the matter of insanity versus legal insanity and was not really enlightened by the medical experts. Here the problem was that Riel's best chance of acquittal by reason of insanity — which we must repeat he opposed desperately — lay in emphasizing his religious visions and voices, not the general nature of his conduct and behaviour. If his direct communion with God meant that he could not distinguish between right and wrong in the conventional senses, then he was innocent by reason of insanity. This book has earlier argued that Riel was not medically insane, but was instead a genuine religious prophet and visionary, to be judged by other criteria. But if Riel was not medically insane, because of those same visions and beliefs in his prophetic status, he certainly was insane in terms of any test of moral responsibility. Almost all the medical authorities in 1885 could agree that Riel was not responsible for his actions if his spiritual beliefs and visions were genuine, and a half century of modern scholarship has determined pretty conclusively that Riel's religion was quite sincerely believed. The trick was for the defence to bring out this feature. In order to do so it would have to overcome both its client's own wishes and the desire of many of the witnesses to see Riel's religious experiences either as playacting, or as deliberate deception.

The Defence Case

Finally, it was the turn of the defence. Their first witness was Father Alexis André. Mr. Lemieux tried to introduce evidence on the communications with government before the invitation to Riel. The Crown objected to the line of questioning. The arguments were interesting. Mr. Osler said, "My learned friends have opened a case of treason, justified only by the insanity of the prisoner; they are now seeking to justify armed rebellion for the redress of these grievances. These two defences are inconsistent. One is no justification at all." Osler indicated that the Crown had allowed them to describe certain writings, but insisted "it is not evidence." The judge asked, what if the writings were actually produced? Osler answered:

> They could not be evidence. They would not be evidence in justification; that is admitted. It cannot be possible for my learned friends to open the case on one defence and go to the jury indirectly upon another. Of course, it is not really any defence in law, and should not be gone into with any greater particularity. If this is given in evidence, we would have to answer it in many particulars, and then there would be the question of justifying the policy of the Government.

Judge Richardson offered the comment that this "would be trying the Government." Osler further insisted that a counter-claim against the government "is not open to any person on trial for high treason." Nevertheless, this was part of the line of argument that Riel wanted his lawyers to pursue. While, as Mr. Lemieux stated, he "did not want to justify the rebellion," the context of the uprising might well be influential with the jury in creating mitigating circumstances, and should have been pursued as far as possible. Lemieux made some small effort, but was not allowed by the Crown or the court to get very far in his questioning of Father André. Beal and Macleod argue in *Prairie Fire: The 1885 North-West Rebellion*, that the defence opened this line to demonstrate to Riel that it would not work.

Perhaps a more promising line of questioning with the priest related to Riel's views on politics and religion. André admitted that Riel "lost all control of himself" when discussing these matters. Mr. Lemieux turned to the priest's experience with people afflicted with mania. André answered by stating that the fathers of the district considered Riel "completely a fool" on these matters, and the defence dropped the line of questioning, allowing the Crown on cross-examination to ask about Riel and the $35,000. Curiously enough, it was the Crown which returned to the question of Riel's religious beliefs. André admitted that a man could be a great reformer without being a fool, but denied that Riel had any fixed principles in his religious beliefs. Riel's spiritual beliefs were pursued by the defence further in the examination of his former secretary, Philippe Garnot, who spoke of the defendant's prophesying and prayers, as well as his unwillingness to brook contradictions in these matters. But Garnot was not actually asked whether Riel experienced visions or whether his spiritual behaviour had any influence on his behaviours or decisions. Father Vital Fourmond was directly asked by the defence about the sanity of Riel. Fourmond spoke about Riel's use of violent expressions when he was contradicted, and described Riel's "extraordinary ideas" about the Trinity. He insisted that at the time of the rebellion, Riel was insane, that he was "not in his mind," but the defence again made little attempt to relate Riel's visions to his decision-making behaviour. All three of these witnesses seemed to be floundering around in their answers, although all agreed under questioning that Riel's behaviour was out of control in terms of his religious beliefs and that he would not be contradicted.

At this stage, François Roy, medical superintendent at the Beauport asylum, was brought to the stand as the first of the "expert" medical witnesses. While the Guiteau trial in 1881 in Washington, D.C. had been attended by more than two dozen expert witnesses, most of whom had degrees in neurology or related disciplines, Louis Riel's trial in Regina was attended by a mere four medical witnesses, only three of whom had any qualifications for the task and none of whom were trained specialists. The defence had been forced to fight to get the court to pay for the transportation and expenses of the two doctors it summoned. The four "experts" offered four different takes on Riel's insanity, which is exactly what one might have expected from such testimony, although the two of the doctors most experienced at dealing with the insane both agreed that he was insane, and all four doctors agreed that he was not responsible if his "delusions" were genuine.

Dr. Roy testified that he had studied the prisoner closely during his stay at Beauport. Most commentators on the trial are not disturbed that Roy had known Riel in a previous incarnation, so to speak. But this intimate knowledge was likely a disadvantage, since it encouraged him to confuse a diagnosis on Riel's medical condition with the provisions of the McNaghten rule, which dealt only with Riel's accountability. The prisoner was suffering, said Roy, from megalomania, a disease in which the sufferer could "show great judgment in all cases not immediately connected with the particular disease with which they suffer." Roy went on to say that "maniacs" like Riel could sound quite reasonable "if they were not starting from a false idea" and could be irritable when their mental condition was questioned, "because they are under a strong impression that they are right." Roy added that the descriptions of Riel's behaviour by the earlier witnesses indicated that his mind "on these occasions" was unsound. He then went on to say that based on the testimony he had heard, he did not believe Riel "was in a condition to be master of his acts." The Crown on cross-examination tried to suggest that Roy had too many patients over the years to be able to remember much about his case, and then turned to attempting to force him to make categorical statements about the nature of the disease under discussion and to produce what Mr. Osler described as a "rule to test this insanity." At one point Roy responded, "I am not an expert in insanity." The defence interjected that if the witness did not understand the questions properly he should answer them in French. Osler's sneering response leaps out from the printed page, "If the man wants to hide himself under the French he may do so."

The cross-examination resumed, with the witness now answering in French. He stated that the prisoner got his "theory from the idea that he has a mission." Mr. Osler then asked whether it was consistent for a man, "having an idea not controllable by reason, that he will abandon that idea for $35,000?" Roy fielded that question well, arguing that this was possible if the individual was reasoning from a false basis. Osler quickly shifted his questioning, asking Roy whether he agreed with the proposition, "An insane delusion is never the result of reasoning and reflection." Again Roy quite properly refused to be categorical, and again Osler pushed him as hard as he could. The defence began complaining about the translations that were now being given of Roy's testimony. Osler answered that it was for the defence to produce a translator for a witness whose testimony required one. The defence objected that although the answers were taken down in French, they were going to the jury in English. Osler replied, "The witness can explain himself in English but was told not to do so, it is not my difficulty." The vehemence of his comments on language suggest that he had determined that the jury would not be alienated by such an attitude. Osler returned to the issue, asking "Do you say that any man claiming to be inspired is insane so as not to distinguish between right and wrong?" Roy answered, "It is possible." Osler asked whether it might not be evidence of fraud. Roy responded that the same idea had been sustained over time, and he repeated this view several times at the end of his testimony.

Toward the end of his lengthy stay on the stand, Roy refused to comment on Joseph Smith's sanity, but agreed that Brigham Young was probably insane. As for whether Young's "idea of prophetic inspiration" was "inconsistent with a knowledge of what was right and wrong," Roy answered, "It would require an examination. If you send him to the asylum for a few months, I will make a study of the case." Still refusing to give categorical answers, Roy was dismissed by the Crown, with Osler's comment, "If you cannot answer…in English or French, I may as well let you go." On the whole, Dr. Roy had made a good witness under difficult conditions. He had stood up reasonably well to Osler's bullying and hectoring tactics, although the jury might take his shifting into French as evidence of weakness, and his answers made clear his opinion that Riel was not responsible for his actions. Whether the latter part of his testimony was damaged by the need to translate it into English for the jury can never be determined. Louis Riel's reaction to Dr. Roy's appearance was fairly predictable. He had regarded Roy as hostile to him in 1877, and saw no reason to change his mind. He actually exulted in Osler's abuse of the Quebec alienist.

Dr. Roy was succeeded on the stand by another expert witness, Dr. Daniel Clark, superintendent of the Toronto Lunatic Asylum. Like his Quebec colleague, Clark was a trained medical man but without any specialization in neurology. Most of his expertise was acquired on the job, but he published extensively in the field. On the other hand, as directors of two of the largest asylums in Canada, Roy and Clark were probably the most important experts in insanity available in Canada in 1885. Unlike Roy, Dr. Clark was not familiar with Riel before the trial, and was able to examine him only three times, as well as attending to the testimony in the case. Clark understandably kept hedging his diagnosis because of his limited contact. He emphasized in the course of his testimony that he did not regard himself as a defence witness, but as an independent medical expert. Unfortunately for the defence plea, Clark weakened his conclusion from the outset in one of the worst possible ways, by raising the possibility that the prisoner was malingering or deceiving. If he was not, stated Clark, "there is no conclusion that any reasonable man could come to, from my standpoint of course, than that a man who held these views and did these things must certainly be of insane mind." Clark further compromised his testimony by attempting to disassociate himself from the McNaghten rule, replying in answer to a question on whether Riel could judge the difference between right and wrong that this "is one of the legal metaphysical distinctions in regard to right and wrong, and it is a dangerous one, simply because it covers only partly the truth." Like many another expert witness, Clark attempted to use the occasion to argue his own views, which were that McNaghten was "one of those metaphysical subtleties that practical men in asylums know to be false." From his standpoint, Clark thought that Riel was quite capable of distinguishing right from wrong, but did not behave as a sane man would have done.

Under cross-examination, he stated that Riel would "know the nature and quality of the act that he was committing, subject to his delusions assuming them to be such." The scrupulously honest Dr. Clark continued to insist that he could not determine the genuineness of Riel's pathology with only cursory examination. He also acknowledged that Riel had told him in the morning's examination that "he was a prophet, and he knew the jury would acquit him, because he knew what was becoming beforehand." On re-examination, Clark dealt in more detail with the question of whether Riel's beliefs were like those of Joseph Smith and Brigham Young, a matter that the Crown had cast aside as soon as he answered that he saw a difference. Smith and Young, said Clark, consistently carried out their system with tact and discretion, employing common sense. From his perspective, Riel was neither a very good Brigham Young or a Mahdi (referring to the Muslim religious leader in the Sudan). Mr. Lemieux closed the defence by asking Clark whether Riel could distinguish right from wrong, subject to his delusions? The answer was yes. This was a disastrous place to end, since it was not at all clear that all members of the jury would understand that what Clark was really trying to say was that it was precisely what were being called Riel's "delusions" that were at issue.

In an academic paper delivered in 1887, Clark recounted that in one interview Riel had mentioned his book, which proved that he was a great prophet. Clark also here acknowledged "there could be no doubt" that Riel "was stating what he himself believed to be true." In 1887 Clark had nothing but scorn for the notion that judges, lawyers, and members of juries could separate the sane from the insane. He emphasized that those at the trial who testified as to Riel's sanity offered worthless evidence, since "A person may be insane and yet rational." For Clark, the witnesses for the Crown had testified to the "prisoner's mental unsoundness," quite apart from the evidence of the defence. Clark went on to opine that Riel had been responsible up to Duck Lake, but "from that time there is no evidence that he was accountable for what he did." Why he could not have been similarly categorical in Regina in 1885 has never been explained adequately. The best explanation is probably that he did not really want to play the McNaghten game and objected strenuously to laymen making judgments.

The Crown called Dr. James Wallace in rebuttal. Wallace was medical superintendent of the Asylum for the Insane at Hamilton, Ontario. He had decent credentials, but had been able to examine Riel for only half an hour, and was honest enough to admit that while what he had seen indicated a perfectly sound mind, it would be presumptive of him to go any further. At this point, he should have been dismissed. Instead, Mr. Fitzpatrick for the defence sought to get more information on megalomania, the particular form of mental illness that Dr. Roy had diagnosed in the case of Riel. Wallace replied that megalomania was a rare term, hardly ever used, at least by those writing in English. He only barely avoided saying "nowadays." He acknowledged the existence of Dagoust's work on megalomania (cited by Dr. Roy), but did not know it. The subsequent discussion of Wallace's understanding of megalomania did not much enlighten the jury, as Fitzpatrick and Wallace argued at length over whether megalomania was a disease or only a symptom. It only served to demonstrate that Wallace was not familiar with French current writing on mental illness — "I don't want to hear of any French authors. I never read them," he exclaimed at one point — and perhaps to call into question the expertise of Dr. Roy, who seemed only familiar with the French authorities.

The final medical witness was Dr. Augustus Jukes, the senior surgeon of the Mounted Police. Jukes was a general practitioner, and his appearance here among the specialists at first glance seems out of place. But Jukes was an articulate man, and one of those bluff sensible non-nonsense and self-assured GPs whom every patient tends to want to believe. He would have little time for hair-splitting or medical mumbo-jumbo, and after a day of the jury listening to the agonizing verbal gymnastics of the professionals, he was a perfect choice to close out expert testimony as a contrast. Jukes had dealt with Riel as a general practitioner while he was in prison, and reported that he seemed perfectly sane. Under cross-examination, he admitted that he had trouble hearing in the court room, especially the translations to the examinations in French, but insisted that nothing he had heard could not be accounted for by other factors, such as fraud or deception. Moreover, he claimed that "A man operating under a delusion was not necessarily incompetent either to perform business in a successful manner or to be responsible for his actions." So, queried the Crown, he would still be responsible despite the delusion? Certainly not, answered Jukes. If it could be proved that a man was operating under an insane delusion — rather than a feigned one — then any act he performed under that delusion he would not be responsible for. He subsequently added that many men were held to be insane until they became leaders of a new sect, and in such cases "It is extremely difficult to tell how far a delusion of that kind may begin as a direct attempt at fraud and may at last so take possession of a man's mind that he may believe himself divinely inspired." But Jukes did not see Riel as another Joseph Smith or Brigham Young or Mahomet — who would have been regarded as subject to delusions if they had not so many followers. Instead, he thought that Riel had acted out visions and revelations for the purpose of influencing the Métis. He found Riel perfectly rational. At the same time, Jukes told the defence that he had not discussed either his mission or religion with Riel. It must be emphasized that Jukes was not arguing that persons who had genuine — if delusive — visions and voices were responsible for their actions, but that Riel had not experienced genuine "delusions."

The Crown subsequently called a series of other witnesses who had contact with Riel during his confinement. Captain Holmes Young quoted from one of his notebooks in which Riel had written about his mission and described the exovedate and its reasons for action. General Middleton found the prisoner quite sensible, and the Reverend Charles Pitblado, who had accompanied him on the boat to Regina, described Riel's account of his plans and schemes in the rebellion. His actual jailers found him of sound mind.

Mr. Fitzpatrick addressed the jury for the defence. Fitzpatrick was an experienced criminal lawyer, and his speech was both emotional and impassioned, although not very persuasive. As he phrased the issues for the jury, they were: first, what proof had been given by the Crown of the overt acts of treason laid at the door of Riel, and second, to what extent was he responsible for those acts? Fitzgerald insisted he had no wish to justify the rebellion, but he did point out that the people of the North-West Territories, especially the Métis, did have grievances which had not be resolved. Even if Riel were a sane man, Fitzpatrick argued that he had some redeeming features in his character and in his leadership of the rebellion. But the defence were bound by their instructions, he said, to represent Riel as "entirely insane and irresponsible for his acts." Unfortunately, Fitzpatrick tried to combine religion and insanity, medical insanity and legal insanity, in the behaviour of Riel. He was not content to label Riel as having religious visions and communications with the holy spirit, but he wanted to diagnose those visions in medical terms instead of leaving them as part of the mystery of faith. He maintained that Riel was suffering from megalomania and was acting under an insane delusion. If the prisoner were truly a "deep, designing man," he would have made a better job of the rebellion than he did. If he were calculating, would he not have manipulated the Métis in more conventional religious terms than he did? Riel's conduct was entirely consistent with an unsound mind. Believing himself to be inspired by God and in direct communication with the Holy Ghost, he led a small group of men into battle against the forces of Canada.

It seemed a powerful argument, but it was immediately followed by Riel himself, making a statement to the jury that his lawyers disavowed in advance. The defence would have been far better served by being able to put Riel in the box and to examine him about his religious beliefs and visions. Unfortunately, this option was not legally possible in 1885. Defendants in a criminal trial were not allowed to testify as witnesses. But even if his lawyers had been procedurally able to quiz Riel about his beliefs, they would not necessarily have had his co-operation.

For Louis Riel, the trial had provided several dilemmas. He had been forced to decide whether or not he wanted to conduct his own defence and break with his friends as well as his lawyers. He had decided to allow his lawyers to act for him, but he was now prepared to sabotage their carefully orchestrated arguments by attempting to demonstrate to the jury that he was not insane, that he was responsible for his behaviour, although he ought to have known that success in this venture would lead directly to the gallows. Louis Riel was a shrewd and capable orator, and he was nowhere more brilliant than in his speech to the jury on 31 July and 1 August 1885.

Riel began by acknowledging his mission, but he did not describe it. His descriptions of his religious sentiments at the beginning of his remarks sounded quite orthodox, and he felt blessed by God for all those who testified that he was not mad. As for the rebellion, it would have remained quite constitutional if "we had not been attacked." As far as his religious beliefs were concerned, he wished to leave Rome, he said, because it divided Protestants and Catholics. He wanted an ecumenical church in America. If he was insane, "of course I don't know it, it is a property of insanity to be unable to know it." But his mission, he insisted, was based on "Practical results." He was pleased the Crown acknowledged him as leader of the half-breeds. "I will perhaps be one day acknowledged as more than a leader of the half-breeds, and if I am I will have an opportunity of being acknowledged as a leader of good in this great country." He went on, "If it is any satisfaction to the doctors to know what kind of insanity I have, if they are going to call my pretensions insanity, I say humbly, through the grace of God, I believe I am the prophet of the new world." Riel concluded by insisting the ministers of an "insane and irresponsible Government" had jumped upon him and his people. He was "ready," and such was his "crime of high treason." He had worked for the people of Saskatchewan at the risk of his life without pay, although he admitted "It has always been my hope to have a fair living one day." Riel's plea was not necessarily a convincing argument for his sanity, but it was certainly persuasive that the accused did not want to be acquitted by reason of insanity. The jury was as likely to respond to the intent as to the argument.

In his concluding remarks for the Crown, Christopher Robinson took the high ground in a clear speech, doubtless recognizing that Riel had himself decided the matter by his arguments in objection to the insanity pleas. He saw no need to go over the evidence, since the defence had not attempted to dispute it. If the government had delayed in dealing with Riel in 1884 and early 1885, they had delayed to agreeing to requests by a man who was now being called insane (thus nicely confusing medical insanity and legal insanity). Robinson's position was that Riel was neither a patriot nor a lunatic. The Crown attorney was quite prepared to play with words, as he did in his use of the term "responsible," knowing full well that it had a particular meaning in the context of an insanity plea. "I should like to know if the prisoner at the bar is not in law to be held responsible for this crime, who is responsible?" Robinson also liked inescapable dichotomies. Either the prisoner was sane or all the half-breeds in Saskatchewan were insane. "You must have it one way or the other." Turning to the medical testimony, Robinson insisted the "very essence of an insane impulse is that it is impervious to reason." The lawyer for the Crown then pounced on the defence's attempt not merely to describe Riel's spiritual state but to diagnose it as megalomania. Robinson insisted that Riel was quite capable of reason, and that he was a man "who calculated his schemes and drew his plans with shrewdness." Any man of intelligence and sense was as capable of deciding on cases of insanity as were the medical experts. Riel had calculated taking up arms as early as December of 1884, and the rebellion was "designed contrived, premeditated and prepared…it was carried out with deliberation and intention."

In his charge to the jury, Judge Richardson began by describing the crime of high treason. He added that to be found guilty, the prisoner must be found by the jury to be implicated in the acts charged against him, and also "he must as completely satisfy you that he is not answerable by reason of unsoundness of mind." On this point, Richardson insisted that the law was now such that "judges may be able to tell the jury fixedly in words what their duties are in regard to responsibility for crime when insanity is set up as a defence." The line was "drawn very distinctly," declared Judge Richardson. But before he drew the line he drew the jury's attention to the $35,000 and to the fact that no-one involved in the rebellion thought Riel insane. Then he turned to the law, which "directs me to tell you that every man is presumable to be responsible for his crimes until the contrary be proved to your satisfaction." To establish insanity, "it must be clearly proved that at the time he committed the act, the party accused was labouring under such defective reasoning from a diseased mind as not to know the nature and quality of the act he was committing, or that if he did know it, that he did not know that he was doing wrong." That, said Judge Richardson, "I propound to you as the law."

The jury then retired, for a mere hour, and returned to declare the prisoner guilty. Then one of their number added, "I have been asked by my brother jurors to recommend the prisoner to the mercy of the Crown." The jury was told by the judge that this recommendation would be forwarded to the proper authorities. This was the same verdict that had been rendered in the trial of Ambroise Lépine in 1874. Given this fact, one might have expected the defence team to be aware of this possibility and to warn the jury against it in its closing remarks, at least if the jury sought to do anything more than attempt to evade full responsibility for the consequences of its actions. In a trial for any capital crime in the 19th century, recommendations of mercy were not very effective, and they would certainly be completely futile in a trial for high treason in which death was the mandatory sentence for the guilty verdict the jury had brought.

We do not know precisely what motivated the jury to this action, but subsequent remarks by several jurymen suggested that some members found that there were extenuating circumstances for the rebellion, and were uneasy about Riel's accountability for his actions. One juror subsequently wrote to Edward Blake commenting on the "dilatoriness of Sir John Macdonald, Sir David McPherson, and Lieutenant Governor Dewdney," and another said many years later that the jurors often commented on the need to have the Minister of the Interior (Sir John A. Macdonald) in the prisoner's box. According to a journalist for the Toronto Mail immediately after the trial: "I saw three of the jurors, who told me that in their opinion Riel should not be hanged, as they think that, while he is not absolutely insane in the ordinary accepted meaning of the world, he is a decided crank." Another juryman was quoted by the Mail as saying, "The unanimous desire of the jury in recommending the accused to the clemency of the court, was that he not be put to death."

When the verdict was announced, Louis Riel insisted on making a second statement. It was very much more rational and analytical (if disjointed) than his earlier one, describing his actions in 1869-70 and outlining the 1884-85 situation as he saw it and what he had done to deal with it. It is basically a justification of the rebellion. George Stanley has argued that this was probably the original statement Riel had intended to make, but which was superseded by the need to argue the insanity business. In the course of this statement, Riel noted that Ambroise Lépine had not been executed in 1874. "Why?" he asked. "Because he was recommended to the clemency of the court," was his answer. This was, of course, a total misreading of the difference between a pre-amnesty murder conviction in 1874 and a high treason conviction in 1885. Riel spent a good deal of time in this statement on his American citizenship. "The idea of the seventh, I have two hands, and I have two sides to my head, and I have two countries," Riel told the court. The reference to the seventh was to the principle of giving a seventh of the lands in the North-West to the half-breeds. If his peoples' views were not heard, Riel maintained, "we will meet as American citizens." He then added, "I am an American citizen and I have two countries, and I am taken here as a British subject." This was not quite true, but it was probably the case that whether he was executed for treason depended to a considerable extent on whether his adopted country would come to his assistance. To the court, Riel concluded by asking that a panel of doctors examine him to determine "if I was sincere or not." Whether he appreciated that if the jury had possibly rejected the insanity plea in part because it doubted his "sincerity" is another matter entirely. Sincerity was different from honour, however.

In any event, Judge Richardson then pronounced sentence, which was that Riel be hanged by the neck until dead on 18 September 1885. For his part, Prime Minister John A. Macdonald pronounced contentment with this result. "The conviction of Riel is satisfactory," he wrote to Lieutenant-Governor Dewdney. "There is an attempt in Quebec to trump up a patriotic feeling about him, but I don't think it will amount to much."

-13-

After the Trial

The Riel case hardly ended with the trial in Regina. Another four months of legal manoeuvring occurred before the sentence was carried out, and even after Riel's execution, the controversy was not ended. In some senses, closure has never been achieved.

The American Appeal

Although Riel's Montana friends had offered to supply him with an American attorney, there is no evidence that they took further action in the matter. What we do know is that on 24 July 1885, the American consul in Winnipeg, James Wickes Taylor, received a letter from Riel dated 21 July and posted on 23 July from Regina. Since Riel was not allowed to send letters, that to Taylor was probably smuggled out by his attorney, Charles Fitzpatrick. Taylor had been consul in Winnipeg in 1870, and had been acquainted with Riel. He immediately forwarded the letter to his superiors in the Department of State in Washington, D.C., along with a letter written by Riel to "a wealthy friend, of Quebec" (presumably Dr. Romault Fiset, who helped finance his defence) and "detailed reports of the trial at Regina."

A direct connection doubtless existed between the rejection by the Regina court on 20 July of the demurrers about Riel's citizenship and his decision a day later to appeal directly to the Americans. Riel described his situation to Taylor and added, "As American citizen I humbly appeal to the government of my adopted land for help through you." If the American government would say a good word on his behalf, wrote Riel, he could obtain a fair trial, which would save him. Riel noted that he had been a good citizen in Montana, and had on several occasions served as a special U.S. deputy marshal. He also begged the American government to help him defray the expenses of his trial, for he claimed he had "no means."

On 5 August Taylor reported to Washington that the trial in Regina was over. The jury had recommended mercy, but Riel had been sentenced to death. The Winnipeg consul observed that he had already forwarded a telegraphic summary of the trial's early proceedings, and now sent a fuller report of the opening arguments of counsel. These presumably included the exchange over the matter of citizenship, although Taylor did not mention this issue. He focussed instead on the arguments of Riel's lawyers "upon the constitution of the court and the competency of a stipendiary magistrate, with a jury of six virtually of his own selection, and without the intervention of a grand jury, to try a person charged with a capital offence."

At about the same time, Taylor received another letter from the Regina Jail, this one dated 1 August. Riel actually wrote two letters to Taylor on this date. One, which began by noting that Charles Fitzpatrick had been entrusted with the missive, apparently did not reach Winnipeg. In it Riel did not refer to his American citizenship, but instead concentrated on defending his conduct in the course of the rebellion. In the letter which Taylor did receive, Riel insisted that "the troubles of '85 in the Saskatchewan are the continuation of the troubles of '69-70, which the Ottawa government have never duly settled," and explained why he wanted a thorough investigation of the entire matter of Métis land claims. This letter was also forwarded to Washington.

In mid-August of 1885, a group of French-Canadians resident in Lawrence, Massachusetts, organized a petition to T. F. Bayard, the American Secretary of State, on behalf of Louis Riel. The petition, signed by 410 names, insisted that the trial of Riel had not been impartial and observed that Riel was an American citizen. It begged Bayard to get the President of the United States to intervene on Riel's behalf. At about the same time, 65 citizens of Wayland, Massachusetts, sent a petition to Mr. Bayard claiming that Riel had been "denied rights to which he was entitled as an American citizen" and asking that the American government secure him those rights. Both these petitions came from communities which Riel had visited in the course of his earlier travels.

Sometime in early September, Riel himself prepared a petition directly to the American president, Grover Cleveland, the original of which was forwarded to Washington without comment by James Wickes Taylor on 12 September 1885. This petition was an extremely curious document which Cleveland could hardly take seriously. It began by establishing that Riel was an American citizen and continued with a highly partisan rehearsal of the events of 1869-70 in which Riel had played such a major role. The petition then went on to discuss the Canadian government's repudiation of the promised amnesty to Riel, concluding that he was entitled "to reject the Pact which England has made with him and she has never fulfilled." Consequently, wrote Riel, "Before God and before men, the undersigned your humble petitioner declares his native land free, and has the honor to ask your Excellency and most Honorable Ministers for the advantage of annexing the Northwest to the great American republic." Only after he had offered the entire western territory to the Americans did Riel "respectfully" request, as an American citizen, presidential protection. He followed up the request for protection by adding that were it granted, he wanted the international border expunged between Lake Superior and the Pacific Ocean, James Wickes Taylor appointed as governor-general of this western region, and himself appointed as first minister and secretary under Taylor. President Cleveland could hardly act upon this request, and there is no evidence of any immediate diplomatic activity on the part of the Americans with reference to Riel.

The American government received one more petition from within the United States on behalf of Riel. It was submitted by Ambrose Choquet, a Rochester lawyer, on behalf of "French Canadians, citizens of the United States, residing in the city of Rochester, N.Y." Choquet acknowledged a "former personal acquaintance with Riel," and added that his most recent information was that Riel was now insane. Forwarding a copy of Riel's naturalization certificate, he asked that the United States Government intervene to prevent "the hanging of an unfortunate insane citizen of the United States." The enclosed petition, signed by 69 individuals, claimed that Riel's trial had been "unfair, partial, and unjust."

Secretary of State Bayard responded to Mr. Choquet on 27 October 1885. He assured Choquet that his request and accompanying petition had received "careful attention." Bayard added that some friends of Riel had already made personal application to the State Department regarding Riel and had received "a full verbal reply, which took into consideration Riel's alleged American citizenship." Even if such citizenship were beyond doubt, thus suggesting that it was not — Bayard observed — it "would not secure the possessor any immunity from Canadian law, when, as it is definitely certified to this Government in the case in the present instance, the offense was committed within the territory of the Dominion."

Bayard returned to this theme in 1889, in responding to a resolution of the United States Senate of 11 March which requested the President "to communicate to the Senate such knowledge or information as may be in his possession or under his control relating to the case of one Louis Riel, otherwise Louis David Riel, with copies of all documents, papers, correspondence, and evidence bearing upon the subject." He observed that compliance with the resolution in its broadest sense would involve a massive amount of documentary material, including correspondence between the American and British governments regarding border neutrality and the involvement of American Indians in the rebellion. In its narrowest sense, the resolution referred to "the personal claim of Riel to protection as an American citizen," and the handful of documents touching on this matter were those transmitted. Bayard repeated his earlier story that some of Riel's friends who presented in person one of the petitions — perhaps the Wayland, Massachusetts one — were told verbally that Riel's "alleged United States citizenship did not give him any immunity from Canadian laws for offences committed within their jurisdiction, and that it had been definitely certified to this Department that the offense had been wholly committed within British jurisdiction." This ended the report to the Senate. The American government closed its Riel file permanently.

The American authorities never officially acknowledged that Louis Riel was an American citizen. Mr. Secretary Bayard had referred in several letters to the "alleged" citizenship. In any event, The State Department was prepared to accept that Riel could be executed for treason on the basis of residence, whatever his citizenship. The State Department was obviously not about to place any strains on Anglo-American relations in order to save the life of Louis Riel. Had Washington shown some interest in Riel's fate, it might well have been different. Riel had not taken out American citizenship for political purposes, but when a life-threatening crisis had emerged in 1885, the United States had failed him. In fairness, it might equally be argued that Riel had failed the United States when he found its citizenship insufficient to satisfy him and decided to return to Saskatchewan.

The Canadian Appeal

Riel's conviction in the court of the North-West Territories under the "North-West Territories Act of 1880" was appealed to the Court of Queen's Bench of Manitoba, as specified in the 1880 statute. As a result of this appeal, the Canadian government instructed the presiding judge, Hugh Richardson, to grant a reprieve from the execution date of 18 September 1885 until 16 October. The appellate court could not overturn the conviction. It could either confirm the conviction or call for a fresh trial. The three judges who heard the appeal — Lewis Wallbridge, Wardlaw Taylor, and A. C. Killam — were all Tory appointees. Another judge of the court who might have been sympathetic to Riel — Joseph Dubuc — was absent. The lawyers who brought the appeal included Fitzpatrick and Lemieux, as well as a Manitoba lawyer named John S. Ewart, who would later appear in the Manitoba Schools Question. The court ruled that it could hear the appeal, but could not have Riel brought to Winnipeg during its deliberations.

The three Manitoba justices all praised the zeal and adequacy of the defence, obviously overlooking the blatant evidence in the proceedings that Riel had disagreed profoundly with his lawyers over strategy. The defence raised four grounds to the appellate court, two technical and two substantive. The technical objections were weak. One claimed that the information had been taken before the wrong magistrate and the other that notes of the trial had been taken in shorthand instead of in full, and had been fleshed out later by the court stenographer. No mention was made of the problems of translation in a supposedly bilingual court in a trial involving many francophones. The first substantive ground of appeal questioned the jurisdiction of the court. This point had been argued at great length before Judge Richardson, and dismissed. The Manitoba court agreed with Judge Richardson. To find otherwise would have been to question a decision rendered by two of these three judges in another appeal on similar grounds, and might have turned the whole administration of justice in the West into chaos. Finally, the appellate judges turned down the defence plea of insanity. They made special points of noting that Riel's lawyers were not complaining about unfairness, or about the charge of the magistrate to the jury, almost as though these would have been important matters had they been raised. Goulet observes that the defence had not complained about the failure to produce documents which Riel insisted that he needed to make his case, or indeed about their failure to call witnesses deemed essential by Riel. This absence of complaint was related, of course, to the line of defence taken by his lawyers, to which those same lawyers could hardly object.

Moreover, nowhere in the appeal was mentioned the involvement of one of the Manitoba justices — Lewis Wallbridge — in planning the Crown strategy to prosecute Riel. Nor could this point possibly have been made, since the involvement was behind the scenes and was only discovered by a researcher more than a century after the event. Wallbridge had not only given important advice to the government about the venue of the trial, however, but had helped orchestrate appeal proceedings in another case involving the Regina court which provided a precedent for the appellate court's decision in the Riel one. Although he admits that judges gave private advice to the government in this era, lawyer Ronald Olesky has asserted that "Wallbridge's behind-the-scenes conduct certainly went beyond the law, even by standards of his own time." Wallbridge probably should have disqualified himself, but he doubtless did not expect his private involvement to become public knowledge. Whether this conflict of interest is sufficient reason for posthumously overturning the Riel conviction is another matter entirely. The question of a pardon turns not on one piece of evidence, but rather on whether one either believes that the Crown — as Olesky charged in his article on the Riel case — "exercised its prosecutorial discretion unfairly" or that for some other reason Riel did not get a fair trial.

The Riel conviction was subsequently taken from the Manitoba Court of Queen's Bench to the Lords of the Judicial Committee of the Privy Council, sitting in London, bypassing the Supreme Court of Canada. The Canadian government was anxious that a decision be rendered by the Judicial Committee before the expiration of Riel's reprieve, since it felt that another postponement would encourage Quebec to think Riel might be spared. The Committee delayed proceedings until 21 October, waiting for Charles Fitzpatrick — Riel's lawyer — to arrive and plead the case personally. The judicial Lords did not actually hear an appeal, it should be noted, but only a petition for leave to appeal. In that petition, the whole question of Riel's insanity was omitted, and the grounds of appeal were reduced to jurisdiction and the recording process using only shorthand. The Privy Council committee in its response noted that neither the facts of the trial nor Riel's commission of high treason were being contested, which meant that Riel's lawyers had not really done their job. It observed that the only fact established before the jury was whether Riel was not guilty by reason of mental infirmity, the jury had "negatived that defence," and it was not now being argued that such a decision was incorrect. The committee then insisted that to doubt the jurisdiction of the court (which meant doubting the right of the Canadian legislature to enact "The Northwest Territories Act of 1880") would have been quite mischievous. As to the recording process, there was "no complaint" of inaccuracy or mistake from Riel's lawyers. Given the feebleness of the petition, its rejection was inevitable.

George Goulet, author of a recent book on the Riel trial, observes that he can offer no explanation of why the appeal went directly from Manitoba to London, thus bypassing the Supreme Court of Canada. Before the trial, the Crown certainly anticipated that the Supreme Court might well hear an appeal. None of the other commentators on the case offer any evidence on this point, which remains one of the many mysteries surrounding the judicial proceedings against Louis Riel in 1885.

Final Manoeuvrings

As we have already seen, the government did not have to execute Louis Riel. The initial decision for his death was, of course, inherent in the decision to charge the Métis leader with high treason. But this decision was not irreversible despite the law's insistence that a jury verdict of guilty could result only in a death sentence. A confirmation of the earlier decision appears to have been made by Sir John A. Macdonald and the Conservative government in late August and early September. From the government's standpoint, whether or not Riel lived or died would be based chiefly on pragmatic grounds. Would it suffer more from permitting the execution to go forward or by appearing magnanimous? Public opinion in Ontario was overwhelmingly in favour of hanging, while public opinion in Quebec was about equally opposed. A good deal depended on which province one thought would have the longer memory and be more punitive in a future election. One correspondent told John A. Macdonald late in August: "If Riel is spared through any action of the Government it means the utter disruption of the Conservative Party in the Province of Ontario as well as the outlying ones. If he is punished it means a mere surface excitement in Quebec — for the Grits of the other provinces dare not form an alliance with them on the question, and if they did, so much the worse for the Grits."

The Orangeman Dalton McCarthy insisted that Ontario's reaction was to Quebec's desire to save Riel rather than about Riel himself. On the other hand, another MP argued that if Riel was not hanged, many "of our friends" had declared that they would not vote for the Tories. By early September, Macdonald had apparently decided, for the governor-general knew before his departure on a British Columbia tour on 12 September that the prime minister's mind was made up and that he would advise that the law take its course. The government, of course, said nothing publicly. Macdonald and his colleagues, but especially the prime minister, had one more chance to change their minds because of a legislative requirement of a final review.

In the subsequent 1886 debate over Riel in the House of Commons, one of the critics of the government (Mr. Amyot) pointed out that the legislation under which Riel had been tried specified in the case of a sentence to death, the magistrate "shall forward to the Minister of Justice full notes of the evidence with his report upon the case, and the execution should be stayed until such report is received and the pleasure of the Governor thereon is communicated to the Lieutenant-Governor." As Amyot noted in debate, "The execution is not left by the Government to take its course, as in ordinary cases, but must be ordered by them." The phrase "the pleasure of the Governor" in practice meant "the decision of the Cabinet." Lord Dufferin had acted on the death sentence of Ambroise Lépine in 1875 on his own initiative, but that action was presumably with the consent of a government which did not wish to be involved in a decision on the matter. In 1885, the Macdonald government could not really avoid sanctioning any sentence of death which it had worked so hard to get.

The law did not specify the nature of the review. Several ministers advocated a private enquiry into Riel's sanity. The cabinet would hardly have taken seriously any argument that Riel had been justified in his resistance to the law, but there remained the question of Riel's mental state, not necessarily at the time of the resistance, but at the time of execution. The government appointed a medical commission to examine Riel's sanity before he was executed, and granted a one-week stay of execution for the examinations to occur. The commission consisted of Dr. Augustus Jukes, who had already testified in the matter, and two new "experts," Dr. Michael Lavell of Kingston Penitentiary (a Tory from Macdonald's home riding), and Dr. François-Xavier Valade of Ottawa. Valade had little experience with insanity, and he was both an Ottawa civil servant and a "client" of the Minister of Militia. The prime minister gave detailed private instructions in advance to the two external members of the commission, instructing them that the issue was not Riel's sanity at the time of the treason, but his present mental condition. Macdonald then confused the issue by adding that the enquiry was "whether he is so bereft of reason as not to know right from wrong and not to be an accountable being" — which is the McNaghten formulation. His intention was apparently to distinguish Riel's earlier accountability — as documented in the trial — from his subsequent unaccountability, because only current insanity would justify holding him in an asylum, but it was an unfortunate use of the formula words.

Two of the members of the commission, Dr. Lavell and Dr. François-Xavier Valade — both of whom "examined" Riel by posing as journalists — came to opposite conclusions on the matter of whether Riel was indeed an "accountable being." Lavell thought Riel had peculiar ideas on religion but was "an accountable being and capable of distinguishing right from wrong." Valade insisted that Riel "is not an accountable being, that he is unable to distinguish between wrong and right on political and religious subjects which I consider well marked typical forms of a kind of insanity under which he undoubtedly suffers, but on other points I believe him to be quite sensible and can distinguish right from wrong." Dr. Jukes initially thought Riel perfectly sane and accountable except "upon certain religious and private matters (re Divine mysteries)," but he had second thoughts and wrote a subsequent letter suggesting that Riel's writings be examined to determine the sincerity of his thinking. In his first letter, Jukes also confessed: "I should be well pleased if justice and popular clamour could be satisfied without depriving this man of life."

Exactly what the government and the doctors thought they were doing on this commission is a real mystery. If the issue was Riel's present mental state, why couch the enquiry in terms of the McNaghten language, which was a test of legal insanity rather than medical insanity? What Sir John A. Macdonald presumably wanted to know in October of 1885 was whether Riel was sufficiently sane to be executed, which is not a question which ought to be phrased in terms of accountability. In any event, the government ignored Valade's opinion and Jukes's recommendation for all the wrong reasons. Riel was probably sane enough in November of 1885. It was his mental state at the time of the rebellion that had been dealt with badly. In the subsequent debates in the Commons, and in a post-execution memorandum, the government manipulated Valade's report for public consumption, omitting his phrase that Riel "is not an accountable being." Beyond the question of the government's bad faith is the larger point that to the end the government had a choice, which it exercised on strictly political grounds. It need not have executed Riel. It need not have pardoned him either. It could have commuted his sentence ("at Her Majesty's pleasure") to a lifetime of imprisonment without possibility of parole or to a lifetime in an asylum. There were precedents for such sentences, including the commitment for life to Broadmoor Asylum of the insane American murderer Dr. William Minor in 1872. Minor had actually done something constructive with his sentence, employing his erudition to provide much of the linguistic evidence for the Oxford English Dictionary. At the same time, it must be noted that the problem with a lifetime sentence or commitment was that it could be revoked by a subsequent government and Riel could be freed, a thought that the government could not tolerate.

The Canadian cabinet met again on the evening of 12 November on the question, and confirmed the decision to go through with the hanging, despite threats of defections by a number of French Canadians. A considerable difference of opinion had emerged before this meeting between Militia Minister Caron and Secretary of State Joseph-Adolphe Chapleau over the implications for Quebec of the execution. Caron argued "that in a month no one will think anything more about it," while Chapleau expected to "be called upon to suffer, my Quebec colleagues and myself, I more than others, at the hands of our people owing to the intense feeling which exists in our province." Chapleau stood by the prime minister, however, preferring "after all, to fight and to fall in the old ship for the old flag." All three French-Canadian cabinet ministers approved of the execution. The meeting produced a statement of policy given to the governor-general, who made a few changes and sent it on to the Colonial Office. The official explanation was that it would be difficult to pacify the North-West if an example were not made of Riel; it would be hard to justify the execution of Indian chiefs if the Métis leader were spared. There were no legitimate Métis grievances and Riel was quite sane. The memorandum emphasized that if Riel's mental state "had become essentially different from that of which the courts had cognizance, and that the sentence of death was about to be carried out upon a person incapable of realizing his own position or the circumstances which had led to his imprisonment and punishment, it would, I believe, have been wrong to allow him to be executed."

The government was prepared to detain Riel as a sentenced prisoner subsequently declared insane, but the medical examination found no difference in his mental state. The government obviously was not prepared to order Riel incarcerated for life without a reason. Some opinion in Quebec favoured mercy, but the Catholic hierarchy were critical of Riel because of his religious positions. All in all, the popular demand in Quebec for Riel's life had to be ignored. So too did the opinions of the medical experts. The cabinet ignored Valade's medical judgment and Jukes's suggestion, and ordered execution. What the official explanation did not say was that the Orange Order and much of Ontario had insisted that Riel must die, and the Macdonald government had decided to listen to that segment of public opinion. "He shall hang," Macdonald is alleged to have said, "though every dog in Quebec bark in his favour." Riel maintained that despite the conditional pardon in 1875 he was really being executed for the death of Thomas Scott. Many contemporaries and a fair number of subsequent experts would agree.

On 16 November 1885, at 8 a.m., the door to Riel's cell was unlocked. Carrying a crucifix, he followed Father Charles McWilliams, and was in turn followed by the Mounted Police escort, then finally by Father André. Before reaching the scaffold, he forgave all his enemies and thanked those who had helped him. After the rope and mask were placed over his head at the scaffold, he and Father McWilliams recited the "Our Father." Before they finished, the trap door was sprung and Louis Riel dropped to his death.

The body was not released for burial until authorized by the government in Ottawa, which took several days. On 18 November the coffin containing the body was opened in the presence of a few witnesses because rumours were circulating in Regina that it had been mutilated. The funeral occurred on the morning of 19 November in St. Mary's Church, Regina, and the body was returned to Winnipeg in an empty railroad freight car on 9 December. Three days later, with the coffin in front of the altar of St. Boniface Cathedral — which was filled with Métis and others who had known him — a requiem Mass was celebrated by Father Georges Dugas. Riel was then buried outside in the grounds of the Basilica, not far from his father.

The Disposition of the Insurgents

The Métis Prisoners

Except for William Henry Jackson, who was found not guilty by reason of insanity on 24 July and shipped off to the lunatic asylum in Manitoba — from which he would escape to the United States — the remaining members of the Exovedate who had been captured by the Canadians had to wait until after the completion of the Riel trial for judicial action. The government had already decided to concentrate the burden of responsibility for the rebellion upon Riel's shoulders, and although it threatened to try all his colleagues for high treason, it is likely that this was to intimidate them into making a deal by pleading guilty to treason-felony and eliminating the need for jury trials. Despite the success in the Riel case, made possible by a combination of Riel's eloquence and his lawyers' inadequacies, there were never any guarantees in jury trials about how a jury — even a six-man North-West Territories jury — would react. Lengthy jury trials would only continue to publicize the events of the rebellion, and either acquittals or heavy sentences would be equally disastrous. Acquittals might seem to justify the rebellion, and heavy sentences would make martyrs out of the Métis. The government therefore had decided against execution because the Métis prisoners "were not leaders or were compelled to take first steps by more or less force," a position consistent with its strategy against Riel. The entire situation, of course, encouraged the other Métis prisoners to heap all the blame upon Riel. Charles Nolin was especially creative in this regard, as he had already shown at the Riel trial. The priests were happy to have Riel as the devil and the poor Métis as misguided victims, and the various prisoners of the Métis were able to add their bit.

On 14 August the Métis councillors were dealt with in court without a jury trial. Eleven of them — including Philippe Garnot, Pierre Parenteau, and Maxime Lépine — got sentences of seven years in prison. Three others got three years, and four more got one year. Seven prisoners were discharged conditionally, and a few others (André Nault, Abraham Montour) were never actually formally brought into court at all. The Canadian justice system decided to concentrate on the Indians instead.

The Métis Exiles

A few Métis had made their way across the border, including Gabriel Dumont and Michael Dumas, as well as a number of aboriginals. According to his biographer, George Woodcock, Dumont spent the summer of 1885 plotting to rescue Louis Riel from the jail in Regina. He apparently managed to establish a series of relay stations to provide fresh mounts for Riel and his liberators. Nothing ever came of these plans, because the government had troops of Mounties guarding the jail until after Riel's execution. Government spies reported that most of the exiles had gone to Sun River, and the Dumonts settled in the Lewiston area of Montana. In the end, Gabriel Dumont accepted an offer from Buffalo Bill Cody to join his Wild West show, performing with Annie Oakley for a part of one season. An amnesty for rebels was declared by Canada in 1888, and eventually Dumont joined other Métis exiles in returning to Canada.

The English Mixed-Bloods and White Supporters

The only white man put in the dock for the 1885 rebellion besides Jackson was Thomas Scott, ironically of the same name as Riel's victim in 1870. Scott's fate offers the best evidence of what an aggressive defence might have done for Louis Riel, although the comparisons between Riel's situation and Scott's are not very close. Scott was another one of those who was around the rebellion and may have given it "aid and comfort," although he did not bear arms. Scott's defence attorney was Henry J. Clarke, the lawyer who had prosecuted Ambroise Lépine. In his opening address to the jury, he discussed the history of the North-West in great detail. The people of the region bore injustice "from day to day, and from week to week, and from month to month, until fifteen years had rolled around, and still they were as far from a settlement as they were fifteen years ago." Clarke insisted that the conviction of a white man was necessary to please Quebec; this was a political persecution, he proclaimed. The courtroom burst into cheers when the jury announced an acquittal within 20 minutes. The English-speaking mixed-blood Magnus Burston was subs quently tried for treason-felony. The evidence was not much different than for most of the aboriginal defendants, but Burston was acquitted.

The Disposition of the Aboriginal Insurgents

The first aboriginal tried after Riel's conviction was One Arrow, who was the chief of the Cree reserve east of Batoche. He was put before Judge Richardson and a six-man jury on 13 August, charged with treason-felony. He pleaded not guilty. According to Beal and Macleod, the indictment, in translation into Cree, accused One Arrow of "knocking off the Queen's bonnet and stabbing her in the behind with a sword." One Arrow asked the interpreter, "Are you drunk?" No witnesses could actually be produced to any wrongdoing by One Arrow, although he had been around Batoche at the time of the battle. Most observers thought him too feeble and confused to be guilty of very much. But B.B. Osler insisted that One Arrow would have to prove that he was hanging around innocently. The case ought to have produced a good deal of jury agonizing, since Osler and the defence counsel Beverly Robinson had jousted at some length over the nature of the evidence required to convict, and Judge Richardson had not helped clarify matters in his charge. The jury took a full ten minutes to reach a guilty verdict. The Judge gave One Arrow — despite his age and general feebleness — three years in the penitentiary. One Arrow declined rapidly in the Stony Mountain penitentiary in Manitoba. He became a convert to Catholicism and was released in April of 1886 because the government did not wish him to die in prison. He was carried to Archbishop Taché's palace in St. Boniface and died shortly thereafter. One Arrow's conviction set the tone for the treatment of many of the remaining aboriginal prisoners. Neither Crown nor juries would show any mercy whatsoever.

Poundmaker was next on the government's agenda, beginning on 17 August in Judge Richardson's court. It was Poundmaker's Crees who had presented the Thirst Dance in 1884. The Crown tried to prove that Poundmaker had been the chief architect of the Indian rebellion, while the defence argued that Poundmaker's band had been taken over by militant elements and that he had tried to stop the violence. Much hinged around the meaning of a warrior's lodge (actually a tent) erected in the middle of the band's camp. Did it mean that Poundmaker was not the military chieftain? A number of witnesses so testified. No testimony dealt with Poundmaker's saving many soldiers at Cutknife Creek by stopping the battle. "Everything I could do was done to stop bloodshed," Poundmaker told the court. "Had I wanted war I would not be here now. I should be on the prairie. You did not catch me. I gave myself up. You have got me because I wanted justice." Judge Richardson gave him three years in Stony Mountain. "I would rather prefer to be hung," commented Poundmaker. He too was released before a year was up, and he died not long thereafter. Father André in a letter to Archbishop Taché pronounced the epitaph on One Arrow and Poundmaker, writing "If there were two innocent people in the world, it was assuredly these Indians against whom nothing has been proved if not that they had always been well-disposed towards the whites."

Big Bear was another older chief who had lost control of his band. His trial began on 11 September in the Richardson court. One of the witnesses related what Big Bear had told him after the Frog Lake killings. "It is not my doings, and the young men won't listen, and I am very sorry for what has been done." A request for a judicial direction to the jury for acquittal was denied, and in his charge to the jury, Judge Richardson insisted that in order to demonstrate his innocence, Big Bear would have to have left his people. Although the defence asked him to recall the jury and explain that aiding and abetting required some positive action, after a second judicial charge, the jury still probably believed that to be around rebels constituted treason. Big Bear's jury found him guilty, but recommended mercy. Big Bear got the usual three years in Stony Mountain. He lived marginally longer than his colleagues, but was released in 1887 because of ill health and died early in 1888.

The wheels of Canadian justice rolled inexorably on. On 16 September, nine Cree from Big Bear's band were charged with treason-felony involving Frog Lake, the sacking of Fort Pitt, and the Battle of Frenchmen Butte. Because of the difficulty of the Cree names, each of the defendants was given a number. Most could be placed at the scenes of the crimes, but little evidence existed that they were involved in rebellion. The Crown itself summarized, "It is not shown conclusively that these Indians took any part in that outrage [at Frog Lake], but it is shown that it was taken by Indians with whom they were living and acting." Judge Richardson reminded the jury that the accused were entitled to the same protection of the British Crown as anyone else, which is probably why it took the jury a half hour to convict. The nine got two years each. Five more numbered natives on the following day were equally swiftly convicted. Whitecap, the Dakota chief released by General Middleton after Batoche, had been around the village. But a white man testified that Whitecap and his people had been coerced by the Métis. Whitecap's attorney observed in his address to the jury that "It has seemed to me it is only necessary to say in this town to a jury, there is an Indian, and we will put him in the dock to convict him." The chief was unexpectedly acquitted, and the Regina trials were over. The remaining cases would be heard at Battleford.

Although Judge Richardson had some considerable trouble in understanding the law he was enforcing, he was a pussycat by comparison with Judge Charles Rouleau at Battleford, who had been meting out justice to aboriginals since the beginning of the summer with a fierce personal vengeance. Rouleau's life had been threatened by the aboriginals, and his home and library of legal volumes had been burnt to the ground. He wired Joseph Chapleau from Swift Current: "Got here safe with family Indians ransacked & plundered my house am left poor as a church mouse god save the Queen." Rouleau, the only French-Canadian appointed to the bench in the West, had initially been sympathetic to the Indians when he had first arrived in 1884, but things were different now. In his overall career on the bench, Rouleau was not a harsh judge, but he treated the Indian defendants in his court in the autumn of 1885 with little mercy. His typical sentence in a case not involving violence was six years in Stony Mountain. Those charged and convicted of the Frog Lake killings, including Wandering Spirit, were sentenced to death in trials in which they were not defended by legal counsel. They were summarily hanged only a few days after Louis Riel.

When the government had finished at Regina and Battleford, nine Indians were hanged and another 50 sentenced to penitentiary terms for their parts in the uprising. The trials, particularly at Battleford, were most improper, conducted without full translation against people who understood little English and less of the law being employed. Few were properly represented in court. Most First Nations leaders and people tried to remain clear of the Métis uprising, but this did not save them from a subsequent campaign of repression by Assistant Indian Commissioner Hayter Reed, who insisted that the rebellion had abrogated the treaties and introduced a series of policies which made the First Nations totally dependent on the largesse of Canada.

Those aboriginal insurgents who managed to cross the border into the United States spent the remainder of their lives wandering the American west.

The Fate of Riel's Family

Louis Riel appears to have given little thought to his family during the period from his decision to return to Canada and his surrender to General Middleton, a period of nearly a year. Marguerite and the couple's two small children accompanied Riel from St. Peter's Mission in 1884, travelling for three weeks before being able to spend a night indoors, and then living with Charles Nolin 50 miles north of Batoche until early November. The little family then joined the family of Gabriel Dumont at Batoche, from which they escaped with the aid of Dumont after the village was overrun by the Canadian militia. Riel's wife and the children had cowered in a cave until led to safety. The ordeal contributed to Marguerite's illness (which was consumption) and to the death of the couple's third child, born on 21 October, who lived for only a few hours. In his jail cell in Regina, Riel did begin to think about his wife and family. Riel wrote Marguerite poetry in English as he waited to die, often with religious themes: "Marguerite be fair and good/Consider now the sacred wood/On which the perfect Jesus/Died to save us…. Margaret! we be the prey/ Of bad spirits? no let us pray…/Be sweet to my words and listen/ When I write you with a golden Pen." According to Riel's prison guard in 1885, writing in the Empire in 1896, Marguerite "was a very dark Cree woman. She possessed all the characteristics of the ideal Indian. She was extremely proud, gentle, and self-sacrificing." She spoke to Riel for two hours in Cree on her last visit.

Presumably they spoke in Cree to be able to converse without being understood by the guards; there is no evidence that Cree was their normal language of discourse. Riel told his prison guard on his last day that his only regret was that he was leaving his wife and children unprovided for. His last letter to his wife, written on the morning of his execution, instructed her to "take good care of your little children," and included a "word of kindness according to God" to his son and "a word of kindness and tenderness also" to his little daughter. The letter was short, its author obviously choked with emotion.

Marguerite Riel died on 24 May 1886, only a few months after her husband. The children were brought back to St. Vital and brought up by their maternal grandmother and aunt. Marie-Angélique died of diphtheria in 1897. Jean Riel, who was given a trust fund raised in Quebec, was educated at St. Boniface College and sent to Montreal for further education. He worked as an engineer for the Grand Trunk Pacific Railway and died in St. Boniface Hospital in 1908 after being injured in an accident involving the upsetting of his buggy.

The Political Consequences

The initial response of the press in Quebec was not particularly sympathetic to Louis Riel, and both it and the people even supported the dispatch of French Canadian units (the 65th and 9th battalions) to the front. But a sense of ambivalence, of being torn between patriotism and loyalty, soon took over. The Métis, after all, were compatriots of the French Canadians. The surgeon of the 65th asked that his battalion not be ordered into battle, writing that "Several of our principal officers are close friends and ex-classmates of Louis Riel, and that all our men look upon the Métis as their compatriots and are not far from thinking that the demands of the Métis are made in the national interest and are as fair and just as those of our ancestors in 1837." Increasingly, the English-language press from Ontario criticized Riel and the Métis, and increasingly, the French-language press came to their support. Impartial justice was required. The Métis had some legitimate grievances, and Louis Riel was clearly insane. On 18 May *La Patrie* wrote, "Yes, we say it again, Riel is just a madman, a visionary entirely without responsibility for his acts. He is a moonstruck fellow whose sickly excitation naturally made a great impression on the minds of the primitive people who took him for a sort of prophet." Riel had to be put away so that he could do no more harm, opined another newspaper, but he should not be severely punished.

The announcement of the death sentence imposed on Riel was the decisive moment when the French press turned to outrage. Quebec believed that Riel was truly mad and the grievances of the Métis provided extenuating circumstances. How could the jury have found him guilty? There must have been something wrong with the trial. The government must have manipulated the result. How William Jackson could get off while Riel could not was explained by the fact that "Jackson is English while Riel is French-Canadian." The hanging of Riel would be a victory for Orange Ontario. The press responded with pleas for petitions, agitations, pressure on politicians, to save Riel. Charles Fitzpatrick, Riel's lawyer, declared in late October that execution would make Riel a martyr, whereas if he were imprisoned or put in an asylum he would soon be forgotten. The Montreal *Herald* declared about the same time that it had been a mistake to charge Riel with treason, since the death penalty had not been imposed on a traitor in Britain or the United States for many years. The *Herald* thought Riel should have been tried for murder, as Ambroise Lépine had been in 1874. The newspaper also reported that a medical commission would question Riel's sanity and he would be saved. A number of lawyers began producing public post-mortems of the trial, most of them unfavourable to the Crown. But the government pressed ahead with the execution, and the Quebec francophone press almost unanimously responded with new paroxysms of outrage at Riel's death.

The execution of Louis Riel on 16 November 1885 did not end the controversy over the North-West Rebellions. The issue had little immediate effect on the federal government of Sir John A. Macdonald, but it was employed in Quebec by the Rouges to beat the incumbent Conservative government in the province. The Conservatives in Quebec reacted to criticism of Riel's execution by seeking scapegoats and exculpation, but they never really recovered from the onslaught. The vast majority of French Canadians believed that Riel had died because he was French Canadian and Catholic. Riel's execution had opened a race war against French Canada. Quebec suddenly discovered that it was being deprived of a legitimate share in Western Canada. It had learned that it had no power in the national government. It responded, as one pamphlet put it, with cries of French-Canadian nationalism: "The province of Quebec is ours; it is our property, and let's tell the English we intended to keep it. No concessions: absolute power in our own house, French governments throughout." By 1886 Honoré Mercier was arguing in the provincial election that the Quebec Conservatives had failed to defend the autonomy of Quebec. From the standpoint of the history of Canada, the death of Riel led inexorably to the election of a government that labelled itself national and devoted itself to a defence of Quebec autonomy. A large step toward separatism had been taken.

J. M. Bumsted

Did Riel Get a Fair Trial?

T wo points need to be made at the outset in dealing with this question. In the first place, the fairness of a trial depends not only how the behaviour of the prosecution but also on the ability of the defence to provide "full answer and defence," at least to some extent in accordance with the defendant's wishes. In the second place, an evaluation of a trial's fairness should not be ended when the jury delivers its verdict and the judge pronounces sentence, but should follow through until all avenues of appeal are exhausted.

The behaviour of the defence was absolutely crucial to a fair trial. A Riel Defence Committee in Ottawa approached the three lawyers — Charles Fitzpatrick, François Lemieux, and James N. Greenshields — who headed west to handle Riel's defence. The Crown paid their rail expenses to Regina and, under pressure, offered to pay the expenses of witnesses within the territory coming to Regina. Of the three, only Lemieux was an experienced criminal lawyer with substantial trial experience, and he did not head the defence. That task went to Charles Fitzpatrick, whose experience in capital cases was certainly limited. In Regina the defence team added Thomas Cooke Johnstone, a local lawyer who was supposed to add experience with the North-West Territories legal system.

Although Riel initially appeared generally satisfied with his lawyers, he expressed some reservations over the team from the outset. Riel wanted a defence based upon "the merit of my actions," in effect justifying his rebellion in terms of the misconduct of the Canadian government in the West. While such a defence might defy the government's own legal assertions and assumptions, the real point is that there is a wild card in the equation: the jury. The jury needed to be given some reason to defy the government and the charges that would be given it by the judge to find the defendant guilty. The government had chosen to go for death by charging high treason, which had always been a difficult charge to sustain because of the understandable reluctance of juries to condemn men to death by finding them guilty. Despite the absence of any decent reasons for sympathizing with him being presented at the trial, the Regina jury found Riel guilty but asked for mercy. If the jury thought Riel might be insane, they should have returned a verdict of not guilty by reason of insanity. So in recommending mercy, they were suggesting that the rebellion was understandable. (As already noted, the defence should have warned the jury of the impotence of a recommendation of mercy). Had the jury been given more reasons for finding the rebellion justifiable, it might well have opted for innocence.

A defence based on the inadequacies of the government, were it made strongly and persistently enough, might well have swayed a jury that was already predisposed to blame the government and call for mercy. Such a defence in a different context had been rejected at the murder trial of Ambroise Lépine, but in that trial the presiding judge had refused to admit any evidence of government cheating and lying that could not be substantiated with documentary evidence, and the defence had no documents, only oral testimony by various witnesses that the government had lied to them. The same ruling might have been given in 1885, but the question was never tested. A defence based on the merits of Riel's actions might have made some sense and some headway, although it would have involved Riel's lawyers in some unseemly arguments with their Crown colleagues. A spirited defence of the rebellion might well have forced the Crown into showing its hand totally, instead of being allowed to present itself persistently as the generous protector of the rights of the accused.

The lawyers for Riel were far too committed to the insanity defence, and then they did not handle it particularly well. There was entirely too much confusion over the McNaghten rule, which the defence never managed to clarify. In a case in which all of the expert witnesses agreed that Riel's religious beliefs — if sincerely held — meant that he was not responsible for his actions in the rebellion, the lawyers should have been better able to marshall that testimony on their client's behalf. On the other hand, the insanity plea itself — opposed by Riel — led him to spend far too much of his statement to the jury in defending his sanity rather than his actions.

If the defence was weak in the trial, it was really perfunctory in the various post-trial actions. The grounds of the initial appeal were exceptionally weak, easily dismissible, and the arguments to the Judicial Committee of the Privy Council were pathetic. In 1886, in the debate over the Riel trial in the House of Commons, critics of the government quoted at length from interviews about the trial conducted with Mr. Lemieux, one of the members of the defence team. Lemieux on this occasion complained that the French translators were incompetent, adding that "The court had to change translators three or four times; that the evidence given in French is mutilated, incorrectly reported, given in the lump, specially that of Dr. Roy and that of the Rev. Fathers Fourmond, André, and the others." Moreover, said Lemieux, there was often no interpreter present. But the defence did not attempt to introduce this information at any point in the appeals or use it to argue for a mistrial.

Two connected observations need to be made about the defence team. First, the two senior counsel did really well in their post-Riel legal lives. Fitzpatrick rose to be Chief Justice of Canada, Lemieux to become

Chief Justice of Quebec. This is not to suggest that they were being directly rewarded for their services in the Riel case, but it is to suggest that
these were ambitious establishment lawyers who were not likely to want
to play too dirty with the system. Politicians in the House of Commons
might condemn the system of justice, but lawyers seeking to avoid blot-
ting their copybooks could hardly do so. Riel's attorneys were far too
genteel in their approach. Fitzpatrick and Lemieux, when they first met
with Riel in June of 1885, were obviously quite pleased to discover that
he seemed quite irrational, for it meant that they could employ a defence
that essentially blamed Riel for the rebellion rather than a defence that
blamed the government. Such a defence would have meant fighting it
out in the trenches with the prosecution, an approach Riel's lawyers carefully avoided. Malcolm Cameron, in his speech in the House of
Commons on the Riel case in 1886, would do a far better job of defending Riel than his lawyers did in 1885, but that was because Cameron went
straight after government policy. In the second place, what Riel did not
have on his defence team was a maverick professional defence lawyer, a
Clarence Darrow or Horace Rumpole-type character whose sole goal in
life was not in the Canadian equivalent of "taking silk" but in defending
his client by whatever means proved necessary. Riel would have found
an American trial attorney like Enos Stutsman extremely useful, or
Henry J. Clarke were he willing to be associated with Riel. Such a lawyer
would either have been given considerable leeway by the Crown or
would have broken down the Crown's professions of fairness. Enough
judicial decisions silencing the defence would have exposed the Crown;
people tend to object to imposed closure. As it was, the possibility of a
real defence of Riel was never really raised, except by the accused.

On 12 March 1885, Mr. Malcolm Cameron, MP for Huron, delivered
in the Commons a speech that represented one of most powerful cri-
tiques of the Riel trial ever presented. Cameron insisted that the Crown
had deprived Riel of his right to full answer and defence, and blamed the
Crown. Cameron concentrated his fire upon the failure of the Crown to
allow the defence the time it had requested to prepare
the case, and upon the Crown's positive refusal to allow documents necessary to his defence to be produced. The matter of the production of the
documents, of course, took the debate into the area of larger
government policy, for the critics of the government regarded the
causes of the rebellion as mitigating the sentence. Cameron was also
quite scathing on the inability of the court to appreciate that, as he put it,
"A man may be responsible, may be clear-headed, may be rational upon
every subject but one, and if he commit an offence within the scope of
this one, he is not responsible." He pointed out that the jury had recommended mercy and had been ignored. Cameron described Riel's reli-

gious beliefs in some detail, and commented on the opinions of the medical experts. Sir Hector Langevin defended the fairness of the trial with some vehemence, pointing out that if the jury doubted Riel's guilt or accountability for his actions, it had but to acquit him. Langevin's protestations of the government's sense of fair play do not ring entirely true, but in saying that the jury could have acquitted, he was quite accurate.

George Goulet, in his recent book *The Trial of Louis Riel*, insists that Riel was "deprived of his right to make full answer and defence," not so much by the Crown as by his own lawyers. Goulet has a legitimate point here. One of the key actions was in caving in on the documentation business in such a way as to leave no possibility of appeal on the point. This raises an interesting question about any posthumous action on the conviction and sentence of Riel for treason. The prosecution does not have to be responsible for the unfairness of the trial. Surely the defence can be equally responsible for a miscarriage of justice. I personally do not think that the Crown was fair. Every time it had a choice, it opted for the course of action least favourable to or most hostile to Riel. But in the end, Riel's own lawyers were the people who were most responsible for his failure to receive justice in 1885.

Conclusion

The military defeat of the Métis, the public execution of Louis Riel in November 1885 for treason, and the campaign of repression against the First Nations supplied only half the reason why that year (and even that month) was so significant, not only in the history of the West but in the history of Canada. For in November of 1885, the last spike was driven at Craigellachie in eastern British Columbia to mark the completion of the Canadian Pacific Railway. The CPR had been resurrected in 1881 as a hybrid corporation controlled by private capitalists and financed chiefly by the state — which, along with public subsidies, gave it about 25 million acres of land along its right-of-way, as well as other concessions. The question of building in advance of settlement — what T. C. Keefer had called "colonization lines" — was actively debated at the time, particularly given the inducements needed to convince hard-headed businessmen to proceed with construction; but the Macdonald government defended the railway on the grounds of national interest. Since this concept is hardly measurable in quantitative terms, it is impossible to know whether the price was too high.

The West was to be an anglophone colony of Canada. Not only were Indians and Métis to be cast aside as quickly as possible, but French-

Canadians were not supposed to move there in any substantial numbers. Most Quebeckers in the years after Confederation had seen the West as important mainly in commercial terms, or at best as a destination for determined Quebec migrants than the United States, although they were prepared to defend the rights of the Métis. As *L'Opinion Publique* (Montreal) stated in 1879: "For five years English emigration has flooded Manitoba, and French emigration has been pretty well nil...The North-West, founded and settled by the French, is destined, like the rest of North America, to be English."

The French-Canadian response to the execution of Louis Riel, however, was hardly so fatalistic. By 1885 Quebec public opinion was prepared to believe in theories of anti-French conspiracies. National consolidation was arguably completed in 1885, but much Canadian "nationalism" still bore the distinctive sting of the Ontario WASP. Two cultures, French and English, were being firmly set in opposition to each other. Trying to satisfy the country's two major components was to become the most challenging task facing the nation. The execution of Louis Riel would hardly make it any easier.

Epilogue

L ouis Riel has never been out of the public eye in Canada since 1869. In recent years, a number of attempts, both in the Canadian House of Commons and outside it, have attempted to rehabilitate him officially, usually by proposing to grant him a posthumous pardon for his activities in 1884 and 1885. (He was given a conditional pardon in 1875 for his activities in 1869-70, and met the conditions in 1880.) In some ways, what is most interesting about these proposals is the vehemence of the debate that ensues, with many Canadians totally adamant against either action or any recognition that Riel was anything other than a murderer and a traitor. In order to judge whether Riel should or should not be pardoned, it is necessary to examine both the historical record and the mythology that has grown up around Riel since his death.

The historical record is a complex one that can be interpreted in almost any way one chooses. This book has attempted to portray Riel as a constructive statesman in the Red River uprising/rebellion of 1869-70. He managed brilliantly to unite two very different mixed-blood communities — and to keep them sufficiently united to force the Canadian government to grant Red River some concessions it would not otherwise have won. It is true that in the process he was responsible for the death of Thomas Scott, but while that death cannot be excused and was a terrible miscalculation on Riel's part, it was understandable in terms of the circumstances of the time. Riel also kept Red River together and peaceful until the arrival of Canadian authority in August of 1870, and even began a process of democratic government in the settlement. However one feels about the death of Thomas Scott, there can be no doubt that Red River's delegates to Canada were promised an amnesty for it in return for their acceptance of the Manitoba Act, a promise which the Canadian government shamefully tried to pretend it had not made and upon which the government shamefully reneged. Had Canada kept its word, Riel would not have spent the years from 1870 to 1875 in hiding and exile, would not have been declared an outlaw, and would not have had to spend the years from 1875 to 1880 in exile, either. While the entire burden of official deceit ought not to be placed on the shoulders of Sir John A. Macdonald — he had lots of help, not least from the racists of Orange Ontario — the prime minister clearly was in the best position to exercise a bit of political courage on behalf of Riel and the government's honour, and his failure to do so represents a substantial blot on his record of accomplishment.

The record in 1884-85 is considerably more ambiguous and complicated. There can be little doubt that Riel returned to the North-West Territories in 1884 to lead a legitimate protest movement against the government of Canada, with no intention to turn it to violent ends. His frustration certainly grew with the failure — or refusal — of Canada to respond to peaceful petitioning, and his strategy became far more confrontational in the spring of 1885. The trigger which set off the rebellion was probably supplied inadvertently by the North West Mounted Police in their advance on Duck Lake, but Riel played some considerable part in the preliminary proceedings which set off that event. Although the aboriginals rose against Canada and the European settlement for their own reasons, they were encouraged by Riel personally and by the general atmosphere of rebellion. If one takes the view of the court in 1885 that treason against the Crown can never be justified by grievances, then Riel was guilty of treason. He should not have been convicted of treason, however, because he was not "accountable for his actions," i.e., was innocent by reason of insanity, whatever his wishes. In his insistence on his sanity in 1885, Riel became a classic tragic figure. Even if he were convicted, however, he need not have been executed. To use the harshness of government vengeance against the aboriginal leaders as a reason for being harsh with Riel seems somehow wrongheaded.

Whether the government of Canada miscalculated in its interpretation of public opinion can never be known. We do know that the execution of Riel played a large role in the ending of Conservative government in Quebec, and a considerable role in the ultimate loss of support for the Tories in Quebec, a political reality that lasted for nearly a century of Canadian history. But we do not know what would have happened had Riel been spared. The wrath of Orange Ontario might well have been just as disastrous for the Conservatives as that of Quebec. What was important, of course, was that the Canadian government of 1885 made a political choice that was perfectly consonant with its overall preferences, particularly in western Canada. In the largest sense, Riel was executed to suit the political needs of a government that represented, when the chips were down, the expansionist interests of Protestant Ontario. In his death, Riel became a martyr, much as Thomas Scott had done 15 years earlier.

Louis Riel v. Canada

All these facts help to explain the position in the Canadian psyche which Riel has assumed in the years since his death. Riel has come to embody some very important themes in the Canadian memory.

In the largest sense, Riel has become a legendary figure — even a hero — of mythological proportions. Nobody doubts that Riel was badly flawed as a hero. The complexities of his personality are part of his attraction, however. He was and remains the Canadian historical personality most often written about, both by historians and by imaginative writers in fiction and poetry. Riel has been the subject of more than a dozen full-length biographies. Since 1885, he has been the protagonist of more than 20 stage plays, many building on the inherent drama of his final trial. He is the central character of the opera usually regarded as Canada's finest, *Louis Riel*, by Harry Somers and Mavor Moore, which was written for Canada's Centennial celebrations and was presented at Kennedy Center as an official Canadian contribution to the 1975 American bicentennial. Dorothy Livesay gave Riel a voice in radio dramas produced by the CBC in the 1940s. There has been a CBC television series dramatizing his life. Riel has also been featured in or starred in countless novels and works of poetry, again stretching back to 1885. He is the only Canadian historical figure whose entire writings have been published in a standard edition. In recent years he has clearly become Canada's major mythical figure. Whether he would have relished the irony of this development is another matter; a sense of irony was not one of his strongest attributes.

Beyond having become a mythological hero, Riel has also become a symbol for some very important themes in Canadian society. In the first place, he serves as the historic spokesman and symbol for the aspirations of his people, writing or helping to write a number of major statements of Métis rights and demands that were submitted to various governments in Canada and the United States, as well as leading two Métis rebellions. Riel first came to public attention as a correspondent to Quebec newspapers in 1868 and 1869, defending the Métis people. Among the many political statements he drafted — or helped to draft — were the "Declaration of the People of Rupert's Land and the North West," dated 8 December 1869, and "Petition to His Excellency the Governor General, of Canada, in Council," dated 16 December 1884.

But over the years, Riel has also symbolized many other causes in Canada, mainly associated with resistance to certain forces in Canadian development. He has come to represent not only Métis but aboriginal resistance to Canadian assimilation. He is a hero of francophone efforts to preserve a language, religion, and culture in western Canada. In a wider context, he has come to stand for all efforts to resist the breakdown of traditional community in favour of cultural and ethnic homogenization. In an even wider context, Riel has served to embody spirited resistance to the centralizing imperialism of a Canada dominated by Protestant Ontario, not merely in political but also in intellectual and emotional terms as well. The Canada which Riel opposed in two rebellions had a very distinct view on how the West should be developed and how the resulting nation should look. That Canada was unilingual and unicultural. It was not sympathetic to minority groups of any description. It believed in one single and integrated version of Canadian historical development. There are those in Canada who still believe in parts or all of this vision, and most of them can be found among the modern critics of Louis Riel.

In the largest sense of all, of course, Riel does not have to symbolize resistance to anything in particular, but simply a spirit of rebellion and protest, of willingness to stand up and oppose the illegitimate exploitation of self and community by the system and even by the inexorable forces of history. Indeed, that his central cause — the protection of the Métis people — is almost certain to be defeated is probably one of its attractions.

Riel was and is many things to many people: madman, prophet, murderer, saviour. Canadians do not have much of a pantheon of great heroes, and there are certainly few resisters in that collection. One of our most enduring heroes is Louis Riel — the righteous rebel.

At the beginning of the 21st century there is little doubt that Louis Riel should receive a posthumous pardon. He should be pardoned partly so that he can take his rightful and undisputed place as the Father of Manitoba. He should be pardoned because he was badly treated by Canada throughout his entire career. But mostly he should be pardoned as a gesture to the memory of a great Canadian.

Index

Louis Riel v. Canada